EL CASTILLO

EL CASTILLO

*The Politics of Tradition in
an Andalusian Town*

RICHARD MADDOX

University of Illinois Press
Urbana and Chicago

*Winner of the 1991 President's Book Award
of the Social Science History Association*

Publication of this book was made possible in part by grants
from the Social Science History Association and the Program
for Cultural Cooperation Between Spain's Ministry of Culture
and United States' Universities.

This book is printed on acid-free paper.

Library of Congress Cataloging-in-Publication Data

Maddox, Richard Frederick.
    El Castillo : the politics of tradition in an Andalusian town /
Richard Maddox.
        p.   cm.
    Includes bibliographical references (p.   ) and index.
    ISBN 0-252-01946-6 (cl : acid-free paper). ISBN 0-252-06339-2
(pbk : acid-free paper).
        1. Ethnology—Spain—Aracena.   2. Aracena (Spain)—History—
Sources.   3. Aracena (Spain)—Politics and government.   4. Social
structure—Spain—Aracena.   5. Country life—Spain—Aracena.
6. Aracena (Spain)—Social life and customs.   I. Title.
GN585.S7M34   1993
306'.0946'87—dc20   92–6842
                                                                         CIP

FOR SHARON AND ZACK
más verdad que pan y la tierra

CONTENTS

Illustrations follow page 168.

Acknowledgments

I began the field research on which this book is based in the summer of 1980 with a visit to Aracena that was funded in part by the Department of Anthropology of Stanford University. I returned to Aracena in June 1981 and remained there until November 1982. During this period, support was provided by an International Doctoral Dissertation Fellowship from the Social Science Research Council and the American Council of Learned Societies, a Fulbright-Hays/Spanish Government Grant, and a Grant for Improving Doctoral Research from the National Science Foundation (Grant BNS81-07146). In 1988–89, support for the writing of my book was provided by a Mellon Postdoctoral Fellowship at the Center for European Studies of Stanford University. In the summer of 1990, I returned to Aracena with the help of a research grant from Augustana College. Publication of my book was made possible in part by grants from the Social Science History Association and the Program for Cultural Cooperation Between Spain's Ministry of Culture and United States' Universities. I am grateful for the generous assistance of these organizations.

I am also grateful to the many townspeople of Aracena who graciously granted me access to the private and public documents on which my research is partially based. Descriptions of the documents are included with the other sources of data at the end of the text. All English translations of Spanish sources are my own.

The late Shelly Rosaldo helped me formulate the questions addressed by my field research and taught me a great deal about the relation between "forms of discourse" and "forms of life." Her valuable guidance and friendship are deeply appreciated and sorely missed.

George Collier and Jane Collier, who have done extensive field research in the village of "Los Olivos" near Aracena, have been sources of encouragement, support, and well-informed criticism during every phase of my research and writing. Extensive comments by Roger Rouse, Mark Handler, Andrea Klimt, Tom Lutz, Peter Kivisto, David Gilmore, and anonymous reviewers have been invaluable in helping me revise many sections of the manuscript. I also owe thanks to Stanley Engerman, James Fernandez, John Modell, Alfredo Núñez Jiménez, Francisco Núñez Roldán, and Salvador Rodríguez Becerra.

Above all, I am deeply indebted and grateful to Sharon Keller Maddox for her many contributions to both the research and the writing.

Because I refer to Aracena by its real name, I have taken a number of steps to protect the privacy and confidences of townspeople, including the use of pseudonyms for all contemporary persons mentioned in the text. In keeping with this policy, I feel it best not to thank townspeople by name, but I wish to express my heartfelt gratitude to the many individuals in Aracena without whose assistance and kindness this project could not have been completed.

Introduction:
Space Inscribed

Of course, he had arrived yesterday, and the Castle
had been here since ancient times.
—FRANZ KAFKA
Original manuscript of *The Castle*

VISIBILITIES: PASTORAL VISTAS AND EPIC MONUMENTS

SIGHTSEERS in the western Sierra Morena, the mountainous region that divides the high plateau of central Spain from the Guadalquivir basin of Andalusia, usually wend their way along the road that runs from the city of Seville to the Portuguese border. At a point eighty-eight kilometers from the city, they round a bend and all of Aracena comes suddenly into view. Most of the town lies in a shallow valley between the highway and a *monte* (hill) that rises in the background. On the top of the *monte* is a church abutting the shattered walls of an ancient fortress, "El Castillo."

Aracena has a population of about 7,000 and is situated in the westernmost extension of the Sierra Morena. The reddish soil of the region is thin and poor, there is little surface water, and much of the terrain is covered with scrubby *matorral*. Although occasional well-tended groves of oak, chestnut, olive, cork, and eucalyptus trees break the monotony of the landscape, the area seems relatively wild and sparsely populated. At certain hours of the day, the traveler can go for kilometers without encountering another vehicle or seeing people along the roadside. In the summer, the sun bakes down and the heavy scent of wild rosemary clogs the air; in the winter rainy season, the fog-shrouded broken lines of hills look like a choppy, wind-driven sea. Each of the towns and villages along the highway turns its ugliest and poorest face to the road, and this magnifies the sense of being in a deserted zone that foreigners and Spaniards alike often feel in the Sierra Morena. Aracena, though more open to view, appears to be just another of the thirty or more settlements that are strung out across the northern third of Huelva province.

The sierra region is geographically divided into two zones, the Sierra de Aroche and the Sierra de Aracena (see fig. 1). The first zone extends west toward the Portuguese border and contains two principal towns, Aroche and Cortegana, with populations of about 4,400 and 7,000, respectively. The second zone lies to the east and includes the highest hills of the province, which rise to more than a thousand meters above sea level and are the heart of the Sierra de Aracena. Scattered among these high hills are ten small *municipios* (incorporated townships) with populations ranging from 200 to 2,000 inhabitants. Along the slope of the hills lies the western boundary of Aracena's large township. Aracena is the seat of the *partido judicial* (judicial district) for thirty-one townships, including those in both zones (see fig. 2).

Aracena's position is a relatively favored one. The present area of the township is 17,797 hectares, and some of the lands are gently rolling hillsides and valleys rather than steep slopes. Along the northern edge of the township, several small streams feed into the Río de Huelva, a tributary of the Guadalquivir. To the southeast is the source of the Río Odiel, which passes near the great mining zone of Río Tinto and then to the capital city of the province, Huelva, where it runs into the sea. Both streams often degenerate into a series of stagnant pools in the dry season from June to late October, but even in this state they are useful sources of water for livestock.

Aracena proper is near the center of its territory (see fig. 3), and six *aldeas* (dependent hamlets) are scattered elsewhere in the township. While the town has little surface water nearby, underground springs and streams provide a dependable year-round supply of good water. Moreover, because of the heights immediately to the west and south, Aracena enjoys a microclimate that brings cool breezes on summer evenings and, more important, relatively abundant winter rains. Although the average annual rainfall of the Sierra de Huelva as a whole is 900 millimeters, Aracena ordinarily receives 1,100 millimeters, while Campofrío, a bordering municipality to the south, can count on no more than 714 millimeters (Avila Fernández 1981:21). This natural advantage has made Aracena's agriculture somewhat more varied and productive than that of most of the other townships in the region.

The town's position has other advantages. Smaller villages and hamlets are scattered in deep valleys and arroyos wherever there is water, but the major centers of population are stretched along the road that arches from the southeast to the northwest and connects

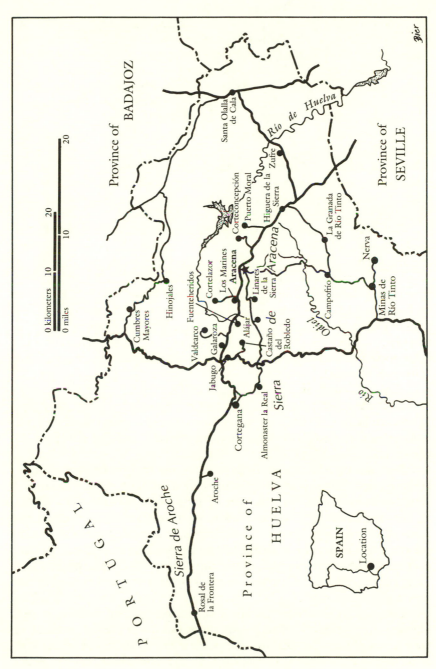

Figure 1. The western Sierra Morena

1. Aracena
2. Alájar
3. Almonaster la Real
4. Aroche
5. Arroyomolinos de León
6. Cala
7. Campofrío
8. Cañaveral de León
9. Castaño del Robledo
10. Corteconcepción
11. Cortegana

12. Cortelazor
13. Cumbres Mayores
14. Cumbres de Enmedio
15. Cumbres de San Bartolomé
16. Encinasola
17. Fuenteheridos
18. Galaroza
19. La Granada de Río Tinto
20. Higuera de la Sierra
21. Hinojales

22. Jabugo
23. Linares de la Sierra
24. Los Marines
25. La Nava
26. Puerto Moral
27. Rosal de la Frontera
28. Santa Ana la Real
29. Santa Olalla de Cala
30. Valdearco
31. Zufre

Figure 2. Townships of the *partido judicial* of Aracena

Seville to Lisbon. Since Aracena is located on the eastern edge of this archipelago, most of the traffic between Seville and the sierra passes through it.

Even so, the appearance of the two *barrios* (neighborhoods) straddling the road into Aracena from the east tends to reinforce the initial impression that it is just another of many essentially similar settlements. The *barrio* of El Cabezo seems to consist almost entirely of oil-stained pavement, rusting metal, cluttered garages, and a bus stop. The *barrio* of Santo Domingo looks like an impoverished mountain village, and its grassless, dusty plaza, where donkeys are tied and children and chickens run about, is surrounded by small one-story houses. But the scene changes abruptly near the center of town. Tree-lined, cobblestone streets, immaculate plazas, a municipal garden, banks, stores, shops, old mansions, and new apartment buildings create an image of urban complexity. Sometimes there are even crowds. Particularly in the mornings and on Saturdays, throngs of women make their way be-

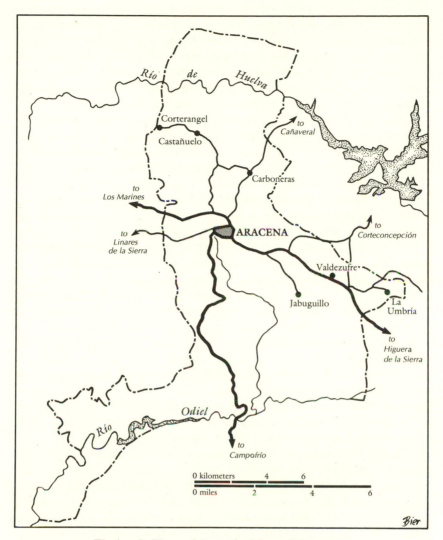

Figure 3. Township and *aldeas* of Aracena

tween the municipal market and a number of grocery stores, doing their shopping as their husbands talk to friends in one of fifty or more bars.

It soon becomes obvious that Aracena is the central marketing town for the whole of the eastern sierra—a place that people from the smaller hamlets, villages, and towns visit frequently for general shopping and specialized services. In addition, the observant visitor will note that Aracena is the seat of a *partido judicial;* a bureaucratic hub where many agencies, ranging from the agrarian extension service to the national health service, maintain offices; and an educational center with a large high school that prepares students for university and technical training. The numerous lawyers, civil servants, physicians, and teachers who live and work in Aracena keep up with cosmopolitan styles and lend a further degree of urbanity to the local scene.

The destination of most visitors, however, is not the town center, attractive and busy as it is. Rather, they are on their way to Las Grutas de las Maravillas, the "marvelous" caverns of stalactite formations that underground streams have sculpted inside the *monte* beneath the castle. The caverns are dramatically illuminated with colored lights and attract busloads of Spanish sightseers, who spend an hour or two touring the caves, shopping for ceramics, and having lunch near the entrance to the caves on the southern edge of town.

Although relatively few of the visitors take the time to climb the *monte* and investigate the collapsed remains of the old fortress and the ancient church of Santa María de Aracena, it is certainly worth the effort because a walk around the hilltop is the next best thing to a grand tour of the sierra and the town. Far to the south, in the direction of the huge mines of Río Tinto, visitors can see the white houses of the village of Campofrío nestled in the rolling hills of the sierra. In the middle distance, there is the ancient stone hermitage of San Jerónimo by the side of a road that meanders through groves of chestnut and oak trees and cuts across the pasture lands of a vast estate on which fighting bulls are raised. Nearer, there are modest country houses whose surrounding gardens are irrigated by water from the same subterranean source that shaped the caves of the *monte*.

Gazing almost straight down from the *monte,* visitors can contemplate in succession the bleached tombs in Aracena's cemetery, the neat compound where highway workers and their families live, the grounds where the livestock fair is held each May, the former tuberculosis sanatorium that now shelters orphans from all over the province, and the stately weekend house of a family from Seville who inherited a large department store in the city. From the other side of the *monte,* where hobbled goats usually graze on the thick grass, visitors can see the *barrio* of San Pedro and the new apartment buildings and modern secondary school. Just to the right are a large corkyard and a bullring, with the *barrio* of Santa Lucía in the background. The center of town is somewhat obscured by the massive edifice of the parish church, but there are clear views of the *barrios* of San Roque, Santo Domingo, and El Cabezo. Finally, completing the circle, visitors can see an elegant villa, tennis courts, and swimming pool. Members of

Opus Dei, a Catholic lay organization that gained great influence during the Franco regime, use these facilities for weekend retreats and regional meetings.

The buildings and artifacts found on the *monte* also make the steep climb worthwhile. The castle, now in ruins, was erected by Castilians in the thirteenth century to protect the hinterlands of Seville from raiding Moors and Portuguese. The adjacent church of Santa María, built around the same time, has been designated a national monument. Although its austere walls give it a somewhat forbidding appearance, the effect is partly mitigated by a fine Mudéjar campanile and elegant Gothic vaulting. Near the portico, in a niche in the castle walls, is a large bronze bust of Don Enrique, a native of Aracena who rose to a position of considerable power in the waning years of the Franco regime and who used his influence to help his hometown in the transition from an archaic, agrarian economy to a service-centered economy.

Especially at sunset, when the castle and church are silhouetted against the sky, the monumental array of the *monte* is irresistibly picturesque. At this hour during the spring and summer, the visitor is likely to encounter young couples strolling along and children scrambling over the walls of the castle. Throughout the year, small groups of elderly men, caps on head and canes in hand, gather to talk of the weather, politics, bulls, and soccer. Even in the worst weather, a steady trickle of elderly women clad in black come to the church of Santa María to make their evening devotions before La Virgen del Mayor Dolor, the patron saint of the town, whose image is sheltered inside. It is obvious that the townspeople feel intensely proud of the *monte* and castle and particularly of the church of Santa María de Aracena. The more conventional among them regard the church as a concrete testimony to the enduring strength of orthodox Catholic faith. But even for the townspeople who are less moved by the institutional grandeur of the universal church, the *monte* embodies much that is important about Aracena's traditions, history, and present circumstances.

The cultural elements that are concentrated in the monumental space of the *monte* are also present but more dispersed in the town below. The walled barracks of the Guardia Civil are only a pale reflection of the fortress on the *monte,* but they and the town's numerous public buildings display the influence of the institutions of the state. More striking are the signs of the impact of religion on local life. The parish church of Santa María de la Asunción, which looms over the center of town, is a huge fortresslike mass of stone that was begun during the Counter-Reformation by Juan de Herrera, one of the architects of the palace of El Escorial, but was never quite completed in the centuries that followed. Four other major places of worship that have all in the past been associated with either the Dominican or Carmelite order are further evidence of the impact of the institutional culture of the church on local life, and several well-kept chapels in the *barrios* reveal the vitality of popular religious customs. The signs of secular, humanistic culture are also highly visible. In the streets and plazas of the town center, there are statues, busts, and plaques commemorating a long line of Aracena's *hijos ilustres* (famous sons and daughters), who as statesmen, soldiers, authors, and artists have added some measure of fame to the town's reputation. Among the most prominent of the town's illustrious children are Benito Arias Montano, a sixteenth-century statesman and biblical scholar; the *marqués* and *marquesa* of Aracena, town benefactors who lived in the first decades of this century; José Nogales, a turn-of-the-century novelist; and, of course, Don Enrique.

Yet because the monumental array of the *monte* contains the most ancient artifacts, it, rather than anything in the town below, is regarded as the authoritative emblem of the community and the heart of local traditions and history. Most people refer to this complex cultural space simply as "El Castillo," and it is by this name that they commonly designate or distinguish not only the old fortress but also the *monte* itself, the church, and the most popular of the town's lay religious brotherhoods. Even the patron saint of Aracena is sometimes called La Virgen del Castillo. In the following pages, a more detailed guide to local traditions, culture, and history will be presented, but we will continue to look at Aracena from the perspective of "El Castillo" and at "El Castillo" from the perspective of Aracena.

Arguments: Tradition and Hegemonic Processes

The fact that "El Castillo" is an archaeological and historical site is less significant than the fact that it reminds the townspeople of "tradition" by evoking an array of customs and ways of viewing life inherited from or at least inspired by the past. The ancient fortress conjures heroic sentiments associated with notions of worldly honor and pride, and the church proclaims the spiritual values of piety and mercy. The figures of the two patrons, Don Enrique and La Virgen del Mayor Dolor, recall the divergent ways in which men and women have been led to realize the abstract values represented by the fortress and the church. Viewed in this light, "El Castillo" reveals that cultural tradition centers on the meanings and values of religion, honor, and patronage.

"El Castillo" dominates the town from the highest point in the immediate area and is understood by the townspeople to be a significant cultural space, not simply a collection of monumental artifacts. This suggests that tradition itself has a governing order, and a sense of this order can be gained by considering the rhetorical and ritual practices that define the place for townspeople. The term "El Castillo" is more than a quaint local usage that betokens a familiarity with community customs. It is also a traditional figure of speech that identifies a peculiar multiplicity which includes a feature of the physical landscape, a set of monumental artifacts, a social group, and a sacred image. Moreover, it names this diverse ensemble in terms of a unifying element that inevitably evokes notions of authority, power, and force. This tends to assimilate the "little" traditions of the community into the "great" traditions of the church and state and to imply that the natural landscape has been domesticated for the purpose of reaching higher human goals. The ritualized activities that regularly occur on the *monte* communicate similar messages by different means. In one way or another, all of the yearly religious rites and secular celebrations convey the notion that the well-being of the community depends on maintaining ties with supernatural or worldly patrons.

Viewed in this light, "El Castillo" appears to be a site where the heterogeneous themes of religion, honor, and patronage converge in accordance with a guiding generic style. This traditional cultural genre can be described as pastoral epic—"pastoral" because it is concerned, above all, with the quality, for good or ill, of life in the town and the sierra, and "epic" because it fundamentally represents the foundations of rural life in terms of the spiritual, moral, and practical relations maintained between rural people and heroic figures of virtue who represent the "higher" values of the church and the state. As expressed in the forms of pastoral epic, tradition can thus be regarded as a complex set of cultural tendencies that serve, on the one hand, to personalize and "parochialize" the encompassing great traditions of Spanish culture (Marriott 1955; Redfield 1960) and, on the other hand, to generalize and universalize the significance of local symbols, values, and customs that townspeople regard as distinctive markers of the community's identity.[1]

But if traditional culture (or at least its overt and explicit aspects) has a governing style, what accounts for this? Influenced by Antonio Gramsci's concept of hegemony, Raymond Williams (1977:115–16) has argued that tradition is never a random array of customs and beliefs inherited from the past. Rather, it is an "actively shaping force" and a "deliberately selective and connecting process which offers an historical and cultural ratification of a contemporary order." In other words, tradition involves an invocation of the past for the purposes of the present, and it is constantly being invented and reinvented in order to secure present social arrangements (for numerous examples, see Hobsbawm and Ranger 1983). Accordingly, an understanding of the enduring strength, coherence, and significance of pastoral epic in Aracena depends on an understanding of the hegemonic role of traditionalism as a means of winning compliance with particular distributions of sociopolitical power and cultural authority over time.

These days, traditionalism remains fairly strong in Aracena, although it is not the primary force influencing contemporary life in the town. However, for most of the past three centuries, traditional meanings and values have been crucially involved in warranting many critical relations of power. The key traditional genre of pastoral epic has operated as a selective mode of historical consciousness that has tended to preserve sociopolitical inequalities by representing the past as an heroic struggle of patrons to bring sociopolitical order and spiritual tranquillity to the town. In addition, the rhetoric and images of religion, honor, and patronage have shaped a pervasive local ethos that has long supported a "whole lived social process" of domination and subjugation (see Williams 1977:106).

Indeed, even in contemporary Aracena, social relations are often influenced by tensions arising between an agonistic personalism that reinforces values of autonomy, loyalty to one's intimates, privacy, and the defense of personal honor on the one hand and a spirit of corporatism that grants moral authority to those who cultivate self-denying public virtues and maintain the broadest range of social ties on the other. Over the long run, this paradoxical traditional ethos has shaped people's habits and actions by informing tacit, commonsense understandings of what is at stake in social interactions. And it has done so in ways that have usually worked to the advantage of the small minority of the townspeople who have been in the best position to mediate between personal interests and communal concerns and between informal customs and official ideologies. Thus, because "El Castillo" embodies the traditions of pastoral epic, it represents the most visible manifestation of a distinctive hegemonic cultural formation that has for centuries been shaped by strategies and tactics of power and domination.

This is not to suggest, however, that traditional culture is either one-dimensional or unidirectional. Although traditionalism tends to reproduce forms of domination, the degree of integration among its disparate elements is never completely adequate to the task. Each traditionalizing strategy has limits, and each sets in motion currents of opposition. For example, the central strain of "pastoral epic" includes stories that highlight the virtues and beneficent actions of extraordinary patrons in order to legitimate relations of domination, but these stories can be countered by "epic pastorals" that turn the tables and portray the people of the sierra as heroic defenders of a common humanity and depict their putative patrons as predators, hypocrites, thieves, and worse. Nothing goes uncontested. Yet it is worth bearing in mind that countercurrents of opposition, to the extent that they must overcome entrenched cultural predispositions, are limited by their lack of autonomy. The presence of "El Castillo" constrains what can be meaningfully said and practically done even by those striving to build another way of life outside its walls.

Nevertheless, the walls of tradition have been repeatedly breached by forces of change, and they have had to be shored up and partly reconstructed in ways that have radically altered the original design. Over the past three centuries, the townspeople of Aracena have continually reinterpreted and reformed (and, on occasion, obliterated) traditional customs, values, and meanings. As political, economic, and social conditions have been transformed, so too has the significance of traditional culture. Improvisation has been necessary to maintain even the semblance of continuity, and ad hoc arrangements have sometimes generated enduring shifts in the play of cultural forces.[2]

To describe the vicissitudes of "El Castillo," the text is divided into three parts that mark epochal shifts in the sense of pastoral epic and the dynamics of local sociopolitical relations since the beginnings of modernity.[3] Part 1, "Tradition and Domination: The Ancient Regime," describes how traditional values grounded in orthodox religious dogmas concerning the nature of the self and the world conditioned the exercise of power in Aracena during the seventeenth and eighteenth centuries. In a social order based on patrimonial, patriarchal, and paternalist principles of corporate organization, patronage was the master strategy of power in Aracena and elsewhere, and religious and secular perspectives were brought to bear in order to contest the legitimacy of the relations between putative patrons and their subordinates. Local processes were partly regulated by higher authorities who granted formal charters, exacted tribute, and periodically lent support to one or another of the local factions and community groups. At the summits of power, the imperial monarchs of Castile in alliance with the Counter-Reformation church buttressed their claims to sovereign and orthodox authority by intervening occasionally in the politics of patronage in order to enforce at least nominal political and cultural uniformity by means of embryonic bureaucratic procedures of governance. Although classic anthropological accounts of Spanish culture (for example, Caro Baroja 1966; Pitt-Rivers 1966) stress the contradictions in principle between religious morality and worldly codes of honor, much evidence from the early modern period in Spain suggests the strategic convergence of religion and honor as mutually reinforcing alternative ways of construing the significance of sociopolitical practices.

Part 2, "Tradition Displaced: Agrarian Capitalism and Class Society," discusses the collapse of the Ancient Regime and focuses on the formative processes and subsequent crisis of rural class society in the nineteenth and early twentieth centuries. The elimination of aristocratic privileges, the weakening of the monarchy, and the decline in the wealth and influence of ecclesiastical institutions diminished religion as a cultural force and altered the formal and legal bases upon which discriminations of honor and relationships of patronage had been based. Although ancient forms of privilege were vehemently defended by some regions and sectors of Spanish society, the transformation of Spain into a liberal, capitalist state shifted the direction of hegemonic processes. As old orthodoxies became less compelling, traditional discourses and practices were displaced and their formerly directive role in sociopolitical life was taken over by ideologies of freedom, property, and progress. In Aracena, however, traditional values were reasserted as moral ideologies that were used to judge the state of civil society by agrarian capitalists and rural proletarians alike. This redeployment of tradition played a critical role in the processes of class formation and political polarization that eventually culminated in revolution and civil war in the 1930s. Nevertheless, an analysis of the displacement of tradition in Aracena challenges conventional views of the premodern and quasi-religious character of the radical social movements that swept Andalusia in the decades before the Civil War (see Brenan 1960; Hobsbawm 1965).

Part 3, "Tradition Liberalized: Re-formations of Class Society," describes the radical transformation of rural life in the decades following the Civil War and especially during the post-Franco period of transition to a democratic regime. In the 1960s, class tensions began to be reduced in Aracena as a result of processes set in motion by the rapid development of the Spanish economy. Yet even as the atavistic traditionalist ideology of the Franco regime lost its force throughout Spain, the more egalitarian aspects of traditional culture in Aracena underwent a partial revival that continued after the end of the dictatorship in 1975. To some extent, the revival represented an effort by the political left to reanimate community traditions that previously had been suppressed. But this backward-looking revivalism was only a secondary factor in reshaping local traditions. The primary factor consisted of the newly dominant forces of cultural and politicoeconomic liberalism. The pressures of liberalism eventually led to a reconfiguration of local traditions that helped townspeople accommodate themselves to their marginal and subordinate position in contemporary Spanish society. By devising a partial and alternative traditional cultural identity for themselves, townspeople were able to represent life in the community as a nearly ideal synthesis of the best aspects of the old and the new. This view of the reconfiguration of tradition in Aracena challenges the notion that the "presence of the past" must recede "into the mists of time" in advanced liberal societies (Behar 1986:287) and also counters the idea that processes of modernization lead inexorably to a "slow, clean, cultural death" (Harding 1984:201). The view of tradition presented here stresses instead the hegemonic capacity of contemporary liberal societies to foster, contain, and depoliticize processes of cultural differentiation.[4]

This threefold ethnographic project is in keeping with the broad shift in the direction of cultural studies that has occurred in recent years (see Marcus and Fischer 1986; Ortner 1984). Among other things, this shift has involved a rejection of neofunctionalist theories that ultimately treat "culture" as a social, psychological, or ideological "control mechanism" and has also involved a sharp devaluation of associated approaches to cultural analysis that center on isolating symbolic systems and structures. The present emphasis is on understanding the complex range of cultural processes, performances, and practices. For some, this emphasis stems from a largely theoretical interest in developing conceptual frameworks that comprehend both sociocultural structures and the dynamics of history, events, and agency.[5] For others, it stems from the conviction that ethnographies in the classic style have overestimated the rule-governed, conventional character of social life and thereby underestimated the theoretical and political significance of people's ability to create meaning and reinterpret their own experiences (see Rosaldo 1989). Recent studies have attempted to redress this imbalance by developing new forms of ethnographic description and critical analysis.[6]

In the case at hand, the aim is to offer a "genealogical" account of the relations between culture and politicoeconomic power in Aracena, an account that maps major lines of descent, patterns of affinity, and points of generation of traditional cultural forms.[7] By tracing the continuities as well as the ruptures in hegemonic processes, it will bring into focus what Michel Foucault (1984:83) called "the hazardous play of dominations" involved in social formations and thereby contribute to a larger and critical task for those influenced by Gramsci's notions of hegemony and Foucault's genealogical projects. This task, which Stuart Hall (1988:70) has described as one of examining "the interchanges between a macrohydraulics of power and a microphysics of power," has the goal of examining how grand strategies associated with the development of capitalism, the state, and civil society are linked to local conflicts, specific practices, and transitory events.

From an anthropological perspective, of course, this task is by no means an entirely new one. At least since the 1960s, ethnographers of Mediterranean Europe have devoted a great deal of effort to understanding how contemporary global processes of political and economic modernization have affected rural life in the region. Yet, until recently, less systematic attention has been given to how these contemporary processes of transformation relate to long-range historical patterns of cultural and sociopolitical domination in particular locales.[8] To further illuminate this relationship, the three chapters that comprise each of the major parts of the text focus on a limited set of processes that best capture the overall directional dynamics produced by specific interpolations of culture and sociopolitical power through time.

While no attempt is made to construct a general social history of Aracena or to provide an exhaustive description of local customs at any historical moment, the first chapter in each part of the text discusses how encompassing institutionalized forms of cultural authority serve to incorporate the town into the larger polity and affect the general dynamics of relations between the local dominant groups and other townspeople (Chapters 1, 4, and 7). The middle chapters provide examples of how local rituals and other cultural forms shape a community ethos of personal and collective identity that helps to render townspeople's specific experiences meaningful and affects their day-to-day sociopolitical practices (Chapters 2, 5, and 8). And the last chapter in each part focuses on how the strategies of community politics that directly maintain or shift prevailing patterns of domination are governed by the manner of articulation of local concerns and values with the versions of the ideologies of higher-level institutions which are embraced by various sectors of the community (Chapters 3, 6, and 9).

In different ways, then, each chapter explores the convergences of and tensions between the domain of formal (orthodox, authoritative, and institutionalized) discourses and practices in the community and the larger society and the domain of informal (improvised, commonsense, and ordinary) speech and dispositions that inform the conduct of everyday life in Aracena. As Michael Herzfeld (1987) has forcefully argued, virtually no aspect of the cultures of the Mediterranean can be adequately analyzed without taking into account this type of critical relationship.[9]

In social terms, the focus on the relation between forms of cultural authority and local customs and practices means that, throughout the text, primary attention must be given to the roles of the local elite. In Aracena, the elite have served as political and economic brokers of the relationship between the community and the larger society. In addition, they have acted as "organic" and "traditional" intellectuals (Gramsci 1971:97) who, whatever their day-to-day occupations may be, also perform the crucial tasks of translating, adapting, and interpreting authoritative idioms and images in terms that are responsive to local values and practices.[10] By virtue of performing this function, members of the dominant groups throughout Aracena's history have usually succeeded in serving their own interests and exercising a directive role over local affairs. Indeed, it appears that Aracena's ruling groups have for centuries been so influential in cultural affairs that they have decisively shaped the townspeople's sense of collective identity.

If this has been the case in Aracena and presumably in other communities of a similar sort, then it may be necessary to revise certain generalizations concerning Andalusian and Spanish culture. Many of the classic and some of the recent ethnographies of Spain have represented the culture and ethos of rural communities as organized around antithetical principles and forces such as hierarchy and individualism (Lison-Tolosana 1983), urbanity and sociocentrism (Caro Baroja 1957, 1963), moral equality and social divisiveness (Pitt-Rivers 1961), class conflict and community solidarity (Corbin and Corbin 1984, 1987), and identity crisis and identity consolidation (Mitchell 1988). Moreover, the tendency has been to represent these forces and principles as enduring cultural and social structures.

But the account of Aracena challenges this sort of representation in two ways. First, it historicizes these representations by demonstrating that the impact of notions such as hierarchy and equality on social action has varied radically over time. Second, it shows that there has not been an enduring equipoise of hierarchical and egalitarian principles, nor have these cultural principles been mutually constitutive of social life. Relations of inequality, conflict, and difference have dominated and have thus defined and shaped secondary and subordinate forms of equality, solidarity, and identity. And as the work of many ethnographers of Andalusia suggests, the cultural and social equation has never balanced.[11] To suppose that it has leads to a reification of dynamic historical processes, an underestimation of the significance of specific strategies of domination, and an essentially functionalist understanding which presumes that in the long run or from a purportedly objective and dispassionate point of view, conflict and change are vehicles of systematic development and integration.[12]

The view of the hegemonic dynamics of sociocultural and historical processes employed here does not imagine culture to be a monolithic mechanism of social control whose principal effect is to produce either consensus or ideological mystification. Instead, culture is understood as a contested mode of power whose dominant manner of articulation with the means of economic production, political regulation, and social reproduction is historically and geographically variable rather than functionally constant.

As Edmund Leach (1964:278) observed, "Culture is a language of argument, not a chorus of harmony." To understand culture, it is necessary to understand how the argument is conducted, who wins, and why. From this perspective, one of the key tasks of ethnographic analysis must be to develop a pragmatics of culture (or a symbolics of power) that adequately describes how particular discourses and images become compelling within specific social formations.[13] The present study aims to contribute to this task by investigating how tradition has been authored, what it has authorized, and to what extent it has been authoritative in Aracena.

Tradition, religion, honor, patronage, pastoral epic, hegemonic processes, genealogy, organic intellectuals, and the pragmatics of culture—these are the foundations for understanding "El Castillo" not as a concrete fortress but as a hypothetical construct and metaphoric figuration of the relationships between cultural discourses and practices and politicoeconomic power, a "possible castle" in Jerome Bruner's epistemological sense of the phrase (see Bruner 1986:44–46). But exactly whose castle is it, anyway? Mine? Theirs? Ours? To ask this question raises immensely difficult problems about the political, moral, and cultural status of ethnographic description that authors of texts are not necessarily in the best position to judge with respect to their own work. However, a partial response to these problems is given in the concluding section of this introduction, which discusses briefly the conditions and considerations that shaped the research and writing of the text and declares what, in light of these constraints, its value may be.

ETHNOGRAPHIC POLITICS: THE STORY OF THE TEXT AND THE TEXT AS STORY

The person from Aracena who has had the greatest influence on what I know or imagine about the town and its history is a man of about forty years of age who works in the local branch office of a government bureaucracy and has a deep interest in and knowledge of local customs and traditions. I will refer to him by the name of Carlos. Telling the story of the early period of our uneasy friendship will help explain a great deal about why this ethnography has the overall shape it does.

I met Carlos during my first visit to Aracena in the summer of 1980. I had asked the proprietor of the local bookstore where I could find a map of the town, and he directed me to Carlos. Carlos was curious about why I wanted the map, so I explained my tentative plans to do research on local religion and politics during and following the Civil War. Carlos was enthusiastic about the project, and I had several conversations with him about Aracena during the following weeks. Informative as these talks were, it was not so much the knowledge I gained but Carlos's hospitality and friendliness that made me eager to return to Aracena for an extended stay, and I spent much of the following year back in the United States reading about Spain and planning research in the town.

At Carlos's suggestion, within a few days of my return in June 1981, I began to do archival research in the office where he worked. As it turned out, I followed the same basic pattern of daily activity for the next year and a half. Almost every morning I would go to one or another of the local repositories of documents and work there until two o'clock, at which time the offices closed for the afternoon meal and siesta. Then I would spend most of the rest of the day visiting and talking with townspeople and writing field notes. This pattern gave a class slant to my research. Most of the public employees with whom I spent the mornings were members of Aracena's traditional middle or upper classes, and my relations with them, while pleasant, tended to be somewhat businesslike and formal. In contrast, when I returned home, I spent most of my time with working-class men and women in the neighborhood where I lived or in one of the local bars, and these contexts made for more familiar, friendlier interactions. My wife, Sharon, also knew these people well, and with some of them our relationship became as close as it is with old friends and even some members of our own families in the United States. Because it was clear that our neighbors were somewhat jealous of our time, Carlos was the main (although not the only) exception to this pattern of having working-class friends and middle- and upper-class acquaintances. I saw Carlos fairly regularly away from the office, and despite a certain formality that persisted in our dealings with one another, I had begun to consider him a good friend.

During the early months of my research in Aracena, it seemed that the most difficult problems I would face were some serious gaps in the documentary record that resulted from the destruction of most of the archives of the parish and town council during the Civil War. The archives had been housed in the parish church and were burned by anticlerical revolutionaries in August 1936. Oddly enough, I got a certain satisfaction from the dramatic way in which the very phenomenon I was most interested in investigating had placed limits on what I could know about it.

A month or two later, however, I was not feeling so complacent. By this time, I had accumulated a lot of information, but my research seemed to have no particular direction other than a disturbing tendency to continue to slip backward into earlier historical periods. I had become convinced not only that in order to understand the events of the Civil War period I had to know more about religion and politics in the nineteenth century but also that what had transpired in the nineteenth century was somehow fundamentally conditioned by how things had been during the Ancient Regime. Moreover, I was faced with this problem of unlimited historical regression just at a time when I was growing bored with archival work and found talking with and interviewing people much more appealing. What was worse still was that my friendship with Carlos was clearly deteriorating, and I was not able to do much about it.

We were seeing less of each other outside the office, and even in the office Carlos seemed to be somewhat remote, often affecting an air of being too preoccupied with his job to be able to talk. The simplest explanation of this was that I had worn out my welcome by working longer in the office than either he or I had anticipated in the beginning. But there was a bit more to it than that. From the beginning, I had been careful to ask Carlos first when I needed a favor or, for that matter, felt like having a cup of coffee with someone. But even though I was grateful for his help and tried to show it, as time passed and I came to know his colleagues and superiors better, I was inevitably less dependent on Carlos. When this was added to other factors, it was not too difficult to understand why Carlos might be feeling some resentment.

Because of his family circumstances, Carlos had not been able to attend the university, despite his intellectual abilities and inclinations. To his credit, Carlos tried to make the best of this situation by cultivating an interest in local culture and history and becoming involved in many aspects of local affairs. Given these circumstances, it is hardly surprising that he would initially be inclined to be enthusiastic about someone who shared his interests but that he might soon come to feel more than a little ambivalent about a foreigner with ample money, education, and time to investigate matters that Carlos knew far more about and was in certain respects better qualified to pursue.

Imagine how Carlos might have felt the first time I came to ask him more about something I had encountered in the archives and he discovered that he was completely ignorant of it. It would have taken a saint not to have felt a twinge of envy or not to have wished to keep some knowledge or information in reserve. Unfortunately, neither Carlos nor I have much potential for sainthood, and our friendship was nearly destroyed by the way we acted when temptation was set in our path. While it would serve no good purpose to go into detail about what occurred, basically Carlos and I became embroiled in a hot dispute over a public document that Carlos was reluctant to give me even though his boss said I could see it. Several of Carlos's coworkers overheard our shouting match through the door of his office and were clearly amused by the whole business.

After a week of tense silence, it was Carlos who took the first step to bring about a reconciliation by calling me into his office one afternoon and asking if I would be interested in borrowing a seventeenth-century biography of a woman of Aracena who has long been revered for her piety and holiness. I was, of course, and Carlos's offer broke the ice in more ways than one. I now think that reading this biography (see Chapter 2) was the single most decisive intellectual event of my field research because it gave a direction to my work by providing a sort of cultural and historical baseline for my inquiries and because it led me to think of traditional culture in new ways. I am still grateful to Carlos for his graceful gesture of goodwill, and we remain friends.

But what does this less-than-towering tale of scholarly passion have to do with the ethnographic account as a whole? At the time of our argument, I largely attributed the problems between us to my general lack of familiarity with how things are done in Aracena and to my misunderstanding of Carlos's motives and intentions. When Carlos and I had first met, we had established a pattern of interaction that was egalitarian but at the same time impersonal, rationalized, and overly serious or professional in tone. Both of us were familiar enough with this cosmopolitan language of international relations, and although neither of us was particularly adept at or comfortable with it, we were unable to move our friendship beyond this phase of businesslike formality. I was therefore convinced that the limitations of this linguistic "code" had led me to misconstrue or just plain miss the nuances of what Carlos said or did not say and that the consequence was a classic "breakdown in communication."

It was not long, however, before I realized that much of what had transpired between the two of us was less the result of a misunderstanding of motives and meanings than an expression of an underlying conflict of interest between a professional researcher and a "traditional" and "organic" intellectual. Such conflicts are, of course, by no means rare in Spain or in other places where ethnographers have worked. On this reading, my undeniably "imperial" and cosmopolitan position as a researcher funded by two governments and my less than fully controlled internalization of a professional will to knowledge had rendered me at least temporarily incapable of preventing our friendship from degenerating into a competitive struggle for control over information. In this sense, I construed the argument as a struggle of cultural domination and resistance that recapitulated in a minor key some aspects of anthropology's dark side of involvement with colonial mentalities and hegemonic forms of power.

It was not until I had returned to the United States that a third way of viewing the matter occurred to me. I had been somewhat aware at the time of our quarrel that considerations of patronage and honor were involved in our relationship, but as I read over my field notes, what struck me most forcibly was how well our quarrel could be understood as a traditional affair. Although Carlos and I had discussed our relationship principally in "modern" terms, we had also occasionally adopted the pose of high-minded "patrons" of local culture, despite the fact that we did little of direct value for the community to justify this pose. Instead, we pursued our own interests and became embroiled in concerns about who was patronizing whom and how our relationship affected our reputations within the community.

The result of these excessive concerns over our dignity and autonomy and of our awkward attempts to occupy the traditional cultural high ground was a public conflict that was embarrassing for both of us. More ironic still was our reconciliation to one another through the gift of the saint's biography, which provided a number of edifying examples of people encountering difficulties in sustaining the role of honorable patrons. From a local cultural perspective, my dealings with Carlos and perhaps my fieldwork as a whole could thus very well be understood as an episode in the long history of interventions in the life of the community by people who claim to be doing good but are more interested in doing well. In other words, I belatedly discovered that I had acted as if I were a minor character within the traditional cultural genre of pastoral epic.

The realization that my efforts as an outsider to understand and adjust to life in Aracena had led me to act not just as an occasionally overzealous practitioner of modern social research but also as an unwitting agent for the reproduction of some of the least attractive aspects of traditional idioms and forms of social interaction directly affected the writing of this ethnography. Having been convinced that the political and cultural dynamics of fieldwork are such that there is no firm ground of tranquil dispassion and neutral contemplation on which to stand, I have tried to write a text that bridges some of the distance between academic and local forms of understanding by presenting a critical view of the genre of pastoral epic. On the one hand, as in pastoral epic, the mode of historical consciousness embodied in the text is discontinuous, episodic, and exemplary; and the plots of the stories told (including the story about Carlos and me) and of the text as a whole center on encounters of townspeople with local patrons and external authorities of various kinds. On the other hand, the interpretive stance taken toward these matters is essentially antiheroic, skeptical, and ironic, rather than laudatory and idealized, and strives to imitate the spirit if not always the letter of popular counternarratives of resistance which have long challenged the legitimacy of the dominant cultural genre by inverting its politicomoral sense.

Even so, like most ethnographies, this one constructs a version of other people's culture and history that runs the risk of appropriating them for purposes essentially unrelated and unresponsive to their values and wishes. In the case at hand, it is doubtful that the risk would be worth taking were it not for the fact that questions concerning the political significance of cultural traditions are on the minds of many people in Aracena and Andalusia. Indeed, how such questions are answered has both a direct and an indirect bearing on some of the issues and options involved in Andalusian cultural and political identity. Like Catalonia, the Basque country, and other areas of Spain, Andalusia now has the constitutional status and governmental institutions of an autonomous region. But in Andalusia, unlike in Catalonia and the Basque country, the sense of possessing a distinct regional identity has been relatively weak. Indeed, Andalusian identity has historically been intertwined and usually subordinated to representations of Spanish national identity.[14] The political concomitant of this has been the domination of the regional government by representatives of the national political parties, especially El Partido Socialista Obrero Español (PSOE), and the continuing inability of regional parties to articulate a compelling alternative vision of Andalusia's future.

Andalusian anthropologists have responded to this situation in two basic ways: they have tried to foster a stronger sense of regional identity by describing the richness and diversity of Andalusian customs (see, for example, Rodríguez Becerra 1980, 1982, 1985), and they have criticized and exposed some of the deleterious cultural effects of the long history of Andalusian poverty, dependence, and subordination (see, for example, Moreno Navarro 1981, 1984, 1985). Both of these basic strategies seem necessary and valuable, but they are not without certain dangers. On the one hand, to celebrate, catalog, and describe the region's customs and traditions may well reinforce the sort of folklorism that represents local cultural traditions as worthy of preservation largely because they attract tourists and add a touch of historical color to national life. On the other hand, to expose and criticize local traditions as vehicles of a culture of dependency that has to be overcome in the interests of material progress and socio-political liberation may well undermine cultural forms that have enabled many Andalusians to resist the increasing rationalization and homogenization of contemporary life in an advanced industrial society. In other words, the paradoxical and to some degree unavoidable risk involved in the ethnographic strategies devised by anthropologists to foster a sense of distinctive Andalusian identity is the risk of devaluing the contemporary significance and diminishing the force of cultural differences in the very act of delineating, celebrating, and comprehending them (see Cuenca Toribio 1984; Santos López 1984).

From this perspective, one of the principal values of the ethnographic account that follows may be to undermine the reifying tendencies of both the folkloric and dependency views of tradition. The examples of the politics of tradition in Aracena from 1634 to 1982 demonstrate that traditional culture, despite its deep involvement in strategies of domination, has never constituted a unified system or fixed structure of meanings and values. It has instead entailed an historically variable range of interpretations of social life, interpretations that have always been and continue to be actively contested and reshaped in accordance with unstable relationships of power and domination. For this reason, cultural traditions are neither to be venerated as living monuments to past forms of social life nor denigrated as impediments to future progress; they are to be employed as resources in the struggle to build a humane present.

PART 1

Tradition and Domination:
The Ancient Regime

1
Local Polities

The Marqués de Leganés... has given his consent in order
that the mercy may be done of freeing you from the
jurisdiction of the town of Aracena.
—[Signed] I, THE KING
Title of *villazgo* (town charter) of Alájar, 1700

PASTORAL, PATRONAGE, AND TRADITION

IN 1634, Rodrigo Caro, an author of the Spanish baroque with a
bent for ethnographic and archaeological inquiry, wrote *Antiquedades y principado de la ilustrísima ciudad de Sevilla . . .*, a work
describing the various towns and antiquities of western Andalusia.
Here is how Aracena appeared to him (1896:208–11):

> The first place that offers itself to us in this account [of the western
> Sierra Morena] is the town of Aracena, the largest metropolis of the
> sierra to which it gives its name. . . .
>
> At its highest point, the town has an ancient castle very strong by
> art and by nature, and by it is a parish church that was the first built
> of the place and was later restored; and afterwards, when times were
> more pacific, the settlement extended down and [the parish seat]
> was lowered to less rough terrain, and there a very large and spacious church of three vaulted naves all of white marble has been
> built. In addition to this church, there are monasteries of Dominicans and Carmelites and a convent.
>
> In the district of Aracena, there are seventeen hamlets [whose inhabitants] all regard themselves as householders of her as much in
> temporal as in spiritual matters, although many of the hamlets have
> churches with the sacraments. [The township] has a thousand
> householders, and the principal occupation of many of them is the
> herding of pigs; and the pastures of the town are good, and for this
> reason the dried meats and hams of Aracena are famous throughout

Spain. There are also many beehives, and the honey is very good; there are many irrigated gardens, and fruit trees supply fruits of all kinds to Seville and other places; the vines are many and the wine excellent. Near the town on the peak of a high hill that rises almost a league stands a hermitage of San Ginés, and it has a holy image of this saint which was brought from Germany by Doctor Arias Montano. There is in this hermitage a very large *cofradía* [brotherhood] founded by the principal people of the place, and many from outside have seated themselves in it as brothers because this saint is invoked against the plague of the lungs.

At three leagues from the town to the west is the remarkable *peña* [place, rock, peak] of Arias Montano, where he had his habitation and where he wrote many of his notable works; and while he lived there, that site was adorned with all of the proprieties and curiosities that pertain to such a great guest. Now aside from its natural aspect, which is in itself admirable, the rest is very decayed; but the renown of its ancient guest will make the place famous down through the centuries.

Caro's account of Aracena is typical of the period in both its generality and its use of traditional formulations, and it is worth examining for this reason. By referring to Aracena as "the largest metropolis of the sierra" at the beginning of his description, Caro stresses the importance of the town as a regional center. His subsequent references to the ancient castle ("El Castillo") and the churches of Santa María de Aracena and Santa María de la Asunción serve to identify local culture with the great traditions of the state and church, thereby linking the town with the larger polity. In describing the township, Caro's observations strike the notes of a rustic idyll of well-ordered prosperity (good pastures and honey, bountiful fruits, famous hams, and excellent wine). His account then shifts abruptly to a discussion of various forms of patronage centering on saints, religious images, lay religious brotherhoods, and "principal people" of the region.

Figuring prominently among the "principal people" in Caro's description is Benito Arias Montano (1527–98), one of the key figures of the Spanish Counter-Reformation (see Bell 1922; Rekers 1973). Montano spent most of the last two decades of his life in semiretirement near Aracena and has continued to be an important focus of historical consciousness in the sierra. Local traditions have generally represented him as an unassailably orthodox and pious scholar, an honorable and prudent statesman, and a patron of the people of the sierra. Caro's observations concerning Montano are fairly typical insofar as they seem designed not only to insist upon the harmonious relationship between local tradition and the high culture of Catholic humanism but also to suggest that the people of Aracena and the sierra were the pious and worthy recipients of the patronage and favors of the great man.

Taken as a whole, Caro's description of Aracena is an exemplary expression of the cultural genre of pastoral epic because it describes a prosperous rural community and associates this prosperity with the institutions of the church and state and with the protection and favors extended by patrons. This traditionalist mode of rhetorical description represents the town's fame and the community's identity in terms of rural bounty, religious devotion, and the virtues of saints, principal people, and a renowned benefactor while it omits mention of the mundane and less pleasant aspects of local affairs.

In the following sections of this chapter, bureaucratic and legal documents from the eighteenth century will be used in order to describe the formal principles, official ideologies, and practical dynamics that regulated the conduct of ordinary political and economic relations in the township. Having gained this broader perspective, we will be able to better understand the relationship between Caro's conventional description of Aracena and broader hegemonic processes of domination.

OFFICIAL VIEWS: PASTORAL ECONOMIES, CORPORATE BODIES, AND LEGITIMATE AUTHORITIES

Although relatively little is known about Aracena in the centuries before Caro, it is clear that by the end of the sixteenth century, the settlement was no longer merely a fortress with a village huddled around its base.[1] Instead, as Caro's description suggests, the town had emerged as a well-developed regional center. From the viewpoint of the city of Seville, Aracena no doubt appeared as little more than a minor dependency sequestered in a rugged hinterland; but from the perspective of its seventeen hamlets and the other settlements of the sierra, it had become a locus of authority, commerce, and religion—a "metropolis," to use Caro's hyperbole. The town's gentry, officials, clergy, and traders stood between the urban, cosmopolitan center of New World trade and the remote mountain villages.

The regional importance of Aracena in the eighteenth century is evident in two descriptive surveys, the first made in 1723 by Zapata, a governor of the town, and the second conducted in the mid-1750s under the auspices of the royal minister, the *marqués* of Ensenada (see Document of Zapata and Catastro de Ensenada in the list of documents cited). Though more detailed than Caro's account, these surveys contain little that is inconsistent with it. This is not because little had changed in a century and a half of plagues, dynastic wars, massive inflation, economic cycles of boom and bust, and the overall decline of Spanish imperial power but, rather, because the basic institutional, social, and economic structures of the sierra were flexible enough to accommodate these changes until the end of the eighteenth century (see Chapter 3).[2] The most obvious long-term local trends were a rise in population and a loss of Aracena's jurisdiction over many of its hamlets, which became chartered towns in their own right. Between Caro's time and 1753, the number of *vecinos* (heads of households) in the township increased from 1,000 to 1,367 (indicating an overall population of about 5,000 people in 1753), despite the fact that five of the seventeen dependent hamlets of the town in the early sixteenth century had won charters of *villazgo* and their *vecinos* therefore were no longer counted as inhabitants of Aracena.[3] Within the township, the majority (about 60 percent) of the inhabitants continued to live in the remaining hamlets, while Aracena proper consisted of the households of 540 *vecinos*.

Caro was not wrong in striking a pastoral note in his description of local agriculture. Despite difficult conditions, the variety of crops grown in the township in the early modern period was notable: olives, grapes, cherries, walnuts, pears, persimmons, figs, peaches, apples, beans, garbanzos, pomegranates, and flax were all cultivated, and about half of the arable land of the township and almost all of the fields of "first quality" were devoted to the production of wheat and barley.[4] As a rule, however, only one crop could be produced every three years because of the poor quality of the land, and yields were always inadequate to meet local demand. More productive were the groves of oak and chestnut trees on which five thousand or more hogs were fattened for slaughter every winter. In addition, twenty thousand goats fed on the stubble of the fields and grazed the uncultivable hillsides that comprised nearly a quarter of the approximately forty thousand hectares of the township.

The local economy was based on these crops and had three interrelated but somewhat distinct tiers oriented to household needs, the requirements of local and regional markets, and a profitable long-distance trade in commodities. To the extent that their resources permitted, households of all sizes engaged in subsistence production. To a greater or lesser degree, all households also participated in a regional marketing system centered on the exchange of grains, oil, wine, and livestock. Cereals were especially important in this trade. Transporting grains was expensive but necessary to overcome chronic shortages and prevent disastrous famines. Thus, the market held in Aracena every

Saturday attracted large numbers of traders from Extremadura with wheat, oats, and rye to sell. Finally, animal products not only supplemented the local diet and were exchanged regionally, but they also provided the main raw materials for a commodity trade that linked the town and sierra to Seville, Cádiz, and more distant markets. The significance of this third tier of the agrarian economy is indicated by the fact that no fewer than 196 dealers in "shoeleather, leather, hides, tallow, lard, oil, and livestock" and nearly an equal number of muleteers depended on it for a large part of their livelihoods (Catastro de Ensenada).[5]

While the majority of the traders were residents of Aracena proper, the householders of the township's hamlets were almost all primary producers of agricultural products. In 1753, the dependent hamlets ranged in size from 8 households in Las Granadillas to 177 households in Campofrío, but there was only a narrow range of socioeconomic differentiation evident among their inhabitants. Most hamlets could count a few humble *labradores* among their numbers. Such men were peasants who owned or had access to enough land that they did not need to sell their labor to others. It was unusual for these hamlet dwellers to own more than a house, a corral, and several scattered, often minuscule plots of land, but they could earn a minimal living by combining several small properties of different types and a few animals to form a small subsistence farm that met most of the ordinary needs of a household. In addition to their small personal holdings, as *vecinos* the *labradores* had the right to graze their animals on the common pastures of the township, and some of the more prosperous among them possessed a pair of mules and leased small parcels of land, usually from the church.

Modest as the estates of most *labradores* were, most inhabitants of the hamlets were not so fortunate. There were fewer than two hundred *labradores* in the whole township, and roughly one-third of them were residents of Aracena proper. The great majority of the householders of the hamlets and between 55 and 60 percent of the total labor force of the township were *jornaleros* (agrarian day laborers) who worked on the lands of others for a wage of two reales a day, an amount scarcely sufficient to buy bread for a small household. These people lived in a condition of chronic and often desperate poverty. The following list of the worldly goods accumulated by a *jornalero* over a lifetime is not uncommon: "a cape, one set of clothes, a pair of shoes, a chair, a table, a knife, a frying pan, a pot, a quantity of charcoal, two chickens, and a pig" (AN/mlv 1757).

Aracena proper was different. Although the town had its share of primary agricultural producers, many of the townspeople earned their livelihoods by other means. The largest group of artisans consisted of those involved in the transformation of animal products. In addition to several butchers and two dozen tanners and leatherdressers, the town could boast of fifty-five master, journeyman, and apprentice shoemakers, of whom twenty were employed in two large workshops. There were also twenty-eight bakers; ten carpenters; sixteen masons; nine vendors of cloth, kitchen goods, ribbons, and other articles; several blacksmiths; a brick and tile seller; nine potters; and numerous practitioners of other basic crafts and trades, including inn and tavern keepers, tailors, hatmakers, silversmiths, surgeons, barbers, and even a chocolate maker. Professions and services requiring highly specialized knowledge were represented by two physicians, two pharmacists, four teachers, four *abogados* (lawyers), and several notaries, *procuradores* (solicitors), and scribes. Such a diversity of occupations in a town whose population could not have exceeded three thousand indicates its importance as a regional marketing center.

The men who carried on professional careers or ran large commercial enterprises were almost entirely drawn from the ranks of the local elite—the group of about fifteen families of notables, *hidalgos* (the lowest untitled rank of nobility), and *hacendados* (large landowners), whose members used the title of *Don* or *Doña* and lived in the town center. Much of the wealth and power of the elite derived from their control of formal institutions and offices, but even apart from their dominant position in public life, the elite families were well endowed with private and personal property, and they were in control of the economy of the region.

The basis of the economic position of the elite was their access to land, the elementary means of production. They were direct proprietors of perhaps 40 percent of the township's area, which they usually personally managed and exploited (although short-term leases and sharecropping agreements were not uncommon). In addition, the largest local landowners were able to administer or lease much of the municipal and ecclesiastical lands, which accounted for as much as half of Aracena's territory.[6] With the control of vast areas of land also came control of the raw animal products essential to Aracena's role in transregional commerce. Indeed, what marks the economic position of the local gentry is just this involvement in all phases of commodity production and exchange—an involvement that not only gave trader-proprietors strategic advantages over the artisans and *jornaleros* whose labor they required but also permitted a high degree of "vertical integration" and coordination of production, processing, and commerce.

The capital goods listed in the testamentary inventory of one landowner of Aracena reflect a fairly typical range of agrarian activities extending from production for household subsistence to production for commodity markets (AN/mlv 1757). The deceased *Don* owned the following: one house with two full wine cellars (valued at 13,330 reales), one new country house (8,000 reales), one tannery (20,000 reales), one mill (5,000 reales), one *monte* with oaks (52,000 reales), one fenced area with olives and figs (7,700 reales), one *huerta* (small irrigated garden) with chestnut trees (8,000 reales), 1,394 hides of various types (109,372 reales), 1,134 goats (48,010 reales), 42 measures of wheat (2,666 reales), and 20 pigs (7,260 reales). The total value of the estate was thus 281,338 reales.

Such an estate, though not an especially large one among those of the gentry, nevertheless indicates that its owner was actively engaged in general commerce. At the time of his death, outstanding contracts to deliver hides to two dealers in Seville and another in Cádiz had yet to be fulfilled. Even so, in his final days it is unlikely that this landowner was very anxious about problems of cash flow, since his strongbox contained 21,446 reales (equivalent to the yearly wages of between twenty and thirty fully employed *jornaleros*). He may, however, have been somewhat concerned to settle accounts with his neighbors, since seventy-eight *vecinos* of the town were indebted to him for amounts ranging from 34 to 4,719 reales. Additional evidence of the gentleman's economic status is revealed in the forty-page list of household goods—including furniture, tools, arms, clothing, linens, pillows, lamps, worked silver plate, strongboxes, crucifixes, religious images, and paintings of the Virgin and saints—all testifying to the prosperity and comfort of the family. Similar documents indicate that some of the local gentry were considerably wealthier than this man and that others were poorer.

Generally, it is clear that although the economic position of Aracena's elite was far below that of the high nobility of Andalusia or even the established commercial families of Seville (see Pike 1972 for an account of both sorts of elite), it was far above that of most of the artisans and workers of the sierra who had to struggle to eke out a bare subsistence. Less than movers and shakers of the realm, the local gentry were nonetheless more than prosperous peasants, and their wealth and power gave them decisive influence over local affairs.

In Aracena, the gentry lived side by side with traders, artisans, *labradores,* and *jornaleros,* and this proximity of the powerful and the humble created far more complex patterns of socioeconomic stratification than existed in the dependent hamlets of the township. One mark of this greater complexity was the presence in the town of more than a hundred domestic servants, some of whom lived in the households of the elite. No such group existed in the hamlets. It was only in

Aracena that the range of wealth and poverty was great enough to create the social conditions for such an occupation. Yet the social character of Aracena itself clearly reflected the town's place in a regional division of labor that shaped the social life of each of the communities of the sierra.

The interrelations among these communities were conditioned in part by the requirements of a system of market production and exchange and in part by critical "noneconomic" mechanisms for extracting wealth (Wolf 1982). A tributary political economy of huge proportions was based on the control of lands and the collection of taxes and rents by the officials and corporate bodies of the church and state. The extraction of tribute by these institutions was legitimated not by purely economic considerations but instead by the archaic tripartite organization of society in estates of nobles, clergy, and commoners.

In principle, the social order was hierarchical and authoritarian, and the estates were bound to one another by complementary sets of duties, rights, and freedoms. The noble and honorable ranks of society were owed deference and had privileges in keeping with their role as protectors and governors of the realm. The clergy deserved support in order to fulfill their spiritual and charitable functions. Commoners had to labor and pay taxes, but in return they were entitled to just government, the pastoral ministrations of the church, and access to economic means sufficient to allow them to earn their own livelihoods. Although this simple scheme was in fact endlessly complicated by the existence of dozens of chartered corporate bodies, such as lay religious brotherhoods, parishes, convents, associations of gentry, and hamlet communes, each of which had a unique set of properties, entitlements, privileges, and obligations, the estate principle was firmly inscribed in both law and custom, and it regulated the conduct of many aspects of practical affairs.

Until the beginning of the seventeenth century, virtually the whole sierra, including the township of Aracena, was *tierra realenga* (royal territory) incorporated into the realm of Seville and subject to the jurisdiction of the royal officials who governed the city (Terán 1976). By 1627, however, *señorío* (lordship) over Aracena had passed to Don Gaspar de Guzmán, count-duke of Olivares, favorite of Philip IV, and one of the most powerful statesmen in Europe (see Domínguez Ortiz and Aguilar Piñal 1976:91; Elliott 1986). Even after the fall of the count-duke, the *señorío* remained in the Guzmán family, but it eventually became a part of the "Principality of the Counts of Altamira." Nominally, all of the inhabitants of Aracena owed respect and obedience to the lord of the House of Altamira. In contrast, however, to the ancient feudal prerogatives of the great noble houses whose heads often enjoyed virtual sovereignty over their subjects, the lordship granted over Aracena was more limited, and the Crown retained some powers. Even so, the House of Altamira had two critically important prerogatives. One was to appoint the *gobernador y justicia mayor* (governor and chief magistrate) of the township, and the other was to receive the income from the *alcabala* tax (AN/mlv 1756).[7] Other than appointing a new governor from time to time and expressing concern over the delivery of their incomes to the court in Madrid, none of the counts of Altamira ever seem to have evinced great interest in Aracena.

Their appointed governors, however, were intimately involved in local affairs, presided over the *cabildo secular* (town council) of Aracena, and held broad executive, judicial, and legislative authority. The remaining members of the council were the *teniente del gobernador* (deputy governor), the *alguacil mayor* (high constable), a handful of minor officials, and up to six aldermen known as *regidores,* who each had different prerogatives, titles, and duties.[8] Unlike the *gobernador,* these *regidores* were all native householders of the township, and two of them, the *regidores perpetuos,* held their posts by virtual hereditary privilege and often rivaled the *gobernador* in influence if not in legal authority. The other members of the council were appointed to their offices for varying tenures either by officials in Seville or by the *gobernador.*[9]

In addition to the *gobernador* and the majority of the *regidores,* many other officials and licensees of the township held their posts at the behest of superordinate authorities. There were, for example, captains and subalterns of the local militia responsible for mustering troops in times of crisis; a customs officer; tax agents; and various licensees charged with overseeing the supply of commodities such as seed, grains, and salt, regulating the soap and tobacco trades, and so forth (AN/mlv 1757). Most of these offices were granted by the House of Altamira or by the Crown. Such positions often provided their possessors with lucrative sources of income and enabled them to control and profit from key sectors of local and regional trade, but they were not generally posts to which great political power was attached.

The ordinary householders of the township had an even smaller voice in the conduct of public affairs. The traditional right of householders to hold public meetings and vote on critical matters affecting the welfare of the community was rarely invoked in Aracena. Moreover, the *gobernador* appointed the *alcaldes pedáneos* (justices of the peace) of the township, whose duties included representing the interests of the common people before the council and the onerous task of collecting taxes from their neighbors as well as the settling of minor disputes. As a result, political power in Aracena was exercised almost exclusively by the town council, which had effective control over many aspects of local affairs ranging from the maintenance of the town's water supply to the celebration of fiestas. The power of the council was particularly critical in three areas of vital economic concern to the ordinary householders of the township: the regulation of commerce, the administration of public lands, and the collection of taxes.

Aracena's weekly market and its annual *feria* (fair) attracted traders in livestock and many other commodities from all over the sierra, and because the town council regulated most aspects of commercial exchange, it functioned as a mercantile board whose economic influence extended far beyond the limits of the township. The council appointed the overseer of weights and measures for the markets, exercised control over who could buy and sell, and served as a board of appeal for settling disputes among traders. In addition, the council awarded exclusive licenses for the supply of goods such as beef, cod, liquors, and munitions to the township and was thereby able to set prices for a number of key commodities. The mercantile prerogatives of the council were therefore of sufficient scope that the prosperity of many householders directly depended on how these prerogatives were exercised.

The public lands of Aracena, though not extensive in area, were important both as a means of livelihood for householders and as a source of income for the House of Altamira.[10] These lands constituted an estimated 8 to 12 percent of the township, and they were divided into two basic categories: the *propios* and the *tierras baldías* (the term indicates that lands in this second category were once directly held by the Crown). The twenty-two parcels of land identified as *propios* were administered by the *regidor de propios,* who was a member of the town council and who ordinarily leased tracts to particular individuals. The incomes thus produced were intended to support public services and benefit the entire community. The *tierras baldías* were administered directly by the *gobernador* and consisted of twelve large tracts and many smaller plots. Three of these twelve tracts and some of the smaller plots were common lands. Most of these commons consisted of hillside pastures of poor quality on which hogs and goats were grazed. According to traditional use rights, all *vecinos* had equal access to these pastures; and for some, such access probably made the difference between want and a minimally satisfactory subsistence. The remaining tracts of the *tierras baldías* were reserved for producing the income for the *alcabala* tax owed to the House of Altamira. In the mid-eighteenth century, this amount was fixed at about 17,000 reales per year.

This tax was only a small portion of the heavy exactions imposed on the township by higher secular and ecclesiastical authorities. Annually destined for the royal treasury were the proceeds of the *bulas de cruzada* (4,261 reales in the 1750s), the *servicios ordinarios* (9,792 reales), and the *servicios de paja* (9,792 reales). The burden of payment of these and other taxes weighed heavily on *pecheros* (commoners), because the clergy, *hidalgos,* and many town officials claimed exemption from most of these obligations. Since the council members determined how the duties listed above would be collected, they acted as fiscal middlemen mediating between the majority of the populace and higher authorities in Seville and Madrid as well as administrators of public lands and regulators of local markets.

The role of ecclesiastical authorities in the tributary aspects of the political economy of Aracena was at least as significant as that of the secular officials. Indeed, the organization of ecclesiastical institutions roughly paralleled that of secular ones.[11] In 1752, there were sixty-eight parish clergy in the *priorato* (priory) of Santa María de la Asunción of Aracena, which formed a part of the Archbishopric of Seville. The *priorato* functioned as a super parish and incorporated the lesser parishes of hamlets and former hamlets of the town within its jurisdiction. It was governed by the *cabildo eclesiástico,* a council whose practical functions within its own sphere were analogous to those of the town council. The senior priest of the parish of Aracena presided jointly over the ecclesiastical council with the vicar of the *priorato,* who also usually held the post of commissioner of the Holy Office of the Inquisition and acted as the principal liaison with the cathedral chapter of Seville. The remaining seats on the council were held by the ten *curas beneficiados* (beneficed priests) of the *priorato,* who were supported in part by the endowments of the various lesser parishes. The council and particularly the senior priest and the vicar were responsible for governing the other parish clergy, conducting the complex temporal business of the *priorato,* and seeing to the spiritual and corporal needs of lay people.

In addition to the parish clergy, there were four regular religious communities in Aracena in the eighteenth century: a house of eleven Carmelite monks (known as El Carmen); a convent of thirty Discalced Carmelite nuns (Santa Catalina); a community of nine Dominican brothers (San Sebastián); and a convent of twenty-nine Dominican sisters (Jesús, María, y José). The wealth of these communities was not great. In the 1750s, the best-endowed house was the convent of Santa Catalina, which had an annual income of only slightly more than 16,000 reales generated from the proceeds from about fifty hectares of leased land and hundreds of small "tributes" attached to the properties of laymen.[12] The small endowments of the convents and monasteries suggest that Aracena had few jolly friars or plump nuns.

In contrast, the parish clergy of Aracena enjoyed far greater incomes from many different sources. Nearly 40 percent of the lands of the township were classified as ecclesiastical, and most of these were administered through the *priorato*. The lands and properties of the parish church fell into four distinct categories. The first consisted of beneficial properties that were endowments attached to the various parishes and destined to provide the livings for *curas beneficiados* and to maintain the physical structure of the church. The second category, which was more important in terms of the incomes of particular clergy, consisted of *capellanías* (chaplaincies). The endowments of the chaplaincies varied greatly in size and manner of exploitation. Most consisted of a single parcel of land, such as a *monte* of oaks, which might be leased to a *colono* (tenant farmer) (AN/mpt 1736). A few included several houses and up to fifteen separate tracts of land, which were frequently worked by *jornaleros* and managed by relatives of the chaplain (AN/mpt 1757). The third category consisted of properties incorporated into charitable and pious foundations. The endowments of these foundations were quite small except for those of the foundation known as El Patronato de Gerónimo Infante, a wealthy and singularly complex organization (see Chapter 3). Finally, the incomes of some of the senior priests and most of the twenty-four clergy who held minor orders in the *priorato* were augmented by the proceeds from a fourth category of land, the patrimonial properties, which accounted for about one-fifth of the total lands of the church. While patrimonial lands were classified as ecclesiastical and were therefore exempt from certain taxes, this was solely due to the clerical status of their owners. Essentially, patrimonial lands were private, entailed properties and were managed as such. Most of the twenty ecclesiastics of the township who engaged directly in commodity trade possessed lands of this type.

Besides receiving rents, the *priorato* and parish of Aracena benefited from the incomes produced by the *diezmos,* the *primicias* (taxes on agricultural production), and other ecclesiastical levies. Local cultivators annually contributed about 50,000 reales in coin and hundreds of *fanegas* of wheat to the church.[13] Thus, the ecclesiastical taxes on the inhabitants of the township were as burdensome as the exactions made by secular authorities; and as was the case with the secular tributes, a large proportion of the ecclesiastical tributes (over half) was destined for distant treasuries and storehouses.

As this summary of the corporate and economic organization of the church and state indicates, it would be difficult to overestimate the impact of formal institutions on the township. Quite aside from all considerations of the church's cultural influence, its sheer wealth and resources gave it a central place in local society, and the town council exercised authority over equally vital aspects of secular affairs. Indeed, the patterns of tributary redistribution and administrative authority were analogous in the ecclesiastical and secular realms: wealth was extracted and transferred upward through the institutional ranks and social hierarchy, while authority was delegated downward by the overlords of the church and state to local officials. Aracena's position within the system of tribute and authority made it an administrative as well as a market center for the sierra, and it was a town of officials, functionaries, and priests as well as laborers, traders, and landowners.

CONTESTING AUTHORITY: OLIGARCHIC POWER AND THE POLITICS OF COMMUNITY INCORPORATION

The concentration of multiple administrative, mercantile, and other functions in the town and church councils of Aracena gave the leading officials of these bodies ready access to higher authorities and effective command of local affairs. These secular and ecclesiastical officials shared not only similar strategic positions of power but also the same general interests and background. The possession of wealth and legal privileges that accompanied honorable rank, the practical exigencies of politics, and other factors such as literacy limited accession to higher local offices to the local gentry. Indeed, those who claimed the rank of *hidalgo* held or controlled all of the positions of *regidor,* several lesser posts connected to the secular council, and the senior clerical and lay offices of the *priorato*. The township was thus governed by a self-perpetuating civil-religious oligarchy (see Chapter 3).

The circles of power and patronage within the township largely excluded the lower ranks of society. In the secular realm, the council members distributed minor offices such as that of constable and lamplighter to their clients among the ordinary townspeople, but they reserved larger favors such as the distribution of mercantile licenses for themselves and their relatives, friends, and allies among the gentry (AN/mpt 1757). Similar patterns existed in the management of church property and the distribution of ecclesiastical posts to laymen. No doubt some ordinary householders also benefited from ties to the elite based on master-servant links, relations of godparenthood, membership in religious brotherhoods, and so forth, but most artisans, peasants, and *jornaleros* (and particularly those residing in the hamlets) were outside these networks.

The dark sides of oligarchic rule were political factionalism and the exploitation and neglect of the poor. Cutthroat competition was particularly rife on the town council, where temptations to profit from office were greatest. Thus, whenever a new junta seized control of the council, most of the lesser offices in the township rapidly changed hands (see Chapter 3). Although the ecclesiastical realm was more stable, there were often conflicts among the priests over chaplaincies and disputes between the priests and secular authorities over such matters as the celebration of religious festivals and the administration of charitable foundations.

Yet in comparison to more general patterns of exploitation, even the worst factional dispute among the oligarchs was a tempest in a teakettle. The absence of any systematic checks on local authorities meant that reasonably clever officials could profit greatly by administering justice, lands, taxes, and markets in their own interest. Officials seldom had to go so far as to violate the letter of written law.[14] Rather, traditional rights were compromised by manipulating the administrative and judicial powers invested in authorities. Mismanagement of the common lands, upon which many householders were particularly dependent for their livelihoods, is a case in point.

The *regidor de propios* and his allies on the council treated large tracts of the township commons and all of the *propios* as spoils of office. Generally, between one-fourth and one-half of the *propios* were under lease for periods ranging from three to thirty or more years to members of Aracena's elite. These "alienations" were justified on various grounds. Most frequently, the pastures and groves of alienated lands were declared to be "exhausted," and the leaseholders undertook to replant them in exchange for exclusive use rights that prohibited ordinary householders access to the parcels. Occasionally, the lands were alienated in order to repay debts incurred by the township to the leaseholder. But whatever the ostensible reasons, none of the alienated lands ever appear to have produced any significant income or benefits for the community as a whole. Ground rents received by the township were virtually nil, and accusations were frequently made that the leaseholders overexploited and grievously damaged the very lands they had pledged to revitalize (AN/mv 1763:10; 1767:12, 189). Moreover, despite the repeated protests that lands deemed by the council to belong to the *propios* were in fact part of the commons, ordinary householders had little success in their efforts to win redress of their grievances.

If the community as a whole did not profit from these alienations, the *regidores* and their allies certainly did. While it was not unusual for one or another of the *regidores* to control parcels of the *propios,* the common practice was for the council members to award the alienated lands to their friends and relatives. A telling indication of the attractiveness of these arrangements for the authorities is the fact that the most bitter factional struggles within the council generally pertained to issues arising from the award of alienated lands (see Chapter 3).

The way in which the township's grain supply was managed indicates that much the same pattern existed in the regulation of other resources. By the mid-eighteenth century, townships were mandated to maintain *pósitos* (granaries) whose contents could alleviate shortages in hard times. In Aracena, the granary was under the supervision of the *regidor de propios,* who was charged with collecting and storing a reserve of three thousand *fanegas* of wheat. In times of relative abundance, this official apparently neglected his duties, and the reserve was rarely near the prescribed quantity. However, when shortages existed, the *regidor* exerted himself to collect debts of grain from the householders. Since the exaction was demanded when there was already a shortage, it was occasionally necessary to resort to coercion. There are records (AN/mpt 1757; AN/mv 1762) preserved of several instances similar to one in 1766 (AN/mv 1766:208) when the *gobernador* clapped two peons of the hamlet of Los Granados in jail until the *alcalde* (justice of the peace) and seven other householders of the hamlet surrendered a large quantity of wheat owed to the granary. It does not appear that this pattern of mismanagement was simply a matter of neglect of duties: during the same period, the less powerful faction of the council charged that the *regidor* was manipulating grain supplies for his own profit, apparently by withholding public wheat from the market to drive up prices. It is small wonder that legal disputes over whether it was the *gobernador,* the council as a body, or royal officials who had the right to appoint the *regidor de propios* seem to have persisted for decades (DZ 1723).

Without question, the hamlets suffered most severely from abuses of power, and documents of the period contain many instances of disputes over common lands that indicate a general pattern of conflict between the gentry of Aracena and the householders of the hamlets. One case presented before the *gobernador* demonstrates both the intensity and the difficulties of resistance. The criminal proceedings were prompted by an incident that occurred in 1758 (AN/mpt 1758) when two swineherds were bold enough to graze their hogs on what they asserted to be common pastures of the hamlets of Corteconcepción and Puerto Gil. One morning they were attacked and severely beaten by a group of men who proceeded to scatter their animals far and wide. Backed by their neighbors, the outraged swineherds sought legal redress and claimed in court that the bullies were instigated by two cousins, one a priest of Alájar and the other an *hidalgo* of Aracena (both related to a *regidor*). According to the swineherds, these two cousins falsely claimed to possess rights to the fruits of the commons. The case was like many others for two reasons. First, the alienation of the common lands was upheld by the *gobernador.* Second, the swine-herds, in addition to being beaten, were fined for their trespass. This reveals the legal and illegal coercion to which ordinary householders were subject when they resisted the manipulations of the oligarchs.

The continuing willingness of the hamlet dwellers to unite in or-der to resist the depredations of the powerful against such odds prob-ably accounts for the survival of the commons of the township, because protest on the part of the *jornaleros, labradores,* and artisans of Aracena itself appears to have been more sporadic. This disparity probably reflects both the stronger linkages of patronage and the more immediate means of coercion and surveillance that were present in the town and tended to deny ordinary townspeople the capacity to sustain popular protest (see Chapter 3). In the relatively isolated and homo-geneous hamlets, however, where the notion of the *pueblo* (village, common people) as a community of equals bound to one another by mutual obligations was less immediately compromised by hierarchical principles of authority, defending the traditional rights of the commu-nity as a whole served as the political rationale both for individual acts of resistance and for collective political action (see Weisser 1976 for an account of peasant resistance in early modern Castile).

The strength of this sentiment of community solidarity in oppo-sition to oligarchic power was no doubt continually reinforced by the knowledge that it was possible for a hamlet to become incorporated as a *villa* (independent township). As a result, over the course of more than three centuries, hamlet after hamlet sought and won indepen-dence from the jurisdiction of Aracena; and by the early nineteenth century, only six hamlets of an original thirty remained dependencies of the town (see Núñez Roldán 1987:55–59, 141). During the eigh-teenth century alone, the hamlets of Alájar (in the year 1700), Castaño del Robledo (in 1700), Linares de la Sierra (in 1724), Campofrío (in 1753), Los Marines (in 1768), and Valdearco (in 1770) were granted titles of *villazgo* by the Crown, as indicated in local archival sources. Thus, during the Ancient Regime, the formation of independent towns through a process of fragmentation into smaller communal cor-porations was the most salient, enduring, and recurrent political pro-cess in the sierra.[15]

The period in which a hamlet sought to win autonomy from the town was conditioned by the interplay of a complex set of factors. Dis-tance from Aracena clearly mattered, for many of the most remote hamlets were among the earliest to become townships. The size of the population and the prosperity of the householders were also influential because the process was expensive and required a community to muster its collective resources. The most important factors were political, however. While all of the hamlets—regardless of their size, distance from Aracena, or the period in which they sought independence—cited in their petitions the same general litany of complaints concerning the extortion of taxes, failures in the administration of justice, and misuse of common lands, the specific political resources that each of them could muster varied considerably from time to time, and this directly affected the chances of achieving a successful outcome.

The case of Valdearco was fairly representative of this process and illustrates how various forces interacted with one another. Valdearco was a small community consisting of about sixty households of *labradores* and *jornaleros* on the northern edge of Aracena's territory. The initial crisis that set the community on the road toward independence was a dispute in 1761 (AN/mv 1761) over common lands with the neighboring and much larger town of Cumbres Mayores. Residents of this town had begun to encroach on some of the pastures of the *tierras baldías* of Aracena, which the householders of Valdearco claimed were theirs to use as an "immemorial privilege." Faced with losing these pastures, the people of Valdearco appealed to the council of Aracena for protection. Unfortunately, no assistance was forthcoming. The council was in internal disarray and repeatedly failed to respond to Valdearco's plight or to defend its own interests in the matter. Thus, by 1763 (AN/mv 1763:56), the *alcalde* of Valdearco was apparently desperate and chose to side with the minority council faction in Aracena. He and the disaffected *regidores* pressed a complaint before authorities in Seville in which they accused the dominant group on the council of dereliction of duty and failure to defend the rights of the householders of the township.

This tactic appears to have backfired. In 1768 (AN/mv 1768:137), the dispute with Cumbres Mayores still persisted in about the same state as before, but the hamlet's relations with Aracena had further deteriorated. Now Valdearco was also charging Aracena with a long list of grievances including unfair taxation, extortion, and the illegal alienation of common lands (other than those that were disputed by Cumbres Mayores, evidently). On these grounds, Valdearco appealed to the king and to the count of Altamira for the privilege of *villazgo*. After some complex negotiations with royal officials took place and a set of suits and counterpetitions by the council of Aracena were settled, Valdearco was granted the title in 1770.

The payments demanded by the Crown in exchange for the title had made it necessary for thirty-five householders of Valdearco to mortgage fifty-four separate properties ranging from a grove of chestnuts worth 6,000 reales to a vineyard valued at 550 reales. Whether this enabled the householders of the new town to fulfill their desire to "increase their capital, traffic, commerce, and families" is not altogether clear, since the disputed common lands remained under the jurisdiction of Aracena. What Valdearco did gain was the right to manage its political affairs through a town council chosen from its own householders (AN/mv 1770:145).

The political dynamics in the cases of other hamlets were roughly similar. Since Aracena ordinarily resisted the process with all the means at its disposal, most of the hamlets seem to have achieved independent status during periods when some critical threat to the welfare of the community arose and galvanized the inhabitants into sustained action. To win independence required in practical political terms the capacity to pursue and endure endless petitions, negotiations, suits, and countersuits with contending powers. At least four separate interests—those of the Crown, the House of Altamira, the hamlet, and Aracena—were usually at stake and had to be accommodated in varying degrees in the process. As a result, the eventual outcome, as in the case of Valdearco, was often manifestly not all that the inhabitants of a hamlet had wished it to be, and the practical benefits of independent status were usually compromised in one way or another. Measuring the length and expense of the process against the limited results achieved gives an idea both of how acute the sense of grievance must have been among the householders of the hamlets and of how much political power was concentrated in the hands of the authorities of Aracena.

HEGEMONIC PROCESSES AND THE RHETORIC OF DOMINATION

The language of the petitions and charters of Valdearco and other hamlets of the sierra reflected the ideological as well as the practical dynamics of the political processes of late estate society. From one perspective, the struggles between the hamlets and Aracena's oligarchs were clearly conflicts between the dominant and subordinate classes of the township, but these struggles were not primarily represented in terms of general conflicts of economic or other interests between social groups. Rather, the discourse of the official documents was shaped by notions of the prerogatives and obligations that ought to exist between the authorities and those they were supposed to govern and protect. A hamlet's attempt to win independence from Aracena was thus fundamentally construed as a direct appeal to a higher patron who was called upon to correct the particular evils done by local authorities and to grant the hamlet a charter of incorporation that established the formal rights of the community. In return for this recognition, the community was obliged to express its gratitude and reaffirm its loyalty to the overlord.

In most documents concerning hamlet affairs, three strands of rhetoric and argument were interwoven. One rhetorical strand consisted of appeals directly to the king or occasionally to the count of Altamira for justice and protection as deserts of loyal subjects. Even though the price to be paid for the title of incorporation was discussed, the quasi-religious rhetoric of the appeals stressed the disinterested role of the king or the count as a fount of "mercy" and "grace" in the affairs of this world and cast these temporal lords in the role of patrons of almost absolute heroic virtue, wisdom, and magnanimity. A second strand of argument sought to convey a sense of the hamlet as a community worthy and capable of self-government. Heavy stress was placed on the cooperative consensus and spirit of unity within the hamlet, and the petitioners customarily claimed that they were seeking autonomy as the only means of restoring their rights to protect and promote "natural goods," such as the increase of family patrimonies. In relation to such claims, the argument was usually made that the natural prosperity of the hamlet had been reduced to an unnatural state of poverty by the extortions of Aracena's authorities. Roughly equal emphasis was thus placed on the economic ability and on the spirit of determination that led the householders of the hamlet to willingly volunteer to bear the costs and burdens required to achieve independent status. The third strand of rhetoric served to interpret the significance of the specific complaints of the hamlet. Exploitative abuses of power were attributed wholly to the personal moral failings and lack of a sense of justice and honor on the part of Aracena's officials. The disintegrating effects of their immorality on the hamlet were emphasized—most often by claiming that many householders had fled to other towns to escape the depredations of the powerful and that the state of those who remained was one of unjust "slavery" (Moreno Alonso 1979:278–81). In this way, the petitions sharply drew the contrast between immoral authorities in Aracena and a hamlet community of moral equals whose members were willing to sacrifice a portion of their wealth for the common good of their neighbors and the kingdom as a whole.

This official rhetoric of protest and compliance is in many ways similar to the rhetoric of Caro's apparently factual but also highly selective description of Aracena that was quoted at the beginning of this chapter. As noted previously, the three major elements in Caro's description of Aracena were a disclosure of the links of the community to the higher institutions of church and state, a description of agricultural variety and rural prosperity, and an evocation of the piety, wisdom, and beneficence of local patrons and "principal people" of the town. In the official documents of the hamlets, the first of these elements appears in the form of the appeal to the prince for justice, and the second element is an argument that the hamlet is potentially capable of supporting itself economically and governing its own affairs politically. The third element is inverted: the "principal people" of the town, Aracena's officials, are represented as the antithesis of beneficent patrons. Thus, the rhetorical form of Caro's description and the ideological discourse of official legal documents mirror each other and represent variations on common themes.

Much the same is true of the rhetoric used by Aracena's oligarchs in their petitions and reports to higher authorities. In dealing with the matter of the hamlets, the oligarchs usually took the position of denying any malfeasance, asserting that their legal prerogatives were well grounded, and accusing the commoners of disrespect, rebelliousness, and the unbridled pursuit of self-interest. However, these direct claims were ordinarily accompanied by protestations of loyalty that displayed an acute awareness of social hierarchy and simultaneously managed to convey a sense of intimate solidarity between local authorities and the higher powers of the realm. The tone of these rhetorical acts of obeisance is well represented in the preamble of a report on local affairs sent by a *gobernador* of Aracena to the count of Altamira (DZ 1723):

> Even before my birth, my fortune was propitious [because] the greatness of Your Excellency placed on me the obligation of consecrated obedience to a House as brilliant as it is illustrious. Ordination is Divine, and it is natural that less worthy and perfect creatures serve and subject themselves to the most worthy and elevated. And since I am the eldest legitimate heir of my father, who received benefits incompatible with his merits by virtue of the renown that came to him from being the Servant of Your Excellency, his legacy has come to me; and by natural obligation, my submission is owing in order to manifest the law of gratitude.

Intimate and elaborate declarations of this kind were well beyond what hamlet dwellers dared or probably desired. By invoking divine and natural law as well as the history of the two families in order to reaffirm the relationship of protective patronage and servile obligation existing between himself and the count, the *gobernador* manages to suggest the close community of interests and unity of purpose of authorities of every kind and degree. While hamlet dwellers depicted the role of the patron as one of formally perpetual but practically intermittent protection and while they in fact sought to establish a relationship with all higher authorities best characterized as one of benign neglect, the *gobernador* suggests in this passage that constant and intensely personal links are the only guarantee of moral and political order. His rhetorical flourishes not only create a sense of identification and solidarity among virtuous and heroic men burdened with the responsibilities of authority, but they also reinforce the belief that the vulgar populace, being naturally of lesser merit, must therefore be carefully watched and closely governed in order to prosper even minimally. This discursive variant of Caro's themes represents the most hierarchical and authoritarian version of pastoral epic. Though far from his master in distance, the *gobernador* is close to him in his convictions.

Despite the differences in tone between Caro's description and the versions of ideological language discussed above, these texts offer examples of mutually authorizing forms of rhetoric that suggest a great deal about the character of cultural and political hegemony in Aracena during the early modern period. Notions of patronage, prosperity, and legitimate institutional authority were central to Caro's ideal portrait of pastoral felicity, and they also constituted the principal cultural means of regulating, negotiating, and contesting relations of domination and subordination of all sorts. Thus, the conventions of pastoral epic by no means wholly misrepresented the effective power structure or political dynamics of the township. Rather, the partial ideological mystification of class exploitation was only one somewhat minor aspect of a cultural formation whose principal hegemonic effect was to channel local resistance and opposition along predictable and manageable lines.

Even though Aracena's oligarchs sometimes chafed at the restraints imposed upon their manipulations by higher powers, they never openly challenged the principles of hierarchy and authority upon which their own advantageous positions as formal mediators between the great princes and prelates and the people of the sierra depended. Moreover, the efforts of the common people of the region to oppose the local oligarchs by direct appeals to the highest authorities always led to their forced reincorporation into the system of legal dependence and tributary extractions in which abuses were more the rule than the exception. In fact, in the course of the common people's efforts to achieve limited relief, their values of egalitarian communal solidarity were partly but quite effectively subverted and limited by their entrapment in a cultural and political process that redefined equality in hierarchical terms as a relationship existing among members of specific corporate groups by virtue of their identical obligations to an overlord or patron. Thus, the principal form of practical political resistance open to the people of the sierra did not pose a serious threat either to the dominant sociopolitical order or to the traditional forms of pastoral epic that legitimated it.

2

The Dominions of Spirit and Flesh

Christianity must be defined agonistically
and polemically in terms of struggle.
—Miguel de Unamuno
The Agony of Christianity

Sources of Traditionalism

WHAT DID tradition mean to the townspeople of Aracena during the seventeenth and eighteenth centuries? While bureaucratic documents—the wills, petitions, legal forms, census reports, and tax surveys on which this account of Aracena during the Ancient Regime has thus far been largely based—illuminate a great deal concerning the legitimate principles of authority, the political economy, and the power structure of the township, there are critical matters that they scarcely touch upon. Caro's concise description of the township is equally formulaic. To gain a better sense of how townspeople understood themselves and the world in which they lived, other sources richer in evidence and more varied in rhetoric are needed. Although much fragmentary information on local customs is available concerning Aracena in the early modern period, only one major document offering a more comprehensive view of cultural life in the town has survived. This is *Vida y virtudes de la venerable Madre Sor María de la Santísima Trinidad . . .* (1854), a biography of a local *beata* (holy woman), first published in 1671.

The *Life and Virtues of Madre María* was written by Antonio de Lorea, a Dominican brother well informed concerning both his subject and her native town.[1] The biography is both a quasi-official document of the church and a work of popular literature. Lorea researched and wrote it at the command of the archbishop of Seville, and nothing in it violated the canons of orthodoxy. On the contrary, the work represented an initial step in a process whose ultimate goal was to determine whether Madre María was worthy of canonization. Nevertheless, in Aracena and even in Seville, there was evidently great interest in the life of Madre María, and the text was also clearly intended to edify and inspire a lay audience with the glories of the faith.[2] Books and pamphlets of this type were extremely common during the Counter-Reformation, as befits a period when education was controlled by the clergy. One bibliography of Spanish books, for example, lists more than seven hundred works that described the lives of Catholic saints and local holy people and were published between 1500 and 1670 (Caro Baroja 1978:609–10).

Lorea's three-hundred-page work tells the story of the *beata*'s life in considerable detail. In thirty-two chapters, he relates how as a child Madre María was known for her gentle character and precocious wisdom; how as a youth she practiced the most rigorous ascetic disciplines and took the vows of chastity and poverty; how as a mature woman she was able to win the favors of Christ and the saints and to heal the sick in body and soul; and how in her later years her renown as a holy woman spread beyond Aracena to Seville, where she was honored by the great families of the city. In his final pages, Lorea describes the miracle following Madre María's death: when her remains were moved from Seville to the newly founded convent of Dominican nuns in Aracena, a convent that she had spent the latter decades of her life trying to establish, the Madre's body was discovered to be in a miraculously preserved, uncorrupted state after two years in the tomb. By representing Madre María's life as a progressive movement from an inherent condition of sin to a state of blessedness so profound that the people of Aracena and Seville revered her bodily remains as sacred relics with the power to heal, Lorea reproduces the universal epic of original sin, redemptive sacrifice, and salvation in microcosm.

In its broad outlines, then, the biography is a fairly conventional example of Catholic hagiography. As such, it is also a somewhat tedious work for modern readers, since it continually oscillates between chapters that focus on the evidences of spiritual discipline and deep faith and chapters that describe the manifest signs of spiritual power and good works. Moreover, in his eagerness to associate the virtues of his subject with those of the great saints of Catholic tradition, Lorea tends to undervalue the particularities of Madre María's life by rushing to compare her every thought and deed with those of figures such as Saint Catherine of Siena and Saint Teresa of Avila. Even so, much evidence of the *beata*'s specific situation manages to pass through the filter of conventional modes of hagiographical representation, and this makes it possible to see the text from other perspectives. In the course of his account, Lorea describes many aspects of local customs unmentioned elsewhere and offers a valuable perspective on what counted as time-hallowed tradition for Aracena's townspeople in the seventeenth and eighteenth centuries.

Lorea's work and other supplementary materials on religion will serve in this chapter as a basis for discussions of how the cultural strands of religion, honor, and patronage were interwoven to fabricate the official ideologies of tradition in Counter-Reformation culture; how community rituals and other forms of popular religion in Aracena represented a local variant of this dominant tradition; and how the authoritative and local versions of tradition interacted with one another in ways that shaped the townspeople's sense of practical morality and personal identity. This threefold perspective on tradition is necessary to fully appreciate how constraining and compelling hegemonic strategies of cultural integration and differentiation were in organizing a whole way of life for the townspeople of Aracena during the early modern period.

LIFE IN A FALLEN WORLD: REGIMES OF TRUTH AND VIRTUE IN COUNTER-REFORMATION CULTURE

Catholic doctrine and scripture alike continually affirm that there are two dimensions of the real: one dimension is spiritual, everlasting, and immaterial; and the other is corporal, temporal, and material. Nearly every page of Lorea's account of the life of Madre María is filled with concepts, narratives, and embellishments of rhetoric that are generated from this opposition, forming a part of what may be termed the discourses of the spirit and flesh. Throughout the work, Lorea represents personal life as a continuing process of "adapting oneself to the temporal so that the spiritual is not neglected or debased, and to the spiritual so that it may be the fount from whence the temporal flows" (p. 272). Moreover, the basic task he assigns himself as an author is an interpretive one based on the faith that "nature is the inscription put on men so that the passions of the spirit may be read" (p. 281). Thus, for Lorea, both the affair of living and the will to knowledge are conceived in terms of the interrelation of the life of the body and the life of the soul. As noted above, there is little that is original in this way of understanding human experience and representing the world. The discourses of spirit and flesh have been at the core of religious interpretations of personhood, society, and power for nearly two millennia.[3]

Within this traditional religious framework, the character and the fate of each individual are determined by the inclination of the soul or will toward one of two possibilities. One mode of existence is represented as a state of harmonious unity in which the corporal dimension of the person is hierarchically subordinated to the authority of the spirit and to the will of God. The other mode is a wholly antagonistic one in which corporal desires subvert the spiritual, sin and death dominate life, and the person is in a state of rebellion against God.[4] The self is represented as if it were a polity in which two antagonistic forces are always in a state of greater or lesser tension.[5] The distinction between the spiritual and corporal dimensions of being has also shaped orthodox sociopolitical thought, and just as the self has been represented as a polity, so too have polities, groups, and institutions been represented in personalist terms as social bodies that require government by spiritual and temporal heads.

What marks Lorea's biography as typical of the Spanish Counter-Reformation, however, is an intensification of the most emotional, agonistic, and authoritarian dimensions of this tradition.[6] Consider, for example, the following passage (p. 48):

> Always among those who travel toward God, one of their great studies is to mortify the body with rigors. They know that the slave who grows sovereign comes to deprecate his master sooner or later. When the body takes dominion over the precepts of the spirit because it abhors hardships and on account of its weaknesses and vices resists all harmonious adjustments and repudiates the spirit, this breeds opposing forces always at arms and in continual warfare with one another. And just as in temporal warfare many types of arms, swords, and daggers have been invented to defeat the adversary, spiritual warfare has invented its own arms and tactics.

This vision of personal life as a state of perpetual civil warfare, though by no means absent in the tradition as a whole, was extraordinarily prominent in orthodox Spanish religious thought during the Counter-Reformation. Its influence is detectable in the military inspiration of the spiritual exercises that Loyola prescribed for the Jesuits, and even Teresa of Avila spoke of the "interior castle" and evoked the supreme mystical experience of rapturous union with God by writing of a spear of divine love piercing her heart—an image at once both erotic and violent.

Similarly, Lorea's descriptions of social institutions and relations entail a heightening and exaggeration of the more agonistic, violent, and authoritarian rhetorical possibilities of orthodox discourse. Although Lorea occasionally praises God as an "all-wise Father of a family" who "makes the wisest distribution of talents, giving to all, but not to all equally, in order that each one, according to his strengths and with divine aid, may work and achieve something of value for his

God" (p. 127), such celebratory visions of universal harmony and order are relatively rare in his work. Far more frequently, he stresses the potential savagery of social life and emphasizes the need for vigilance and authoritative control in human affairs. Here, for instance, is how he wrote about the governance of monastic communities (p. 97):

> Republics are scarcely efficacious in preserving peace. Since if judges and superiors do not care for a community like a garden, pulling the weeds and cultivating the plants according to the nature of each one, and if they are not able to cut out the plant that wants to possess more than its estate permits it and they instead let it grow according to its vice, then all heads are filled with vice and everyone wants more, and the garden reverts to a mountainous wilderness, full of evils. The most licentious thrive and confound the humble, and the garden that used to produce roses, carnations, jasmine, and fruits becomes a cave of boars, bears, tigers, and lions.

As the passage makes apparent, Lorea basically understands society in traditional terms as a social body composed of persons, groups, and estates with natural inclinations toward various spiritual and material functions. However, as he sees it, social life quickly degenerates into a state of sinful anarchy without the firm restraints imposed by superior powers. His use of the imagery of the great mythic drama of the rebellion and fall of man, the expulsion from paradise, and the corruption of natural creation to argue in favor of maintaining strict surveillance over the day-to-day affairs of a small community of nuns communicates a sense of grave urgency and creates the impression that social life in general is in a perpetual state of crisis not unlike war. In the absence of judgment and rule, the pastoral garden of the spirit inexorably collapses into the brute cave of the flesh.

Undoubtedly, the intensification of the violent rhetoric in Lorea's spiritual account owes a great deal to the long history of the interconnection of religion and politics in Spain. The centuries-old tradition of religious crusade against the Moors, which Castilian knights fought under the banner of Santiago the Apostle, had established the intimate association of religion and politics. During the sixteenth century, this link had been further strengthened as the Jews and Moors were forcibly converted or expelled from Spain and as the conquest of the New World was legitimated as an evangelical mission. In addition, the struggles against Ottoman Turks and Protestant heretics and the use of the Inquisition as an instrument of cultural and political repression that served and was controlled by the interests of the Crown had bound church and state in an imperial alliance unparalleled elsewhere. By the seventeenth century, religion was virtually the only unifying ideological force other than loyalty to the Spanish Hapsburgs that even nominally linked the diverse peoples and polities of the world's largest empire to one another. But what Ramón Menéndez Pidal (1966:43) termed the "Christianization of the Reason of State" involved more than just an institutional alliance. It also led to a crucial, if never wholly complete, cultural integration of disparate religious and secular discourses, images, and values.[7]

The most critical effect of this integration was to make the idioms, representations, and practices of religion, honor, and patronage mutually reinforcing and easily convertible or translatable in terms of one another in ways that contributed to a practical sanctification of a "nobiliary social morality" (Maravall 1986:273) by the church.[8] This hegemonic integration is readily apparent even in Lorea's most comprehensive statement about the significance of the life of Madre María (p. 5): "Inasmuch as the sins of this age are so great that the majesty of God has been offended, our Lord deigned to give us in these calamitous times the venerable Madre, Sister María of the Most Holy Trinity, for the fame of her *patria* [native land], honor of her lineage, glory of the Order of Santo Domingo, [and] consolation of the afflicted."

In this passage, Lorea (who was, it must be remembered, a friar) understands the value of the spiritual life of this saintly woman—a woman who dedicated herself to the harshest ascetic disciplines of self-abnegation—almost exclusively in terms of the honor, fame, and glory she brings to her native town, her family, and her religious order. Clearly, whatever tensions Lorea may perceive between the evangelical imperative to surrender oneself to God and serve others and the noble ethos of honor and prideful self-assertion have been suppressed, presumably because of a deep-seated conviction that the dominant values of secular princes, lords, and masters essentially conform to and support the revealed truths of religion. Moreover, in seeking a way to reaffirm the orthodox principle of the superiority of spiritual over worldly values, Lorea expresses himself in an aristocratic language of honor and concludes his reflections on the topic by writing that "the spirit is more noble than the flesh" (p. 60). By employing the rhetoric of nobility and by subsuming talk of the spiritual within the worldly discourse of honor, he unintentionally undermines the very hierarchical distinction he was attempting to reaffirm. In the long run, rhetoric such as this merely served to buttress the power of established authorities.

To better understand the hegemonic effects of this cultural integration of spiritual and secular meanings and values on life in Aracena, the remainder of this chapter will be devoted to describing the dynamics of practical religion and morality. As argued below, the convergence of the idioms of honor and religion generated a dominant personalist and corporatist ethos that represented patronage as the most critical sociomoral relation among unequals in rank and virtue.

RITUALIZED SOCIAL RELATIONS AND THE POLITICS OF PRACTICAL RELIGION: PATRONAGE, PERSONALISM, AND THE PLAGUE OF 1647–48

As the mystical body of Christ, the Catholic church links heaven to earth and is a channel and repository of grace. The intercessory and mediating role of the church is expressed through all of its pastoral, charitable, and evangelical activities, but the critical embodiment of its mission is in the administration of the sacraments instituted by Christ. The sacraments are the outward signs of inward spiritual grace, and their efficacy lies in their transformative power that establishes or renews the relation of the person to God and to others. Yet while the sacraments are viewed by the church as the very core of religious life and as indispensable aids for salvation, it would certainly be misleading to claim that the sacraments were at the center of collective religious practice in Aracena during the Ancient Regime. As William Christian (1981b:175) has stressed, local religion in early modern Spain was based on the vow and the patron. Sacramental religion was secondary to ways of dealing with the supernatural in which priests played only a subsidiary role. While the clergy preserved and promoted the essential rites of the church, their most important functions in communal religion were to guide and to sponsor forms of worship centered on cultic images of the saints, the Virgin, and Christ.[9]

In Aracena, the central role of devotion to the saints in collective religious life was continually reaffirmed as the annual cycle of community rituals unfolded. Many days of every year were set aside to renew relations with one or another of the holy patrons whose images were sheltered in the churches, convents, and chapels of the township. While Holy Week and Corpus Christi were the most important holidays of the year (see Chapter 8 for a discussion of contemporary celebrations of these occasions), scarcely a week passed without one of the lay brotherhoods offering a public demonstration of devotion to its patron on the appropriate feast day. San Antonio Abad, San Ginés, Santa Lucía, San Roque, San Pedro, and San Jerónimo were especially important in the township, but many other saints were honored as well. In addition to the saints' days and the great holy days marking events in the life of Christ, all of the celebrations in honor of the Virgin were fully observed, and each of the many images of the Virgin that were to be found in the township had its own group of devotees. Thus, on the first Sunday of every month, those loyal to La Virgen del Rosario demonstrated their faith by carrying her image from church to church.

Regular observances were augmented by occasional special processions organized in times of crisis—for example, whenever drought, famine, war, or other general maladies threatened the townspeople. Rather than being simple acts of devotion, these processions entailed active and direct expressions of supplication and gratitude to the patron for benefits sorely needed or already received. In 1610, for example, on or about the day of San Marcos (25 April), an extraordinary procession was organized by the town's authorities to request the saint's aid in procuring relief from the excessive rains of that year (AA 1610). Several hundred people joined the procession as it began on the outskirts of Aracena in the early morning. As the hours passed, the procession made its way from the Dominican monastery of San Sebastián to the convent of Santa Catalina, where a mass was said, and then on to the *priorato* church of Santa María. After a long pause there, visits were made to the chapels of San Jerónimo, San Ginés, Santa Lucía, and San Roque. At each chapel, supplicatory prayers were offered to the special patron of the place and to San Marcos. By the end of the day, the procession had completed the circumambulation of the town.

Notice has also survived of a large procession in 1629—this time one of thanksgiving rather than supplication (AA 1629). Youths of the neighboring town of Cumbres Mayores sponsored a march to Aracena in gratitude to San Roque for relief from a plague of *garrotillo* (probably diphtheria) that had claimed the lives of hundreds of victims in the region. When the young men and women of Cumbres Mayores approached Aracena, they were met by a welcoming group carrying the image of the saint. After a mass was said, the youths of both towns joined together for dancing and celebrations that lasted several days.

The frequency of popular rituals gave life in Aracena something of the character of a never-ending cavalcade of saints and devotees, and the circumambulatory pattern of the processions as they moved through the streets and around the outskirts of town represented the paramount ritual expression of the cultural genre of pastoral epic. Each ritual was virtually a mini-epic in which the community as a whole or one of its constituent groups carried the adorned image of a saint and through this act of homage reestablished its identity by accepting the dominion of a supernatural patron of heroic power and virtue.

Within this framework of elementary religious forms, many patterns of social relations and identity could be ritually expressed, and membership in lay religious brotherhoods was evidently only rarely determined by purely individual devotion to a particular saint. Social bonds based on factors as various as residence, rank, occupation, and kinship strongly conditioned the direction and subject of devotion. At the same time, the forms of ritual practice redefined all forms of social solidarity, including those of an egalitarian character, in hierarchical terms of the fraternity created by obedience and loyalty to a superior in merit, power, and authority. This dynamic of social patterning and cultural reconfiguration linked the organization of religious practices to dominant notions of authority and enabled the direct expression of secular interests and concerns. Thus, processions were not only the primary spectacles of collective religious life, but they were also public demonstrations of the unity and vitality (and often wealth and power) of corporate groups.

Dedicated to a saint, an image of the Virgin, the true cross, the holy sacraments, the trinity, or some other figure or image worthy of veneration, the score or more of lay religious brotherhoods were the most important focus of day-to-day collective religious life, and membership in them created a double bond: a bond of aid, protection, and respect between the saint and the devotee and a bond of honor among the brothers who were formally pledged to maintain good relations with one another. The brotherhoods varied greatly in their religious, economic, and social character, and each was linked to an *ermita* (rural chapel), a parish church, or a monastic house. While some of the most important brotherhoods were almost exclusively devotional in character, others functioned as mutual aid and burial societies and were endowed with properties whose incomes helped them meet these practical ends.[10]

Instances such as that cited above in which religious expressions of devotion to a saint and thanksgiving for a particular favor were combined with what seems to have been an occasion for courtship between youths of the two towns were anything but exceptional in the affairs of the brotherhoods. The intermingling of the spiritual and the worldly was a constant cause for concern among the higher clergy, and they made intermittent efforts to curb popular excesses.[11] More than once, for example, La Cofradía de la Vera Cruz (Brotherhood of the True Cross) of Aracena was threatened with disciplinary action by emissaries of the Archbishopric of Seville for sponsoring feasts, games, and bullfights that the urban clerics regarded as "festivals purely profane which cause turbulence and inquietude and other effects very contrary to the penitential ends of the institution of the brotherhood" (DPS 1757). Generally, however, such warnings seem to have had relatively little impact on local customs. The local secular and religious authorities directly responsible for the conduct of public life usually officially supported and often fully participated in the activities of the brotherhoods, and most of the forms of religious action had a strong civic character and were deeply embedded in the forms of everyday life. In this context, the guardians of the purest orthodoxy did not find it easy to reform lay customs, although they clearly exercised a restraining and guiding influence on them. The result in cultural terms was a set of idioms and customs that were delicately balanced between a religious interpretation of life in the world and a worldly perspective on the usefulness of religion.

The logic of patronage depended on the notion that real benefits would be deserved and received in return for loyalty, service, and homage to the saints, the Virgin, and Christ. While some of these benefits were, of course, understood in purely spiritual terms of peace, love, and solace, most of the benefits sought were more concrete. What was most needed was aid and protection to fend off all the ills that flesh is heir to in a fallen world of strife and suffering; and as a result, both individual and collective religious practices were oriented toward attaining the intervention of the saints in the affairs of the natural world.

To accomplish this, relations with supernatural patrons were largely conducted and informed by two basic idioms of alliance. The first idiom was the formal and legalistic one of vows, pledges, and promises. In its simplest expressions, practical religion entailed the forging of an almost contractual relationship between the devotee and a saint: favors could be sought and services rendered nearly on a quid pro quo basis despite the fact that the parties involved were unequal in spiritual merit and power. Thus, many religious pledges and vows were rather formulaic and consisted of promises to perform penitential or charitable acts, to pray and attend mass, or to mark the favor received with the offering of an ex-voto. Ideally, however, the relationship between a supernatural patron and the devotee would develop from the formal, contractual mode into the second idiom, an informal and intimate alliance based on mutual respect, confidence, and familiarity. The more complex forms of religious life depended on solidifying the bonds between saintly patrons and mortal clients by acting in ways that were designed to ensure a continuing relationship of protection and devotion between the parties involved. At this level of religious devotion, the dominant idiom for representing the relation between human devotees and supernatural patrons was one of honorable friendship rather than contractual obligation.

Madre María and other *beatas* like her were particularly expert at building and maintaining such intimate relationships with the saints.

They knew that what their patrons desired was homage that would recognize their spiritual merit and honor their persons. Perhaps the most important way this was accomplished was through the adornment and care of their images and the proper observances of the saints' days. Lorea describes the basis of the relationship with supernatural patrons in the following terms (p. 104): "The servant of God [Madre María] called the saints for whom she had special devotion 'friends.' And as one of the duties of friendship consists of caring for the friend in those things that are conducive to the friend's reputation and pleasure, she wanted the fiestas of her friends to be solemnized with great devotion and attention."

Friendship between the saint and his or her favorite represented the crucial means through which the domain of the spirit was positively linked to the natural world of human affairs. Patronage essentially represented a channel of grace and merit apart from the sacraments of the church, and the flow of spiritual power through relationships of patronage was full of social consequences for interpersonal relations among ordinary people. A special friendship with a saint enabled the favorite to aid family, friends, neighbors, and others; to become their patron and ally; and to renew natural social bonds among people. The hierarchical chain of patronage, virtue, and obligation that constituted these socioreligious alliances is evident in Lorea's description of Madre María's friendship with Santiago, the patron saint of Spain (pp. 105–6):

> The favors of the Holy Apostle [Saint James] were not limited only to the venerable Madre; the saint also worked by his intercession for all the members of the household and for whomever Madre María requested him. And having favored as we have seen the mother and two daughters, he also extended his favors to their relatives. Sister Juana de la Ascensión, of the same habit as Madre María and a relative of hers, was ill from a sciatic pain so great that for more than six months she cried out night and day. The venerable Madre saw the affliction of the sick woman and the disconsolation that was growing in her house because she had tried every remedy imaginable and had no relief and seemed incurable. Finally, Sister Juana promised the Holy Apostle that if she were cured, she would go to the church of Los Granados to visit him. The evening before the festival of the saint, Madre María carried Sister Juana to the parish church so that she might hear vespers, and with great affliction Sister Juana prayed to him of the misery of her illness. . . . She made a good friend of him, and suddenly he took away her pain, which never returned again.

As this passage shows, popular religious practice was motivated by an intensely personalistic discourse of social relations grounded in the realities of everyday life. There was little discontinuity between the manner of dealing with family, friends, and patrons of this world and the conduct of spiritual affairs with supernatural patrons. As here below, so in heaven, the conduct of social relations hinged upon the establishment of more or less formal alliances and obligations whose real vitality nevertheless depended on the exercise of political tact to create a sense of enduring intimacy, trust, and confidence among the parties involved. This and much else of importance in understanding the far-reaching effects of the dominant cultural formation of the Ancient Regime are apparent in one of the most interesting accounts in Lorea's biography of Madre María—the story of the great plague of the 1640s—which reveals how the politics of this world intersected with the politics of the next.

According to Lorea, the story of the plague began in 1647 when Madre María adorned the image of San Blas in the monastery church of Santo Domingo with a new miter, cape, and other vestments. Not long afterward, the saint appeared to her in a vision to demonstrate his gratitude for the service.[12] He revealed that God was going to send "a great punishment of plague to fall on Seville," and complaining that the ecclesiastical estate of Aracena was "very distracted" from spiritual concerns, he instructed her to see to it that a number of saints including himself were named patrons and protectors of the town (p. 191).

Within eight or nine months, the people of Aracena began hearing reports of many deaths from plague in Seville. (This was the great plague of 1648, which according to modern estimates probably reduced the city's population by half.) When the reports were confirmed, the town council took strong measures to seal off Aracena. Guards were posted on the outskirts of Aracena to prevent the entrance of goods and people from Seville. When the town and church councils met together to consider which patrons should be declared the town's benefactors, they decided on San Ginés, San Sebastián, and San Roque, as well as Nuestra Señora de los Remedios, whose image was venerated in the parish church.

But a few days before the joint council was to swear the oaths making the bond between the town and the chosen patrons a formal one, Madre María was granted another vision. San Blas was very annoyed that the *beata* had failed to obey his instructions: Why had she not gone before the councils and revealed that it was God's will that he be named Aracena's patron? Madre María explained that she lacked the "audacity" to appear before the town's secular and ecclesiastical authorities and that, in any case, she was certain they would not "credit" her in the matter. San Blas as a former bishop was evidently no stranger to the politics of this world, for he wisely instructed the abashed *beata* to tell her vision to Don Sebastián de Rioja (a leading figure on the secular council) or, if she lacked the courage for this, to reveal it to Doña Isabel de Rioja (the sister of Don Sebastián and a friend of Madre María). The Madre, however, ignored part of the saint's advice and on her own initiative decided the better course was to first confide in Friar Roque de León, the prior of the Dominican monks. Fortunately, the prior found her vision credible and straightaway presented it to Don Sebastián. At the next meeting of the councils, Don Sebastián proposed that San Blas be named the patron saint of the town, and the councils in due course voted to approve his petition.

Meanwhile, Madre María was having further visions, and Saint Ursula appeared to her and commanded that a painting be made of the eleven thousand Virgin Martyrs of Germany so that they would "beseech God not to discharge his justice on Aracena" (p. 193). This time, the councils acted quickly (presumably on the clear principle that if a half-dozen or so patrons are good, eleven thousand more can't hurt), and they commissioned the painting, which was duly hung in the parish church.

As the plague rapidly spread throughout western Andalusia, the action of the councils sparked a revival of religious devotion in Aracena (pp. 193–94):

> The churches [were] often visited for communion, the confession boxes attended, public penances done and solemn fasts observed, hospitals refurbished, lives reformed, and the streets filled with processions carrying the images of greatest devotion. During the day there were these public exercises; at night there were so many penitents and their penances were so many and continuous that magistrates were necessary to organize them. One saw a Nineveh reformed, with the penitents all asking God's mercy that the whip of his justice should be spared them although they merited punishment for their sins.

All this would have been for naught, however, without the direct intervention of San Blas at a moment of supreme danger. Lorea describes the events leading to this intervention as follows: Aracena had thus far been spared the plague by its prayers and the "extreme vigilance" of the guards who protected the town, but "the Lord wanted to demonstrate that his punishment could pass into the town without being perceived by the sentinels and that it was his mercy and the supplications of saintly intercessors [not the vigilance of the watchmen] that had extinguished the fire of the plague" (p. 194). When rich clothing embroidered with precious stones had been sent by a high official of Seville to adorn the image of San Blas in Aracena, the secular authorities ordered the Dominican friar who was to receive the gift to burn it. The friar protested, and a dispute arose over the matter. After Don Sebastián de Rioja had a conversation with Madre María in which she convinced him that God would not punish the town by bringing the plague in this way, he gave his permission to allow the entry of the clothing.

Madre María's sister (also a Dominican *beata*) collected the clothes and brought them to the house of the *beatas* near the monastery. She immediately began to feel ill and by nightfall had a terrible headache and fever. The plague had come to the town and, indeed, to Madre María's own house. Still full of confidence in San Blas, Madre María visited his image and prayed for help. The saint appeared once again and told her, "Do not fear; . . . By the time you return to your house, all will be well," and so it happened (p. 194). Madre María's sister was immediately cured, and Aracena escaped the threat of the plague once and for all. The town had been spared through the mercy of God, the intercession of San Blas and several thousand other saints and martyrs, the faith of Madre María, and the actions of the authorities who sponsored the spiritual revival and swore the oaths that had made San Blas a patron and protector. For Lorea, the period of the plague clearly represented a crucial episode in the life of Madre María because it was at this time that her reputation for holiness began to spread beyond her intimate circle of friends and family.

Although Lorea's story of the plague may not be a trustworthy guide to the town's history in the 1640s, the descriptions of the quarantine, the religious revival, and the way the lines between temporal and spiritual power were blurred when the secular and ecclesiastical officials banded together to form a joint council to meet the emergency have the ring of truth.[13] However, hegemonic processes involved more than the direct ideological integration and alliance of religious and political authority, and indeed Lorea's account was shaped by a complex set of narrative strategies that affirm notions of personhood, power, and politics at the core of the dominant cultural tradition of the Ancient Regime.

From the perspective of orthodox faith, Lorea represented the natural disaster of the plague as a punishment for the sins of humankind and as part of a divine plan of retribution and repentance. God acted in the manner of the authoritarian Jehovah of the Old Testament, dispensing harsh justice to lawbreakers. But other cultural idioms and concerns clearly entered into his account. Lorea also represented the plague as an affair of divine honor and vengeance and compared his Andalusian contemporaries to the ancient Israelites who worshipped the calf of gold. This led him to observe that God was offended by their irreligion and wished "to take their lives in order to restore his honor, which [was] defamed by their adoration of a beast" (p. 189). This intrusion of the discourse of honor into the story has the effect of politicizing relations between the human and the divine in a way immediately comprehensible to Lorea's readers and transforms an orthodox parable of divine judgment into an extended narrative of the politics of honor and patronage in this world and the next.

All the principals in the story whether supernatural or mortal reacted to the plague by engaging in a complicated set of political tactics that were designed to secure or obtain the favors and good will of higher authorities. Moreover, the protection, services, favors, and mercies that constituted the religious relationship between Madre María and San Blas were similar in kind and quality to those which determined the venerable Madre's this-worldly friendship with Don Sebastián de Rioja, and the fate of the town depended on how these personal, delicate, and difficult relationships of alliance and subordination were conducted by the key parties. Errors and mistakes, such as Madre María's failure to approach the town council, were always possible in a situation in which every actor—from God, who initiated the somewhat gratuitous ploy of the contaminated gift, to the guard, who was prevented from burning it—behaved in light of motivations determined by his or her position in hierarchies of authority, power, honor, and prestige. However, the capacity of the people involved in these relationships to tack back and forth between spiritual and worldly understandings of patronage as circumstances demanded is clearly depicted by Lorea as critical in determining the fate of the community and as an essential aspect of the exercise of power and authority. Unequal relationships of patronage are thereby construed as the single most important social, moral, and political counterweight to all the spiritual and natural forces that threaten human life.

Thus, the story of the plague is more than an essentially orthodox tale of punishment and redemption in a fallen world full of sin, suffering, and death. It is also an exemplary instance of the dominant cultural genre of pastoral epic both because the narrative shows the high degree to which the heterogeneous discourses and representations of religion, honor, and patronage were integrated in Counter-Reformation culture and because everything in the story proceeds as if the very survival of the community depends on the heroic exertions of local authorities aided by both human and supernatural patrons.

Moreover, the story of the plague reveals how the conduct of social relations in early modern Aracena was imbued and shaped by a
distinctive corporatist ethos and personalist spirit. The way in which
secular power and religious authority operated during the plague and
other times of crisis reanimated the traditionalist notion that the
worldly lot and ultimate fate of each person were irrevocably conditioned by and dependent upon the manner in which he or she participated in the spiritual and worldly life of corporate groups. The agony,
chaos, and sinfulness of life in the corrupted state of nature could
only be mitigated and partially transformed by recognizing the formal
bonds, obligations, and powers one had as a member of the collective
body of society. Accepting one's prescribed position within a larger
whole was the precondition for the emergence of personal relations
of mutual support, sentimental allegiance, trust, and intimacy, which
could counter the natural tendency for things to fall apart and evil
to triumph.

Yet even though this dominant corporatist ethos represented an
integrating cultural force, it also produced countervailing tendencies
that politicized social relations of all kinds by encouraging a personalist spirit that magnified the cultural significance of ascendancy over
others even as it stressed the importance of social interdependence and
intimate ties of trust. From the perspective of both religion and honor,
personal virtue and righteousness tended to be construed in extensional terms: the greater one's capacity to extend care to others and to
incorporate them into a moral community of reciprocal love, respect,
and good will, the greater is the good accomplished. Thus, although
moral and honorable bonds such as those involved in patronage were
represented as strongest among natural intimates (members of the
same family, household, community, and so forth), the sign of great
merit and virtue was the ability to "domesticate" relations with more
distant persons and to expand the domain of spiritual and moral life to
an ever-widening circle of others, as Madre María and her intimates
did in the story of the plague.

But the dark side of this extensionalist ethic of incorporation was
that it bound the sense of self to the sense of social relations in a
manner that fostered an agonistic logic of struggle and domination at
least as much as it supported a logic of shared identity and common
interests. Indeed, the subjective sense of self-worth depended on the
ability to distinguish oneself from others and at the same time to remain intimately involved in their lives. This, coupled with the desire
for salvation and the concern for personal dignity and integrity, lent a
moral reasonableness to the drive to act as a benefactor, guide, or governor of others.

PRACTICAL MORALITY, CULTURAL AUTHORITY, AND THE POWER OF INTERPRETATION

Consideration of another story written by Lorea will help us explore how the dominant personalist and corporatist ethos of the Ancient Regime influenced practical morality and the conduct of ordinary social relations in ways that accustomed people to the notion that the interventions of higher authorities in local affairs and the general inequalities in power, if not always just and desirable, were at least necessary and inevitable. The following story, which concerns Madre María and her nephew, is a miniature version of pastoral epic in that it indicates how the micropolitics of daily life in rural Aracena were conjoined to the grand strategies of domination employed by higher authorities (pp. 205–6):

> The venerable Madre María had a nephew named Juan Moreno de Peraza who was *alférez* [lieutenant] of infantry of the people of Aracena. He went to Seville and in an inn of Triana exchanged words with another man, whereupon the man dealt him a blow. . . . Some people of Aracena told the lieutenant that it would be bad not to avenge himself, since he had been dealt a blow and would live without honor all his life until he took satisfaction. With this, the lieutenant decided to leave Aracena to search out his enemy in order to kill him. But the servant of God [Madre María] discovered what was happening and beseeched her nephew, reduced him with reason, and told him such things that he forgot the insult he had suffered as a *político* [political man, officeholder] and left his vengeance to God as a Christian.
>
> However, the captain of the lieutenant's company learned of the case, and because the injury had not been avenged he wanted to take away the *bandera* [the "stripes" or commission] of the lieutenant and give it to another. To this end, he wrote to the *conde* of Villainbrosa, who was the *asistente* of Seville [i.e., the highest royal official of western Andalusia] and the captain-general of the people of that realm and thus had jurisdiction over the case. The *conde*, believing that the lieutenant was a man unworthy of a military position, decided to take away what the lieutenant possessed.
>
> The captain of the lieutenant's company had conducted the matter and treated the challenge to his militia as if there were no Evangelical Law, and the venerable Madre knew that he had written to Seville and that his advice had ruined her nephew. Fearing now that her nephew would remain both without vengeance and without accommodation, Madre María wrote to Don Gerónimo de Avendano [a former governor and chief magistrate of Aracena]. Sometimes the

soul better explains itself with the pen than with the tongue, and although the venerable Madre was eloquent, it seemed on this occasion that she had partaken of the spirit of Chrysostom. By letter alone she was able to restore the memory that many men have forgotten: the counsels of Christ to pardon injuries and enemies and leave the right of vengeance to God and his justice.

Marveling at the letter, Don Gerónimo was emboldened with a fervent spirit and went to see the *conde*. For some time when he was before the *conde*, Don Gerónimo did not put forward his petition, but when the occasion offered, he said that he was burdened with a complaint concerning a captain of Aracena and told the *conde* the case of the captain and the lieutenant. The *conde* then asked him what he thought of the case and Don Gerónimo responded, "Sir, it seems to me that if the position of captain of that company were to become vacant, I would give it to the lieutenant." Admiring the response, the *conde* asked him the reason for his opinion. Don Gerónimo introduced the reasons of the letter of the servant of God, and put them forward himself; thus, the dead letters made an effect as great as if the one who had written them were persuading the *conde* with her own words. The *conde* was convinced and immediately wrote to the captain and ordered him not to pursue the case any further because he had disposed of it and instead of punishing the lieutenant because he had not avenged himself as a soldier, he favored him because he had proceeded as a Christian.

In this story, Lorea seeks to convince the reader of the *beata*'s sanctity in a manner that reflects the extensionalist ethos of personalism and corporatism generated by the dominant cultural formation of the Ancient Regime. The immediate and primary focus of Madre María's moral concern is her nephew, but because of their intimate family relationship, there is no extraordinary spiritual merit manifested in her ability to convince him to forgo vengeance. However, her influence over the former governor of Aracena and the persuasive impact of her argument on the *conde* betoken the great magnitude of her virtue, which is further driven home by Lorea through the rhetorical device of contrasting bodily absence with spiritual presence.

Yet one of the most striking things Lorea's story reveals about practical morality in traditional society is the difference in the moral requirements that honor imposed on men and women. For both sexes, challenges to personal honor arose when real or symbolic violence threatened the integrity of the person. For men, however, threats to personal honor were primarily represented in terms of blows, insults, and overt or covert warfare and battles, and the sentiments and codes of masculine honor were centered on the perception that the natural life of men is essentially political and unfolds in public arenas, such as the inn of Triana where passions flared in the case of Madre María's nephew. Unanswered challenges in such arenas almost invariably led to dishonor, humiliation, and the public shame of defeat. When Juan failed to immediately return the blow he received in the tavern, he became the subject of scandal and gossip among the townspeople of Aracena and appeared to be left with only two choices: either to seek delayed satisfaction or to endure the disgrace that results when men appear to lack the courage to defend themselves aggressively.

Considerations of pride, courage, and honor were so strong for men that they practically overrode countervailing principles of religious morality. Honor demanded neither forbearance nor withdrawal but an active engagement in worldly struggles, and it represented an "aesthetic" rather than an ascetic code of conduct in the sense that maintaining the appearance of dignity and integrity was crucial to holding one's social position and forestalling the challenges of others. What linked honorable notions of masculine nature to religion was not explicit moral imperatives but the agonistic conception of the suffering and sacrifice demanded by life in a fallen world. But as Madre María's nephew discovered, actions contradicting the normal imperatives to maintain one's integrity were sufficiently anomalous that it was more than likely that others would view a failure to defend honor and reputation as sheer cowardice rather than religious virtue.

In contrast, Madre María, though not indifferent to the imperatives of masculine honor or the consequences of its loss, had little patience with her nephew's desire for vengeance and willingness to risk his life because of an insult. Her attitude toward the youth was essentially protective, and she sought ways to guard him from the slings and arrows of political fortune and to prevent his "ruin." She adopted this stance not only because it conformed with religious morality but also because feminine honor was constituted differently from masculine honor.[14] Whereas masculine honor was basically assertive and required a willingness to risk the body, feminine honor was defensive and required the cautious, circumspect protection of the body. As a result, practical ethics and the politics of moral reputation for women were centered on the virtues of modesty and prudence. Above all, a woman's sense of shame had to shield her from exposure to the power, especially the sexual power, of men.

The critical issues governing estimations of feminine virtue are evident in the following passage in which Lorea describes the concerns of the mother of the young Madre María for her daughter's reputation.

The incident (p. 55) occurred when María was returning from the church of Santo Domingo.

> [María's mother] heard a great noise made by boys as if they were running a bull. She went to her window and saw her daughter being followed by the boys and persecuted with pushes, stones, and taunts. She left her house and as well as she was able she defended her daughter from the boys. . . . [Afterwards] her mother turned the anger she had for the boys against her daughter and said to her, "What is this, daughter? How can a mother behold an affront like this? Is it possible that every day my heart must worry that you might dishonor me as a *beata* more than you would as a lost woman?"

As this anecdote indicates, women were involved in the honor of other women as guardians of reputation, but the critical focus of feminine virtue was on relations between women and men. If masculine disgrace came from unanswered blows, then feminine shame derived primarily from exposure to real or symbolic violation.

Because the values of feminine honor were focused on themes of purity and protection, they were far more congruent with the ascetic tendencies of religious morality than were the masculine values. In terms of norms of conduct for women, less tension existed between the religious demand to withdraw and protect oneself from the cares and sins of this world and the imperative of honor to avoid even the appearance of vulnerability to natural passions and male aggression.

This overwhelming emphasis on the virtue of prudence for women closed off many avenues of action for them, and given the character of feminine morality, Madre María's actions in the affair of her nephew were quite daring insofar as they involved an intrusion into the public political arena of men, an arena from which women were ordinarily barred. Such an intrusion was inherently dangerous, and Madre María's reputation was far more vulnerable than that of most women; as an uncloistered *beata,* she was neither safe behind the walls of a convent nor protected by the arms of a husband. Thus, in seeking to restore Juan's honor and reputation, she necessarily risked her own.

That she was willing, able, and even bound to do so was in large measure, of course, because the affair of her nephew was a family matter. Expressing support for and solidarity with relatives was the most direct manifestation of the personalist spirit and corporatist ethos that pervaded the various aspects of day-to-day social life.[15] To act for the welfare of a family member was the closest thing to acting on one's own behalf, and the practical political and material logic of family solidarity (see Chapter 3) was buttressed by the notion that loyalty, honor, piety, and virtually all of the other secular and religious virtues had the most force and efficacy among kin. Thus, although Juan's apparently weak will during and after the affair in the inn raised serious doubts about his capacity to fulfill his obligations not only to the soldiers under his command but also to his family, Madre María's desire to see her nephew's reputation restored was deeply congruent with conventional feminine notions of the family as an intimate community of love. Since the *beata* had no children of her own, her nephew was her closest descending male relative—her natural heir and spiritual son. To protect him was her obligation as a relative, and this imperative was reinforced by her moral perception that vengeance should be left to God. Indeed, by acting for his protection, Madre María both invoked and in a sense realized the sacred image of a Virgin Mother caring for a son and lamenting his suffering. For a woman, no other disposition was more natural or more spiritual. Viewed from this perspective, the Madre's practical interest in preserving the "accommodation" of her nephew was consistent with but subsidiary to a broader and more profound set of moral concerns, desires, and values shaped by fundamental notions of womanhood.

Nevertheless, Madre María was confronted with the problems of how to overcome the difficulties all women had in acting outside the domestic domain and how to convince others of the importance of supporting the religious and feminine values of love and forbearance in the larger social domain where considerations of political honor were ordinarily dominant. As Juan's relative, she could plausibly lay claim to an intimate, personal knowledge of her kinsman's character, but to avoid criticism of herself and at the same time convince others to suspend their doubts concerning Juan, she had to proceed with great tact and caution into the public arena.

Apparently confident of the strength of his charges, Juan's principal adversary in the affair, the captain of his militia company, had acted directly and according to bureaucratic procedures and had lodged a formal legal complaint that threatened Juan with the loss of his post and his honor. In contrast, as a woman, Madre María was forced to pursue an indirect and discreet "domesticating" strategy of argument and action. However, the great advantage of this strategy was that it enabled Madre María and her ally, Don Gerónimo, to move the debate from a legal to a higher moral plane and to exploit to the greatest extent possible the informal and interpersonal dimensions of the exercise of moral authority. By pointing out that the captain had acted as if "there were no Evangelical Law," they sought to redefine the issue by turning the narrow problem of deciding the nephew's absolute honor or lack of it into a subtle but broader question of the relative degree of moral excellence manifested by the nephew and the captain as near-equals in rank and office. Thus, at the very core of Lorea's story, there is evidence that the politics of moral reputation among the local elite of Aracena proceeded through the formulation of rival religious and worldly interpretations of the meaning of social acts and relations. Like other sorts of agonistic competitions, these small-scale ethical and political struggles required both careful calculation and the mustering of the support of family and close friends in order to prepare and present a successful "case."

Madre María's and Don Gerónimo's efforts were successful in large measure because their actions and words invoked representations of the moral community as an extended but ideally intimate spiritual-corporal hierarchy. This view of the community was deeply appealing and useful to those at the highest levels of power, such as the *conde,* who held the most important judicial and military offices in western Andalusia. His exalted position made it necessary that Don Gerónimo—a man of honor and office himself—be "emboldened with a fervent spirit" before he even approached the *conde.* Lorea's description of the deferential and roundabout way in which Don Gerónimo presented the "burden" of his petition suggests a social ritual of respect for rank and authority that involves more than an expression of mere etiquette. The petitioner's deference ceded control of the interview to the *conde* in such a way that it initiated and became an essential aspect of a procedure of inquiry. The *conde* listened to Don Gerónimo's story and then asked a series of questions designed to draw out Don Gerónimo's opinions on the case. But it is clear that the *conde* was not particularly interested in the raw "facts" of the episode. What he wanted to gain was a sense of intimate knowledge of the persons involved. It is as if the *conde* was interrogating Don Gerónimo to bring the petitioner's client, Madre María's nephew, under his scrutiny and into his presence so that he could judge the young man's virtue. In this sense, the chain of patronage in corporate society represented a path to intimate familiarity of a remote other. The *conde*'s admiration for Don Gerónimo's responses to his queries led to the reestablishment of the personal reputation of the nephew, and having never seen either of the men directly involved in the incident, the *conde* judged the case in favor of the nephew and against the captain.

The tact, sense of timing, and eloquence of Don Gerónimo and Madre María won the day, but only because there were indirect hegemonic political, institutional, and cultural forces at play, and these forces predisposed the *conde* to heed the arguments of Madre María and exercise his authority in the way he did. In supporting the nephew, the *conde* chose to act as a protective patron rather than a judge following the letter of the law. Such a decision was possible because no firm line of demarcation separated acts of judgment from acts of patronage during the Ancient Regime. The *conde* and others who occupied the highest reaches of the sociopolitical hierarchy were invested with multiple forms of cultural authority in addition to the administrative control of political and economic resources. As an officer of the Crown, the *conde* was a primary source of secular justice who was charged with administering the civil law and maintaining the good order of society. As a noble servant of the king, the *conde* was also a "fount of honor" who distributed specific "favors" (gifts, offices, incomes, and all the other graces of rank and high status) in formal recognition of each recipient's worthiness and past services and in practical exchange for personal and political loyalty. Finally, because of the marriage of the institutions of the church and the monarchy, the *conde,* like every orthodox prince, had binding religious and moral obligations to defend the faith. Thus, as a head of the body politic, the *conde* had the duty to exercise, manifest, and harmonize the range of spiritual as well as legal and political virtues that bound the members of society to one another.

The convergence of these multiple responsibilities meant that the *conde* had necessarily to weigh his options carefully in cases such as that of the nephew. For the *conde* to have maintained his initial decision to remove the nephew from his post would have been an action difficult to criticize on legal grounds but also one that involved little more than doing one's duty as an officer of the Crown. In contrast, for the *conde* to reverse his decision when Don Gerónimo appealed to him suggests both considerable political acuity and the ability to adjust to changing circumstances. The advantages of reversing his judgment were twofold. First, it was politically prudent of him to favor rather than to humiliate Don Gerónimo—his immediate subordinate and an important official in his own right—and thereby expand or strengthen the personal network of clients directly indebted to him. Second, to dare a bold stroke and dispose of the case in an unconventional way held an intrinsic appeal. To make a decision that ran counter to normal expectations was an act which permitted the *conde* to clothe himself in the mantle of the wise and subtle patron rather than the uniform of a dull official. It could be construed as an exemplary manifestation of the magnitude of the personal wisdom and spirituality of one who could see deeply into the hearts of distant subjects and in so doing validate his role as a head of a great moral community. Only such exceptional acts could make it apparent that the virtuous, righteous, and just ruled.

The great responsibilities of princes and prelates therefore brought with them great freedom to make the unusual interpretation, to stretch the boundaries of the plausible, and to make use of the arts of reason in ways that had an immediate impact on the lives of others. Only they were fully endowed with the formal prerogatives, status, and practical resources necessary to traverse the cultural space opened up by the discontinuities and ambiguities existing among the multiple discourses, values, and images of gender, kinship, community, law, religion, honor, and patronage that gave corporate society its complex form. And like Madre María, Lorea, and other spiritual virtuosos, they could also lay claim to a traditional high ground of cultural authority concerned with such ultimate realities as sin, salvation, and the inner life of the soul, and this enabled them to exercise cultural hegemony by assuming the role of patrons and rendering social life significant in terms of the adjustment of the life of the flesh to the life of the spirit.

More was involved in this process than a crude ideological adjustment of orders of moral reputation, virtue, and righteousness to orders of politicoeconomic interest and power. The one pattern was ineradicably inscribed in the other and shaped a whole way of life that was simultaneously a form of domination muting the voices of some as it magnified the capacities of others. Thus, the significance of the story of Madre María and her nephew is not simply that it reveals how such parables served to legitimate the social order or that it illustrates how the powerful could buttress their own influence and prestige by intervening in disputes among subalterns vying with one another for position and reputation. More important, the story indicates how the cumulative pressures of overlapping ideological representations, popular traditions, and commonsense views of practical morality that townspeople and princes alike encountered in the ordinary affairs of daily life induced them to constantly adjust and, if need be, sharply revise the social identities they presented to others in ways that not only were acutely sensitive to politicoeconomic power differentials and in essential compliance with hegemonic forms of cultural authority but were also bound to affect their deepest sense of themselves as pious and honorable men, women, and family members.

3
Patronage, Patrimony, and Oligarchic Domination

The argument which such people generally use, and on
which they most rely, is that the labours of the spirit
are greater than those of the body.
—MIGUEL DE CERVANTES
The Adventures of Don Quixote

THE FOUNDATION OF GERÓNIMO INFANTE

IN THE LAST years of the seventeenth century, Captain Gerónimo
Infante, a native of Aracena who had emigrated to Peru as a young
man and made his fortune by cultivating wheat, sent eight strongboxes of gold and silver to the town of his birth.[1] Each shipment was
accompanied by a letter addressed to the head priest of the parish of
Aracena and providing instructions about how the treasure was to be
used. These letters represent the charter of the foundation that came to
be known as El Patronato de Gerónimo Infante y La Cofradía de San
Pedro y Pan de los Pobres (the Foundation of Gerónimo Infante and
the Confraternity of Saint Peter and the Bread of the Poor) (AA 1693;
DPS 1693).

The letters reveal that the aging captain's first concern was for the
fate of his soul. He therefore established two well-endowed chaplaincies whose occupants were charged with saying hundreds of masses
each year on his behalf. Each chaplaincy was to be awarded to a descendant of the captain if possible; if no such candidates were available, then two other priests of the parish of Aracena were to be
chosen. The captain's second concern was for the maintenance of the
nonclerical members of his family. His two surviving sisters, who lived
in Aracena, were each to be given large gifts of money, and if any of his
other relatives or descendants were in need, they were to be among the

first provided for by the endowments of the *patronato*. And the captain's third concern was that the poor of the town be provided with a permanent source of relief from hunger. Most of the small fortune he sent was to be used to purchase properties whose incomes and fruits could be devoted to this charitable purpose. Thus, he stipulated that two thousand *fanegas* of wheat a year were to be baked into bread and distributed to the impoverished at half the prevailing market price and that any surplus was to be given freely to those who most needed it in the period from the first of April to the first of November, the season of greatest need in the year. In addition, twenty-four people a year were to be given complete sets of clothing.

The captain was obviously a generous and devout man, and his act of patronage was in several respects an exemplary expression of the moral priorities that shaped the personalist spirit and corporatist ethos of the Ancient Regime. In making provisions for the care of his soul first of all and then the maintenance of his family and the support of the poor, he balanced spiritual requirements against worldly necessities and his personal loyalty to his lineage against the general demands of charity in a way that permanently secured his local fame and honor. In addition, the good captain was astute enough to realize that some of his wishes would be neglected if he did not specify in some detail how the wealth of the *patronato* was to be managed. Thus, he took care to distribute administrative responsibilities among several clerical and lay officials. The council of the *priorato* (priory) of Aracena was charged with general oversight of the foundation; the vicar of the parish was to award the chaplaincies; and the head priest of the *priorato* and the lay *hermanos mayores* (senior brothers) of La Cofradía de San Pedro y Pan de los Pobres were assigned joint control of the portion of the endowment intended for charitable purposes. Yet for all his foresight, things did not work out as the captain had planned. Aracena's oligarchs followed the captain's instructions but not quite in the spirit he intended. It is to this theme and to the practical actions and strategies of the town oligarchs with regard to the captain's patrimony as well as to their own patrimonies that the remainder of this chapter is devoted. By considering the various strategies involved, it will be possible to address the question of to what extent traditional cultural forms of authority remained dominant or were subordinated to emergent capitalist economic tendencies during the final decades of the Ancient Regime.

BASIC STRATEGIES: THE PRIMACY OF THE PATRIMONY

The Infante family, of whom the good captain was the offspring and eventual benefactor, was one of the more illustrious *hidalgo* lineages of Aracena. During the seventeenth and eighteenth centuries, members of this lowest untitled rank of the nobility formed the core of the local elite, and they were careful to set themselves apart from commoners. Their sense of their separate and unequal cultural identity is evident in many documents of the period, including their wills. The following introduction to the will of José Villafranco, an aging *hidalgo* patriarch, is representative: "I, . . . , an old Christian, pure of all bad blood of Jews, Moors, *Moriscos,* mulattos, gypsies, or other evil sects, and having committed no abominable sin and not punished by nor a penitent of the Holy Inquisition, and being of the estate of *hidalguía* and not subject to marks of infamy, do hereby bequeath . . . " (DPS 1769).[2]

By 1769, when this declaration was sworn, its affirmation of a traditionalist ideology must already have had an archaic ring to it for some townspeople. The Moors and Jews had long vanished from Spain; the power of the Inquisition had declined; and evil sects were hardly a serious threat to religious orthodoxy or royal power. In addition, the values of honor had lost their strict identification with the military virtues and profession and were becoming more closely associated with the attitudes and values of a nonwarrior governing elite of officials and even with certain "bourgeois" values directly related to commerce and the accumulation of wealth. Indeed, within a few years of Villafranco's death, even tradesmen would no longer be denied legal recognition as honorable persons in Spain.[3] Nevertheless, the aging and ailing patriarch of the Villafranco family—a family intimately involved in the administration of the captain's patrimony—had taken pains to associate himself and his lineage with ancient traditions of honor, orthodoxy, and nobility both in his formal rhetoric, which implied that spiritual and worldly virtues were inherited through the blood, and in his actions, such as leaving his sword and breastplate as a legacy to his eldest son.[4]

This was far from unusual in Aracena. During the eighteenth century, the possessors of at least twenty different surnames among the town's inhabitants either securely held or could lay some claim to the rank of *hidalgo.*[5] Members of these various lineages formed the "brotherhood" of *hidalgos,* which was centered in the church of "El Castillo" and was headed by an official who held the largely ceremonial post of *alcalde* (justice) of the castle. A dozen of these families could trace their ascension to noble status to the exact date of 28 March 1394, when King Enrique III of León-Castile elevated some of his soldiers to the rank of "Caballeros Farfanes de los Godos" and specified that they and their descendants were exempt from the payment of all taxes (DZ 1723). These ancient lineages, as well as the descendants of other notable persons who had been granted the status of *hidalgo* in succeeding centuries, jealously guarded the reputations of their families and not merely because of the direct tax exemptions this rank brought them. Rather, their whole way of life depended on their ability to preserve their social position in the face of powerful forces and difficult circumstances that continually threatened them with a decline in prestige and authority.[6] Because the *hidalgos* formed the core of Aracena's civil-religious oligarchy, the political life of the town and sierra cannot be understood apart from the strategies used by *hidalgo* families to compete for power.

At the center of *hidalgo* concerns were the preservation and, if possible, the expansion of the family patrimony.[7] In most families of Aracena, the principle of equal inheritance of property was usually endorsed in wills and testaments and evidently was virtually unchallenged in practice. Either at the time of their marriage or more frequently when their parents died, children—male and female, youngest and eldest alike—were entitled to an equal share of the family patrimony (AN/bta 1748; AN/mlv 1774). However, the principles and practices informing the transmission of property among the *hidalgos* and other notables of the township were different. More than half of the estates of *hidalgo* families took the form of *mayorazgos*, entailed properties divided into unequal parts called *vínculos*, which heirs could not alienate (see Clavero 1974; Domínguez Ortiz 1976:327–32). Most of the remaining gentry families also practiced some form of unequal devolution of property through the exercise of testamentary rights. The principle of equal treatment of heirs was thus subordinated to an ideal of sacrifice that required daughters and younger sons to accept lesser shares of the estate in order to preserve the patrimony, honor, and rank of the lineage. Even so, great efforts were made to secure minor heirs a suitable match or office, for to do less threatened the principal heir and the whole family with disgrace.

The period when children reached marriageable age was especially critical for gentry families, since in this phase of the domestic cycle the amount of women's dowries and men's marriage portions represented the most important issue in the negotiations that decided whether two estates and two lineages would be united. The daughters of the gentry tended to receive virtually the whole of their inheritance in the form of dowries at the time of marriage. These dowries were often quite large, a few exceeding a total value of 100,000 reales (AN/bta 1748; AN/mv 1759:68). The marriage portions for men were generally smaller, although young men received properties sufficient to enable them to set up a household by the age of majority (twenty-five) if not earlier (AN/mv 1759:86; 1765:147) and could often expect to receive additional property when a parent died. Yet the period of marriage was so crucial that transfers of property at the time of the death of a parent were often a matter of delivering to the succeeding generation an inheritance that had been pledged and determined years earlier.

With the gentry, as with the ordinary townspeople, the ideal of a suitable marriage alliance was expressed in terms of "equality of estates," and this phrase implied both equal rank and equal wealth between marriage partners (AN/mpt 1763). In practice, of course, the determination of equality was subject to negotiation and interpretation. While those able to offer a potential marriage partner both great wealth and honorable rank could look far afield (usually in the direction of Seville) for an alliance, over the course of many generations most of the gentry of Aracena married within the town or at least the sierra, where the pool of even remotely suitable marriage partners was rather small. Flexibility was thus required in arranging matches, and the usual expression of this flexibility involved a trade-off of wealth for rank. The favored path here was a marriage between a daughter of a wealthy *pechero* (taxpaying commoner) and a younger son of an *hidalgo,* since such a match promised a permanent rise in status for the family of the former and a secure livelihood for the latter. Marriage between an *hidalgo* daughter and a *pechero* son appears to have been less common, probably because it made the future generation's claims to *hidalgo* rank more easily disputable (AN/mpt 1759).

The attractions of attaining high rank involved a good deal more than prestige. With *hidalgo* rank came concrete economic advantages and entitlement to hold various types of office, and the income from offices was a source of wealth nearly as dependable as land. Indeed, because offices were held in the same families for generations, marriage contracts treated them essentially as a form of heritable property. Thus, the basic assets involved in marriage negotiations were rank, wealth, and office, and it was through the alliance of real property and social prospects that gentry families and couples sought to maintain their own status and that of their descendants.

Despite the flexible strategies employed in the creation of marriages and the conservative effects of the unequal patterns of inheritance, the gentry were continually faced with the threat of gradually sinking status and declining fortunes, generally because there were simply too many heirs for whom some provision had to be made. In this situation, the relative stability of the gentry as a group and hence the whole power structure of the sierra could not have been maintained if the church had not been available to provide secondary heirs with a vocation and a living. Whatever the intrinsic attractions of the religious life, its social advantages were enormous.

Although in principle the church was an open institution, in practice it took both money and connections to enter a convent or join the ranks of the parish clergy, and it appears that virtually all of the clergy of Aracena were from families of the local elite. The costs, though high enough to exclude the humbler ranks of society, were generally far less than those imposed on a gentry family to secure a suitable match for a son or daughter. Furthermore, despite the sacrifices entailed by religious vows, a clerical vocation had many of the desirable features of both a good marriage and a lucrative office. To become the bride of Christ or the son of Holy Mother Church was eminently honorable, maintained family prestige, and eased both immediate and (assuming celibacy was sustained) long-range pressures on the family patrimony. In addition, for the priests of the *priorato* there were the prospects of securing a more than adequate living from a large chaplaincy or some other type of ecclesiastical endowment and also the possibility of playing an important role in community affairs. In short, one of the primary reasons why the church was a crucial institution of local society was that it functioned as a safety valve that permitted the gentry to dispose of their excess heirs and as a sort of reserve officer corps or junior service for the most powerful lineages of the township's *hidalgos*.

For the gentry and particularly for the larger *hidalgo* families of Aracena, the creation of marriage alliances, the devolution of property to heirs, the pursuit of secular offices, and the dedication of children to the church represented options that could be employed in the development of an overall domestic strategy designed to ensure the conservation of the family patrimony and the prestige of the family name. Actions taken in one of these areas inevitably altered the possibilities open in the others, and general success required a spirit of family pride, cooperation, and solidarity. Moreover, as a result of these strategies, there was no split between the politics of the domestic domain and the politics of church and state for the local elite of the township. The degree of coordination possible in the elaboration of domestic and political strategies is illustrated by the following brief history of three generations of a powerful *hidalgo* family in Aracena (DPS 1730–80).

In the 1730s, there were four surviving heirs of Gavino Villafranco, the deceased paterfamilias of the line (see fig. 4). The eldest, Andrés, was the *mayorazgo* heir and possessed the bulk of the family estates, which were certainly very large and probably amounted to several hundred hectares of land in addition to numerous other properties. Andrés had married María de Aronja, the offspring of another *hidalgo* family of considerable property. His brother-in-law was Juan

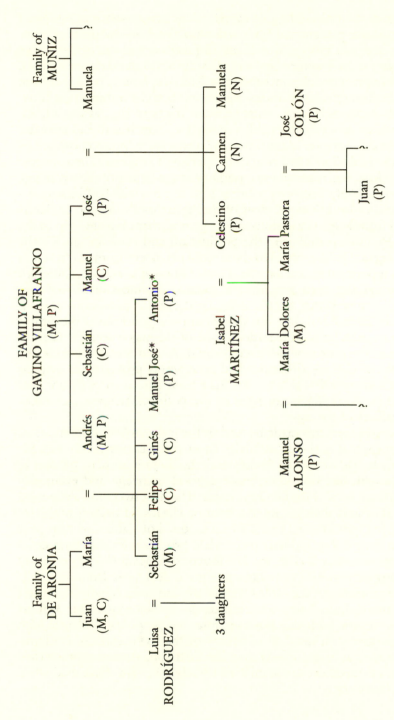

Figure 4. The family of Gavino Villafranco (c. 1730–90). M = *mayorazgo* heir; C = clerical office; P = political office; N = nun; * = marital status unknown. Pseudonyms have been used.

de Aronja, the only sibling of María and a priest who was endowed with extensive patrimonial lands and who also held the posts of commissioner of the Holy Office of the Inquisition and vicar of the *priorato*. Two of the younger brothers of Andrés had also become priests, and although they had inherited little from the family, both had been granted substantial chaplaincies. Moreover, both held important ecclesiastical offices. Sebastián controlled vast tracts of land as the administrator of an *obra pía* (charitable foundation) attached to El Patronato de Gerónimo Infante. Manuel was the *comendador* (prefect) of the Order of the Holy Spirit and vicar of the parish of Aracena. The youngest brother, José, had married into another *hidalgo* family of the township, the Muñiz family. However, neither José nor his wife had inherited a great deal of land. Rather, most of the household's income evidently derived from José's possession of the rights to manufacture soap in the township and to administer the production and trade in salt for the whole sierra. He had inherited these royal privileges from his father, as well as a permanent seat on the town council as a *regidor*. Although Andrés had also been a *regidor* for some years, most of his energies seem to have been devoted to managing the family patrimony and engaging in trade. Thus, José was the paramount politician of the family, and for decades he was the leader of one of the major political factions wrestling for control of the town council. As can readily be seen, the four sons of Gavino Villafranco had been amply provided for by their father in many different ways and had been placed in positions that allowed them to play major roles in the political, religious, and economic affairs of the town.

The arrangements made by Andrés for his own five children, all of whom were males, closely paralleled those made earlier by Gavino. Sebastián, the eldest son of Andrés and the *mayorazgo* heir, resided in Aracena and, like his father, made a good marriage and eventually managed the bulk of the family's estates. The next two sons, Felipe and Ginés, followed their uncles and became clerics. However, both also became lawyers attached to the Royal Council of Cádiz and were able to assist their father and later their eldest brother with the commercial affairs of the family in that city. The fourth son, Manuel José, inherited some property from his parents and a good deal more from his uncle, the commissioner of the Holy Office of the Inquisition, who as a priest was without direct heirs. The records do not show whether Manuel José ever married. He did, however, form a close political alliance with his uncle and won the post of notary of the town council. Little information is available concerning the fifth son, Antonio, other than that he was an officer of the militia of Niebla. He may have died when still fairly young.

The junior, collateral branch of the Villafranco family (José and his children) fared as well as the *mayorazgo* line (Andrés and his children) in the descending generation, largely thanks to an adroit use of the more limited assets at their disposal. Far less wealthy than his eldest brother, José Villafranco was nonetheless able to provide his son, Celestino, with sufficient resources to make a good marriage. This was accomplished through a number of measures. Most significantly, Celestino's two sisters were placed in the convent of Jesús, María, y José near the time of Celestino's majority and several years before they themselves reached marriageable age. In effect, this made Celestino the sole heir of the family, and his parents were able to endow him with a marriage portion consisting of two houses and some good lands valued at 46,500 reales. His father immediately loaned him an additional 3,300 reales, and with this money Celestino bought a garden from the same convent his sisters had joined. All of this was sufficient for Celestino to attract a bride whose dowry was two or three times more valuable than his own property. This was no doubt possible for two basic reasons. First, the family of his bride, Isabel Martínez, though rich, had recently failed in its efforts to win control of the council of a neighboring town (Los Marines), largely because the town's householders had protested to higher authorities that the Martínez claims to the rank of *hidalgo* were unfounded. An alliance with the Villafrancos could scarcely fail to aid the Martínez family in its efforts to overcome this obstacle. Second, Celestino's prospects for the future were bright. Within a decade of his marriage, he took over the family's business in soap and salt and succeeded to his father's position of *regidor* and leader of the Villafranco faction of Aracena's oligarchy. Indeed, Celestino's power and probably his wealth as well soon rivaled and finally exceeded that of any of his cousins, the heirs of the *mayorazgo* line, who acted as his supporters in local politics.

Celestino eventually entailed his own estates, but fate denied him a son who could succeed to his offices. However, he was able to grant his elder daughter and principal heir, María Dolores, a dowry of nearly 100,000 reales, and she married Don Manuel Alonso, the treasurer of the *propios* (leased common lands) of the city of Seville. Celestino's younger daughter, María Pastora, was provided with an almost equally large dowry and married a scion of a local *hidalgo* family. This union, which occurred in the late 1780s, was to have far-reaching consequences both for the family and for the town (see Chapter 4).

The history of the Villafrancos indicates a few of the many strategies used by *hidalgo* families to maintain and enhance the prestige of their lineages. The *mayorazgo* heirs of the Villafrancos received the bulk of the family property, but the patrimony included much more than property. In the course of the eighteenth century, members of the family occupied at least fourteen of the most important secular and religious offices in the town, and these offices provided them with livings, prevented the fragmentation of family lands, and at the same time gave them such power that they constituted the core of the most powerful group of the gentry oligarchy. For such a family, there was no real line separating the domestic from the public domain, and it would be difficult to overestimate their interest in maintaining connections with the institutions of the church and state. Their social position depended on their rank and reputation as honorable *hidalgos* and servants of the church. It is not surprising that in most documents, such as the will quoted at the beginning of this chapter, the Villafrancos offered proclamations of the orthodox faith and stainless honor of themselves and their forebears. They were not alone in affirming the codes of honor and orthodoxy or in utilizing strategies of devolution of property and office to gather the cords of power in their hands. Everywhere the ordinary householders of Aracena looked, they would be sure to encounter a Villafranco—or a Granvilla, a Garay, an Infante, or a Fernández—claiming precedence and competing for offices and spoils.

TACTICAL MANEUVERS: RANK, HONOR, AND THE POLITICS OF FACTION

While the long-range social strategies of the gentry were keyed to processes involved in the maintenance of family patrimonies, the day-to-day political affairs of the town were dominated by competition among gentry to take advantage of the access to patronage, spoils, and other prerogatives of rank that provided them with the resources with which to pursue their more fundamental goals. To a certain extent such competition over resources occurred within families as well. But it was rare for close relatives to oppose one another in the larger arena of community politics. On the contrary, the public politics of the town was based on the solidarity maintained by family-based factions, usually formed around a core of close blood relatives—fathers, sons, brothers, and cousins—sometimes in alliance with in-laws.

For most of the eighteenth century, the civil-religious oligarchy of Aracena appears to have been composed of three primary factions of *hidalgos*. As noted above, first among these factions were the Villafrancos, who occupied crucial ecclesiastical and secular posts. The principal rivals of the Villafrancos in community politics were the Granvillas, who also occupied seats on the town council and other secular offices. Finally, there were the Garays, a clerical family whose position was altogether weaker and different in character because it depended on the passage of the office of head priest of the parish and *priorato* from uncles to nephews—a shaky business at best and one that seems to have collapsed after three generations as a result of the lack of male heirs.

On the peripheries of these factions were a number of more independent officials, *hidalgos,* and notables (including the key figure of the *gobernador* [governor]), who were usually aligned with one of the dominant factions but who occasionally switched sides or simply withdrew from the fray. Many of these gentry in peripheral positions were related by ties of blood or marriage to more than one faction of the oligarchy, and, indeed, the leaders of the opposing factions were not all that distantly related to one another. As a result, even fierce factional disputes had something of the character of a feud within one large extended family.

The normal state of factional politics in the town consisted of an unceasing round of petty charges and countercharges exchanged between officials concerning such matters as the breaking of contracts, the overstepping of prerogatives, the failure to aid the poor of the township, and general accusations of incompetence. Periodically, though, this background noise of contention was punctuated by cries of self-righteous outrage and offended dignity that marked the beginning of serious struggles for power among the oligarchs. Such struggles invariably arose when one party or another perceived that offices and spoils were not being distributed equally among those whose rank entitled them to consideration (that is, not enough power or wealth was finding its way into the hands of the protesters). When no compromise could be reached, the factions tended to coalesce and plot the downfall of their rivals.

One such bitter factional dispute dominated the proceedings of the town council and the political life of the town for most of the period from 1757 to 1768. The roots of the conflict dated back to a few weeks in 1749 when the *gobernador* and the leading members of the Granvilla faction were out of town. The members of the Villafranco group took advantage of this situation and leased themselves several of the largest tracts of communal land at a nominal rent for a period of ten years. José Villafranco's position on the council was sufficiently strong that he was able to prevent the cancellation of the leases despite the protests of members of the opposing faction when they returned (AN/bra 1749:94). Several years passed more or less quietly, but tensions rose again in 1757. The Villafrancos persuaded the *gobernador* to take action against Nicolás Granvilla (a *regidor*) and a number of others for leasing the houses of a widow without authorization of the full council (AN/mpt 1757). While the circumstances surrounding this incident are unclear, the upshot was not. From this point forward, the conflict escalated; by 1758, the Granvilla group had taken the serious step of filing complaints with the *asistente* of Seville (the highest royal official of western Andalusia) against the "excesses" of José Villafranco and his two principal allies among the *regidores*, Andrés Muñiz and Tomás Lobo (AN/mv 1758:93).

These complaints must have had some effect because most of the leading members of the Villafranco faction were out of office in the early 1760s, and even José Villafranco's hold on the office of *regidor* was made insecure by the *gobernador*'s petitions to Seville, which accused José of defrauding the township by illegally occupying common lands and by stealing water from El Fuente del Pilar (AN/mv 1761:67). This period represented the nadir of the fortunes of the Villafrancos. The vacant seats of the Villafranco faction on the council as well as a number of subordinate offices in the township were filled by allies of the Granvilla group. Furthermore, Nicolás Granvilla and the *gobernador* had forged a close alliance and evidently had sympathetic patrons in the court in Madrid, since they were confident enough to begin sending royal officials a series of petitions charging José Villafranco with manipulating the tax list of the township in ways that caused "grave injustices" in the assignment of fiscal obligations (AN/mv 1761:68, 77).

Finally, to add insult to injury, the Granvilla faction lodged a suit in Granada alleging that the Villafranco family's claims to the rank of *hidalgo* were fraudulent and that family members had used their offices to defraud the township of twenty-eight thousand reales through the illegal possession of common lands (AN/mv 1761:72). This was an extremely serious threat not only to the personal honor of José Villafranco but also to the honor of his whole extended family, and it threatened loss of the privileges that accompanied their rank. Moreover, the official normally responsible for investigating such charges within the township was the head of the Holy Brotherhood of the Estate of Hidalgos of Aracena. This post was held at the time of the charges by Isidro Fernández de Granvilla, one of the new *regidores* and a cousin of Nicolás Granvilla. It was thus not difficult to force a resolution through the town council. Accordingly, the council declared that the Villafranco and Muñiz families as well as their "consorts" were not *hidalgos*, had no rights to their offices of *regidor,* and should henceforth be subject to all of the obligations of *pecheros* (AN/mv 1762:57, 65).

Although they were damaged by this formidable onslaught, it did not take the Villafrancos and their allies long to counterattack. One of their first successes was to have Andrés Muñiz appointed by the Sala of Hidalgos of the Royal Chancellery of Granada to investigate the rights of the Granvilla family to *hidalgo* rank—a case of check and counter-check facilitated by the Crown's eagerness during this period to reduce the number of *hidalgos* throughout Spain and thus increase royal revenues (Moreno Alonso 1981:364–65). An equal and opposite reaction also quickly developed over the issue of taxation. Charging that tax funds were being used illegally by the Granvilla faction on the town council to pay for the expenses incurred in the course of political maneuvers motivated by "passions, ill-will, and private ends," the Villafranco faction assumed the mantle of public decency and declared that "it is unjust that householders must contribute to the support of the council when no public benefit is secured." Acting together, Celestino Villafranco and his cousin Manuel José, both of whom were becoming actively engaged in politics for the first time, demanded that the *regidores* be obliged to redistribute twenty-two thousand reales in misspent funds to the local householders (AN/mv 1762:60).

Not surprisingly, the Villafrancos were able to win the support of all of the *alcaldes* of the hamlets and of more than twenty householders of Aracena for this measure, and since the Villafrancos were well connected to Seville officialdom, the *asistente* sided with them and ordered that an "open council" of all householders of Aracena be held so that a vote could be taken on the issue (AN/mv 1763:12). However, forging alliances with the populace at large was a rare tactic in local politics and did not prove effective in this instance. As Manuel José rather ruefully complained in the course of filing yet another appeal to Seville, the Granvilla *regidores* were able to subvert the meeting by bribing, cajoling, and threatening the populace, and as a result of their "sinister operations," the "ignorant householders" voted against the redistribution (AN/mv 1763:13). Nevertheless, the *asistente* forbade the *regidores* to use council resources to defray the costs of future legal proceedings against the Villafrancos. This order, as well as the general goodwill with which Seville officials favored the Villafrancos, more or less restored the balance of power between the contending groups. Thus, by 1764, José Villafranco's position on the council was secure, and his two most important allies had regained their seats at the expense of the friends of Nicolás Granvilla (AN/mv 1764:70).

For the next four years, the two factions jockeyed for position in various ways, but neither side did much damage to the other. The Villafrancos had the backing of officials in Seville, and the Granvillas were favored by bureaucrats in Madrid. Neither group was able to break this deadlock, although each made attempts. For example, on one occasion in 1766 when the *gobernador* and Nicolás Granvilla were absent from the council, the Villafrancos sent an emissary to the count of Altamira with petitions requesting him to appoint a new *gobernador* and to certify the council's right to award the office of *regidor* currently held by Granvilla. The grounds for the requests were that the Granvilla group members had exercised their offices with a "partiality and prejudice" that had led to a situation in which "for some years the community has been in a very deplorable state because of these malintentioned people who have threatened the town with total ruin through costly litigations and unjust actions that have notoriously destroyed the union and good harmony of the council" (AN/mv 1766:221). But despite the implicit warning that the incomes of the House of Altamira might be threatened by the mismanagement of finances under the Granvillas, the count stood fast behind his dependents, and eventually the Villafrancos were forced to offer a humiliating apology stating that they had never had any intention of defying the authority of the House of Altamira (AN/mv 1767:17).

The outcome of this decade of political struggle was essentially a stalemate. The Villafrancos had regained their power on the council but had failed to dislodge the Granvillas. Nothing came of the attempts of either faction to challenge the *hidalgo* status of the opposing group. Indeed, without much ado, Celestino Villafranco succeeded Isidro Fernández de Granvilla as head of the Holy Brotherhood of the Estate of Hidalgos of Aracena in 1768 (AN/mv 1768:73). All charges of fraud, misappropriation of funds, and subversion of justice (many of which are not discussed here) came to naught, and not one official was fined, imprisoned, barred from holding office, or even disgraced. In the years following these disputes, the Villafrancos and Granvillas alike continued to bicker and to share the power, spoils, and prestige of office with their arch rivals and brother *caballeros* (gentlemen, horsemen).

What these political struggles of the 1760s reveal is the linkage between the domestic realm and the political order of the Ancient Regime. The basis of local politics was the competition for spoils of office, and ordinarily this competition was conducted in terms of disputes over prerogatives and procedures. Disputes occasionally moved beyond this level, and the contending factions attacked the public virtues and personal honor of their opponents, sought the patronage and protection of higher authorities, and challenged the fundamental rights to office that came with *hidalgo* rank. When this occurred, the political and social fate of the town's oligarchs depended on their ability to maintain the unity of their family-based alliances and to use the collective resources of the group to thwart the designs of near-equals in wealth, rank, and power. The extent to which any group was capable of doing this was dependent on whether its members had been able to establish connections with others both within the town and outside it through strategies of marriage, inheritance, and office. While in the dispute described above, both the Villafrancos and the Granvillas were able to maintain their positions of power in the community, this was not always the case. Over the course of decades, there were definite winners and losers in the oligarchic politics of faction, with some families rising while others fell. Although the rules of the game were open-ended enough to permit considerable social mobility, what seems to have remained more or less constant were the strategies and tactics employed in the contests for prestige, wealth, and power.

GRAND DESIGNS: CHARITY BEGINS AT HOME

The strategies and tactics used by Aracena's oligarchs to maintain or enhance their dominant position in the township affected the religious domain as much as the political domain. As noted above, the clergy all came from gentry families, many clerical offices were inherited, and church property was administered in ways that favored the local elite. As a result, Captain Gerónimo Infante's decision to leave control of his charitable foundation in the hands of the senior clergy of Aracena, a decision discussed at the beginning of this chapter, did not prevent his legacy from becoming an opportune target for the local oligarchs. On the contrary, the history of the foundation and especially of La Cofradía de San Pedro y Pan de los Pobres reveals the extent to which all important aspects of social life were affected by the oligarchs' efforts to conserve the patrimonies, rank, and power of their families. Even an institution specifically dedicated to providing charity for the poor could be turned into a means for the exploitation of the underprivileged.

Before Gerónimo Infante's gift was bestowed, La Cofradía de San Pedro appears to have ranked about equal with the numerous other lay religious brotherhoods in the township (see Chapter 2). But with the huge increase in its endowments, the organization quickly became attractive to Aracena's gentry. Indeed, the town council attempted to wrest control of the *patronato* and the brotherhood from the senior clergy of the *priorato* despite the good captain's explicit instructions. For reasons that are unclear, this gambit failed; but in any case, it was not long before the character of La Cofradía de San Pedro was radically transformed. The seat of the brotherhood was moved from the *barrio* chapel of San Pedro to the parish church of Santa María de la Asunción, and soon most of the parish clergy and the gentry of Aracena were counted among its members. As a result, the brotherhood became one of the bulwarks of orthodox faith within the township, and its select members often boasted of their *esclarecidos linajes* (illustrious, honorable lineages) and *pureza de sangre* (purity of blood). In addition to the more worldly benefits that membership in the brotherhood brought, the brothers (and sisters) of La Cofradía de San Pedro were ordinarily afforded a prestigious burial within the walls of either the *priorato* church or the church of "El Castillo" as a mark of respect for their status. Thus, while in principle this brotherhood differed little from the others, in fact it became a singular and exclusive association of the town's lay and clerical elite.

Unfortunately, the social character of La Cofradía de San Pedro did not make it a particularly effective organization for the distribution of charity. Although some sense of paternalist patronage influenced its policies and there is no doubt that the poor benefited to a certain extent from the ministrations of the brotherhood, charitable donations were far less than they might have been. The maximum known amount of wheat ever distributed for one year was a bit more than fifteen hundred *fanegas*—a quantity considerably short of Gerónimo Infante's expectations—and the amounts distributed in other years appear to have been far less. Moreover, even when there were adequate stores of wheat on hand, the brotherhood seems to have been rather tightfisted. For example, in 1793, during a period of severe shortages and high prices, *regidores* of the town council had to plead with the officers of the brotherhood to release more of its substantial stores to meet the pressing needs of the community. The brotherhood complied with this request but only after exacting a personal pledge from the *regidores* to restore the quantity of grain depleted.

Such niggardliness was not due to a lack of means. The wealth of the *patronato* had enabled the brotherhood to acquire hundreds of hectares of land in the years immediately before and after 1700, and for the next century no private persons could muster anything approaching the brotherhood's economic resources. As a result, the brotherhood steadily accumulated lands, houses, tributes, and other capital. The largest single property of the brotherhood was known as the *obra pía* and consisted of several wooded *montes* and some cultivable fields. Simply to complete the periodic clearing of brush from these lands required (in 1766) two months of labor by 380 *jornaleros*. The wealth of the brotherhood thus seems to have been more than sufficient to enable it to carry on its charitable work. That the poor profited relatively little was due to the fact that the brotherhood acted more as a joint stock company for the local gentry than as a charitable association.

The leading figures in the brotherhood were the head priest of Aracena, two *hermanos mayores,* and two salaried administrators of the brotherhood's property. For most of the eighteenth century, a member of the Garay family was head priest, and the four other positions were rotated among leading *hidalgos:* a Fernández or Granvilla was often to be found among the officers; a Villafranco almost always held one of the key posts; and for one period in the 1760s, all four offices were in the hands of the Villafrancos. Through the actions of this self-perpetuating board of directors, the income that might have aided the poor was held to a minimal level or was diverted to benefit the governors of the brotherhood or others among the gentry. Part of the income of the *obra pía* was used to pay the salaries of the lay administrators, and by local standards these salaries (totaling more than five thousand reales a year) were substantial. Some income from the endowment was used to support the clergy who performed services at the funerals of members of the brotherhood. More important, extensive tracts of the brotherhood's land were leased to the gentry at low rates of rent for long periods.

Such favoritism in the use of institutional endowments was predictable. What was unusual was the self-interested banking and investment procedures that the administrators followed in order to augment the capital of the brotherhood. The charter of the *patronato* enjoined the officials of La Cofradía de San Pedro to "buy and sell at opportune times," and this they did with considerable acumen even when the directive conflicted with the association's charitable mission. Furthermore, a considerable portion of the working capital of the brotherhood was used to make loans. Few of these loans were large, for short terms, or taken out by the gentry. Rather, the standard loan was from one thousand to five thousand reales and was granted to a *labrador* or other small householder who mortgaged his property as security. In most cases, loans were repayable at a yearly rate over several decades or *censos* (annuities) were required in perpetuity. However, repayments of this sort often went uncollected for several years on end until the brotherhood's officers recalled their sense of duty and demanded immediate fulfillment of all obligations. This cycle of neglect and demand was apparently repeated several times in the eighteenth and early nineteenth centuries, always with the same results.

The best records date from 1780, a year in which the brotherhood had satisfactory supplies of wheat (1,348 *fanegas*) but the townspeople involved in agriculture were experiencing difficulties. The officers of the brotherhood nevertheless chose this "opportune time" to demand back-payments on all lapsed obligations. Many of the hard-pressed small householders of the town were naturally unable to comply, and within a few weeks the officers resorted to outright confiscation of property. For a week in early summer, the senior brothers of the association accompanied by the *alguacil* (constable) of Aracena went from street to street claiming what they were owed. The list of attachments was long: Francisco Barrera, one mule; Juan Paneagua, one vine and fenced plot; Pío Díaz, his houses; Francisco Díaz, the same; Vicente Barrera, a large table, a box with lock, and a frying pan; Nicolás Márquez, a grove of oaks; and so on. Forty-seven householders lost significant property during the week, and some apparently had their whole means of livelihood expropriated. The chronicler of the event noted that when the people of a street heard the officials of the brotherhood approaching, they locked their doors and hid themselves and their most precious possessions. The most serious problem the officials faced was in finding townsmen who would agree to guard the seized properties until they could be sold or leased to those more fortunate than their previous owners. A few years later, there still remained another two hundred properties with similar liens against them listed in the brotherhood's account books.

Such were the workings of charity and patronage in a ranked social order organized by the institutions of church and state but pervaded by struggles among officials, families, and councils, as well as between the town and its hamlets. What one hand gave in the form of bread, charity, charters, and paternalism, the other took away in the form of spoils, tribute, status, and power. Founded on the wealth of empire, the *patronato* lent glory to the name of Gerónimo Infante, honor and wealth to his lineage, and influence to the clergy of Aracena. Its dependent arm, La Cofradía de San Pedro y Pan de los Pobres, became a bastion of the local gentry's claims to honor and orthodox faith and a vehicle both of charity and of exploitation. It would be difficult to discover institutions that better expressed the contradictory tensions shaping the oligarchic power structure of the Ancient Regime. The social order was based on paternalist relations of dependence and authority and on the notion that formal prerogatives and obligations of patronage bind unequals in rank and power to one another. But in all domains of life in Aracena—domestic, political, and religious—the fierce loyalties of persons, families, factions, and corporate bodies that helped them maintain and enhance their rank and social position also served to alter and subvert the significance of formal obligations and duties. This generated a form of social life in which inequalities between persons and groups were extreme.

The practical basis of the commitment of Aracena's elite to the values of orthodoxy, honor, and patronage lay in the fact that religious, political, and economic elements were inextricably interwoven in the local power structure. Each of these interdependent elements had a crucial place in the strategies of the town's oligarchs, and the intensity of the competition among these members of the gentry as well as their common preoccupation with maintaining the overall pattern of unequal social relations between themselves and the commonfolk of the sierra continually spurred the active regeneration and reaffirmation of the institutional ideologies of estate society. Nevertheless, the force of these official ideologies in Aracena was not wholly derived from their direct relevance to the conduct of micropolitical and economic affairs. In equal measure, the official ideologies of orthodoxy, honor, and patronage were compelling because they provided the means through which relations of power could be represented, established, and maintained in day-to-day life and because they were derived from fundamental discourses and images of personhood, power, and society that had been at the core of Catholic culture for more than a millennium. These discourses and images structured an ethos and mode of social consciousness that shaped the basic character of interests and motivations for people of the Ancient Regime. While moral and social prestige were associated with charitable acts and with patronage extended to corporate groups and the community as a whole, the economic and political conditions demanded that, for the most part, charity had to begin and end at home. This meant that there were large gaps between the ideals of patronage and the reality of agonistic struggles for power and authority within the township.

Yet despite the existence of such gaps, it would almost surely be misleading to describe Aracena as a community in which traditional cultural idioms and images represented little more than a cracked and warped ideological veneer that barely concealed an exploitative class system, as some scholars have been inclined to describe other communities in Andalusia and Spain (see Artola, Bernal, and Contreras 1978; Bernal 1979; Herr 1989).[8] To be sure, there is considerable evidence from the township to support the view that the agrarian economy was dominated by market forces and that the local oligarchs who controlled the private and corporate means of production sought to maximize profits and accumulate capital by overcoming some of the legal obstacles that the corporate patrimonial system presented to the free exchange of land and labor. Indeed, as discussed above, the Infante patrimony appears to have been aggressively managed as a capital-intensive financial enterprise and thus provides some grist for the mill of those who discern the critical earmarks of agrarian capitalism and class society in the Ancient Regime.

There are, however, two immediate difficulties in representing the Ancient Regime in Aracena in this way. The first is the absence of any evidence of emergent oppositional liberal ideologies or even a current of opinion that challenged the patrimonial institutional structure of the Ancient Regime. There are no signs, for example, that the enlightened views advanced by the ministers and intellectuals of the court of Carlos III in regard to the state and national wealth (see Herr 1958) had any audience in Aracena. The second difficulty is the massive evidence that Aracena's oligarchs and other townspeople wholeheartedly embraced the fundamental ideals and institutions of the old order. Thus, despite the Infante Foundation's strategies of accumulation, its use of wage labor, and its foreclosures on poor debtors, it never entirely neglected its charitable mission; nor did its agents and officers, who were members of La Cofradía de San Pedro and undoubtedly sincere Catholics, show any desire to do so, even though their generosity was less than it might have been. More generally, although the oligarchs in Aracena manipulated market relations, exploited the poor, and sought to accumulate capital, they did so in order to pursue traditional goals: the preservation of their patrimonies, the purchase of masses to be said for the salvation of their souls, and the winning of fame and honor through exemplary acts of patronage. In other words, their goals—and probably their means to obtain them—were the same as those of the "good" captain Infante.

In light of these factors, an alternative way of describing the final decades of the Ancient Regime in Aracena is to represent it in terms of a sociocultural formation that was neither purely fish nor purely fowl. This would be consistent with recent scholarly work (see Holmes 1989; Rebel 1983) that has emphasized the tendency of local oligarchs in much of early modern Europe to move back and forth between traditionalist and rationalized contractual ways of construing socioeconomic relations in accordance with where they perceived the greatest advantage. Mercantile patrimonialism would thus seem to be a more accurate term for describing the operations and structure of the Infante Foundation and accounting for the mixed motives of those involved in it. Indeed, from this perspective, many facets of life in Aracena could be construed in terms of a dynamic but precarious balance between the ideology of interdependence and the ideology of proto-individualism or, similarly, between archaic cultural, political, and economic institutions and practices and emergent liberal ones.

Yet, based on the evidence regarding Aracena, even this dynamic and balanced view is somewhat misleading if it fails to stress that rationalized contractual forms of sociopolitical and socioeconomic relations (forms often labeled in retrospect as signs of the emergence of liberal class society) were not only extensively used by the old order but were also easily assimilated by that order without much ado. In other words, their use was not regarded as a cultural contradiction and certainly did not generate fear that a radical social crisis was at hand. For one thing, certain types of highly rationalized, formal, and official ways of organizing and construing socioeconomic relations and even relations with supernatural beings (for example, the types used by Gerónimo Infante) were every bit as time-hallowed and traditional in Aracena as were the informal, customary ways of conducting local affairs. The processes involving the bureaucratization of community affairs do not seem to have dramatically intensified during the eighteenth century. For another, the institutional structure of the Ancient Regime in the town, for all its emphasis on corporate rights and patrimonial obligations and the existence of institutions such as *mayorazgo,* does not seem to have presented insuperable obstacles to the cruder forms of manipulating labor, markets, and capital or to pursuing individual economic self-interest. Nor does it seem to have hindered those with wealth from converting their capital into social prestige and power by means such as making political and marital alliances, arranging for excess heirs to enter the church, and purchasing secular offices and even the rank of *hidalgo.*

Most important, the pursuit of self-interest, both economic and political, was widespread in traditional society and went hand in hand with commonsense notions of what the limits of corporate interdependence or the necessity to struggle for the sake of one's honor and position were in an agonistic world. Indeed, the marked vacillation of the powerful between acts of domination, exploitation, and venality and acts of generosity, charity, and patronage, which encompassed the range of relations of domination and subordination in Aracena during the early modern period, indicates the extent to which the personalist sense of self as a virtuous spiritual and natural person in an agonistic world was tied to the achievement of advantage over others. Even the life story of such a traditional and venerated figure as Madre María (see Chapter 2) demonstrates that she saw no contradiction between the goal of ensuring her nephew's material and political accommodation and the higher workings of charity and grace. And, as Lorea's biography shows, Madre María's lifelong project of founding a Dominican convent in Aracena was undertaken in large part because of her desire to better not just the spiritual but also the material conditions of a group of women that included a number of her close relatives. Furthermore, to accomplish her goal, she became deeply involved in calculating just what was required of her and her allies both politically and economically.

As was shown in Chapter 2, cultural hegemony during the Ancient Regime was exercised by rendering the life of the flesh significant in terms of the life of the spirit. One critical aspect of this involved continually justifying practical egotism and exploitative social relations in terms of higher values and purposes. In the final analysis, the strategies and projects that the oligarchs of eighteenth-century Aracena pursued were not discontinuous with those of the saintly *beata,* nor were their justifications. They could rationalize cold-hearted, tough-minded calculations of interests within the framework of traditional ways of representing personhood and community. Because it was not especially difficult to incorporate heterogeneous practices within the dominant framework of the images and idioms of religion, honor, and patronage, the local elite of Aracena apparently had no inclination to advance alternative visions of the social and institutional order.

From this perspective, it would be inaccurate to represent the scales of socioeconomic power as being delicately balanced between traditional and rationalized forms of representing and conducting social relations in late eighteenth-century Aracena. Rather, things were tipped in favor of the conservation and reproduction of traditional forms, since they were able to accommodate a great deal of innovation. No doubt the dynamics of social production and reproduction differed in other sorts of community (see Herr 1989), but caution is in order before the Ancient Regime is represented essentially as a capitalist class society *avant la lettre.* Although some aspects of rural agrarian economic life were liberalized, the way in which these aspects articulated with the exercise of political power and cultural authority is what is crucial when it comes to characterizing the social formation as a whole. And at least on the evidence of Aracena, what seems most notable is the persistence and resilience of the old order. It survived both the presence of new economic possibilities and the less-than-definitive shifts in the policies of the enlightened monarchy as handed down to the community. Any distant echoes of revolution that the townspeople may have discerned in the late eighteenth century appear to have given them little reason to expect, much less hope for, the collapse of the old order. Rather, it seems that when the Ancient Regime fell, as it did within a few years after the turn of the nineteenth century, it did so because, thanks to the catastrophic disasters of war, virtually all of the complex modes of articulation of cultural, political, and economic power of a hitherto resilient social formation were simultaneously disrupted. Yet even though the hegemonic formation of the Ancient Regime in Aracena did not survive the early nineteenth century, its fragmentary remains have continued to exert critical influences on local life down to the present day.

PART 2

TRADITION DISPLACED: AGRARIAN CAPITALISM AND CLASS SOCIETY

4

Liberalism, Caciquismo, *and Cultural Enterprise*

It affirmed principles in legislation and violated them in practice; it proclaimed liberty and exercised tyranny; ... it professed to abominate the ancient iniquities and nourished itself on them alone.
—Francisco Giner de los Ríos
Description of the Revolution of 1868

The Agonies of the Ancient Regime

In 1807, when Napoleon was planning to invade Portugal, Carlos IV of Spain granted the emperor's armies right of passage through his domains. This proved to be an unwise decision. After Portugal was defeated, the imperial armies occupied Castile. Unprepared for French aggression, Carlos IV was disgraced and forced to abdicate in favor of his son, Fernando VII, in the early summer of 1808; and by July, Napoleon was able to depose Fernando and install his own brother, Joseph Bonaparte, on the Spanish throne. Popular resistance to the new regime had already begun, but this dynastic chicanery rapidly transformed sporadic outbreaks of violent protest into the full-blown guerrilla struggles of the War of Independence. The war was the crucible of modern Spain, and from this crucible emerged the liberal ideologies that contributed to the formation of the constitutional monarchy and agrarian-based class society of the later decades of the nineteenth century.

The townspeople of Aracena were full participants in the events of the war and its aftermath. As early as 23 July 1808, the "immense majority of the *pueblo*" rallied under the banners of "King [Fernando VII] and Religion" in thanksgiving for the defeat of the French at Bailen (AA 1808). A mass was celebrated in the church of "El Castillo," and

La Virgen del Mayor Dolor was named "Madrina de la Guerra" (protectress or godmother of the town in time of war). As in past centuries, Spanish nationalism and local pride were identified with the defense of religion. A few months later, a local militia was formed of four companies of fifty soldiers each, led by twelve officers.

War came to Aracena in the early months of 1810. Outnumbered by French forces, Spanish troops under the command of General Ballesteros fought a pitched battle to protect Aracena. But when Ballesteros learned that enemy reinforcements were approaching, he prudently decided to retreat to the more easily held village of Alájar, leaving Aracena without defenders. The undefended town was quickly occupied and became the base camp for French forces in the region. Property was confiscated or damaged, and many of Aracena's places of worship, including "El Castillo," were desecrated and put to use as stables and barracks by the foreign troops (AA 1810). The French troops were fiercely anticlerical, and religion became a focal point of tension in the town. Some of the local nuns renounced their vows in panic, and members of the senior clergy "with the motive of the present notorious circumstances" began to sell the endowments of the local convents and monasteries in order to support themselves (AN/jms 1812:22).

The more or less voluntary sales of church property in 1810 extended a process of corporate disintegration that had begun a decade earlier when the royal government had mandated the auctioning of the endowments of certain ecclesiastical foundations to increase wartime revenues.[1] In Aracena and its dependent hamlets, the auctions had been confined at first to the properties of the lay religious brotherhoods.[2] The sales had undercut the vitality of the brotherhoods by making it difficult for them to provide aid to their members or charity to the poor, and it was not long before most of these organizations ceased to exist for all practical purposes. Another round of sales had occurred in 1807 and primarily involved the auction of the endowments of the town's religious orders. In Aracena, as elsewhere in Spain, war, internal political disorder, and foreign pressures had steadily disrupted traditional patterns of social life and decisively altered the dynamics of local and national politics by undermining long-established institutions and forms of authority. The dramatic occupation of "El Castillo" in 1810 thus marked a crucial juncture in the process of the dissolution of the Ancient Regime in Aracena.

In 1812, after the French had withdrawn from the sierra, the Cortes of Cádiz adopted a liberal constitution—a step that marked the beginning of the end for royal absolutism in Spain. In Aracena, an *ayuntamiento* (town council) was formed in keeping with the new constitution; the *cabildo* and *regidor* system of the Ancient Regime was temporarily abolished; and the counts of Altamira lost their *señorío* (lordship) over the township. The constitutional government was short-lived, however. A "royal council" took office in 1814 after a restored Fernando VII disbanded the Cortes and abrogated the liberal constitution. Locally, these changes in regime at first seemed to make little difference. But by 1819, sharp lines of political cleavage between traditionalists and constitutionalists developed. The traditionalists dominated the royalist town council until mid-1820, when it was replaced by a constitutional *ayuntamiento*. This occurred as a result of a *pronunciamiento* (coup) of liberal army officers led by Major Rafael Riego, who forced the king to accept the Constitution of 1812. A new Cortes met in July 1820 and rapidly passed legislation ending *mayorazgo* entailments and laying the groundwork for further sales of church lands. In Aracena, these measures were evidently supported by the new town council, which was controlled by three or four men from the most illustrious and wealthiest of the old *hidalgo* families.

Although the traditionalist leaders, who in general came from less prestigious and less wealthy gentry families, were out of office, they did not lack popular support. On the contrary, it is clear that most townspeople were on the side of old-time religion and absolutist monarchy and that Aracena's clergy actively agitated against the liberal minority (see Moreno Alonso 1979:154–58, 298–306).[3] By July 1822, opinions were polarized to such an extent that traditionalists placed a placard reading "Long Live Spain and Religion / Death to Those Who Want the Constitution" in the town's principal plaza. In February 1823, a serious disturbance erupted when traditionalists refused to accept the replacement of one of the foremost agitators among the local priests. In the course of the dispute, eighteen members of the pro-liberal local militia were assaulted and disarmed. The regional political chief of the liberals arrived with another force to arrest the culprits, a pistol was discharged, a riot began, and the chief and his militia were driven from town. The state of rebellion was deemed serious enough that the liberal governors of Seville posted an official notice declaring that Aracena was in a condition of "perfect anarchy." By the end of the month, five hundred militiamen and regular soldiers (mostly from Seville) had returned to restore order. The regional political chief exiled two priests from the town, and they were subsequently hidden in neighboring *pueblos*.

The populace of Aracena rose again in June 1823, destroyed several monuments erected by the constitutional regime, and freed clerics and other prisoners from the liberals. Once again, La Virgen del

Mayor Dolor was named "Madrina de la Guerra" to protect the township's one thousand militiamen who were sworn to fight for the restoration of the king's prerogatives and the institutional order of the Ancient Regime. This time, however, the supposed "enemies of Spain, the King, and Religion" were not foreigners. They were liberal Spaniards, fellow townspeople. The identification of loyalty to the church with partisan faction, ideology, and party had begun. By the autumn of 1823, the traditionalist forces had triumphed both locally and nationally.[4]

The essentially reactionary alliance between the lesser gentry and the laboring poor of the township did not prove a durable one, however. By the mid-1830s, the leading traditionalists of Aracena no longer demonstrated much hostility toward the principles or political order of constitutional monarchy. Indeed, their political attitudes varied little from those of their liberal opponents. The interests of the majority of townspeople who had so recently defended the Ancient Regime were hardly represented by either of the local factions, and except during the brief interlude of the First Republic, for the remainder of the century there was no organized popular political force in the township. Thus, in the course of a few decades, the corporate political order of the Ancient Regime, an order based on notions of rank, honor, religion, and patronage, had been decisively undermined by the disasters of war and partisan conflict. Nevertheless, the old faction-riven oligarchy of Aracena had managed to survive and eventually succeeded in reconstituting itself on a new institutional basis.

In the remainder of this chapter, the kind of agrarian class society that developed in Aracena in the period from 1830 to 1920 is described. As noted below, the particular character of this society was shaped by new forces of political, economic, and ideological liberalism, forces that subverted and were themselves deflected by the fragmented institutional structures and displaced cultural traditions of the Ancient Regime.

THE IRONIES OF LIBERALISM AND THE EMERGENCE OF CLASS SOCIETY: SOCIAL DISTANCE AND CULTURAL DISPLACEMENT

In the 1830s, the key principle of political liberalism—the principle that sovereignty resided in the nation and its people rather than in the Crown (first expressed in the Constitution of 1812)—triumphed in most of Spain. One direct consequence of this was a movement for the creation of a centralized state with a rational bureaucratic structure that could express the will of the nation. In keeping with this point of view, the division of Spain into provinces, each with its own administrative apparatus, was accomplished in the mid-1830s. Aracena, for example, was incorporated into the new province of Huelva and became the head of a *partido judicial* (judicial district) that encompassed thirty-one municipalities of the sierra. In 1840, with the passage of a new law of *ayuntamientos,* municipalities were defined as "subaltern corporations" of the state (see Herr 1974:98; see also Castro 1979). And in the remaining decades of the nineteenth century, the bureaucratic reorganization of Spain set the stage for the more conservative governments of the period to enact a series of other measures that consolidated state power and cumulatively redefined the character of civil society. Among the most important steps taken were the establishment of the Guardia Civil, a quasi-military national police force, in 1844; the reorganization of the local-level judicial system in 1858; and the establishment of civil registries, registries of property, a census bureau, and other similar agencies in the 1850s, 1860s, and 1870s.

Within the emerging liberal Spanish polity, the counterbalancing force to bureaucratic centralization was political individualism—the legal (and, too frequently, purely nominal) recognition of the abstract rights of the citizen. By the late 1830s in Aracena, the declining role of the ecclesiastical council in local affairs, the final abolition of the *señorío* of the House of Altamira, and the denial of special political prerogatives to those of *hidalgo* rank had eliminated the last vestiges of the corporate political order of the Ancient Regime. With the collapse of the Ancient Regime, the rights of adult males to hold local office and to vote for town councilmen and national deputies to the lower house of the Cortes were based on property qualifications rather than rank.[5] But the concentration of power at the highest levels of the state and the rather narrow franchise ensured that power would continue to reside in the hands of a faction-ridden oligarchy that represented the interests of the propertied classes.

In Aracena, the terms "moderate" and "progressive" served to distinguish the competing factions of the local oligarchy, but differences in ideology between these factions seemed to have mattered very little. The "moderates" (i.e., the political heirs of the traditionalist group of the 1820s) were usually able to secure a majority of seats on the town council, but their control of the township was never total. Particularly when the "progressives" (i.e., the political heirs of the liberals of the 1820s) were supported by a sympathetic *alcalde* (mayor), they were capable of causing enough ruckus about the award of spoils to disrupt municipal government. At such times, the political infighting became so intense that the *jefe político* (political head) of the province would intervene in the fray and disband the council in order to bring an end to "anarchy."

It was not until the late 1870s that the political dynamics of Aracena began to shift away from pitched battles between the oligarchic factions. After the collapse of the First Republic, leaders of the nation's Conservative and Liberal parties agreed to alternate in power, and this *turno pacífico* (peaceful succession) in national politics required predictability in electoral results. Provincial authorities thus began to consistently support whoever could ensure that deputies from the right party were elected. In Aracena, the figure who got official support for his unofficial role of *cacique* (political boss) was Don Juan Duro, a landowner of the middle rank who had long been one of the principal politicians in the "moderate" faction. In exchange for producing the desired electoral outcome, Don Juan was apparently given a free hand in local affairs, and soon his friends and clients occupied most municipal and judicial offices in Aracena. As a result, "tranquillity and peace," as his far more powerful successor (see below) to the role of *cacique* termed it, began to prevail in local politics.

In the economic realm, the emergence of liberalism in Aracena was accompanied by freewheeling activity and intense competition from 1840 to 1875, followed in the last decades of the century by consolidation and exploitation of previous gains. During this period, two key processes interacted to transform the local economy: the progressive concentration of land and property in the hands of the local gentry and the thoroughgoing incorporation of critical sectors of the local economy into the national and international commodity markets. The accumulation of land and other property by the old gentry families of the town was a century-long process, but it reached its high point in the middle decades of the century. As noted above, a critical factor in this accumulation was the sale of ecclesiastical and communal lands.[6] While existing documents show that 2,408 hectares (about 14 percent of Aracena's total area) were transferred from the town's commons and ecclesiastical corporations to individual proprietors, this figure does not include all the lands that changed ownership.[7] In addition, many ecclesiastical properties, particularly the endowments of occupied chaplaincies, were never auctioned or sold but instead became the private property of the clerics who had benefited from their incomes (AN/fgl 1837:24; AN/jgf 1860:50; RP 1876:1344; RP 1896:2737; see also on this point Moreno Alonso 1979:163). The old elite, the local officials, and the wealthiest stratum of *labradores* (laborers who owned the land on which they worked) were virtually the sole beneficiaries of the sales in Aracena. As large tracts of lands were added to their already existing properties, they were able to form the great estates or latifundia that dominated the local agrarian economy in later years.[8]

The formation of extensive private estates in Aracena was occurring just as market demands for local agricultural commodities began to increase. In the years following 1855, the population of Spain rose precipitately, cities grew, railroads were built, roads were improved, and the infant industries of Catalonia and the Basque provinces emerged. A few kilometers to the south of Aracena, British capital was invested to exploit the largest pyrite deposits of Europe; and by the 1880s, the Río Tinto mines employed thousands of workers. These developments had far-reaching effects on local agriculture. The mining communities, Seville, and other cities of Spain needed to be supplied, and Aracena's traditional products of hides, hams, and sausages were in ever-increasing demand. The greatest impetus for local agrarian commerce, however, was the new demand for cork, which accompanied the huge expansion of the viticulture industry in Catalonia after 1868. As documents regarding the sale and lease of cork trees and products indicate, cork production in Aracena had become a booming sector of the economy by the 1870s.

In 1890, universal suffrage for men became a permanent feature of political life (see Carr 1982 and Herr 1971b and 1974 for extended discussions). By this time, in the economic sphere as well, liberal principles and legislation had expanded the formal liberties of male citizens. Nevertheless, in Aracena, as in other places in southern Spain, members of the old gentry were in the best position to take advantage of the new conditions, and the result was a rather magnificent if familiar historical irony. While the theoretical equality and freedom of Aracena's people expanded, the practical capacity of most of them to control their lives declined because of the new and massive concentration of power in the hands of a ruling class of political *caciques* and agrarian capitalists. Indeed, the underside of the process of political and economic liberalization was the impoverishment of the common people of the township and the emergence of a class-divided rural society.[9]

In 1900, about 80 percent of adult males in Aracena were directly engaged in agricultural labor as *jornaleros* (agrarian day laborers) or small landholders; another 13 to 17 percent of the male work force consisted of "industrial" workers, artisans, and *comerciantes* (merchants and shopkeepers); and the great landowners and professionals accounted for the remaining 3 to 7 percent of the adult male population (EL 1890, 1910, 1920, 1930). These proportions were not much different than they had been in 1840 or even 1750. However, a number of factors made Aracena a radically different place in 1900 than it had been a few decades earlier. The most important of these factors was a massive increase in the population of the township from about 4,300 people in 1840 to 6,300 in 1900 and a consequent expansion of the potential supply of labor as well as the number of people to be sustained. Another factor was a decline in subsistence and intensive agriculture as more land was devoted to tree crops and raising hogs.[10] This shift was coupled not only with a loss of the traditional use rights of *jornaleros* and small landholders as a result of the privatization of communal properties but also with a decline of the least exploitative forms of sharecropping, leasing, and other such arrangements and a corresponding increase in the direct exploitation of estates by owner-managers. Despite a good deal of emigration,[11] these factors acting together led to a proletarianization of the working poor of the township as population pressures mounted, the means to win an independent living were reduced, wages were held to minimal levels, and unemployment assumed proportions unknown in the past.

By contrast, the conditions of life for Aracena's elite families dramatically improved during this period, widening the gap between classes. As Aracena became a favored spot for bourgeois families from Seville to escape the summer heat of the city, the local elite began to adopt urban fashions and habits, and some of them built large mansions in the center of town and spent part of the winter in the city. And to meet their demands for manufactured consumer goods and entertainment, a general department store, two pastry shops, two stationery and bookstores, seven beauty salons, a printing shop, a photographic studio, several other stores, and a theater were established in the town by the turn of the century. The radical differences in the basic conditions and forms of life of the rich and the poor led to the formation of remarkably segregated class subcultures (see Chapter 5) that affected virtually every aspect of life in the town.

A sense of the revolutionary scope and cultural impact of this restructuring of local life in the nineteenth century can be gained by briefly examining the local history of the church and religion during this period. For centuries, the church had been the key institution of Aracena, and despite the more recent blows delivered to its endowments and prestige, it had remained so as late as the 1820s, when the clergy had mustered the populace to fight liberalism and support the Ancient Regime. By the last decades of the nineteenth century, however, the situation of the church had radically changed, and virtually the whole working class had been alienated from orthodox religion.

A number of factors contributed to the deterioration of the church's power and authority within the liberal regime.[12] The political turmoil of the first two decades of the nineteenth century significantly reduced the opportunities for clerical engagement in many aspects of local affairs by undermining the role of religious brotherhoods and by reducing clerical endowments. More important, though, the loss of virtually all ecclesiastical properties after 1836 was accompanied by a sharp decline in the number of parish clergy. In 1822, twenty-seven parish clergy still remained in the township, but their number fell to eleven by the late 1840s and declined still further in succeeding years. In addition, by mid-century the laws designed to eliminate the influence of the religious orders in Spain had dealt a severe blow to Aracena's convents and monasteries. Although a few nuns remained in the convents of Santa Catalina and Jesús, María, y José, both the Dominican and Carmelite monasteries had been deserted (Mádoz 1845–50).

This decline in the number of clergy led to an increasing lack of involvement of the church in many aspects of social life, especially in the hamlets and smaller *pueblos* of the sierra, where it became difficult to secure a priest to perform baptisms, weddings, and funerals much less celebrate regular masses. The impact that this more or less forced clerical withdrawal had on popular attitudes toward the church and formal religion was aggravated by two other developments. First, the local clergy and ex-clergy of the town acted in ways that underscored a growing popular perception of abandonment by the church. After the collapse of the traditionalist resistance to liberalism, many members of the clergy came to identify their own interests with those of the local gentry who had already set about procuring the ecclesiastical and communal "patrimonies of the poor." There was nothing very surprising in this. Tax records of the incomes of twenty-seven parish clergy in 1822 indicate that although no clerics were truly wealthy, half of them enjoyed sufficient incomes to fall in the upper-middle range of taxpayers and were clearly comfortably well-off. Not only these wealthier clergymen but also most of the poorer priests of the township were related to leading gentry families and were inclined to support the interests of their kinspeople. Moreover, several priests and former members of the clergy became substantial private landholders themselves when they inherited patrimonial lands or became the owners of properties that were previously part of endowed chaplaincies. Thus, those clergy or ex-clergy who were able to maintain or secure incomes through the period of disentailment became property holders whose interests were for the most part in opposition to the majority of their poor parishioners, and this no doubt contributed to the popular sense of abandonment by the church.

The second factor that aggravated the consequences of the withdrawal of the clergy was the alliance forged between the church and the most conservative elements of national and local liberalism in the late nineteenth century. With the Concordance of 1851, the church accepted the confiscations of ecclesiastical property and agreed to the restrictions on the activities and number of religious orders in return for the recognition of Spain as an officially Catholic country, the provision of state salaries for priests, and the right of the church to acquire property in the future. From this time forward, the church devoted most of its energies to defending these and related privileges (such as its decisive role in elementary and secondary education) from the threats of radical liberals and republicans who regarded the church as the principal block to social and cultural progress. In the struggles with the left wing of liberalism, the church became the ally and supporter of the conservative oligarchy. Thus, by the last decades of the nineteenth century, the landowning elite of Aracena had fervently re-embraced the church as a bulwark of the social order and had begun to sponsor new orders of nuns, religious education, and all sorts of devotional and lay organizations. However, this revitalization of local Catholicism did nothing to narrow the distance between the church and the rural poor of the sierra, who were almost entirely illiterate and hardly aroused by the supposed evils of social anarchy, Protestantism, and secular humanism. Rather, the poor were further alienated from the church because they recognized the alliance of the church and the landowning elite.

The identification of institutional religion with oligarchic interests added an active perception of betrayal to an already strong sense of abandonment. This was further exacerbated by the fact that by the turn of the century, the more remote villages of the sierra had become notorious dumping grounds for bad priests (see Ordóñez Márquez 1968). These conditions laid the foundations for the fierce anticlericalism of the agrarian laborers of the sierra and most working-class townspeople of Aracena in the first decades of the twentieth century (see Chapter 6). Religion, once the glue of local society, no longer bound social groups to one another; instead, succumbing to the pressures and constraints of liberalism, religion became a critical line of cultural cleavage marking class allegiances and antagonistic sociopolitical ideologies.

While the cultural effects of hegemonic processes of class formation were clearest in the case of religion, there were also analogous displacements of the traditional discourses and values of patronage and honor (see Chapter 5). These displacements created a crisis of moral and religious authority that was simultaneously a crisis of political and economic legitimacy. The concluding sections of this chapter deal with how working-class townspeople experienced and fomented these crises and how the agrarian gentry responded to them in the first two decades of the twentieth century.

The Conditions of the Working Class in Aracena and the Economies of Political Order

In the first issue of the *Geographical Review* in 1916, J. Russell Smith made the following comment about the agrarian system of the highlands of western Andalusia and Extremadura (quoted in Parsons 1962:233): "If I wanted to be comfortably and permanently rich, I could ask for few more secure bases for it in the line of agricultural lands than the undisturbed possession of a few hundred acres with a good stand of cork-oak trees . . . with its crops of cork and pork." A few hundred acres of cork-oak trees is precisely what each of the wealthiest landowners of Aracena had in the period of the town's greatest prosperity (from 1890 to 1936), and if their possessions were not wholly "undisturbed," they managed to accumulate fortunes nonetheless. But the great houses of Aracena's agrarian gentry were surrounded by the miserable hovels of day laborers, and few townspeople failed to perceive the intimate connections between the two phenomena. Because of the rudimentary techniques of the archaic agrarian system, virtually the sole determinant of profits over which landowners could hope to exercise some control was the price of labor. The stark and simple realities of the economic situation "poisoned" the social life of the town, as rich and poor alike readily admitted.

As table 1 indicates, the agrarian economy of Aracena throughout the first part of the twentieth century was based on a classic latifundia-minifundia distribution of land in which 7 percent of the proprietors held 75 percent of the township's surveyed lands in large estates while the bottom 62 percent of the landowners divided a mere 5 percent of the surveyed lands among themselves in small holdings of five hectares or less.[13] *Fincas* (agricultural properties) from the smallest to the largest varied little in their methods of exploitation or patterns of land usage,[14] but the commodity production of cork, pork, and (to a lesser extent) olives and chestnuts was primarily an enterprise of the large estates. These great estates required a substantial labor force only during a few months of the year.

The yearly agricultural cycle began after the livestock fair of September with the harvests of olives and chestnuts. Both crops were gathered by hired *cuadrillas* (teams) of men and women who were employed from periods of two to eight weeks. While neither the olive nor the chestnut crop was very large, the harvesting, processing, and transporting of crops required the employment of a considerable labor force, even if only for a short period; for this reason, these harvests represented a high point of the yearly labor cycle. After a long summer of idleness—and, all too often, undernourishment—the poor workers

Table 1. Ownership and Distribution of Surveyed Land in Aracena during the 1940s

	Land Ownership		Land Distribution	
Description of Land Holdings	Number of Individual Landholders	Percentage of Landowners	Number of Hectares	Percentage of Land Surveyed
Small holdings				
Under 1 hectare	73		52	
1–5 hectares	285		680	
Subtotal	358	62	732	5
Medium holdings				
5–20 hectares	129		1,152	
20–100 hectares	47		2,098	
Subtotal	176	31	3,250	20
Large holdings				
100–300 hectares	26		4,317	
300–500 hectares	9		3,398	
Over 500 hectares	5		4,036	
Subtotal	40*	7	11,751	75
Total	574	100	15,733	100

Source of data: Catastro of the *ayuntamiento* of Aracena, early 1940s.
*Records show that these 40 individuals comprised only 30 households, since the spouses of 10 of the individuals were counted separately as land-owners; i.e., there was not joint ownership, although the lands were worked jointly.

of Aracena looked forward to the harvests as the beginning of the winter season of relative bounty.

The last weeks of the olive and chestnut harvest usually overlapped with the first part of the *montanera* (the period when hogs were fattened on acorns in the countryside in preparation for slaughter). Although the *montanera* usually lasted for a period of two to three months and involved several thousand hogs, it required the labor of only a few dozen swineherds for most of this period. But as the *montanera* drew to a close in February and early March, many more hands were needed to bring the animals to town for local processing or for shipment to slaughterhouses in Seville or the neighboring *pueblo* of Jabugo.

After the winter season, there was little work available for hired hands. The harvest of cereals was in late May and June, but in any given year only a small proportion of land was planted and most of this was worked by sharecroppers. Early summer was also the season when cork trees were stripped of their bark. However, a single tree could be harvested only once every eight or nine years, and the delicate process of cutting *planchas* (bark strips and sections) required an expert *corchero* and experienced assistants who were hired seasonally. The only other agricultural work that required much temporary labor during the year involved the clearing and pruning of the oak, cork, and olive groves.[15]

The labor force of some fifteen hundred men and hundreds of women and children who at least occasionally had to accept work on the great estates was so large and the demand for work so limited that most workers were unemployed most of the year. Only a few *obreros fijos* (permanent employees) and the handful of *encargados* (foremen or estate bailiffs) who supervised them could depend on steady employment and sometimes food and shelter supplied by their employers. Most day laborers could count themselves fortunate if they were employed locally more than 150 days in a year.

Added to the problem of unemployment, the low daily wage kept the agrarian labor force in a state of perpetual poverty and debt. Local proprietors recognized that neither more intensive cultivation nor new agricultural techniques would significantly increase crop yields and that holding down the price of labor was the principal way to maintain or increase their profits. With dubious legality, the town council succeeded in setting the average daily wage rate at minimal levels. In 1915, for example, the minimal agrarian wage was about one peseta and seventy céntimos a day, and the price of a kilo of bread was about thirty-five céntimos. This meant that simply providing each member of a four-person household with a kilo of bread (or the equivalent) a day would absorb nearly all the earnings of a fully employed worker. This situation drove large numbers of women and children into the already overcrowded labor market and created an even cheaper pool of labor, since women and children were paid one-half to two-thirds of the rate paid to men.

Thus, it is clear that the huge profits reaped by the great proprietors of Aracena and the sierra were predominantly determined by the chasm separating wage rates and market prices.[16] In a fairly typical year, such as 1913, sellers could expect to receive between 160 and 190 pesetas for a hog weighing fifteen *arrobas* (one *arroba* equals approximately twenty-five pounds). This amount of money was sufficient to pay the wages of a swineherd who could care for thirty to fifty hogs for the entire season of the *montanera*. In the same year, a *cuadrilla* of eight men led by a skilled cutter could harvest up to fifteen quintals of cork a day and earn wages totaling 20 or 25 pesetas—roughly equal to the price of one quintal of cork on the local market. Of course, there were costs other than these involved in agrarian production, but they were not very great and there is no doubt that in a good year cork and pork offered immense profit margins. Furthermore, many of the town's large landowners greatly increased their incomes through involvement in aspects of the agrarian economy other than production, and the wages of shoemakers, leatherworkers, and corkmakers were only slightly higher than those of *jornaleros*. For the rural workers of Aracena, most of whom were intimately acquainted with every facet of local agriculture, it took no great genius to arrive at a concrete sense of the power of capital, extraction of surplus value, or class exploitation.

Though resentment of economic injustice was rife in Aracena, a working-class movement expressing resistance to exploitation and seeking the redress of economic grievances developed only slowly during the first two decades of the century.[17] The ordinary people of the sierra had little political experience, and this was particularly true in Aracena, which was a conservative stronghold sheltering the richest stratum of the region's population, many government and legal authorities, and a large contingent of the Guardia Civil (the force that above all others was dedicated to maintaining social order).

Sporadic and ill-planned working-class protests against local conditions occurred in Aracena in 1905 and perhaps earlier, but it seems that sustained efforts to organize the working class only began in 1909.[18] According to townspeople interviewed recently, a group of "socialists" began to meet in 1909 in a small inn near the center of town. The inn was run by a family whose eldest son became one of the leading left-wing organizers and politicians of Aracena in the pre—

Civil War period. As the story is told, the core group included the inn-keeper and a number of small shopkeepers and artisans. Over the course of several months, these men began to convince many artisans and *jornaleros* to strike for higher wages. However, in December, just when it seemed that they had enough support to take action, local landowners pressured the Guardia Civil to close the inn, and the strike disintegrated.

The events of 1909 reveal some of the key features that character-ized the nascent working-class movement in Aracena and the sierra be-fore the advent of the Second Republic in 1931. Throughout the period, the "natural leaders" or "men with ideas" who had met in the inn were politically committed, aware, and able to muster broad, if in-termittent, support. Like many popular leaders of the period, they were literate, lived near the town center, and had occupations that brought them into contact not only with many rural workers but also with other townspeople and outsiders attuned to radical political cur-rents and events happening elsewhere in Andalusia and other parts of Spain. The most important of these outside groups was that of the nearby miners of Río Tinto. Owing to the influence of some of the miners, most of the popular political leaders of Aracena aligned them-selves with the socialist rather than the anarchist movement, even though they evidently did not formalize their ties to the socialist party (El Partido Socialista Obrero Español, or PSOE) until the late 1920s and even though the rhetoric of some members of their movement fre-quently invoked anarchist themes and ideals. Moreover, it appears that, like many subsequent protests, the aborted strike of 1909 was not simply prompted by an aggravation of local economic conditions; it followed the example set by the heightened militancy of the miners just to the south, who had themselves been momentarily galvanized by reports of the struggle of the "tragic week" in Barcelona in July (see Ullman 1968). Thus, the leaders of the aborted 1909 strike had begun to meet in that year not particularly because of an aggravation of local conditions but because they were imbued with a new sense of political possibilities.

The aborted strike of 1909 was not an altogether auspicious first step, but it set a precedent for what occurred in 1912. This was a year of agrarian unrest throughout the sierra, but the event that had the greatest impact on Aracena was the successful protest of the *taponeros* (corkmakers) of the nearby town of Cortegana, which prevented the shipment of virtually all of the town's unprocessed cork crop for that year to a Seville wholesaler. Inspired by this victory, Aracena's working-class leaders formed a union of *campesinos* (peasants, agrarian workers) and *artesanos* (artisans) whose aim was to force concessions from local proprietors. In 1912, no effective strike was organized, but La Unión de Campesinos y Artesanos acquired many nominal members and held several large demonstrations. Though none of the promises made by the proprietors in the face of these demonstrations were kept for long, the union clearly alarmed them. As a countermeasure to the establishment of El Centro de Obreros (the workers' center or club) by the local artisans and day laborers, the proprietors sponsored church-related agrarian associations that included both proprietors and workers (see Chapter 5), and this temporarily succeeded in blunting the force of the popular union of *campesinos* and *artesanos*.

The brief work stoppages or demonstrations that flared again in early 1914, 1915, and 1919 were also closely linked to developments in the mining zone.[19] In 1915, agrarian laborers demanded a *reparto* (distribution) that would make it the responsibility of each landowner to provide a certain number of the unemployed with food. While some proprietors were not without sympathy for the poor and attempted to ease their plight by contributing to public relief funds, hardly any were willing to accept a full-scale *reparto*. As the situation of the rural workers worsened, what the local authorities characterized as a "black wave of anarchy" broke over the sierra and led to demonstrations for work and some minor attacks on agricultural property in Aracena. These activities did not subside until some months later, when a substantial amount of money was awarded for road-building projects.

The largest work stoppage occurring in Aracena before the Second Republic was the one that began in October 1919, during a period when revolutionary violence that pitted socialists against anarchists and both against proprietors was erupting in the mining zone and throughout Spain. This work stoppage was organized by the reawakened Unión de Campesinos y Artesanos, whose basic demand was for an increase in the *jornal* (the agrarian wage for day laborers). As always, however, the demand was fiercely resisted by local landowners, who refused even a modest increase of one-half peseta per day. Such adamant resistance as well as the harassment of strike leaders and related measures increased the tensions, and during such crises, discussion of a permanent *reparto* or expropriation and redistribution of the estates of the large landowners became a commonplace of talk though not a genuine goal of organized, collective action. In this situation of practical stalemate, the *alcalde* of Aracena was prevailed upon to request reinforcements for the local Guardia Civil, and the arrival of armed police discouraged the militancy of the protesters and eventually restored order.

The capacity of local landowners to defeat working-class actions by using the powers of the state to defend their interests was usually the decisive factor that prevented the popular forces from winning enduring or significant concessions from employers and landowners. The lack of political power kept the working class and the union movement relatively weak throughout the period. In contrast, nothing ever broke the solidarity of the agrarian elite. Their ability to maintain a united economic front was in large measure a result of their position as the key supporters and, in some respects, the clients and subordinates of Aracena's grand *cacique,* Don Francisco, the man who had succeeded Aracena's first political boss, Don Juan Duro, in the last years of the nineteenth century.[20]

Don Francisco's power and influence far surpassed that of his predecessor, and except during a brief interval in the mid-1920s (see Chapter 6), he exercised almost unchallenged control over the political life of Aracena and the eastern sierra until his death in 1931. For most of this period, he served as the deputy to the Cortes for the district of Aracena; and toward the end of his political career, he became head of the Conservative party in the province of Huelva and eventually accepted the largely honorific position of senator in the higher house of the national legislature. During Don Francisco's political prime from 1903 to 1923, he won ten straight elections to the Cortes with no or only nominal opposition. For this reason, Aracena was characterized as a "non-competitive" and "docile" district by Javier Tusell (1976, 1977) in his studies of oligarchy and *caciquismo* in Andalusia.[21]

Don Francisco's personal history illustrates the stability of some of the principal families of the elite stratum of rural society over centuries and provides a revealing example of how great political power often was constructed on the basis of microsocial connections. Don Francisco's heritage was an extraordinarily fortunate one. Through his father, he was a member of one of the great bourgeois families of Seville; and through his mother, he was a direct descendant of both the Villafranco and Granvilla families who had ruled Aracena during the Ancient Regime. Moreover, Don Francisco's father had added at least twenty properties to the united portions of the Villafranco and Granvilla patrimonies in the mid-nineteenth century. When he died in 1890, his sons, Don Francisco and Don Miguel, became the largest landowners of the town and the proprietors of over seventeen hundred hectares in Aracena (one-tenth of the township) and a minimum of a thousand hectares in neighboring townships as well as large and immensely valuable properties in the province of Seville.

The other legacy shared by the two brothers was a set of influential family and social connections. Both Don Francisco and Don Miguel found wives among the great families of Seville, and both were careful to cultivate long-standing family ties with the urban elite. These ties proved exceptionally valuable to Don Miguel, who eventually became one of the leaders of the Liberal party in Seville. For Don Francisco, who made Aracena his political base, local connections were equally important. Through his maternal aunts and his great aunts and uncles, Don Francisco was related more or less distantly to virtually every one of Aracena's leading families, and during the first two decades of the twentieth century, a group of his "cousins" formed the core of Aracena's ruling oligarchy, occupied most of the town's important municipal posts, and ran local affairs in Don Francisco's and their own best interests.

Even though Don Francisco's wealth and social position made him an ideal candidate for a political career, his success owed just as much to developments at the provincial and national levels as it did to his own qualifications. During the mid-1890s, Manuel Burgos y Mazos, a minister in several governments during the reign of Alfonso XIII and one of the most astute politicians of Spain, managed to establish himself as the master of the province of Huelva by forging alliances with local notables such as Don Francisco. As a result of the efforts of Burgos y Mazos, Huelva became a bastion of the Conservative party from the 1890s to the 1920s, and Don Francisco and the other leading Conservatives of the province were assured of seats in the Cortes even during periods of Liberal party rule.

The basic mechanism of electoral politics employed in Huelva (as in much of Spain during the period) was the *encasillado* (electoral pact), which was negotiated by national politicians and party leaders who decided what the composition of the Cortes and Senate should be and selected the deputies for most electoral districts. The *encasillado* and the techniques of political manipulation associated with it made the pretense of universal suffrage a continuing source of scandal under the constitutional monarchy of Alfonso XIII, but owing to the power of Burgos y Mazos, the system operated with remarkable smoothness in Huelva even at times when urban protests put national politics in a state of turmoil.

Because of the predictable character of provincial political arrangements, electoral campaigns in rural districts were cursory affairs and involved little more than taking the appropriate steps (for example, buying votes or making threats of economic retaliation) to bring a sufficient number of voters to the polls. Indeed, after the passage of the electoral law of 1907, which made it possible for unopposed incumbents to retain their seats without running (article twenty-nine), Don Francisco was spared even minimal bother. Moreover, the system required only a rudimentary party apparatus with few of the features of organizations that actually have to win votes. In Huelva, Don Francisco's party activities were largely limited to exchanging visits with other Conservative deputies and holding banquets for a few large landowners. The same situation prevailed in much of Andalusia. In Seville, for example, a newspaper editorial (quoted in Tusell 1976:351) described the Liberal party there as consisting of "a half a dozen gentlemen . . . and the money of Sánchez-Dalp."

Shallow party organizations did little to mask the fact that the real power structure of the state consisted of a multilayered and faction-riven patron-client hierarchy. From the perspective of Aracena, this hierarchy had four significant tiers. Burgos y Mazos occupied the highest (ministerial) level of politics and had a strong voice in determining the policies of the national Conservative party and in negotiating with his Liberal counterparts. Below the ministerial level were a few grand *caciques,* such as Don Francisco, who were secondary actors in national affairs but central players at the provincial level and virtual rulers of their home districts. The third level of the political hierarchy consisted of the *tertulia* (circle of "cousins" and friends) of Don Francisco in the sierra. All of these twenty to twenty-five men were either large land-owners or professionals and lived either in the larger towns of the region or in Aracena itself. Members of this group rotated through a series of district and local posts such as town councilman, municipal judge, district judge or prosecutor, *alcalde,* and provincial deputy. The lowest tier of the political structure consisted of the minor town officials and village *caciques* who could call on a handful of henchmen to bribe, threaten, or intimidate those who opposed them. Such town toughs and village tyrants had very little to gain by being uncooperative with the ruling circle in Aracena and indeed required the favors or at least the toleration of district and provincial officials to maintain their local positions.

Although from the top to the bottom, the power structure of Spain during the period from 1890 to 1930 depended on generally illegal, back-room arrangements and the classic carrot-and-stick strategies of developed patron-client systems, it was at the lowest level of the political hierarchy that the strongest motives of direct, personal economic gain spiced the political stew. Thus, although Don Francisco was rarely accused of personal dishonesty and corruption (perhaps because on the few occasions when accusations were publicly voiced in the press, he quickly brought suit for slander), such charges were frequently lodged against his political allies and subordinates in Aracena and the sierra. These denizens of the town halls took full advantage of their positions and usually managed to avoid taxes and "eat" most of the local funds intended to maintain public services. Local complaints about corrupt practices and formal accusations of wrongdoing (the latter brought mostly by people in other towns and the provincial capital) intermittently produced much sound and some fury but had few practical results.

Despite the prevalence of minor corruption, it was not so much by crude graft as by serving the broader interests of the agrarian elite that Don Francisco won local acquiescence and support. Throughout his political career, Don Francisco did all he could in Madrid to win public funding, licenses, permissions, and, sometimes, private financing for projects to improve the economic infrastructure and amenities of Aracena and the sierra. He had considerable success in these efforts and was instrumental in establishing a number of schools and in bringing a railroad spur, telegraph and telephone lines, and electricity to the region. While such services rarely reached the smallest *pueblos* or outlying hamlets and, even in the larger towns, the poor scarcely benefited, the upper classes were appreciative both because they used the services and because Don Francisco gave his friends the opportunity to invest in and reap the fruits of progress.

But by far the most critical way in which Don Francisco served his district was to quickly secure state funds for road building and improvement during times of massive unemployment and working-class unrest. Local *comerciantes* received the contracts for such projects awarded by the town hall and reaped more than ample profits, as did the landowners who extracted exorbitant payments for rights-of-way through their groves and fields. More important, though, such projects were the main source of public relief and served as a safety valve that relieved landowners from the unemployed workers' demands for a *reparto* and somewhat eased their paramount fear of social revolution.

Providing public funds in times of crisis was the most direct way that Don Francisco's political fortunes hinged on the "social problem." However, more generally, Aracena's elite were willing to forgo the pleasures of factional disputes among themselves in order to close every path along which the rural working classes could conceivably gain power. For this reason, the system of political patronage in which Don Francisco occupied a strategic position between local and higher authorities was not, as it is sometimes presented, essentially a political formation that mitigated the worst aspects of social inequality by enfolding rich and poor in relations of mutual interdependence. To regard it in this way is to overemphasize some of the incidental mechanisms (such as public work relief extended to the unemployed and favors given to a few clients and roughnecks) that it used for its fundamental strategic ends. Politically, the patron-client pattern excluded most people from a role in local and national affairs. Economically, it served the "haves" far better than the "have-nots." Rather than being a system that overcame the worst features of class exploitation, it was the political form that class domination took in liberal society; and as rich and poor alike realized, it was designed to preserve the social arrangements upon which agrarian capitalism depended.

Still, it would be a mistake to focus almost exclusively on the political machinations and economic interests that were involved in *caciquismo,* as most studies of the phenomenon have done, without also considering the ideological and cultural authority that a man like Don Francisco was able to exercise. His domination of local life and especially of Aracena's agrarian gentry was based not only on his political and economic power but also on his crucial role as a cultural mediator between urban and national elites and their provincial supporters in Aracena. In fulfilling this role, Don Francisco followed a traditionalizing strategy that subsumed and incorporated archaic cultural forms as subordinate elements within a progressive ideology in order to lend an aura of legitimacy to a class-divided social order in a state of acute crisis. Thus, under the rule of Don Francisco, the so-called docility of Aracena and particularly of its landowning elite extended considerably beyond the narrow realm of electoral politics.

THE GREAT *CACIQUE* AS GRAND PATRON: PRIVATE CHARITY AND CULTURAL ENTERPRISE

Although Don Francisco and his family were absent from Aracena for most of the year and generally spent only the summers and some holidays there, they directed most aspects of Aracena's social and cultural life for decades by molding the aspirations of local "society." Their two "palaces" (decorated with marble and frescoes) dominated the center of town, and their great country house two kilometers away (with fountains, gardens, and bullring bordering well-kept groves of oaks) presented an image of the ideal way of life of a country gentleman. Most important, Don Francisco acted the part of a great patron of culture and throughout his life was careful to head the list of contributors to every civic, religious, and charitable project. His contributions to such projects were by no means ungenerous. His many gifts to the town included several fountains and a large, costly, two-story brick building that eventually became the town hall, although he and his brother intended it to be used as a school. In addition, Don Francisco and his wife donated works of art to the local churches and were instrumental in bringing teaching and nursing orders of nuns to Aracena. But perhaps their most important act of beneficence was to transform the caves beneath the *monte* of "El Castillo" into a tourist attraction that was intended to provide the town with a continuing source of income to finance public projects. Thanks to the exertions and funds of Don Francisco and others of his circle, paths through the caverns were cleared and illuminated with eight thousand light bulbs.

Such enlightened acts of patronage did not go unnoticed at the highest levels of power, so on 7 August 1915, the king and queen of Spain, Alfonso XIII and Victoria, honored Don Francisco with a royal visit. It was a glorious day for Aracena, despite the rain, and most of the town and many of the notable figures of the sierra turned out to greet the monarchs, who arrived by car from Seville at about one o'clock in the afternoon. After a brief welcoming speech by the *alcalde,* the king demonstrated his rather archaic sense of grace by favoring a poor man of the *pueblo* with a royal gift of five pesetas, and the royal party was then whisked off to lunch at Don Francisco's great country house, where the host's private guards had great difficulty in preventing the crowd from laying siege to the estate in pursuit of their monarch.

During the elegant luncheon, the king and Don Francisco discussed the "social problem" of the sierra and the need for commercial and industrial development to improve the general life of the town. In particular, the king agreed with his host that the region's roads urgently required upgrading so that the beautiful panoramas of the sierra and the artistic wealth of its towns could be more easily admired by tourists. After dining, the king granted a short audience to the *alcalde,* the archpriest, the judges, and other officials of Aracena, and then the royal party, accompanied by Don Francisco and his wife, set off to visit the marvelous caverns, Las Grutas de las Maravillas. The king was much impressed by the geological wonders of what he agreed was a "colossal temple of nature" (*El Distrito,* 20 Aug. 1915). At the conclusion of his visit to the caverns, the king consulted with his party about the inclement weather and expressed regrets that he would have to give up his plans to visit La Peña de Arias Montano and the chapel of La Reina de los Angeles, which overlook the neighboring *pueblo* of Alájar.

Despite the king's hasty visit and early return to Seville, Aracena's leading citizens quickly proclaimed the royal excursion a great success. Word spread that the king had found the caverns eminently worthy of being visited by tourists and had declared them to be the most fantastic he had ever seen in Europe. As a matter of fact, the visit of the king and queen sent local writers and supporters of Don Francisco reeling into rhetorical ecstasy. Aracena "had a new affirmation of its illustrious nobility." Don Francisco had shown "exquisite courtesy," and the people of Aracena owed him "profound thanks" for his patronage of his native town. Those among the townspeople who "every day, as a holy rite, exercise the obligation of adding another stone to the pedestal of the glory of Aracena and who every hour intone a song full of optimism for their beloved town" found themselves blessed with new hopes and inspiration (*El Distrito,* 15 Mar. 1915). In sum, Don Francisco was deserving of "every honor and glory" and, of course, of continuing political support. Apparently, the king shared these sentiments with the agrarian elite of the sierra, for not long after his visit, Alfonso XIII ennobled Don Francisco by giving him the title of *marqués* of Aracena.

The people of Aracena responded by renaming two of their three main squares La Plaza del Marqués and La Plaza de la Marquesa de Aracena, thereby placing Don Francisco and his wife among the most illustrious patrons and *hijos del pueblo* (sons and daughters of the town) in local history. The descendant of *hidalgo* oligarchs and his wife thus became bourgeois aristocrats. But what ends did this resurrection of archaic cultural forms serve? The significance of this strategy of cultural displacement and resignification can best be shown by describing the cultural dynamics and political effects of another of the projects of the *marqués* of Aracena, a project intended to promote the fame and advance the fortunes of his native town.

The ability of the *marqués* to guide and direct the public life and culture of the town and even the surrounding *pueblos* was most evident in a celebration of regional pride and local color organized by him in 1924 and called "El Día de la Sierra" (Sierra Day). This event was scheduled to coincide with the traditional *romería* (pilgrimage) to the chapel of La Reina de los Angeles in September to honor the day of the Virgin's birth, a religious observance that had been undertaken for centuries by the people of the village of Alájar. In 1924, however, the *marqués* and a circle of his friends had conceived the idea of greatly expanding the rite by organizing processions from all the towns of the sierra. The intention was both to express devotion to the Virgin and to use the opportunity to promote regional patriotism and a sense of the common social aspirations of the sierra's inhabitants.

Planning began months in advance, and a commission with the *marqués* at the head was formed. On the appointed day, seven thousand people arrived at La Peña from all the *pueblos* of the sierra and proceeded to amuse themselves—eating, dancing, singing, and strolling past dozens of booths set up by craftsmen, food vendors, and others. Speeches were made by the heads of the lay brotherhoods, who praised the miraculous healing powers of the waters of the springs of La Peña. Local politicians identified themselves with the "progressive" legacy of Arias Montano, the sixteenth-century scholar and statesman who had sought refuge at La Peña from the cares of the world, and they spoke of expanding railroads, commerce, and industry.[22] A concourse of men on horseback was held, and there were displays of the traditional folk arts and dress of the sierra. As Moreno Alonso (1979:247–50) describes it, the celebration was brilliant and unforgettable, although something of the religious character that had typified the holiday in earlier years was lost. The high point of the day was the arrival of the *infantes* of Spain, dressed in regional costume for the occasion and accompanied by the *marqués* and *marquesa* of Aracena, who basked in reflected glory as the royal progeny received medals from the majordomos of the lay brotherhoods. "El Día de la Sierra" inspired local poets and initiated a tradition in the region that has continued to the present. For his part, the *marqués,* whose prestige was enhanced by the success of the celebration, was more than willing to make up the difference between the cost of the event and the donations of the various civic and devotional associations involved.

Like many of the acts of patronage of the *marqués,* "El Día de la Sierra" enfolded distinctively modern forms of civic boosterism in the hallowed mantle of traditional images and customs. La Peña was an ideal site for this sort of effort because it was a regional shrine (not too closely associated with any one town) whose layout and symbolic structure, like that of the *monte* of "El Castillo" in Aracena, reflected the ancient cultural genre of pastoral epic. From the heights of La Peña, a number of the more isolated *pueblos* situated in the most rugged country of the sierra could be viewed, but the space of the shrine itself was a thoroughly domesticated and intimate one protected by the holy and heroic patrons, La Reina de los Angeles and Arias Montano.[23]

While the character of the site and some of the ritual aspects of the celebration reanimated traditional images of religion, honor, and patronage, other dimensions of the event tended to cast traditional culture in a nostalgic light. For example, the display of regional costumes and the self-conscious cultivation of the folkloric by performers and commentators served as a reminder that many local customs and crafts were being supplanted by modern products and fashions in music, literature, and dress. Moreover, the explicit rationale and keynote speeches of the celebration were progressive in tone and designed to promote rural development. This convergence of different themes, which on the one hand invoked aspects of the communitarian and corporate ethos of the Ancient Regime and on the other hand stressed the ancillary relation of traditional cultural meanings and values to progressive forces of historical transformation, suggested that the revival of ancient values was dependent on continued material progress. Similarly, "El Día de la Sierra" enhanced the prestige of the *marqués* and his associates because their sponsorship and support of the event enabled them to represent themselves both as enterprising private individuals whose voluntary initiatives demonstrated a practical concern for the economic prosperity of the region and as honorable and devout patrons conscious of the religious and moral burdens that their heritage placed upon them.

More, however, was involved in the event than the pursuit of fame or an exercise in public relations. The celebrations represented an attempt to define the region in a way that countered and obscured antagonisms between the classes by accentuating the importance of membership within the distinct *pueblos* of the sierra. To some degree, this cultural strategy of divide and rule appears to have been momentarily successful because the efforts of each town to organize the most impressive procession and construct the most elaborate *pasos* (floats carrying the image of the Virgin) created an atmosphere that reactivated traditional forms of rivalry between communities. In fact, the competition led to several nasty brawls among working-class men from Aracena, Higuera de la Sierra, and other *pueblos*. However, the significance of the various effects of cultural domination generated by "El Día de la Sierra" emerges clearly only when the timing of the celebration is considered.

By 1924, working-class social and political movements were in a state of disarray and exhaustion after nearly four years of violent postwar social turmoil that had pitted socialists against anarchists in a contest for leadership of the revolutionary masses. Momentary disillusionment with the prospects for radical change no doubt made many rural workers of the sierra more than ordinarily susceptible to traditional images of social order because the conflicts and strikes in the nearby mining zone had been particularly bitter. In addition, the national government's failure to quell the postwar disturbances and its defeat in Morocco had led to the final dissolution of the liberal constitutional regime that had prevailed since 1876. Blaming the nation's sorry state on the "vices of political organization," Spain's new leader and "gentle dictator," Primo de Rivera, called for political reform, a return to respect for authority, and a revival of traditional patriotic virtues under the banner of "Nation, Church, and King." The political power of the *marqués* and the other oligarchs and *caciques* of the liberal order who had suddenly found themselves stripped of their offices seemed to be in great jeopardy because of Primo's determination to root out corruption (a determination that turned out to be more rhetorical than real, as discussed in Chapter 6).

Under these circumstances, the public reaffirmation of a posture of progressive traditionalism, as manifested by the events of "El Día de la Sierra," represented in great measure an effort on the part of the *marqués* both to deflect class antagonisms and to reinforce by cultural means his own threatened political position in the region. The embrace of local patriotism, religious custom, and loyalty to the monarchy was also part of a strategy designed to emphasize the nonpolitical, personal, and informal dimensions of his leadership of the local elite and to declare his adherence to the more authoritarian regime that had momentarily substituted for the discredited liberal political order. Thus, the cultivation of traditional discourses and practices by the *marqués* and his friends and allies of the Conservative party was a response to a shift in the direction of hegemonic processes, a shift that seemed to mandate a more intense revival of archaic forms of cultural and political authority in order to preserve the basic socioeconomic arrangements of agrarian class society in a period of acute crisis.

This and similar efforts, however, had limited success. While the gentry and middle classes of the sierra were largely persuaded by the *marqués* and his allies, neither private charity nor public patronage ultimately did much to assuage the working classes or dampen the resentment and resistance that sprang from their miserable conditions of life. No doubt working-class people of Aracena were momentarily impressed by the royal visits and the ritual pageantry that garlanded notions of commercial modernization with the images of pastoral epic and linked gestures of noblesse oblige with the promise of social progress. But such strategies of incorporation had little enduring impact, and there is scant evidence that local workers were long delighted by such diversions or finally seduced by Don Francisco and the local gentry into happy acceptance of their subordinate position. Even today, under drastically altered economic conditions, the most common epithet attached by working-class people to the names of the great landowners of the heyday of agrarian capitalism in Aracena is not *patrón;* it is *ladrón* (thief). And even today, in the streets of Aracena (and Seville), one can hear people rebuke someone who has said or done something especially hypocritical, manipulative, or tyrannical with the words *"Tu eres tan mal como [Don Francisco]"* (You are as bad as Don Francisco). The expression condemns a whole order of class exploitation, prejudice, and ideology as much as it does the personal actions of the grand *caciques* who preserved it.

5

Class Cultures and Ideologies

It is not the Old Spain overwhelmed by the sun and muttering
about traditions in glorious tatters; . . . the must of new ideas
has risen to their heads and there is [talk of] everything from
railroads to spiritualism.
—José Nogales
El último patriota

Displaced Traditions and the Ideologies of Progress

THE CENTRAL and unavoidable "social fact" in Aracena during
the early part of the twentieth century was the chasm separating the rich and powerful from the poor and subjected.
However, different classes and individuals in accordance with their
experiences and social positions attached different meanings to this
"fact." In a general way, everyone in Aracena was a progressive, and
few townspeople denied the need for strenuous efforts to overcome the
miserable conditions of the rural poor. The conservative majority
among the local elite maintained that the best chance for ameliorating
the "social problem" lay in gradual socioeconomic development and
believed that the forces of property and free markets overseen and regulated by the vested authorities of the state could be trusted to eventually increase the wealth and well-being of all. The small group of
local left-wing republicans felt that the development of real rather than
sham democratic processes and representative government would offer
the best hopes for the emergence of an educated, modern society that
would guarantee reform and social justice. Increasingly, the majority
of artisans and agrarian laborers viewed a general redistribution of
land and other property to the poor or to collectives and cooperatives
as the ultimate goal of working-class parties and unions, but opinions
varied as to whether this goal could be best achieved by participation
in electoral politics or by a direct revolutionary seizure of power. Thus,

a full spectrum of the progressive ideologies that developed after the triumph of nineteenth-century Spanish liberalism existed in Aracena, and one or the other of these ideologies structured the dominant sociopolitical perspectives of each of the town's key social groups.

Although the traditional discourses of religion, honor, and patronage were no longer at the core of the explicit political ideologies of class society, they nonetheless strongly influenced many aspects of sociopolitical relations among townspeople. Yet because the conditions of life of each class differed so dramatically, the practical significance of traditional meanings and values also differed for each group and became intertwined with the more "modern" aspects of class identity. The outcome of this process of cultural displacement and rearticulation was the emergence of readily distinguishable and opposed class "subcultures." What these subcultures shared was a highly moralistic vision of interclass relations, but what distinguished them were radically different visions of how the contradictions between traditional notions of social interdependence and authority and modern ideals of freedom and equality could be resolved. This chapter is devoted to showing how the selection, elaboration, and interpretation of traditional and modern cultural discourses by the contending individuals and groups of Aracena's gentry, middle, and working classes played a critical role in the processes of sociopolitical and ideological polarization that eventually led to the violent confrontations of the Civil War period.

The Gentry: Cultivation, Paternalism, and Social Hygiene

The members of Aracena's agrarian gentry were distinguished from other townspeople by their large incomes and, above all, by their freedom from the burden of manual labor and the need to be fully engaged and preoccupied with earning a living.[1] The social distinction of great proprietors and their families was in many respects a result of the amount of time that they could dedicate to "higher pursuits," such as politics, expensive recreations, education, religion, and the arts, or simply to the conspicuous display of having little to do and doing it with style.

In its ideal form, the life-style of the gentry was oriented to the imitation of nobility and aristocracy or, rather, to bourgeois images of what a noble style should be.[2] Although few among the gentry had the background, wealth, or connections of the *marqués* and *marquesa* of Aracena, most attempted to imitate their manner. For men, the ideal posture was that of a *caballero andaluz* (Andalusian gentleman or horseman), a man whose life was devoted to pursuing the masculine virtues and maintaining his reputation as an honorable, decorous, and, above all, autonomous individual, strong-willed and worthy of respect. *Caballerosidad* implied a combination of complex dispositions and values—an "open soul . . . a beautiful and *arrogante* [haughty] attitude . . . a paternal authority," as the writer of an obituary of a local *Don* described it (*El Distrito*, 25 Oct. 1913). For married women, the ideal posture was one of noble cultivation, feminine moral probity and piety, and matronly pride and reserve. Younger unmarried women tried to create a romanticized vision of the delicate sentiments of well-chaperoned, carefully presented, and rather immobile beauty. For both sexes, cultivation meant the formation of a self-contained person accustomed to all the codes and courtesies of civilized life—a person of *gracia* (grace, charm, wit) and *formalidad* (formality, a sense of proper conduct) at ease in every social context.

The style of life embraced by Aracena's gentry was designed to take advantage of the best elements of rural and urban culture.[3] The stimulus of urban example and the need to fill the many hours of idleness prompted many of the town's elite to cultivate the arts and belles lettres. Indeed, trying one's hand at painting, poetry, and essays in order to express the sensitivity of one's soul or the acuity of one's intellect seems to have been almost a fad among the younger generation of the upper classes. The *marqués* himself was capable of constructing ornate speeches, which he delivered before the Ateneo (literary club) of Seville, and one of his tougher local political allies was a poet much given to the expression of tender sentiments.[4]

Other aspects of gentry culture emphasized the rustic virtues and benefits of life in a small provincial town. Few great landowners were immune to pastoral sentiments, and despite the manifest evidence of poverty and unrest, they celebrated the "tranquillity," "peace," and "harmony" of existence in the sierra. Romantic visions of the simplicities of rural life were embellished by hymns of praise to local wine, ham, and other fruits of the land. To be the master of a well-kept prosperous estate, the husband of a respectful and reserved wife, and the father of obedient sons and loving daughters was the unchallenged aspiration of the majority of men of the local elite. Above all, the pastoral version of the ideal of good breeding and careful cultivation at the core of upper-class culture was represented by the *ganaderías* (ranches dedicated to raising fighting bulls for the ring) that were maintained by three or four of the town's wealthiest proprietors. No notion was more aesthetically satisfying to the true *caballero andaluz* than that of populating his lands with magnificent and dangerous black bulls watched over by skilled horsemen and destined to die in an epic spectacle that could bring honor and money to their master. In El Casino de Arias Montano and the elite bars—exclusive sanctuaries of the agrarian gentry where local proprietors spent many hours in the afternoons and evenings playing cards, gambling, and sipping drinks—talk of bulls was rivaled only by conversations about politics and local agriculture.[5]

Both the pastoral and urbane foci of gentry culture were most visibly manifested during Aracena's greatest secular celebration of the year, the week-long *feria* (fair) of September. The principal practical focus of the *feria* was the livestock auction and exhibition, which attracted landowners from all over the sierra. But the *feria* was also a great fiesta with amusements of all kinds, and every year it was the occasion for outpourings of local pride and affirmations of love for the *pueblo*. According to a local essayist (*El Distrito*, 25 Sept. 1915), it was a time when "the city is adorned and pristinely clean; there are lights, tents of games, of silver work, and of leather work. Music reigns over the balustrades of pretty passages, and the joy of the fiesta is spread in many notes."

Some of the *feria*'s amusements, such as dancing to folk music, gambling, drinking, and enjoying the *tapas* (snacks) and sweets sold by vendors, were popular in character, and anyone with a few coins could share in them. But at least as early as the turn of the century and perhaps under the influence of the great spring *feria* of Seville, many aspects of Aracena's *feria* began to have an exclusive and elite character; and the poor, excluded from numerous activities because they either lacked money or were the subjects of overt social discrimination, were increasingly cast into the role of resentful onlookers of the recreations of the rich.

The larger social significance of this segregation of the gentry from other townspeople was lost on no one. All knew that one of the principal attractions of the *feria* was its role as a marriage market for the elite society of the town and sierra and that most of the business of courtship and romance was conducted within the inviolable precincts of the *caseta* (canvas pavilion) that served as the central gathering point of the gentry during the *feria*. Only "the most select of good society" (*El Distrito*, 15 Sept. 1914) could gain entrance to the *caseta*, which served as a showplace for the display of fine clothes, food, and manners. Ordinary townspeople could only watch as the private orchestra played. During the seven nights of the *feria*, the "daughters of the sierra," protected from all rudeness and vulgarity by their chaperones and parents, danced with "enamored, delicate souls" in quest of their true loves among the *señoritos* (young gentlemen; also a term for the idle and arrogant rich). Like the stockyards at the edge of town, the *caseta* at the center of the *feria* was a place where good breeding and "cultivation" were clearly of paramount importance in reproducing local socioeconomic arrangements.[6]

The *buñuelada*, another of the customary events of the *feria*, reiterated this message in an especially colorful way. The event was a promenade sponsored by a local association in order to help young people pursue their quest for a suitable husband or wife, and what was especially noteworthy about it was the peculiar site where it was celebrated: the local bullring. Photographs from the early 1900s show young men and women dressed in the highest fashions of the day, seated uncomfortably on a few benches, nibbling pastries or scuffling awkwardly through the sand as a group of musicians plays in the background. Evidently, the *buñuelada* was as much an ordeal as a pleasure, but the temporary transformation of the bullring from one type of "field of honor" into another doubtless gave the trials of courtship a certain epic quality as well as making it easier for the official gatekeepers to perform their task of denying undesirable suitors entrance to the affair. Diversions such as the *buñuelada* made the *feria* the high point of the social season among the "good society" of Aracena and revealed to everyone the raison d'être of many aspects of gentry culture.

The political opinions and rhetoric of Aracena's upper class were largely an extension, justification, and elaboration of gentry culture and had the same emphasis on the superiority of the cultivated elite that characterized their general social attitudes and life-style. So much is evident in *El Distrito*, a biweekly review that was published from 1912 to 1916 with the financial assistance of the *marqués* and served as "the organ of the league for the foment of the material and moral interests of Aracena and its district."[7] The community of opinion represented by the review was united by a common attitude toward the causes and solutions of the "social problem" of the rebellious, embittered, and impoverished rural masses. *El Distrito*'s position on the social issue was pragmatic and paternalistic, and its articles were characterized by a distinctive reformist rhetoric that was moralistic in tone but nonetheless conveyed a sense of adamantine resistance to radical change. The following passage (*El Distrito*, 11 May 1914) typifies the review's bedrock sociopolitical stance: "The patron needs strong workers for his exploitations, and thus he should protect and favor them. The worker requires his daily subsistence from the patron and should serve, respect, and honor him."

The central tenet of *El Distrito*'s social ideology was "mutualism," a concept inspired by Catholic social thought as expounded in the 1890s by Pope Leo XIII in his encyclical on social justice and as explicated in Spain by the leading thinkers of Acción Católica. Mutualism was based on the premise that to fulfill the injunction to love one's neighbor under the conditions of liberal society, all social classes had to give up the pursuit of separate class interests and respect the "obligations of each class to the others." The practical vehicles of mutualism in Aracena were to be the "agricultural syndicates" of proprietors and laborers, organizations whose governing bodies were to mediate labor disputes and promote the local economy.[8] It was hoped that workers linked to these organizations would be instilled with a belief in "the sacred principle of authority," "the sacred rights of property," and the value of voluntary "free associations" and "social harmony." The goal was "evolutionary progress" guided by "Science and Faith" (*El Distrito*, 6 Jan. 1912).[9]

Mutualism was initially greeted with overwhelming enthusiasm as a solution to the "social problem"—at least by the local gentry (*El Distrito*, 15 Feb. 1913): "At last the *pueblo* has been awakened by the call of Acción Católica. Fortifying themselves with religion and Christian law, generous men show the *pueblo* that what all our little brothers ask for in chorus like little birds in the nest can be immediately advanced." The "little birds," however, were singing their own song, and neither in Aracena nor for that matter in the rest of Andalusia did mutualism win many working-class converts. The failure of mutualism to strike a responsive chord among the working class or to develop practical means of ameliorating social conditions meant that it soon degenerated into a set of ideological postures whose purpose was to provide a rationale for the authority and power of the agrarian gentry.

From the perspective of *El Distrito*, the social crisis was a result of the ignorance, lack of understanding, and vulgarity of the rural poor, and any change in the status quo was dependent upon moral and cultural education. To cast the poor and disempowered into the role of the creators of their own misery involved no easy task of obfuscation. In order to accomplish this, *El Distrito*'s essayists tried to establish the superiority of the upper classes by adapting and recasting the cultural discourses of religion, honor, and patronage, and the arguments they developed made use of a modern "naturalized" version of the traditional discourses of spirit and flesh, a version congruent with liberal notions of historical progress and evolution.

Invoking an ancient image, the writers of *El Distrito* portrayed class society as a corporate body with interdependent organs, limbs, and functions. They felt, however, that the social body in its modern state was clearly diseased and that "social medicine," "social hygiene," and "social doctors" were needed "to protect and repair and make antiseptic the ambience which is irritated in order to attack the ravages of the neurosis, threat, [and] danger" (*El Distrito*, 25 Oct. 1913). The disease that the men of *El Distrito* (15 Dec. 1912) were intent on diagnosing and curing was highly infectious and spread rapidly under conditions of unrest when the weakened extremities of the social body—namely, the radicals and members of the working class—were most vulnerable: "Who is the anarchist? The anarchist is the contagious subject, the poor, sick person who has caught the virus from the environment, the lacerated member of society; he is perturbed by collective disequilibrium; he is the moral patient who has a right to his cure."

But anarchists were not the true cause of the social disease. They were merely the agents and symptoms of disturbance. The underlying cause was more serious and not represented as essentially economic or political. It was a "pathology of the spirit," a "virus of passions," that incapacitated the social organism. It was nothing other than that ancient affliction born in the Garden of Eden—*egoísmo* (worldly pride and selfishness) in its modern forms of *individualismo* and *egolatría*— the disease of those who "want to ignore their obligations; those who by mental laziness accept as facts dangerous revolutionary utopian ideas; those who are the enemy of all because [they are] the enemy of themselves; those who show their unhappiness with work and with those that apportion it and with those who pay for it" (*El Distrito,* 25 Oct. 1912).

Moreover, *egoísmo* was not just an occasional failing of the working classes; it was an integral characteristic of every aspect of their personal and social being. The *clases pobres* (poorer classes) had been fundamentally corrupted and seduced by vanity, blasphemy, and the "love of vices." The tavern of working-class people was "the institution that contributes most to the increase of criminality and the anguish of poor families." After the tavern came the brothel, where "public women, . . . poor slaves who deal in their flesh, convert themselves into mere things." Finally, many of the poor suffered from *cursilismo* (the love of vain dress), which led families "to sacrifice indispensable foods [to buy] a silk skirt and blouse" (*El Distrito,* 25 Oct. 1913).

If poverty and political radicalism were caused by the disease of *egoísmo* and the weakness of the flesh, then the cure for the "social problem" had to be spiritual. The depravities of *egoísmo* arose from cultural, religious, and moral deprivation. Ignorance and illiteracy "condemned" the *clases pobres* "to perpetual obscurity, blindness of soul, and enslavement to the flesh and malice." The lives of the humble could only be bettered by "the saturation of their homes with the true doctrine . . . a rigorous order . . . a healthy morality which constitutes the basis of honorable happiness." The "antidote of the book and the example" was required, and members of the dominant class were confident that only they could provide it (*El Distrito,* 15 Dec. 1912).

The claims of the agrarian gentry to paternal authority over the poorer classes were ultimately based on the equation of their greater degree of "literacy and cultivation" with the "rational will of society." Class hegemony and political domination were simultaneously "sacralized" and naturalized through a rhetorical confluence of progressive scientific and traditional religious discourses channeled to communicate the notion that the possession of "knowledge and wisdom" created an unquestionable right to social power (*El Distrito*, 15 Dec. 1912): "The governors, true fathers of the *pueblos*, true doctors encharged with attending the great hospital of society, should know the pathology of the collective soul. . . . To govern is to direct society between science and faith without losing these two poles of life. . . . To govern is to imitate God, . . . who coordinates the inscrutable secrets of the worlds and the atoms."

In tandem with the high-blown rhetoric of "atoms" and the frantic talk of "social disease," which supported upper-class domination, mutualist ideology had another, more subtle dimension. To justify gentry paternalism and authority, it made use of certain aspects of traditional notions of gender, family, and honor to offer a "feminized," depoliticized view of the working class and show that ordinary townspeople were a properly subordinate and "domesticated" group. The tactic involved denigrating the honor and moral capacities of working-class men and praising the virtues of their wives. These women were represented as the natural guardians of domestic piety and honor and, indeed, of all virtues that could be construed as consistent with the notion that the poor sectors of the community consisted of isolated families with discrete and particular rather than common interests.[10] Thus, local commentators always ignored the fact that many women were wage earners—full members of a working class—and instead idealized them as virtual priestesses of family religion. One essayist (*El Distrito*, 5 Oct. 1914) described his emotions on seeing a poor but well-kept house in the countryside as follows: "Before that house . . . I felt as if I were near the altar of the Lord. . . . [Because the mistress of the house] guarded her honor which is the hearth, her home [was] a sanctuary of honor suffused with the health of body and soul."

In striking contrast, male peasants and laborers were described in overwhelmingly negative terms and were usually represented as moral and political idiots. Lacking the "light of understanding" and "brakes on the will," most working-class men were "drawn to vices filling them full of envy and hate which cause the evils that we lament in social life" (*El Distrito*, 5 Dec. 1913). It was therefore the egoistic men, rather than the women with a sense of shame, who were principally responsible for the congenital social disease of the poor. Given the inherent weaknesses of working-class men, the most positive image of them was one of disciplined and suitably humble "heroes of work" who "conquer frenzies and depressions in themselves, are able to persist in their honorable place, and enjoy translating their strength into coins that can be carried to the hands of their wives, the guardians of the home and the domestic economy" (*El Distrito,* 15 Jan. 1912).

The casting of virtually all working-class men into the role of simple, dull laborers imprisoned them within the domestic, nonpolitical sphere and left them in a state of permanent social and moral passivity. To fill this void, the upper classes identified themselves with the general "masculine" will of society and claimed the role of patrons and protectors of feminine honor and domestic virtue. Thus, authorities were enjoined to inflict the most "severe punishments on those who forget the respect and consideration that the most elementary laws of *caballerosidad* impose on men in their treatment of women" (*El Distrito,* 25 Feb. 1913).

These chivalrous flourishes embellished the claim that the rural gentry, as the de facto or de jure representatives of the higher institutions of the state and the church, had the right to intervene in domestic life and to educate the working classes because the gentry were the only positive, active sources of authority and moral order for rural communities. According to this view, which represents a modern variant of the old cultural genre of pastoral epic, the morally weak (working-class men) and the vulnerable (working-class women) stood in dire need of paternalist patronage and the attentions of authorities. The formless, chaotic mass of families whose circumstances were precarious and whose only strength lay in the "feminine" virtues of reticence, shame, humility, and respect for paternal authority needed to be molded by those who "have honor and legality" on their side. This stance was the basis of an authoritarian conception of class relations in which popular education was viewed almost exclusively as a means of social control ("Morality! Morality! Morality! [is] the object of education!") and in which freedom was viewed as largely the prerogative of the cultivated elite (*El Distrito,* 5 Oct. 1914).

The appeal of mutualist ideology for the rural gentry derived from the way in which it supported ingrained class prejudices by weaving together traditional and modern discourses into a more or less coherent justification for the dominant politicoeconomic order of agrarian society. On the one hand, the traditional discourses of religion, honor, and patronage were invoked to establish the greater cultivation, moral authority, and piety of the gentry—in short, their greater spirituality—in ways that conformed with a "noble" ethos emphasizing formality, grace, good breeding, and "the dignity of a haughty manner."

On the other hand, the modern rhetoric of progress and reform sounded optimistic and urbane, while talk of social health, disease, and treatment lent an air of rational, scientific respectability to the exercise of power. Catholic social thought knit together the traditional and modern aspects of the culture of the gentry elite by conflating the naturalistic idea that society was a complex, differentiated, and evolving organism with the archaic representation of society as an authoritarian spiritual and corporal hierarchy. This permitted the rural elite to predict a brighter future for their "little brothers" and, in the meantime, to legitimate their own rule by maintaining that it was a "principle of universal evolution" that in the early stages of development the "intellectual and spiritual functions" were not equally disseminated throughout the social body (*El Distrito,* 15 Dec. 1912).

This displacement and partial resignification of the traditional discourses of the spirit and the flesh reflected the transformation of the hegemonic strategies of the Ancient Regime in accordance with the secularizing and historicizing influences of liberalism. In place of imitating the exemplary acts of patrons, princes, and saints, there was a stress on general education, personal cultivation, and social discipline; in place of the sanctification and legitimation of apparently immutable hierarchical institutions and social estates, there were the ideals of voluntaristic paternalism and the free, dynamic association of classes; and in place of a concern for the ineluctable antagonism between the spiritual aspirations and corrupted nature of humankind, there was an analysis of the health, diseases, and treatment of the social body. The ideologies of other groups in agrarian society were characterized by different but closely related transfigurations of archaic cultural forms.

THE MIDDLE CLASSES: SUBORDINATION, RELIGION, AND THE APOTHEOSIS OF IMPOTENCE

From 10 to 15 percent of Aracena's population were neither rich agrarian gentry nor poor artisans and laborers. The core groups of the fragmented middle sector of local society were the families of the town's *comerciantes* (merchants and shopkeepers) and medium-scale *labradores* (landowners who had plots ranging from twenty to one hundred hectares). Although the lower and upper boundaries of the middle sector were vaguely defined and although the *comerciantes* and *labradores* did not share a distinctive life-style or earn their living in the same way, what the people of these groups had in common was a semblance of economic autonomy and a reliance on family labor to run their businesses and farms. Ultimately, however, both the *comerciantes* and the *labradores* were dependent on and subordinate to the agrarian elite, who controlled the town government and the "industrial" commerce in raw and processed agricultural products and could therefore exert decisive pressure on the middle classes by denying them jobs, licenses, trade, or access to mills, slaughterhouses, and cork-processing facilities. Nevertheless, the middle ranks of society cherished the ideal of independence and were, at least in terms of their day-to-day lives, somewhat insulated from the worst aspects of the capital-wage relationship in the township.

It appears that the *labradores* did not think of themselves as members of a cohesive social group. As property owners, most of them identified with the interests and aspirations of the gentry, while a few regarded themselves as *campesinos* and expressed solidarity with the artisans and landless laborers. The *comerciantes* had a sharper sense of their distinctive position within local society. This was especially so with the most prosperous stratum of business people who owned the larger hardware, department, and dry-goods stores and who were involved in other enterprises such as bakeries and apothecaries. Although the surnames on the signs above these businesses numbered more than a dozen, most of the commerce of the town was, in fact, managed by three or four large, extended families. The heir to a hardware store might well be the son-in-law of the baker, the brother of a building contractor, and the nephew of the dry-goods man. This nexus of kin ties contributed to the *comerciantes'* sense of separate identity and gave them a strong local orientation. While *labradores* were generally regarded as unsociable, "closed," and absorbed by their own narrow, private pursuits, the *comerciantes* felt themselves to be the responsible "solid citizens" of the town and were actively engaged in civic projects in which they generally played supporting roles to the local elite.

Partly because the economic status of many *comerciantes* and *labradores* was insecure, the values of both groups were distinguished by a strong work ethic. Hard work and careful husbandry of resources were essential to prevent a loss of household independence and slippage into the ranks of the poor, while frugality was perceived as the key to social mobility. Whether members of the middle classes labored in the fields or in town, their success usually depended on the cooperation and coordination of the family as a working unit. To avoid paying hired labor and to increase household incomes, the heads of families looked to their wives and children for help with almost every sort of task; and especially among the *comerciantes,* the normal practice was to bring brothers, nephews, and other relatives into the business as partners or employees when additional hands were needed.

Long hours and years of cooperative family labor, again especially among the *comerciantes,* had far-reaching effects on social attitudes. For example, relations between the sexes were somewhat more egalitarian in commercial families because shops and homes were ordinarily adjacent to one another and husbands and wives commonly worked together or at least in close proximity to one another. In addition, independent shopkeepers and farmers who were imbued with the spirit of hard work and accustomed to struggling to make a living had little desire to fritter away money on "diversions." Instead, they sought to use their resources to raise the status of their families. The favored strategy to achieve this end was to provide at least one son with a good education in hopes that he might become a civil service functionary, priest, or teacher. Thus, although *labradores* and *comerciantes* were not generally well educated themselves, many of them stressed the value of disciplined study, formal education, and the pursuit of "careers."

While the cultural and political conservatism of most members of Aracena's middle-class groups was expressed through attitudes toward family, work, and education, the most deeply felt basis of this conservatism among the *comerciantes* was their intense loyalty to the church as an institution and to orthodox Catholicism as a religion. The agrarian gentry were staunch supporters of the faith for ideological as well as spiritual reasons, but their adherence to orthodox Catholicism was just one of the many sources of their sense of class identity. In contrast, religion occupied a central place in the lives of Aracena's leading *comerciantes,* and their adherence to the church's social, political, and religious teachings was close to absolute. Unlike most Andalusian men, many *comerciantes* attended mass almost daily, and virtually every family had a son or daughter or at least a nephew or cousin who had discovered a religious vocation. As the town's most ardent Catholics, the *comerciantes* staunchly defended the church's role in education, often donated considerable sums to the town's teaching and nursing orders of nuns, and always constituted most of the membership and much of the leadership of Aracena's lay devotional and charitable brotherhoods and associations. They were particularly active in the more modern devotional associations promoted by Aracena's clergy, such as the brotherhoods of Saint Vincent de Paul and of the Patriarch Saint Joseph, whose teachings emphasized charitable works and stressed the moral and spiritual importance of the values at the core of middle-class life.

The religiosity of the *comerciantes* gave Aracena the reputation of being a "Catholic town," and in comparison with other towns of the sierra where anticlerical feeling was steadily mounting, the reputation was well deserved. A report sent from the parish to the archbishop of

Seville in the early 1930s estimated that from 800 to 900 of the 6,150 nominal parishioners attended mass regularly in Aracena's churches and that about 1,000 adults and children annually complied with the Easter duty, which obliges Catholics to receive the sacraments during the most sacred season of the year (Ordóñez Márquez 1968:179). Without doubt, these estimates of participation included virtually all of the commercial middle class of the town, as well as the upper class.

Adhesion to the church was the most important cultural factor binding the *comerciantes* to the agrarian gentry and distinguishing them from the 80 percent of the population who were working-class "nonpractitioners" of the faith. In combination with the pressures created by the *comerciantes'* dependent economic relationships with the gentry, the shared religious orthodoxy of the two groups reinforced a prevailing style of interaction that was familiar and cordial but characterized by all the gestures of respect and deference that wealthy patrons could wish of modest clients. This dominant pattern of partial identification with and deference to the gentry also conditioned the way in which *comerciantes* participated in public affairs. Although the numerous civic and religious associations established in the name of Catholic mutualism and usually headed by the gentry attracted few participants from the working class, leading *comerciantes* (and some *labradores*) were often prevailed upon to accept the lesser (but most burdensome) offices of these associations, and their membership lists were filled with names from the middle sectors of local society.

Nevertheless, there were some members of the middle ranks of society who did not identify with or support the general pattern of elite domination. In addition to the poorer *labradores* and small shopkeepers (barbers, grocers, and tavernkeepers) who were sympathetic to the *clases pobres* and embraced "socialism," there was a smattering of republican opinion among younger, better-educated, and disaffected *comerciantes,* clerks, and professionals. Although republicanism did not serve as a rallying point for serious political opposition to the rule of the *marqués* and the Conservative party until the advent of the Second Republic (see Chapter 6), it is worth mentioning this sector of opinion not because of its practical importance or broad popular appeal but, rather, because of the light it casts on the cultural constraints and pressures that more generally influenced the forms of class consciousness in Aracena.

During the first two decades of the century, an exotic variant of middle-class ideology was embraced by a handful of people in Aracena, who because of their interest in freemasonry and spiritualism can be best described as "esoteric republicans." While the esoteric republicans did not entirely lack a political perspective, it was a rather anemic one whose central tenet was that the church (especially the Jesuit order) was the great impediment to the spiritual and material regeneration of Spain. This opinion was consistent with that of more active and organized liberals and republicans elsewhere in Spain who wished to transform the country into a modern and essentially secular society by disestablishing the church and eliminating its role in education. It was not, however, a view that was particularly pertinent to the urgent socioeconomic and political problems of the sierra, and for the most part, the disaffected republican spiritualists of the town occupied themselves with concocting theosophical interpretations of local "signs" that revealed profound connections between metaphysical universals and Aracena's "customs and colors." For example, they interpreted the town's name as signifying a divine or spiritual feast (from *ara* = "communion table" and *cena* = "dinner"), and by contemplating the rock formations of Las Grutas de las Maravillas (the caverns beneath "El Castillo"), they believed that they could discover the secrets of the origin of the physical universe. Indeed, the unknown depths of the caverns were thought to be connected by subterranean passages to La Peña de Alájar, the peak where the earthly and heavenly spheres most deeply interpenetrated.[11]

This baroque structure of spiritualist speculation was knit together by a legend that Arias Montano, the sixteenth-century scholar and patron, had secretly been a cabalist, occultist, and one of the "Wise Men of the Universe."[12] Montano was therefore venerated as the founder of this theosophical tradition, which had survived the centuries and the Inquisition and had been preserved by a few secret initiates, the *hermanos mayores* (senior brothers) of certain of the religious brotherhoods of Aracena and Alájar. These visionary revelations served as embellishments to the belief that humankind would be saved from the present "time of troubles" when people realized that the world was a "universal republic" governed by "eternal ones"—purely spiritual beings free of the chains of "dead materiality"—who wished to liberate lesser immortals from their illusionary bondage to the life of the body (Roso de Luna 1920:105).

To the extent that it expressed resentment against the "mere religious exteriority" evident in the mutualist social Catholicism of the leading members of the gentry, esoteric republicanism represented a form of resistance to the dominant ideology of the day, but it certainly posed no threat to the rule of the local elite. On the contrary, the esoteric republicans were interested in an almost exclusively spiritualist variety of freemasonry and tended to disdain anything so mundane as direct involvement in practical politics. Although a number of Aracena's republicans were probably affiliated with a Masonic lodge in Seville, they represented no more than a group of like-minded men who lacked significant power or influence and (even had they wished to do so) stood little chance of winning support from either Catholic conservatives or working-class radicals.[13] Indeed, they were derided, mocked, and even mildly persecuted by both groups for their otherworldly and mysterious air and their fondness for what was regarded as bizarre symbolism.[14]

Yet idiosyncratic as esoteric republicanism may have seemed, it was by no means unrelated to other cultural and ideological currents in Aracena. In its inflated styles of rhetoric and representation, the influence of the gentry's attempts to create a noble image of themselves and to cultivate the "higher" arts and literature can be detected; in its infatuation with mystical experience, elaborate ritual, and moral dogmatism, there are reflections of the piety and narrow religious orthodoxy of the town's *comerciantes;* and in its identification of Aracena and the sierra as a blessed land where the spiritual and natural planes of being deeply interpenetrate thanks to the beneficent spiritual force of patrons both manifest and invisible, it recasts some of the central images of the genre of pastoral epic in its own image. Moreover, like the proponents of Catholic mutualism, the esoteric republicans sought to reconcile the tensions between liberal ideals and traditional forms of cultural authority by celebrating individual freedom of conscience and at the same time honoring ancient spiritual masters; and like the orthodox *comerciantes,* the esoteric republicans tried to separate themselves from the dominant culture of the gentry by stressing to an even greater extent than the elite the paramount importance of the higher religious and spiritual dimension of their sense of self.

Indeed, because the esoteric republicans and orthodox *comerciantes* alike were caught in the middle of the ideological and social conflicts between the gentry and the working class and lacked most of the resources needed to ameliorate the "social crisis," both groups sought a kind of refuge from these struggles by forging alternative religious identities that distinguished them to some degree from the rich and the poor. Yet by building their castle on a shaky foundation of spiritualist fantasies, the esoteric republicans only managed to construct an unintended parody of the dominant culture of the gentry and middle classes. In effect, the esoteric republicans reproduced in a particularly exaggerated form the central tendency of every ideological current in Aracena—the tendency to seize the spiritual high ground by explaining every sociopolitical problem as finally attributable to the moral corruption of adversaries too sunken in greed, selfishness, and "materiality" to act for the good of others or the community as a whole.

THE WORKING CLASS: AUTONOMY, OBLIGATION, AND MORAL OUTRAGE

In Aracena in the period between 1900 and 1930, there were about 350 men who each owned less than five hectares of land. Barely distinguishable from these *campesinos* (peasants) in their manner of life were the roughly 750 *jornaleros* (agrarian day laborers). In addition, there were about 200 *artesanos* (shoemakers, corkmakers, and so forth) who comprised the work force of local "industries." These men and their families constituted the working class of the township, and they resided either in one of the five peripheral *barrios* (neighborhoods) of the town or in one of the six outlying *aldeas* (hamlets) that were scattered in the countryside. What these people shared in greater or lesser degree were lives of poverty, poor wages, endemic unemployment, and often hunger.

For most working-class men, social life revolved around two or three bars in the immediate neighborhood (of the scores of bars and taverns in the town) where they spent most of the time they were not working. These meeting places usually consisted of little more than a front room of a house with a few tables and chairs and a bar made from a board laid across two wine casks. A few céntimos would buy a glass of wine or *aguardiente* (a strong anise-flavored whiskey), and there was frequently a card game in progress; however, the bars were primarily places to meet and talk. Because most men were without work or were seriously underemployed, they had many hours free for conversation and there were few stories that were not retold, rumors that did not spread, or opinions that remained unvoiced. Witnessing every day the penury and drudgery of their own lives in the lives of their neighbors and friends, working-class men of the town had ample time to envisage solutions for their common problems, and the bars were the hothouses of radical politics.

Women and children rarely visited the bars in the period before the Second Republic, and while they were therefore somewhat excluded from the political discussions of men, the range of opinions they held was just as broad and certainly no less radical. For women, life in the *barrios* was centered on the house and extended into the street, where they met their friends and neighbors. During the winter months, groups of female friends and relatives frequently visited one another's houses in the late afternoons to sew and chat, and in the summers women were often to be found near their doorways, where they could greet and talk with their neighbors. Months and years of face-to-face communication among the families of the *jornaleros*, artisans, and the few peasant farmers who lived in Aracena's *barrios* created a sense of working-class community similar to that found in the more isolated rural hamlets.

Most working-class people had few direct contacts with the town's elite, and as a rule relations between the classes were narrowly focused on practical concerns. In the early mornings or late afternoons, the large landowners or their foremen and bailiffs came to certain bars and street corners to hire laborers. A man's reputation as a good worker and a suitably respectful attitude could make the difference in determining who was hired and who was passed over among the crowd of workers that were gathered. Similarly, the manner in which the employer conducted the brief negotiations concerning wages, the type and duration of work, and whether a meal was to be provided led workers to arrive at judgments about the employer as a relatively "good" or "bad" *patrón*. Yet beyond such minimal necessary contacts, the sense of social place, personal pride, and many other factors normally limited the interchanges between proprietors and proletarians. In these circumstances, the postures of working-class men toward their social superiors tended to alternate between attitudes of humble deference and silent, glaring, and sullen resentment.

In addition to generating hostility between the classes, the conditions of subordination, poverty, and exploitation had far-reaching effects on working-class values and attitudes. While poor men and women longed to achieve a state of socioeconomic autonomy and self-sufficiency that would free them from dependence on others, the harsh realities of their lives meant that they often had to compete with their neighbors for scarce resources as well as rely on the help of friends and family in times of need. The pushes and pulls of the desire for autonomy, the necessity to struggle for survival, and the practical and moral imperatives to cooperate made the conduct of daily affairs a difficult and delicate matter, and in these circumstances it is hardly surprising that the most striking feature of working-class culture during the period was the breadth and depth of concern expressed for understanding what people owed and could expect of one another. Notions of honor, personal integrity, and reputation were heavily influenced by a moral economy of *obligaciones* (obligations) and *deberes* (duties).

For working-class people, the primary meaning of *obligaciones* was and still is both eminently practical and fraught with moral implications. The term is used most frequently to describe ordinary work done for the sake of others, and this usage spans the conceptual distance between a concern for the material exigencies of everyday life and the more elevated moral responsibilities people have to others as human beings. In this sense, a busy person wishing to break off a conversation may say, "Well, I ought to go; I have my obligations," in order to convey both the notion of practical pressures and the message that he or she is sacrificing personal pleasure to fulfill his or her moral commitments.

Like other critical aspects of traditional morality, the notion of obligations was extensional and personalistic. Above all else, men and women had the strongest material and moral obligations with respect to immediate family members, and only after these obligations were fulfilled could practical aid be given and moral commitments made to other members of the community. It was also recognized that the precise character of obligations varied according to the people and circumstances involved. Since beyond (and to a lesser extent even within) the narrow circle of the immediate family what one person owed another was often highly problematic and variable, claims and counterclaims about obligations were central to the politics of everyday life and constituted the heart of gossip about honorable or shameful behavior and the theme of arguments over favors extended or denied, inheritance, cooperative work, generosity, and so forth. To invoke primary obligations was a way for a person to proclaim and defend immediate interests of the household while still fending off accusations of purely individual selfishness and *egoísmo*. All working-class people understood (even if they did not entirely accept) the principle expressed by the saying that "a poor man with six children makes a bad friend"—but, of course, not necessarily a bad person.

The general obligation to cooperate with and help other members of the community was strongly supported by some well-established customs, and neighbors felt bound to give certain types of aid when it was needed. For example, when it was time for a rural family to slaughter its hogs, the household usually required help to ensure that all the work of butchering and curing was completed before the meat spoiled. Anyone invited to attend the *matanza* (hog slaughter) was obliged to come. In return, when it was time for invited helpers to slaughter their own animals, there was no need to extend another invitation. People arrived at the appointed hour without having to be asked. To reject or obviously avoid requests for help in situations where customary expectations prevailed was taken as a deep insult and almost invariably resulted in a total, though often temporary, rupture in social relations between households. To a certain extent, such practically grounded customary obligations to neighbors both counterbalanced and complemented narrower personal obligations to family.

The discourse of obligations and duties served to guide the conduct of working-class social relations because it provided the primary means of interlinking concerns for personal honor, integrity, and reputation to the practical fulfillment of both the material needs of oneself, one's family, and others and the broader moral ideals of community harmony and solidarity. Even though in many situations the sociomoral loyalties produced by multiple obligations might conflict with one another and create serious disputes among people, the constant push and pull of obligations and duties in day-to-day affairs nonetheless reinforced the fundamental perception of a common collective life and shared values and was at the root of working-class notions of equality. Although particular loyalties and duties varied from person to person, everyone had obligations and aspirations of the same general sort because everyone had the same life of poverty, hardship, work, and worry and recognized the values of both autonomy and cooperative interdependence. As one woman stated, "Everyone has his or her *faena* [work, tasks]; we are all equal here." The idea expressed in the statement represents a direct way of affirming what Julian Pitt-Rivers (1961:13) has identified as the main premise of popular political thought among the *campesinos, jornaleros,* and *artesanos* of Andalusia: "the moral unity of the *pueblo.*"

It is from the perspective of the moral economy of obligations that working-class political ideologies can best be understood. Conceptions of class conflict were ordinarily expressed in a direct language that stressed the differences between two diametrically opposed groups, *los ricos* (the rich) and *los pobres* (the poor). The rich were thought of as those who did not have to work (perform physical, manual labor) and still had the means to be autonomous and at no one's beck and call. The poor lived by the sweat of their brow and were subordinate to others. As the saying goes, "The poor do what they have to; the rich do what they want." Nothing was clearer to most working-class people than that the rich had the means but not the desire to fulfill a moral obligation to help the poor. Thus, from the perspective of the poor, the moral failure of the rich and not the ignorance of laborers or the stage of the evolution of society was the cause of the misery of ordinary townspeople and the root of the "social problem."

Nowadays when working-class people describe the past, they do so in tones of profound moral outrage. In recalling their poverty and their dealings with Aracena's landowners and authorities, they constantly repeat a few key words and phrases: "robbery," "slavery," "hypocrisy," "shamelessness," and "lack of justice." From a sociopolitical perspective, the recollected past for them is mostly a series of negatives and absences (even though in other contexts they sometimes express great nostalgia for many aspects of a fading agrarian way of life). The prevalent way they express their bitterness is to deny the piety and moral virtue of the upper classes, and they use traditional cultural discourses in a manner that suggests the "negative" force that religion, honor, and patronage had in shaping working-class consciousness.

When asked about the role of the rich as patrons of the community and benevolent "friends" of the poor, the response is often something like the following: "*Patrón? Patrón* is only a word. *Sí, patrón. No, patrón.* It meant nothing. . . . Some friends! Those who worked you to death and paid nothing. Sons of whores!" The denial of gentry patronage and the emphasis on the basic injustice of the economic system are habitually contrasted with the willingness of laborers to work diligently and hard even if for a pittance. One of the words used to describe this perceived obligation to fulfill one's duties as a worker is *cumplir* (to comply); and as Juan Martínez-Alier (1971:174–206) notes in his extended discussion of the term's usage in the province of Córdoba, the word implies not primarily a contractual relationship between employer and employee but a moral obligation for the worker to do what is just and appropriate. In their recollections of the past, the workers of Aracena draw a contrast between their willingness to "comply" and the failure of landowners to *patrocinar* (to act as patrons). This is one of the strongest bases of their perception that working-class misery was a direct consequence of the personal and collective immorality of the gentry.

In a similar way, people contrast the family and communal character of popular religious life to the adherence of the rich to orthodox and institutional religion. The working-class sense of injustice was deeply aggravated by the perception that the rich were not only lacking in moral sense but were conscious liars and hypocrites intent on maintaining a false image of the community and of their own cultural superiority through the manipulation of elaborate ritual forms. As a result, the *clases pobres* saw church-centered religion as the facade that the rich used in a futile attempt to hide their greed, selfishness, and *egoísmo*. As one old man who had been a leatherworker stated: "Yes, the rich were very Catholic. They went to the church to see each other in their fine clothes and say an Ave Maria and Paternoster so that everyone could hear their 'My Gods,' 'Mother of God,' and 'God protect me.' In this manner, they were able to steal from the poor without fear and without shame. The women were the worst—'Oh, Padre! . . . Padre, please! Come to my house!' [the speaker imitated an infatuated and impassioned woman as he related this]. It is still the same. They love the priests."

False piety was viewed as the mask of worldly passions, and village gossips and working-class political leaders alike saw a close connection between social injustice, the love of wealth, and the "shameless" behavior of rich *señoritos* who were reputed to be adulterers, gamblers, and drunkards. All signified the same sort of moral depravity, and in large measure the intensity of working-class anticlericalism and hatred of the church as an institution was based on the perception that the church openly supported the rule of the rich and secretly tolerated corruption and hypocrisy.

Another element in the working-class condemnation of the rich centered on the sense of the deep insult and offense against the honor and integrity of the self that the poor suffered at their hands. The tensions arising from fundamental socioeconomic inequalities were made worse by social prejudices that affected every aspect of class relations. Few working-class people failed to mention the highly segregated styles of life separating rich from poor. In particular, they resented the fact that during fiestas and the hours of the daily evening *paseo* (stroll), the poor were forbidden to mingle in the town's main plaza, a semi-enclosed, raised space where the rich socialized with one another. The poor had to mill about in the streets a few feet below the level of the plaza. More generally, people complain that the rich never recognized the poor as persons. With tears of anger one woman recalled: "When a *rico* passed a *pobre* in the street, he passed by him as though he did not even exist. Not even a word, not a *buenos días,* nothing." These insults and slights—grievous breaches of etiquette and the social values of "formality" and "openness"—were taken as confirmation that the rich "shamelessly" refused to recognize the minimal "respect" owed to all members of the community.

On the basis of such perceptions and judgments, a large and growing segment of the working class came to believe that the rich for all practical purposes denied the humanity of the poor and masked this denial by invoking the idioms, images, and values of religion, honor, and patronage. Again and again, people recall the "slavery" of the working class: "We were their slaves. They had us working in their houses, and they did nothing and in return paid us nothing. They were thieves; they robbed us of life." The conviction that the rich robbed the poor of "life" represents the most forceful way of expressing the moral outrage of the working class because by "life" people meant not just the material resources to clothe and feed themselves and their families decently but also the capacity to fulfill the obligations to others that were at the core of the practical morality of the working class. The worst consequence of "slavery" was that it denied the poor the means and sometimes the will to be fully human. Poverty generated a sense of hopelessness, futility, and misery that often had disastrous consequences. One elderly man described the early years of his life in this way:

That life—it was no life at all to break your bones sacrificing yourself for what? For nothing. Day after day to rise before dawn, to walk to the *campo* [countryside], to work all day, and to come back to your house without enough to buy a piece of bread. First, my father and brother worked and I went to school, but after a year, my father was sick, and there was no money and I had to work. We worked years and never had a *duro* [five pesetas] in our pocket. After my father was better, he went away; he deserted us, and then my mother had to work in the *campo,* too. I don't know. Maybe he left because he could not take it anymore—to see us suffer without any recourse. The rich had everything in those years and there was nothing he could do. . . . We had no life. I remember him. He was a good father.

Class exploitation led to class hatred because the poor perceived that poverty and prejudice robbed them of more than material welfare. It diminished and sometimes destroyed their capacity to maintain their own sense of dignity and self-worth by forcing them to live as "brutes." In this context, to condemn the rich for their religious hypocrisy, lack of patronage, and absence of shame was a way to set right the moral balance sheet. Piety, honor, and paternal authority were precisely the traditional virtues that the rich claimed almost exclusively for themselves, but the poor responded to these claims of cultural superiority by hating the rich for depriving them of the material and moral power to lead respectable lives.

The radicalism of popular working-class political ideologies was conditioned far more strongly by the sense of moral outrage engendered by this cultural dialectic of blame and fault than it was by explicit revolutionary programs, utopian dreams, or millenarian hopes for the future. For example, a report on Aracena that was written by a local working-class man and appeared in the newspaper *El Socialista* (9 Nov. 1930) invokes the same rhetoric of moral outrage that pervades the recollections of townspeople. The account refers to the "tightening of the chains of slavery" around the working class, contrasts this with the heroic fight of the workers for "justice" and "true life," notes the lack of resources that local workers had for the "physical and moral education of their children," warns workers against approaching "the feet of the bourgeoisie [and] crying like a flock of sheep," and attributes primary responsibility for working-class misery to the moral "infamies" and greed of local "capitalists." The report represents a melodramatic inversion of the paternalist ideology of *El Distrito* and, indeed, of the traditional cultural genre of pastoral epic that ascribed exemplary virtues to patrons rather than to the common people.

Above all, the working class of Aracena wanted minimal "social justice," and what this meant was more conditioned by their practical material and moral concerns than their enthusiasm for rationalized ideologies. What counted politically were general ideals of *unión* (unity), *libertad* (liberty), and *igualdad* (equality), all of which expressed in explicit modern terms the traditional values that shaped working-class culture. Until the Second Republic, the majority of working-class radicals in the town were hardly concerned with sharply discriminating among the various shades of left-wing opinion. For this reason, it is difficult and largely pointless to differentiate local "anarchists" from "socialists" (or for that matter from radical republicans, as Calero [1977:78–79] points out) except in the case of a few leaders.

Yet while most working-class people were united in support of efforts to win concessions on wages and working conditions from employers through strikes, demonstrations, and so forth, and while the conviction was steadily growing that to achieve the ultimate goal of a *reparto* (distribution) of land and property would require intense class struggle and perhaps even revolutionary violence, there was still no consensus about whether independent peasant exploitations, agrarian cooperatives, or wholesale collectivization would provide the best form of economic organization for a more egalitarian sociopolitical and moral order. Differences of opinion about this crucial issue reflected the tensions in working-class culture between ideals of personal and family autonomy and ideals of community cooperation, tensions that ultimately derived from the personalist and corporatist foci of traditional morality. Even so, it seems fairly clear that most politically aware working-class people were primarily concerned with creating a new social order that would permit them and their neighbors a degree of socioeconomic autonomy and personal dignity. This priority is evident in statements such as the following, which encapsulates two basic contrasting points of view on how to solve the "social problem": "I have always believed that until there is no private property, there can be no true peace. This I believe, but what I want is my own life; you don't rob me and I don't rob you. This is social justice and nothing more." As the statement indicates, having one's "own life" was a far more pressing desire than abolishing private property and was viewed as the sine qua non of a just society. It seems that the poor, for the most part, demanded no more from the rich than this. Yet the resentments were so intense and the moral dichotomy between the opposing class groups was so sharply etched that many among the rural working class had come to believe there was little hope for bettering their lives short of resorting to the most radical political measures.

Thus, within all of Aracena's class groups in the early decades of the twentieth century, highly charged sociopolitical ideologies emerged, some linked to the conservative offshoots of a faltering liberal regime and others expressing radical alternatives to it. Each of these ideologies incorporated both modern and traditional elements and gave explicit political form to a set of diverging values that were rooted in the particular conditions of life experienced by the members of each class. However, the cultural discourses of religion, honor, and patronage were crucially important in the development of these opposing ideologies because the way in which each class reinterpreted traditional notions of the person, community, and polity exacerbated the tensions that were inherent in the political and economic inequalities of rural class society. The dominant tendency to cast conflicts of interest in terms of almost absolute contrasts between the moral virtues of class allies and the vices of class adversaries led the members of one group to deny the humanity of others and to accuse them of unbridled *egoísmo,* ignorance, or hypocrisy. Under these circumstances, the already difficult social situation became intolerable. This dramatic ideological displacement of traditional discourses and images generated the cultural conditions for the violence of the Second Republic and the Civil War by socially isolating class groups from one another and eventually dividing Aracena into two hostile and armed camps.

6

Tradition in Ashes

In those days in Aracena the law of terror reigned. The miners
of Nerva and Río Tinto, the envenomed hamlet dwellers, and
all the lower depths of the city had formed a common front
against order, decency, and religion.
—Juan Ordóñez Márquez
*La apostasía de las masas y la persecución religiosa
en la provincia de Huelva, 1931–1936*

Revolutionary Anticlericalism and
Hegemonic Processes

THE EPIGRAPH to this chapter describes the situation in Aracena
in the late summer of 1936, a few weeks after the beginning of
the Spanish Civil War. Although the description reveals the
right-wing sympathies of the author, there is no doubt that most of
the local working-class radicals would have agreed that they were
united against what local conservatives called "order, decency, and religion." The starkest demonstration of revolutionary ardor occurred
on 10 August 1936, when a crowd sacked and burned the churches of
Aracena. Similar attacks against both the church and the clergy were
occurring throughout the sierra and in much of the rest of Spain at the
time.[1] Indeed, according to José Sánchez (1987:8), the violent deaths
of nearly seven thousand Spanish priests, nuns, monks, and seminar-
ians, most of whom were slaughtered during the early months of the
war, represent "the greatest clerical bloodletting in the entire history
of the Christian church."

Who attacked the church, and how did they justify it morally and
politically? Were they fanatics engaged in an archaic form of quasi-
religious protest and motivated by an inflated millenarian expectation
that an earthly paradise was at hand, as some historians have maintained? Or were they coldhearted ideologues launching a carefully

calculated and ruthless attack on the most highly visible institution of an oppressive social order, as others seem to suggest?[2] To answer these questions, this chapter examines the church burnings in Aracena in terms of the dynamics of political and ideological polarization that dominated local class relations during the period preceding the Civil War, in terms of the urgent tactical demands of the revolutionary situation, and in terms of long-range strategies of cultural domination, resistance, displacement, and resignification. It argues that the emergence of revolutionary anticlericalism in Aracena was governed by the convergence of immediate, middle-range, and long-term hegemonic processes and that the people who burned the town's churches were neither frenzied fanatics nor ruthless ideologues but were instead committed radicals whose actions were intended to have the maximum cultural and political impact on their allies and adversaries alike.

THE POLITICS OF POLARIZATION FROM 1923 TO 1936

The *marqués* of Aracena died in the autumn of 1931, just as the Second Republic was being born. In a relatively free and open election earlier in the year, the aging *cacique* had lost his bid for a seat in the Constituent Cortes of the new republic. But well before this humiliating defeat, he had endured some important reversals in his political career. In 1923, when the "gentle dictator," Primo de Rivera, had seized the reins of state power and ended the rule of the discredited Liberal and Conservative "parties of the turn," the *marqués* and his friends were ousted from the offices they had controlled since the late 1890s.[3] To make matters worse, Primo's promise to excise the evils of *caciquismo* from the body politic had encouraged a public outcry against the *marqués* and his circle, and denunciations and letters of protest (many of them anonymous) were sent to newspapers in Huelva and Seville and to one of the governmental "action commissions" appointed by the dictator to investigate corruption. The charges were the familiar ones of thwarting electoral processes, misusing funds, and so forth, but the complaints were of unprecedented number and received great publicity.

As a result, in early 1925, a newly appointed town council largely composed of members of a younger generation of reform-minded gentry spent weeks debating what, if any, actions should be taken with respect to past abuses by the *marqués* and his allies. The official outcome of this debate was a timid declaration that the *marqués*, a former *alcalde* (mayor), and a few others had not acted "altruistically or for the public good" in their administration of the local caverns (AA 1925). But the formal recognition of any impropriety at all was broadly seen as a de facto confirmation that the *marqués* and his cronies had personally profited from their offices, and this permanently damaged their local reputations. Even after the *marqués* was appointed by Primo to the National Assembly and subsequently became head of the resurrected Conservative party of Huelva at the end of the dictatorship, he was unable to claim much popular support in Aracena.

The partial loss of control by the *marqués* unleashed social forces that had long been restrained. By 1931, three main political blocs had emerged in Aracena and began to play the leading roles in the polarized party and class politics of the Second Republic.[4] On the far right were the gentry, *comerciantes* (merchants and shopkeepers), professionals, and civil servants who were initially committed to the old Conservative party of the *marqués* but who soon embraced Acción Popular, the political wing of the Catholic social organization, Acción Católica. During the Second Republic, Acción Popular became the dominant party in the national coalition known as La Confederación de Derechas Autónomas (CEDA) and led by José María Gil Robles (see Montero 1977). Locally, those who embraced Catholic and monarchist principles deriving from the doctrine of "mutualism" were led by a handful of the richest men of Aracena (including members of the family of the *marqués*), who usually chose to exercise their influence behind the scenes and left local offices in the hands of their somewhat less affluent supporters.

On the far left of the political spectrum were the Socialists and their more radical allies and occasional opponents, who could count on the support of the great majority of the *artesanos* (artisans), *jornaleros* (agrarian day laborers), and *campesinos* (peasants) of the township. The working class of Aracena was represented by two primary organizations: (1) a branch of El Partido Socialista Obrero Español (PSOE), whose leaders actively campaigned for local office and had established a *casa del pueblo* (house of the people) in order to promote the moderate Socialist message; and (2) La Sociedad de Obreros, Campesinos, y Artesanos (Society of Workers, Peasants, and Artisans), an offspring of the old Unión de Campesinos y Artesanos whose ideological stance was less well defined but tended to be more radical than that of the Socialists, since it included a number of men of anarchist inclinations who affirmed the ideals of *comunismo libertario* (libertarian communism) and social revolution and were highly critical and suspicious of the Socialists' participation in electoral politics.[5]

The center left of the political spectrum was occupied by the Radical Republicans, a group consisting of small or medium landowners and some workers, shopkeepers, and young professionals. The Radical Republicans followed the lead of a lawyer who was elected to represent the sierra in the Constituent Cortes, and because of the importance of their party in national politics during the early years of the Second Republic, they secured local offices and exercised influence out of proportion to their limited numbers and shaky support in Aracena.[6]

Although even some of the most conservative politicians of the town greeted the prospect of a republic with guarded optimism, a precedent that boded ill for the future of democratic politics was set well before the new regime was in place. In the weeks before the critical municipal elections of April 1931 (the elections whose outcome drove King Alfonso XIII into exile), Aracena's conservative authorities attempted to employ the usual techniques of electoral manipulation (such as the elimination of names from voting lists) that had worked so smoothly in the past. For the first time, however, popular leaders vigorously resisted these maneuvers, and the result was an election whose outcome was hotly protested.

A second election was held in May, and once again the outcome was disputed. At this point, the new civil governor of the province ended the fray by ordering eight Republicans and six Socialists to form a new town council (ACM, 1 June 1931). This was the first of many interventions in local affairs by civil governors of the left and the right who continually sought to impose political "conformity" between municipal and higher-level authorities. Unfortunately, these administrative cures for political ills usually only served to infuriate the losing side and further exacerbate local tensions. In the case at hand, the far right was unfairly deprived of representation, and when members of the Republican majority awarded themselves all of the important municipal offices during the first council meeting, the Socialists walked out in protest.

Despite their lack of an electoral mandate, the Republicans did not hesitate to exercise their power during their first few weeks in office. Among the measures exuberantly adopted were a proposal to expel the Jesuit order from Spain (ACM, 1 June 1931), a requirement that all surplus municipal funds be used to provide jobs for unemployed laborers (ACM, 1 June 1931), and a request to the provincial delegation that a commission be appointed to investigate and correct past abuses in the administration of public accounts (ACM, 28 June 1931). The reforming zeal evident in these measures set the tone for local government in the period from 1931 to early 1933, and while the council members' first actions won them some sympathy and gratitude from workers, their decrees quickly alienated the town's conservatives, who were annoyed by the anticlericalism of the council and complained that there was no source of funds available for an ambitious program of public works.

The council responded to these complaints by taking actions guaranteed to infuriate the gentry. It informed twenty-five of Aracena's upper-class landlords that they must improve the sanitation and the overall condition of their rented properties within two weeks. If they failed to respond to this ultimatum, a "commission of carpenters" recommended by La Sociedad de Obreros and appointed by the council would do the work at the expense of the landlord (ACM, 27 July 1931). This and a number of other directives concerning the maintenance of local houses and streets were designed to impose a de facto tax on the rich, who were unaccustomed to being threatened by local authorities.

Relations between the council and the gentry deteriorated further in 1932. In January, despite protests from the rich, the council responded to worker demands by initiating a project to repair the road connecting one of Aracena's more remote hamlets to the town. In the spring, the council forbade any price increases in "articles of first necessity" such as bread and oil (ACM, 13 Apr. 1932) and established the first day of May as a "Fiesta de Trabajo" to be observed within the township. Around the same time, Republican reformers imposed an increase in the basic agricultural wage to four and a half pesetas a day.[7] All of these measures were decided upon in an atmosphere of increasing labor unrest and escalating demands. As early as February, a vineyard of a landowner openly hostile to the council had been burned, presumably by angry workers.

In late May, a group of proprietors adamantly opposed to the wage increase responded by agreeing not to harvest the year's cork crop, thus denying any work to the hard-pressed *jornaleros*. In turn, La Sociedad de Obreros staged a general strike in protest. Fearful of damage to their property, landowners prevailed upon the Guardia Civil for protection; and in the course of a demonstration, a weapon discharged (apparently accidentally) and a worker was killed. The alarmed town council immediately appointed a new commission to mediate between the landowners and workers, and this led to a small reduction in the wage increase. During these events, the Socialists who had been appointed to the town council played an increasingly crucial role in local affairs because they acted as go-betweens for the Republican majority on the town council and the more radical union leaders of the township.

Later in the year, the landowners were further angered by the town council's approval of a report that was sent to the national commission on agrarian reform and recommended the expropriation of fifty-five underutilized parcels of land in the township.[8] With the exception of some lands owned by the family of the *marqués,* most of the parcels identified for expropriation were small, but the resentment generated by the move was not. Not only were the gentry enraged, but many small and medium landowners were bothered by this threat to private property and began to turn their backs on the reformers just at the moment when labor disputes were swelling the increasingly militant ranks of La Sociedad de Obreros.

In late autumn, landowners expressed their opposition to increased wages by once again withholding work. In response, La Sociedad de Obreros organized another mass protest and demanded a wage increase greater than the rate of four and a half pesetas that had been set but then reduced the previous spring. In December, the civil governor of the province ordered the Guardia Civil to end the "illegal" disturbances; imposed a new wage compromise, which reestablished the old rate of four and a half pesetas; and replaced the reform-minded *alcalde* with another Republican, who was much more conservative. These actions were in keeping with a general policy of repression that had been established by an alarmed national government in the hope of bringing an end to social disturbances throughout the country, and the threat of using the Guardia Civil to implement them was largely successful in curbing organized strikes and protests in Aracena throughout most of 1933 and 1934.[9] Nevertheless, what the council called a "bad social ambience" punctuated by sporadic "social conflicts" (ACM, 11 July 1934) continued in the town.

Matters took a turn for the worse in August 1934 when a new civil governor dissolved the Republican-dominated town council and replaced it with one made up exclusively of large landowners, *comerciantes,* and other supporters of the CEDA (ACM, 21 Aug. 1934), which had formed a national government following the elections of November 1933. For Aracena, this marked the beginning of the period when the full impact of the so-called *bienio negro* (the two-year "black" period of right-wing government in Spain) was felt. Locally, during its first months in office, the conservative council succeeded in undoing many of the reforms and suspending most of the programs initiated by the Republicans. Decrying the town's financial situation and arguing that Aracena had already done more for its poor than most townships, the council canceled public works projects and made only a token appeal to proprietors to take over the burden of providing work for the desperate (ACM, 27 Sept. 1934). As a sop to their political supporters, the council members approved a revision of the municipal tax list that lowered the liabilities of many landowners and landlords (ACM, 29 July 1935). However, the act creating the most resentment was the council's declaration that the daily agricultural wage should be lowered to four pesetas a day (ACM, 4 Jan. 1936).

For the working class, this amounted to an official declaration of economic war.

These harsh economic measures were accompanied by successful efforts to repress the opposing political forces of the left. Almost all municipal workers hired during the early years of the Second Republic were dismissed and replaced by active supporters of the right. Attempts were made to close the *casa del pueblo* of the Socialists, and La Sociedad de Obreros was declared an illegal organization. Working-class leaders were denounced, sometimes jailed for short periods, and then hauled before hostile judges on trumped-up minor violations of the law. The town council not only threatened to prosecute former Republican officials for misuse of municipal funds but also sought to cow ordinary workers by bringing charges of trespassing and theft against them. When in early 1935 a national state of emergency was declared and civil rights were suspended as a result of the uprisings in Catalonia and Asturias, a recently expanded and armed force of thirteen municipal guards in Aracena used the slightest pretext to harass and often beat known leftists residing in the township.

The year and a half of what amounted to political reaction and retaliation on the part of the right-wing council forced most townspeople to take sides either for or against repression, and this polarization was reflected in the returns from Aracena in the national election of 16 February 1936, which indicate that the population had divided into two hostile camps roughly equal in size.[10]

After the sweeping national victory of the Popular Front in the elections of 1936, the civil governor ordered the formation of a new town council in Aracena. This council, which was led by Socialists and included former Republican officials, immediately declared that the right-wing council of the *bienio negro* had been brought into office by an unconstitutional seizure of power, and it announced that it would dedicate itself to seeking "reparation and justice" and a "republic renewed" (ACM, 20 Feb. 1936). During its first meeting, the council received a statement from La Sociedad de Obreros, whose members proclaimed that "the illegal interregnum [of the conservative town council] opened wounds in our hearts very difficult to cauterize" and went on to make an ominous and scarcely veiled vow to seek revenge against the oppressors of the working class (ACM, 20 Feb. 1936). The first concrete measure of the Popular Front council was to fire the hated municipal guards. Many other town employees were subsequently dismissed, and this created bitter personal animosities among the leading figures of the left and the right.[11]

The chaotic situation in the town hall made it difficult for local officials to achieve much during the Popular Front period. A committee of "patrons and workers" went from door to door collecting taxes from those who had failed to pay a suitable amount because of the previous council's "illegal" adjustments of the tax lists (ACM, 1 Mar. 1936). A kilo and a half of bread was dispensed to each person on the "poor list" during the livestock fair in May (ACM, 3 May 1936), but not much else was accomplished apart from a number of symbolic gestures such as changing the name of the main square from La Plaza del Marqués to La Plaza de la República.

By the spring of 1936, the town council was losing its ability to moderate the demands of the workers who had become truly revolutionary in their actions and aims. Gangs of young working-class men engaged members of the Catholic youth organization in street fights, and there was an increase in vandalism of property and theft of livestock, fruits, and other crops. Local officials were unable to stop the fights and vandalism, and many people shut themselves up in their houses at night or else only went about in groups.

In April, La Sociedad de Obreros petitioned the town council to cede control of the underutilized areas of a large private estate to a body of workers who would cultivate the lands as a common property of the township. The petition concluded with the warning that if the council did not respond favorably within eight days, the section of La Sociedad from the hamlet of Valdezufre would act independently to "realize" the seizure (ACM, 1 Mar. 1936). This development threw the town council into confusion; but after some debate, one of the Socialist councilors visited the leaders of La Sociedad, convinced them that such an expropriation was a "legal impossibility" under the laws of the Republic, and offered some of them places on a land reform commission. This had a momentary chilling effect on the plans of the most radical workers. But a few weeks later, when a young boy herding goats in a pine grove on another estate fell into an abandoned well and was killed, La Sociedad renewed its demands, and militants established a camp on the estate.

Despite the illegality of this seizure, the town council could not agree on a response. When a statement condemning the expropriation was proposed, one of the Socialist councilors was infuriated and resigned his seat on the council. He was prevailed upon to withdraw his resignation only after his colleagues promised to take no position on the issue. This internal discord was an indication of the disintegrating position of the legally constituted authorities of the town.

By the end of June, the revolutionary embers were already smoldering. Both the left and the right had armed themselves and were openly preparing for more conflict. Only a bit more tinder was needed for the embers to burst into flames, and this was supplied when news reached the town shortly after 18 July that General Franco's troops in northern Africa had risen in rebellion against the Second Republic.

Revolutionary Melodrama: 17 July to 10 August 1936

In the first two weeks of the Civil War, the forces on the left in Aracena had little difficulty in taking control of the town. The land-owners, *comerciantes,* and other groups hostile to the Republic were outnumbered, uncertain about either the aims or prospects for success of the military uprising, and hesitant to openly challenge the legiti-mate authorities. In contrast, the leaders of La Sociedad de Obreros had immediately foreseen that the greatest single threat to the rule of the left in the town was the local Guardia Civil, whose members were anything but reliable supporters of the Republic. Accordingly, the left-ist leaders acted quickly to neutralize this danger by posting armed watchmen around the Guardia's barracks and thereby effectively seiz-ing the political initiative not only from the right but also from the Popular Front town council.

The resulting split in the Republican forces widened further when a well-organized contingent of workers from Río Tinto and other towns of the mining zone arrived at the end of July. The presence of the miners galvanized those who favored a radical social revolution over simple preservation of the Republic, and the radicals organized a "Communist revolutionary committee" composed of miners and the radical leaders of La Sociedad de Obreros. Popular forces under the control of the committee seized the centrally located church of El Car-men and transformed this place of worship favored by the local elite into a command post, armory, and union hall. From this center, the miners and rural workers issued communiqués to the people, sent out patrols to the countryside, and negotiated with the increasingly iso-lated Socialist officials of the town hall about such matters as how to house and feed the large numbers of *campesinos* who had gathered in the town from the more isolated hamlets and *pueblos* of the sierra.

Although the town council continually tried to reassert its author-ity, real power clearly rested with the revolutionary committee. In this situation, the most that councilmen could do was try to persuade the committee of the wisdom of pursuing a policy of moderation in deal-ing with the crisis. The council's influence was limited, and the revo-lutionary committee was itself under considerable pressure from its most ardent supporters to overturn the old order once and for all. In response to popular demand, a commission was established to formalize the expropriation and redistribution of land that *jornaleros* and *campesinos* had already taken steps to initiate, and many thought that the day of the long-awaited *reparto* was at hand.

Demands for *reparto* were accompanied as well by talk of vengeance against the rich. Many people apparently wanted to see their class enemies suffer, and there was some danger that summary executions might occur. In these circumstances, the town council and members of the revolutionary committee began discussions on how to establish revolutionary tribunals of justice. Many of the town's large landowners and right-wing leaders had already been taken into custody by the popular forces, and those who had not been arrested tried to hide themselves behind locked doors and barred shutters. Hearing rumors of reprisals and improvised trials did little to calm their fears. In an account of this period (quoted in Ordóñez Márquez 1968:184), Don Manuel Siurot, a visiting Catholic educator who had been caught in Aracena at the outbreak of the war, described the feeling of terror that prevailed among the upper classes:

> The privation of liberty had reached such an extreme that one could not laugh, because this was a provocation; one could not be serious, because this was for some purpose; one could not open the window onto the street, because this was espionage; and one could not close it, because this was conspiracy. In the hotel, we lived always surrounded by communists; bombs, rifles, dynamite, and blasphemies were our house companions. . . . With the jail full of honorable men, what sort of death would be given the prisoners was discussed around the table of the hotel's dining room. In this discussion, I applauded in my soul those from Nerva and Río Tinto [i.e., the miners] because they tenaciously opposed killing the poor detainees without a previous judgment, while those from Aracena wanted to burn them alive with no trial. When things were at this height, the Communist revolutionary committee ordered that I was to be conducted to the jail willingly or by force, because as a Catholic I was highly dangerous. They did not imprison me for being a political man, but for being a Catholic.

But, in fact, no massacre of the local elite by popular forces took place in Aracena. Indeed, there is no trustworthy report or record that even one of the "enemies of the Republic" was killed or seriously injured in the days of crisis that followed. What cannot be doubted, however, are the terror felt by the rich and the rage of the left against their class enemies. By the end of the first week of August, the fears and anger of the townspeople reached a climax as rumors of the approach of a column of rebel troops spread and as the news that "Nationalist" forces had captured Seville and many towns in the province of Huelva was received. Most people on the left realized that their barely organized and ill-armed revolutionary militia would stand little chance against regular troops. Faced with the prospect of rapid defeat, the revolutionaries nonetheless prepared to resist, but even in these straits, the popular forces refrained from attacking the supporters of the right. Instead, they turned against the churches and the images of the saints in a ritualized melodrama of violence.

On the morning of 10 August 1936, a hostile crowd of two hundred to three hundred working-class men gathered in front of the parish church of Santa María de la Asunción in Aracena. It seemed at first that municipal guards were going to prevent anyone from entering the sanctuary. Then a group of ten or fifteen militants stepped forward, and after a few minutes of heated discussion, the guards withdrew. Accompanied by other members of the crowd, the leaders entered the sanctuary and began to strip the walls, altars, chapels, and treasuries of their images, paintings, chalices, crucifixes, and other furnishings that had been the gifts and donations of generations of the town's gentry. All of these objects were gathered into a great pile in the center of the sanctuary and set ablaze. As the flames rose, dynamite charges exploded. Although the weakened stone walls did not collapse, the whole edifice was gutted. The municipal and parish archives housed in a room below the altar were destroyed, along with all of the church's sacred objects and artistic treasures, including over thirty images of the saints, the Virgin, and Christ.

In succession, the other churches and chapels of the town met a similar fate. The church of Santa Catalina lost at least fifty paintings, and the church of Santo Domingo and the chapels of San Pedro, San Roque, and Santa Lucía were stripped and severely damaged. The religious furnishings of El Carmen, the new revolutionary command post, were piled in carts, taken to the edge of town, and burned. For the most part, the anticlericals went about their job in a calm, orderly, and systematic way with their work occasionally punctuated by curses and jibes that mocked the church, priests, and even God, the Virgin, and the saints. In the course of the day, the chapel of the school of the Esclavas Concepcionistas (an order of nuns who taught the children of the town's elite) was ruined, and the sisters of the convents of Santa Catalina and Jesús, María, y José were expelled from their cloisters. While not physically harmed, the nuns were taunted and forced to put on secular dress. The sacristan and priests were saved from a similar or possibly much worse fate because they were already in the custody of jailers sworn to protect them. In all of the churches, the images of the lay religious brotherhoods, the most important objects of popular devotion in Aracena, were destroyed. In the late afternoon, the church of "El Castillo" was sacked, and the image of the town's *patrona*, La Virgen del Mayor Dolor, was also consigned to the flames. By the end of the day, only the chapel and nuns of the old people's home were left unmolested.

What was the meaning of this revolutionary melodrama for those who witnessed and participated in it? There is no simple answer to this question, but it is clear that an attack on the churches could be construed in part as an engagement in class warfare by proxy. Under the influence of the *marqués* and the Conservative party, Catholic social thought had long been the basis of the gentry's political ideology; and in a somewhat more reactionary form, it remained so in the 1930s when the local elite gave their support to the CEDA and Acción Católica. In light of this close association, the *campesinos* and *jornaleros* of Aracena regarded the church as the unqualified defender of upper-class domination and exploitation and, indeed, commonly referred to the right-wing politicians, landowners, and *comerciantes* of the town simply as "the party of the priest."

But more was involved in church burning than a direct attack on an ideological institution. Generations of the town's elite had donated the paintings, images, and other furnishings sheltered inside the churches and thought of themselves as the patrons and in a sense the proprietors of the churches' artistic treasures. For the working-class militants to enter and sack what they sometimes called "the houses of the rich" was not only to destroy the most visible representation of the elite's cultural and political values but was also symbolically tantamount to entering the homes and violating the persons of the gentry. It was a way of chastising and humiliating them by demonstrating their vulnerability and impotence. The estates of the gentry had already been effectively seized, and short of murder, there was no more dramatic means of demonstrating control of the town available than burning and sacking the churches.

Thus, it is clear that church burning was, in part, an act of political terrorism intended to ensure the demoralization of the class enemy at the most critical juncture in a decades-long history of class struggles and escalating ideological conflict. By 10 August, Aracena's gentry seemed to be cowed. Some were prisoners, and the majority had locked themselves inside their houses, anxiously awaiting emancipation by the Nationalist forces. The feelings of helpless fear and repugnance that the Catholic gentry and *comerciantes* felt then is readily apparent in their recent recollections of the event, and many of them readily admit that they were unwilling to challenge the popular forces of the town because they felt that the revolutionaries had gone "crazy."

Terrorism was, however, only one dimension of the politics of church burning. Another dimension was the imperative to unify the radical left as the revolutionary crisis approached. To understand the dynamics behind this aspect of revolutionary anticlericalism, it is critical to know who participated in the events of 10 August. When townspeople are asked about this, they usually respond with one or the other of two answers: "a few fanatics" or "the Marxist hordes." Such stock responses have to be treated with some caution,[12] but more extended accounts of the day substantially agree that the crowd was primarily composed of many young men from the hamlets and a smaller number from Aracena (i.e., "the hordes") who were led by miners and a handful of radicals from La Sociedad de Obreros (i.e., "the fanatics"). These leaders orchestrated the day's events and directed the small nucleus of men who actually stripped the churches and burned the sanctuaries and objects of devotion.[13] The church burnings thus brought the most organized, committed, and knowledgeable radicals into extended contact with the least experienced and most ill-organized and isolated *campesinos* of the sierra. This lent the church burnings something of the character of a political rally staged by revolutionary leaders whose authority was informal and whose effectiveness was heavily dependent on winning the support of a large number of followers.

From this perspective, attacking the churches represented a means of rekindling revolutionary ardor and uniting the various subgroups that constituted the popular forces in the town.[14] There was clearly a pressing need to do this on 10 August. As noted above, news of Nationalist advances had disheartened the left in the days immediately preceding the church burnings, even as members of the town council were calling for restraint and caution. In these circumstances, the revolutionary leaders evidently felt that some morale-building militant act was needed. A number of men who at the time of the church burnings had been sympathetic with the aims of the miners and town revolutionaries recently stated that the principal people involved wanted to "unify," "wake up," and even "ignite" the masses. One aging working-class man underscored this rationale by associating the church burnings in Aracena with events of the same day in the neighboring town of Higuera de la Sierra, where a group of miners had killed six members of the Guardia Civil in the course of an attack on their barracks. According to this man, Aracena's radicals were aroused by news of the battle in Higuera and undertook the assault on the churches both as a sort of victory celebration and in anticipation of imminent violence. A time had come when words and plans alone no longer carried sufficient persuasive force and had to be supplanted by great deeds. Burning the churches was an irreversible act—a crossing of the Rubicon—that directly communicated this message and irrevocably sealed the commitment of leaders and followers to one another and to the aims and ideals of social revolution.

The argument that church burning had the dual practical aims of terrorizing the right and rallying the divided left is further supported by evidence that the revolutionary anticlerical actions were a consequence of the politicization of religion, a process that developed in the course of the polarized political struggles of the Second Republic. While anticlerical actions in Aracena had been surreptitious, minor, and sporadic before the 1930s, the subsequent shift in the balance of political power both locally and nationally made religion an immediate and major focus of conflict and confrontation in Aracena. In the early 1930s, officials of the Second Republic expressed their hostility toward the church as an institution by adopting several measures concerning the "religious issue." These measures infuriated the right and provided many opportunities for bitter local disputes. For example, a dispute arose in the first months of Republican rule when the town council of Aracena considered a request to remove a stone cross from the central plaza of a working-class *barrio*. This prompted a vigorous public protest by Catholics, which in turn engendered a counterprotest by Republicans and a lengthy debate that was resolved only when the town council declared that the cross was to be considered henceforth as "an historical monument" and "a relic of the past" rather than an object of religious devotion (ACM, 4 Sept. 1933).

The continued attempts of local officials to implement reforms designed to secularize education and reduce the influence of the church on social life provoked increasingly strong reactions from Catholics and anticlericals alike. The most serious confrontation of the period developed when the Republican town council ordered the removal of the crucifixes from the town's schoolrooms. Acción Católica responded by organizing a march to the town hall to present a petition of protest. When news of this reached workers employed on a road-building project nearby, hundreds of them picked up their tools and marched en masse to head off the Catholics and prevent them from delivering the petition.[15] A riot was averted only because the forces of public order, armed with guns instead of shovels, appeared on the scene and dispersed both groups.

Ideologically motivated confrontations of this type set the stage for the exercise of symbolic violence on 10 August 1936. As working-class leaders had learned during the Republican period, anticlerical actions could be counted on to intimidate the class enemy and unite the popular forces, and this double motivation was a key to the political tactics and timing involved in their actions. What the revolutionaries needed was a dramatic but relatively low-risk victory, and this is what burning the churches provided.

But this is not the whole story. To regard anticlerical violence largely in terms of specific practical aims and political tactics still leaves many questions about the event unanswered. Why, for example, did the revolutionaries take great pains to destroy the most important images of popular devotion when it would seem that burning the church buildings would have accomplished the pragmatic ends discussed above? The question may seem trivial, but it is, in fact, of vital importance. One of the most striking features of accounts of the day is how shocked all but the most militant radicals were by the destruction of certain images of the saints, Christ, and the Virgin; and many working-class people were especially disturbed by the loss of the image of the patron saint of Aracena, La Virgen del Mayor Dolor, which had long been in the care of the most popular and broadly based of the town's lay brotherhoods. At the time, few working-class people greatly regretted and many openly approved of the assault on the churches and even the harassment of the nuns, but the destruction of the most popular images was a different matter. Indeed, in neighboring towns, though not apparently in Aracena, some working-class people and Popular Front officials acted vigorously to prevent popular images from falling into the hands of those who wished to destroy them.

This discord within the working classes on the matter of the popular images indicates that something more than immediate tactical aims was involved in anticlerical violence. To understand the significance of this discord and the broader motivations of the church burners, it is necessary to gain a sense of how revolutionary anticlericalism was related to long-term hegemonic processes that shaped the character of traditional anticlericalism.

Long-Term Displacements and Hegemonic Ironies: Church Burning, Resistance, and Reaction

For most of its long history, anticlericalism in Spain has represented a cultural undercurrent that has occasionally emerged as a focal point of popular movements of protest in opposition to direct domination by elite groups or by the institutions of the church. However, for the most part, traditional forms of anticlericalism have been grounded in everyday concerns and practices and primarily focused on the politics of interpersonal relations rather than on broader social and political issues. Although traditional anticlericalism has varied considerably in its intensity and modes of expression, its central themes have always been derogation of the hypocritical worldliness of the clergy and noncompliance with important aspects of orthodox religious practice. Despite much evidence to the contrary, the general notion of rampant clerical misconduct has persisted. Popular criticisms have been expressed through direct complaints about the venality, abuse of privilege, greed, and arrogance of members of the ecclesiastical hierarchy and also through the countless stories and jokes whose theme is the misadventures and especially the sexual dalliances of ordinary priests and exalted prelates alike.

The reputed lapses of the clergy from ideal standards of behavior are significant largely because tales of clerical corruption and frailty are used (explicitly or implicitly) to challenge the notion that taking a vow or exercising ritual functions can alter or suspend human nature in a way that justifies the priests' claims to a special authority or privilege to instruct lay people, absolve them from sin, and intervene with God or the saints on their behalf. Thus, anticlericalism embodies a particular strategy of social, moral, and spiritual leveling, and the principal practical manifestation of this leveling strategy has ordinarily been the refusal of the great majority of rural Andalusian men and many women to comply with orthodox religious practices, especially those practices which most smack of submission and subordination to priests, such as confession and communion. Such ritual forms of compliance with religious authority are resisted because they set cultural limits to personal autonomy and make it nearly impossible for most lay people to regard or approach priests as moral equals.[16]

Yet in spite of the fact that traditional anticlericalism has egalitarian sentiments at its core, it has at least partly served as a vehicle of hegemonic domination rather than as a mode of resistance to it. This is because the egalitarian sentiments have been diluted by preoccupations with male prestige, honor, and patriarchal authority, which reinforce the notion of male dominance and divert attention from the role played by the church and priests in preserving the general pattern of class domination. This aspect of anticlericalism is particularly evident in the countless tales and jokes focusing on the supposed sexual conspiracies that flourish between lustful and wily priests and wanton women. The socioerotic tensions evident in this cultural subgenre are readily apparent in the comment of one man who explained his refusal to receive the sacraments by saying, "The priest gives the bread and wine with the same hands he uses to embrace other men's women." The association of communion and cuckoldry and other analogous representations indicate that traditional anticlericalism often represents a two-edged sword whose main functions are to undercut the moral distinction of priests from laymen and to defend men's prerogatives to control the actions of their wives and daughters in the course of everyday life. By creating doubts about both priests' and women's capacities to achieve a higher state of spiritual and moral purity through the sacrifice and control of bodily desires, traditional anticlericalism reaffirms the secular, agonistic ethos of honor at the core of traditional representations of masculine identity and thereby creates an apolitical, generalized sense of solidarity among laymen. However, it does so at the cost of deflecting attention from other patterns of domination and the differences in power, wealth, and prestige that shape class relations among laymen and women alike.[17]

The emergence of revolutionary anticlericalism in Aracena necessarily entailed a displacement and reinterpretation of this protopolitical anticlerical tradition. The process of cultural transformation occurred as a result of the convergence and long-term interaction of a number of events and processes such as the desertion of the working class by the clergy, the decrease in the number of clergy, the conservative policies of the church hierarchy, the ideology of mutualism, and the connection perceived between the supposed greed and hypocrisy of the gentry and their attachment to the forms of orthodox religious practice, all of which have been discussed in earlier sections and chapters. However, the final phase of this transformation began with the direct politicization of religion during the years of the Second Republic, when working-class militants began to regularly preach against the evils of religion.

Especially in the hamlets, the militants of the Socialist *casas del pueblo* actively spoke out against the church, promoted secular practices such as civil marriage and burial, and criticized popular religious customs. As early as 1932, only eight men and fifty women among the roughly two thousand parishioners of the hamlets complied with the Easter duty, and regular attendance at mass was limited to a handful of elderly women. In addition, many working-class people were no longer bothering to have their marriages sanctified or their children baptized, and the proportion of hamlet dwellers who refused or neglected the last sacraments ranged between 50 and 90 percent (Ordóñez Márquez 1968). Moreover, the constant diatribes of committed radicals against popular religious traditions led to a sharp decline in the memberships of lay religious brotherhoods, and as a result of the disruptions and counterdemonstrations staged by the most committed anticlericals, many processions in honor of local patron saints on days of fiestas were suspended during the 1930s. Thus, among the considerable number of working-class people who remained devoted to Christ, the Virgin, and the saints if not to the church, relations with the divine necessarily became an increasingly private matter. In light of these circumstances, a concerned Catholic declared that "the Christian life is almost dead" among the working class of the sierra (quoted in Ordóñez Márquez 1968:179).

The decline of public ritual observances and the rise in systematic hostility that working-class leaders demonstrated against not only orthodox but also popular religious culture mark the emergence of revolutionary anticlericalism as a counterhegemonic force in Aracena and a critical point of rupture in the cultural history of the town. Nevertheless, the emergence of revolutionary anticlericalism was influenced to a greater degree by some of the cultural tendencies intimately related to traditional anticlericalism than it was by modern, secular notions of disbelief in the supernatural. In particular, the significance of burning popular images of the saints must be understood in light of what it meant to be irreligious in traditional culture.

While traditional anticlericalism by no means necessarily entailed a lack of faith in God or the saints and indeed tended to strengthen certain aspects of popular religion by stressing their popular as opposed to priestly character, anticlerical attitudes have nonetheless always been closely linked to irreligious ones. The principal forms of irreligious expression in traditional culture involve blasphemous statements and curses such as the following: "Man, I tell you that there is not a day that goes by that I don't shit in the milk of *la puta madre* [the whore mother, meaning here the Virgin Mary] for this lack of rain that is ruining me." In such curses, a verbal defilement of spiritual purity takes the form of a direct insult delivered in response to an evident lack of divine patronage, protection, and favors. Though such remarks are frequently spontaneous outbursts uttered because of some immediate frustration and are often made quite casually, their effect (and often enough their intent) is to level the moral difference between the divine and human, to overturn at least provisionally the notion of a spiritual-corporal hierarchy, and to convert a perception of religious estrangement into a defiant assertion of personal autonomy. Thus, while traditional anticlericalism reflects hostility and resentment concerning priest-mediated relationships between the human and the divine, irreligious blasphemy extends the logic of anticlericalism to the domain of unmediated spiritual relationships as well, and like traditional anticlericalism, it represents an effort to restore or reassert personal or human honor by rejecting a religious subordination that appears to be without moral justification or practical benefits.[18]

Blasphemous, irreligious curses involving intensely personalized, direct accusations lodged against the divine were far more central to revolutionary anticlericalism as a mode of thought and feeling than coldhearted refusals to assent to sacred doctrines for intellectual or po-

litical reasons. Among the handful of vehement older anticlerical people who still live in Aracena, hatred of priests and the church is
accompanied by a conviction that all religious practices and devotions
are pointless and futile. When these people are asked to explain why
the churches and the images of popular devotion were destroyed, the
responses that seem most deeply felt are those which express a sense of
religious alienation and evoke a painful feeling of the absence of divine
love and mercy strongly reminiscent of the curses and blasphemies that
punctuate ordinary male working-class speech: "You don't understand
why the images of the Virgin were burned? . . . I will tell you. Because
the Virgin was a shameless whore and God had no sense of justice. . . .
A mother who sees her children go hungry and turns away is a
whore. . . . What a little mother she is. . . . Tell me, has she ever answered [your prayers]? Does she speak to you? Has she helped you?
No? Well, now you understand [why the images were burned]. It's all
lies. Those images were lies and lies have to be destroyed for the truth
to live."

The rhetoric of this explanation of revolutionary anticlericalism
resonates with both the gender-biased and blasphemous elements in
protopolitical anticlericalism, yet its sense is different not only because
of the notion of disbelief implied by the contrast between "lies" and
"truth" but also because of a difference in affective tone that distin-
guishes this diatribe from ordinary anticlerical and blasphemous tales,
jokes, and curses. The impassioned and bitter irony of the man's remarks do not echo the disdainful and sardonic mockery of traditional
anticlericalism but are virtually identical in feeling and forcefulness to
the expressions of moral outrage that were at the heart of working-
class ideological representations of the gentry as false and hypocritical
patrons. This convergence of the anticlerical, the irreligious, and the
hypermoralistic, ideological elements of working-class culture into a
single current of cultural resistance linking the specific evils of the reg-
nant social order of class domination to traditional religious culture
was characteristic of revolutionary anticlericalism. For this reason, the
most striking anticlerical statements of working-class radicals transform and reinterpret the significance of core religious images such as
that of the figure of Christ in ways that suggest that the indifference
and failures of the divine are of the same moral order as the venality,
pride, and hypocrisy of the gentry and their priestly allies.

This critical aspect of revolutionary anticlericalism is exemplified
by the ironic rejoinder that one older radical offered to a passage from
a catechism favored by Aracena's elite in the years before the Civil War.
The passage declared, "The *patrón* will treat his workers like sons of
God, and the workers will serve the *patrón* as if they served God" (*El*

Distrito, 15 Jan. 1913). To this injunction, the man responded, "Yes, clearly we were like sons of God to them; they saw us dying and did not save us." For this man, the figure of the crucified Christ signified the extreme of human suffering imposed upon the poor by God and humankind alike rather than an act of redemptive sacrifice.[19]

Through such blasphemous inversions of orthodox doctrine, religious discourse was used to put forth a moral indictment that was not only shaped by but also molded class antagonisms. Revolutionary anticlericalism thus stripped away the supernatural and otherworldly aspects of religious culture in order to drive home the contradiction between legitimating ideals of beneficent patronage and the perceived reality of antagonistic social relations. By combining the strains of working-class resistance to sociopolitical and cultural domination, it challenged fundamental notions of patronage (whether human or divine), insisted on the unacceptability of continuing human suffering, and reasserted the integrity, honor, and moral claims to power that notions of spiritual hierarchy, authority, and orthodoxy had served to deny the poor. To the extent that revolutionary anticlericalism transformed religion into an agonistic affair of honor in order to undermine the notions of patronage and hierarchy, it thereby asserted the cultural primacy of the practical, egalitarian morality of personal autonomy and communal obligations that informed day-to-day life among the working class over the "higher" values of "order, decency, and religion" of the gentry and their allies. In contrast to traditional forms of anticlericalism, which tended to identify the immutable frailties of human nature as the source of social evil and to focus on the uncontrolled lusts and desires of the clergy, revolutionary anticlericalism tended to view virtually all aspects of religious culture as a means to further the domination and exploitation of the poor.

From this perspective, the iconoclastic act of burning the images of the saints marked the momentary collapse and failure of religion as a vehicle of hegemonic domination in Aracena. The long process of political and ideological class polarization that reached a crisis point in the summer of 1936 had brought to the fore residual and radically egalitarian aspects of traditional anticlericalism that led the revolutionary leaders, youths, and poor men of the township to act as implacable enemies of a whole cultural tradition and a strongly entrenched way of life.

By 10 August 1936, it was clear that the popular forces in Aracena were likely to be defeated by the approaching Nationalist troops. In this context, the attack on religion was probably not initiated as an attempt to bring about a new age of equality, justice, and freedom but, rather, to achieve a partial but ineffaceable break with the past by destroying the physical artifacts and cultural foundations of local tradition. This destruction could not in itself accomplish a revolution, and it is highly unlikely that the revolutionaries thought that it would. But by destroying or permanently defacing "El Castillo" and other principal monuments of a hegemonic cultural formation, the revolutionaries made a declaration that the dominant order was not eternal, inevitable, or invincible, and they also created a sort of cultural vacuum that could potentially be filled with other ways of perceiving and representing social relationships. Thus, burning the churches and religious images represented an exemplary revolutionary act of rupture whose ultimate motivation appears to have been to recast local history not as an epic chronicle of heroic acts of charity and spiritual guidance that divine and human patrons bestowed on humble countrymen but as a dramatic story of the continuing struggle of the rural poor to seize control of their own lives. In the long run, what the anticlericals hoped to achieve was a *reparto* of meanings that would outlast the temporary and doomed redistribution of land and seizure of political power by the popular forces of the town and sierra.

Yet because many working-class men and women had deep investments in traditional notions of personal and communal identity that were associated with the images of patron saints, Christ, and the Virgin, they naturally associated these images primarily with the popular culture of the people rather than with the orthodox dogmas and ideology of the church as an institution. It is not surprising, then, that many people sympathetic to the left would be shocked and dismayed by the burning of the images and would disagree with the revolutionaries concerning what was at stake. Given this fact, the militants would have been aware that burning the images would alienate some of the people whose support they sought while it would galvanize the support of others. In light of this, the extremity and violence of the anticlericals' actions appear to have been less the result of being swept away by the enthusiasms and anxieties of the moment than they were the consequence of a practical sense of the nature and strength of the forces arrayed against them.[20]

The strength of these forces soon became evident to everyone in the town. A few days after the church burnings, the revolutionary militia fought a short but fierce battle with a column of Nationalist troops and irregulars outside the nearby *pueblo* of Higuera de la Sierra. The untrained workers were no match for regular troops and were quickly routed. Realizing the futility of engaging in open battle with the Nationalists, the miners and local radicals in Aracena decided to flee. Some merely retreated into the countryside, where they mistakenly thought that after a period in hiding they would be able to return to their homes. Others fled north and west toward Extremadura and the Portuguese border. Thus, when the Nationalist column arrived in Aracena on 18 August, there was no organized resistance, and several contingents of cavalry, infantry, artillery, and irregulars were quickly billeted throughout the town. A few paces away from the recently deserted and wrecked headquarters of the revolutionaries in the church of El Carmen, the Nationalists established a command post in the elite Casino de Arias Montano.

After the capture of Aracena, the military commander of the district quickly named a new municipal administration headed by an *alcalde* who had held the same position before the beginning of the Second Republic. The *alcalde* was assisted (some say controlled) by two or three civil service officials, including a former secretary of the *ayuntamiento* who had been dismissed by the town councilors of the Popular Front. These officials as well as a handful of large landowners from Aracena and surrounding towns soon developed a reputation for being "extremely active in hunting Reds." As a result, the town was not spared the acts of political reprisal that were colored by personal vengeance and occurred throughout the Nationalist zones of Andalusia during the first months of the Civil War.

In late August and throughout September, squads of troops and irregulars scoured the sierra in search of leftists. Those discovered in hiding were either summarily shot or turned over to officers in town for interrogation. At night in Aracena, soldiers went from house to house, taking suspects into custody. Most of these people faced hours of questioning and beatings; a few met death by firing squads. During the day, soldiers paraded the wives of known leftists through town. On the way to interrogation, the women were sometimes forced to drink large quantities of castor oil, many had their heads shaved, and all of them were subjected to one form or another of public humiliation. Estimates of the number of those executed in the first months of Nationalist rule range from seventy to two hundred men.[21] Most of the killings occurred in a series of shootings in September, but there were still a few executions as late as the spring of 1937. Virtually all of the prominent revolutionaries who failed to escape the region were shot. Several of the more moderate members of the town councils of the Republican period were jailed, released, and jailed again; a few were subsequently sent to prisons and camps where they either were shot or died of illnesses.

Well into 1938, the military pressured town officials for information that would help them in their systematic reprisals against the working class. However, by this time, even the rabidly "anti-Red" town council was growing weary of the violence against fellow townspeople, and to their credit the council began to resist requests for documents that would reveal the names of adherents of the Second Republic. At one point, council members were compelled by the military commander to swear that they were unable to recall additional names of Popular Front supporters. An uneasy calm gradually returned, however. Aracena was far from the front lines, and most men of military age (regardless of their political sympathies) were soon in Nationalist uniforms and on their way to distant parts of Spain.

At the same time that the Nationalist forces were vigorously pursuing a policy of repression and vengeance against the defeated Republicans, revolutionaries, and anticlericals, efforts were made to reimpose religion on the oppressed populace. One of the first official acts of the military commander of the district had been to order impressed crews of working-class women and men to clean the desecrated churches. A short while later, the Catholics of Aracena enthusiastically spread the news that the bishop of Salamanca and other prelates had glorified the Nationalist uprising as a "religious crusade" (Sánchez 1987:91). To further demonstrate the resurrection of the faith militant, in early 1937 local authorities sponsored a grand procession of more than a thousand people who marched, singing Falangist songs, to the church of "El Castillo," where they listened to a series of sermons delivered by prominent visiting churchmen in support of the Nationalist cause. Almost immediately afterward, the town's parish priest held a ceremony that named La Virgen del Mayor Dolor the godmother and protectress of the "combatants for the authentic Spain led by Generalísimo Franco" (ACM, 3 Feb. 1937).

Throughout the remainder of the war, masses were held and prayers said almost daily for the victory of the anti-Republican forces. The repressive peace of the early postwar period brought an increase in politically motivated religious activity. Veterans of the Nationalist army formed La Cofradía de la Victoria to further seal the connection of faith and patriotism. A committee for the restoration of the local churches and images had been established by the gentry in 1939, and a state donation of 150,000 pesetas allowed reconstruction to begin in earnest in 1940. Despite the difficult economic conditions of the period, fund-raising campaigns throughout the 1940s and early 1950s permitted considerable strides to be made in rebuilding the churches and in obtaining new images of the saints. These local projects were a small part of the national effort to construct a neotraditionalist "organic," hierarchical, authoritarian, Catholic, and monarchical state apparatus inspired by the example of the imperial and spiritual glories of the Ancient Regime.

In considerable measure, this attempt to impose an atavistic vision of the nation and Spanish culture represented a direct response to the challenges to traditional forms of cultural authority by the revolutionary forces of the 1930s. From this perspective, it would appear that burning the churches and related actions were instrumental in eventually bringing full circle the processes of hegemonic displacement that had originated in the liberal revolutions of the nineteenth century, since it was these church burnings that drove the victors in the Civil War to attempt to transform religion and other aspects of traditional culture into the reactionary counterweight of classic liberalism rather than the conservative consort of it. However, this attempt was bound to fail in the long run because no parallel exertions were made to eliminate exploitation of the rural working class and alter the basic conditions that had led to the revolutionary upheavals. Indeed, the main effect of grafting a supposedly "unified and integral" corporate institutional apparatus onto the socioeconomic structure of agrarian class society was to convince people who experienced oppression, deprivation, and exploitation in their daily lives that the gap between ideological representations and social reality was widening. Thus, for many of the working-class people who had beheld the events of 1936 in Aracena, the ruins of "El Castillo" and other churches bore silent witness that despite all the official speeches and rhetoric about restoring the glories of the long-dead past, the project of reconstructing the Ancient Regime would never amount to much more than an attempt to build illusory castles in the air.

Pastoral epic: a view of the sierra from the church of "El Castillo."

Photographs from the late nineteenth and early twentieth centuries were donated for an exposition sponsored by La Hermandad de la Borriquita in Aracena and are included courtesy of the hermandad. Other photographs were taken by the author.

Central Aracena, with its two major churches, the church of "El Castillo" at the top of the hill, flanked by the castle walls, and the parish church of Santa María de la Asunción, below and to the left.

The church of "El Castillo."

The statue of a twentieth-century patron of Aracena, located on the *monte* of "El Castillo."

The portal of El Convento de Jesús, María, y José, the Dominican convent founded in the late seventeenth century by Madre María de la Santísima Trinidad and now abandoned.

The statue of Julian Romero de la Osa, a nineteenth-century patron of Aracena, standing in La Plaza Mayor, with El Casino de Arias Montano in the background.

The central plaza, La Plaza Mayor, of Aracena.

The central plaza of Carboneras, a small hamlet of Aracena.

Leading members of Aracena's gentry, circa 1920. Photo courtesy of La Hermandad de la Borriquita.

La Peña, a revered site located in the township of Alájar and honoring Arias Montano, a patron of Aracena and nearby towns, and La Reina de los Angeles, the Queen of the Angels.

Visitors to La Peña on "El Día de la Sierra" (Sierra Day) in 1923. Photo courtesy of La Hermandad de la Borriquita.

The *buñuelda*, circa 1920, an event held in the bullring during Aracena's annual fair and sponsored by a local association to help young people of the upper class find suitable marriage partners. Photo courtesy of La Hermandad de la Borriquita.

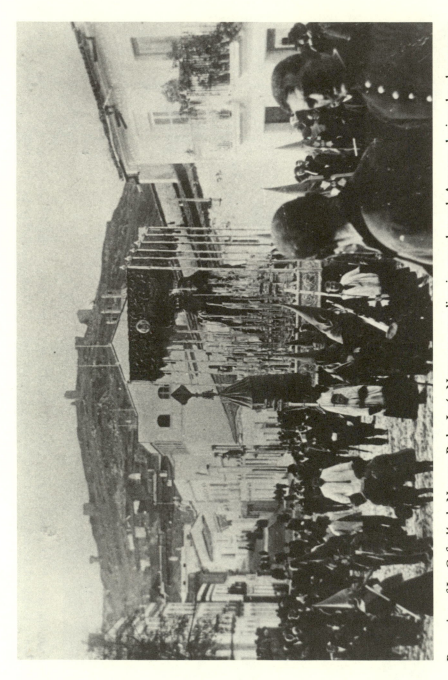

Procession of La Cofradía de Nuestro Padre Jesús Nazareno wending its way through Aracena during the observances of Holy Week in the late nineteenth century. Photo courtesy of La Hermandad de la Borriquita.

Procession of La Cofradía de la Vera Cruz descending from "El Castillo" during Holy Week in 1982.

La Virgen del Mayor Dolor, patron saint of Aracena, carried through town by members of La Cofradía de la Vera Cruz during Holy Week in 1982.

The children's *pasos*, or floats, which were paraded through Aracena a few days after Holy Week in 1982.

The main commercial street of Aracena, 1982.

Friends gathering during the *paseo,* or stroll, 1982.

An Andalusian *caballero* singing to a tourist during the *romería,* or pilgrimage, to La Peña in 1980.

A view from "El Castillo," with central Aracena in the foreground and a new housing project in the background, 1990.

Tradition and modernity in Aracena: the ancient chapel of San Pedro and a sculpture from the new open-air museum of contemporary art, 1990.

A view of the sierra from "El Castillo."

Pastoral epic: La Virgen del Mayor Dolor and the church of "El Castillo," circa 1900. Photo courtesy of La Hermandad de la Borriquita.

PART 3

TRADITION LIBERALIZED: RE-FORMATIONS
OF CLASS SOCIETY

7

Mass Culture and Local Custom

It is not a *pueblo* of cultivators, because now the people do not
have to work the earth. Nor is it the new Spain, because industries do not exist. How does the community survive? Why
by being the seat of a judicial and electoral district; by the one
or two hundred heads of livestock; . . . by the salaries of police-
men and the meritorious Guardia Civil; by the litigious entan-
glements of the villagers; by the salaries of public employees
with open houses; and when these and other things are not
enough, by delightful memories, by sweet hopes, or by miracles—like the ordinary Spaniard.
　　　　　　　—José Nogales
　　　　　　　El último patriota

Tradition and Contemporary Rural Society

WHEN I FIRST went to Aracena in the summer of 1980, I
thought I had stepped into the pages of Julian Pitt-Rivers'
classic ethnography of an Andalusian community in the late
1940s, *The People of the Sierra*. To show their hospitality, local men
bought me drinks in the tavern, just as the Alcareños had done for
Pitt-Rivers. Townspeople were also anything but reticent in offering
highly sententious characterizations of their community that bespoke
what Pitt-Rivers (1961) called the "moral unity of the *pueblo*" and the
virtues of the *patria chica* ("the little country," homeland, native region). Again and again during this initial three-month visit, I heard
statements that echoed this theme: "We are all equal here." "We all
live together here." "Everyone here is like a great family." "Here one
finds the best people of Spain and the authentic life and customs of
Andalusia." At the same time, I found that people were not unwilling
to tell tales on their neighbors and that many of their stories reflected
long-running class resentments. For example, pointing to a forlorn

group of men who gathered every day in a bar, one woman whispered that they were unrepentant Francoists who were plotting to undermine the new democratic order that had emerged in Spain after the death of the dictator in 1975. The apparently backward-looking character of exaggerated accusations such as this and the equally exaggerated affirmations of the town's unity led me to believe that I had chosen an extraordinarily traditional and class-divided community in which to live.

But when I returned in 1981 to undertake eighteen more months of fieldwork, my impressions shifted dramatically. After a few months in the town, what struck me most was the familiarity of the local way of life. I had already lost the sense that the people I was living among were a peasant version of the exotic "others" of such importance to classic anthropology. After all, the clothes the townspeople wore, the food they ate, the television they watched, the sports they followed, the vacations they planned, the hopes they expressed, and the things they complained about appeared to vary only slightly from those of my friends and family in the United States. From this perspective, the traditional affirmations of the fundamental "sociocentric" values of local patriotism that I still heard seemed more quaint than definitive, and most of the differences I experienced in townspeople's ways of talking and acting seemed to me quite trivial in comparison with what I more or less shared with them. Indeed, I continue to feel that most of my basic convictions and values are far closer to those of many people in Aracena than they are, say, to those of my local congressman.

And, of course, Spain in the 1980s was not really much like what it had been in the late 1940s and early 1950s, when Pitt-Rivers researched and wrote his ethnography (see Serrán Pagán 1980). Nor was Aracena like the town he described then. As virtually every book about Spain in the postwar period indicates, there were drastic changes throughout the country. In the years after 1955, Spanish society became increasingly urbanized, industrialized, and modernized; and by the 1970s, the country was no longer "backward" and predominantly agrarian. Indeed, as sociological analyses indicate, by most criteria the general structure and dynamics of Spanish society had become similar to those of the most highly developed countries in western Europe.[1] In other words, corporate capitalism, the bureaucratic welfare state, and (after 1975) liberal, pluralistic democratic principles had triumphed.

Far from being insulated from these developments, Aracena underwent a transformation that was at least as profound and far-reaching as the liberal revolutions of the nineteenth century. Within a single generation, the archaic agrarian economy of the sierra collapsed; a service-oriented commerce developed in the town; local politics gradually became more populist in tone and then became democratic in form; old inequalities in wealth and power were rapidly reduced or mitigated; and ideological cleavages along class lines though not entirely obliterated became less a source of social conflict than in the past. In the course of these sweeping changes, local culture was also profoundly transformed as local people adopted or sought to emulate the most modern and urbane values, attitudes, and life-styles.

Yet I was wrong about the relative insignificance of traditional culture in contemporary Aracena. Rather than being a residual set of customs and idioms that had less and less relevance to the present, as I had once thought, the sense of tradition among townspeople was in fact vital to their sense of personal and collective identity. And rather than fading away, what counted as tradition was being revised and recreated in accordance with dominant and emergent contemporary interests, pressures, and constraints. Among other things, this means that the "sociocentric" affirmations of the moral unity of the *pueblo* that I heard when I came to Aracena have a new and different significance. Instead of manifesting defiance and resistance to class and state domination, as they did during the Civil War period, such affirmations these days primarily express practical compliance with and accommodation to the status quo.

In the remainder of this chapter, I describe the interaction of the political, socioeconomic, and cultural forces governing the transformation of Aracena in the postwar period in order to show how the contemporary configuration of cultural tradition in the town enables rural people to distinguish themselves and their community from other sectors of Spanish society in a way that inclines them to accept a marginal and subordinate position within this society.

Containing Multitudes: From Epic Atavism to Authoritarian Populism

The rule of the revolutionary forces in Aracena had lasted about a month, from shortly after the military uprising of 18 July until 18 August 1936. The rule of the local supporters of Francisco Franco endured almost forty years. During this period, the intensity of political reaction and repression varied and the regime was reorganized several times, but its authoritarian character was never radically altered.[2] The final Nationalist victory in 1939 brought with it an end of more or less direct military rule of Aracena, but the oppressive sociopolitical situation persisted long after the withdrawal of the army from the region. Inquiries into the "moral and political character" of persons continually passed between judicial authorities and the town council. There was constant harassment of poor people, and many were arrested on minor charges. Proprietors denied work to those they felt to be of "bad character and opinions." Those whose political status was secure used their influence to persecute their enemies and pay off personal grudges. The reprisals sometimes reached an absurd level of petty vindictiveness. For example, in 1940 when a landowner complained that his fences had been damaged in 1936 in the course of a road-building project sponsored by the Popular Front council, the new municipal authorities ordered the surviving workers who had been employed on the project to pay the costs of a new fence out of their own pockets or else go to jail (ACM, 22 May 1940).

In addition to political oppression, almost everyone suffered from the dire economic conditions of the 1940s. The Civil War had disrupted agriculture in the sierra and by one estimate had reduced the number of livestock in the region by more than two-thirds. As a result of the war's costs and the combined effects of droughts, bad harvests, inflation, depressed wages, and the international isolation of Spain as the only surviving "fascist" power after 1945, the decade of the 1940s is remembered by working-class people as *el tiempo de hambre* (the time of hunger), when "people thought of nothing but their stomachs" and food shortages were as chronic as the illnesses that attended malnourishment. As a result of discrimination, the situation of the wives and families of dead, imprisoned, or exiled workers was especially desperate, and some of these people say they would have starved if their neighbors had not been able to give them food from time to time. But even the town's conservative middle classes were in bad straits because they could ill afford to pay the high prices on the black market.

As noted in Chapter 6, the cultural hallmark of the reactionary period of the 1940s and early 1950s in Aracena was the reimposition of religion as a dominant ideological force. During this period, the church had a voice in all matters of public concern, and the parish priest was always highly successful in winning concessions and donations of public funds from the town council for religious and educational projects of all sorts. Indeed, the parish priest became one of the more important agents of local government and administration in the new regime and held considerable power over the populace by means of such devices as his capacity to grant or withhold permission to marry and to provide good or bad character references for persons seeking employment. However, the bureaucratic role of clergy members was secondary to their ideological functions, and strenuous efforts were made to "re-Christianize the masses" and indoctrinate them in the principles of "National Catholicism" (see Lannon 1982; Tusell

1984). These efforts were strongly backed by secular officials and lay organizations, and in Aracena they met with widespread if somewhat superficial success owing to the political and economic pressures that could be exerted on the recalcitrant. Since few people were willing to criticize the church publicly and thereby endanger the livelihoods of their families or risk harassment by the authorities, Aracena appeared once again to have become an exceptionally pious and orthodox town by 1950.

The reimposition of religion was, of course, a reflection of much broader political and ideological processes. During the 1940s and early 1950s, the Catholic church was established (along with the army and the political movement of the Falange) as one of the key pillars of the new institutional order in Spain and was more influential and intimately linked to the state than at any time since the fall of the Ancient Regime. In Aracena, as elsewhere in rural Spain, the organs of the new "corporate state" consisted of the triumphalist church, a branch of the "Council of the National Movement" (i.e., the Falange), a section of El Sindicato Agrícola (a "vertical" union of proprietors and workers that handled labor relations), and a number of other entities or representatives of "social corporations" such as a teachers' commission and the "heads of families" of the township. Each of these bodies— along with the appointed civil governor of the province, who chose the *alcalde* (mayor) of the town—had a voice or a vote in selecting the municipal council. The control of these neocorporate groups by members of the local or regional elite ensured that only those with the "correct" political opinions were permitted to participate in public life.

Although the secular, hypernationalistic, and populist rhetoric of the Falange had a strong influence on those who strived to develop an ideological legitimation of the regime, the theory of the "organic state" owed more to Catholic social thought than to any other source after the decline in the fortunes of the fascist powers in 1942. In particular, the key concept of an "integral" state in which each hierarchical body was designed to incorporate members of all classes and thereby "harmonize" the social order constituted a reconfiguration of the ideals of "mutualism" and Acción Católica. But in contrast to earlier forms of Catholic social thought, whose adherents had attempted to come to grips with modern class society by partly embracing liberal political and free market values, the "integralist" ideology of the post– Civil War period involved a radical rejection of classic liberalism. For the ideologues of authoritarianism, the true model of the organic state was to be found in the Catholic monarchy of the Counter-Reformation. Advocating the values of tradition, order, and hierarchy, Franco himself declared that "the nineteenth century, which we would have liked to eliminate from our history, is the negation of the Spanish spirit" (quoted in Carr and Fusi 1981:109).

The attempt to obliterate Spanish liberalism and resurrect an archaic vision of Spain led defenders of the regime to represent the tragedy of the Civil War as an epic struggle of the spiritual forces of order, morality, and religion against the evil demons of materialism, freemasonry, egotistical license, and communism. The dissemination of such reactionary interpretations of Spanish history by means of the organs of the integralist state encouraged local supporters of the dictatorship to promote "traditional" cultural forms and customs. Thus, in the years from 1940 to 1960 in Aracena, there was a revival both of popular religious celebrations and of *cofradías* and other lay religious associations, and no patriotic holiday went without elaborate celebration. Homage to a state-sponsored church and dedication to the sacred honor of the *patria*, together with the formation of hierarchical and nominally paternalist corporations based on notions of elite patronage, were viewed as devices for preserving the "Spanish spirit" and transforming the nation into a great "fortress" defending the religious values of Western civilization against modern heresies. The Concordant of 1953 between the Franco regime and Rome appeared to put the seal of papal approval on the participation and integration of the Spanish church into this ideological state apparatus and represented one of the most important propaganda victories of the early period of the dictatorship.

Yet the atavistic vision of Spain as a fortress protected from the evils of modernity was never compelling to more than a limited sector of the population. In Aracena, most townspeople regarded what came to be known as National Catholicism as an ideological sleight-of-hand trick and spoke of Spain as the "spiritual reservoir of Europe" only with irony. Recognizing that the regime, despite all of its talk of "organic unity" and "social harmony," had in fact merely facilitated the rule of the local elite and formalized the subordinate position of the poor and disempowered, they viewed the professed ideal of cooperation between the classes as a transparent effort to contain the masses. Moreover, despite the repressive tactics of the armed guardians of the dictatorship, working-class people managed to express their resentment of continuing exploitation and domination by various indirect means. For example, townspeople tell the story of a fervently Catholic man who had been one of the most active "Red-hunters" in 1936 and had subsequently been ostracized as a result of his actions. As the story goes, this man sank deeper and deeper into depression and alcoholism and finally hung himself in 1948 or 1949. Working-class people interpreted his suicide in terms of the slow but sure operations of conscience, guilt, and retributive justice, and they responded to news of the decision that the "Red-hunter" would be buried in hallowed ground by gathering outside his house to insult his corpse and jeer the judgment of the local overseers of "order, decency, and religion."[3]

Broader socioeconomic forces were also at work and began to undermine the local foundations and raison d'être of the integralist system almost as soon as it had been established. By the early 1950s, it seemed as if the old agrarian system was going to revive. Cork and pork production was slowly approaching prewar levels; fifteen olive and wine presses were back in operation; and nearly 80 percent of the working population was directly engaged in agriculture, although the daily wage of *jornaleros* (agrarian day laborers) was being held at the woefully inadequate rate of fifteen pesetas a day by local political authorities.

This partial economic revival was short-lived, however. In Aracena, as throughout Spain, agrarian producers began to feel the squeeze of increasing costs and low returns by the mid-1950s. In many areas of the country, landowners managed to survive and eventually to thrive with the help of government loans and other programs that enabled them to mechanize their operations and employ new fertilizers.[4] But in the sierra, where the land was of poor quality and tree crops were grown, modern agricultural techniques and equipment were of little value in increasing production or cutting labor requirements.[5] As a result, when labor costs rose in the mid-1950s owing partly to legislation that set the basic wage rate for agriculture at little more than half the industrial rate, local landowners were trapped. Stagnant prices for cork and pork in combination with the higher cost of labor left them with two grim alternatives. Either they could reduce expenses by hiring fewer workers and letting many groves and fields go unhusbanded or else they could go into debt and hope that the situation would improve. Unfortunately, however, economic conditions deteriorated even further after 1960 with the emergence of two additional factors that affected local agriculture. The first factor was the growing consumer preference for the leaner meat of imported, grain-fed breeds of swine that could not be profitably raised in the sierra.[6] The second was the infestation of indigenous, acorn-fed swine with an endemic parasitic disease known as the *peste africana* (African plague), which began to cause serious losses of animals in the late 1950s.

Some local landowners attempted to adapt to the new economic circumstances by switching to other products such as beef, milk, eggs, and poultry. A few of them were successful, but this did not lead to a general revival of agricultural prosperity in the region. Instead, during the 1960s and 1970s, many of the latifundia of one hundred to three hundred hectares that had been worked by *jornaleros* for centuries were transformed into large but only marginally profitable farms worked primarily by the owner, family members, and in a few cases two or three permanent employees. These small-scale operations were sufficient to meet the limited demand for traditional products such as cork, olive oil, chestnuts, and fruits, but they had to compete with crops grown elsewhere according to modern techniques. And although regional firms continued to buy some indigenous hogs in order to produce canned sausages and the luxury *jamón serrano* (cured hams) for which the sierra is famous, local officials estimated in 1975 that the number of hogs in Aracena had declined by 80 percent in twenty years.

The handful of large estates of over three hundred hectares underwent an even more radical transformation. Large tracts of many of these estates (amounting to nearly 15 percent of the township's territory) were leased or sold to government-industrial consortiums. Employees of these enterprises uprooted cork and oak groves and planted eucalyptus trees whose wood was destined for paper mills in Huelva and Seville. Thousands of hectares more became hunting reserves, and one large tract was converted to a ranch for breeding fighting bulls. None of these ways of using the land provided much employment for local workers. By the early 1970s, much of the countryside (in appearance if not in reality) seemed to be rapidly reverting to wilderness.[7]

The collapse of the archaic mode of agrarian production in the sierra in tandem with the oppressive political conditions of the period stimulated another development that had profound consequences for life in Aracena. Beginning in the early 1950s, people began to migrate.[8] At first, the trickle of migrants consisted primarily of the workers who suffered most from the discrimination of landowners and officials because of their political sympathies (see G. Collier 1987). Soon, however, these workers were joined by many of the privileged sons and daughters of *comerciante* (merchant) and gentry families who wished to pursue careers and the pleasures of urban life in Seville and foresaw that the future of local agriculture was not bright. In the late 1950s, the trickle of migrants became a steady stream as entire working-class families moved to Seville and Barcelona in search of higher-paying and steadier jobs in factories or construction. During the 1960s, there was virtually a mass exodus from the region as 20,200 people, a figure representing one-third of the inhabitants of the *partido judicial* (judicial district) of Aracena, migrated (Moreno Alonso 1979). Over half of them settled in Catalonia; a quarter went to Seville; and most of the remainder were scattered throughout

Spain, southern France, and the industrial cities of West Germany (Fourneaux 1980).

In general, the smallest *pueblos* of the sierra and especially those with the greatest number of landless *jornaleros* witnessed the sharpest drop in population. The decline in larger towns was somewhat less dramatic. In Aracena, the number of inhabitants (about 7,000) remained more or less constant in the period from 1950 to 1980 because the departure of many native-born people was compensated for by births and by an influx of some middle-class public employees and a considerable number of people from Aracena's *aldeas* (dependent hamlets) and from smaller *pueblos* of the sierra.[9] Even so, by the early 1970s there were few families in the town that lacked close relatives in Seville or Barcelona.

The exodus of both the wealthiest and poorest segments of the population from the sierra and the collapse of local agriculture transformed the character of the authoritarian regime in Aracena. The previously overriding interests of local political authorities and large landowners in suppressing working-class dissent, maintaining public order, and controlling wages, labor, and working conditions were no longer paramount. Instead, local officials recognized and responded quickly to the challenge of finding new sources of jobs and income that would help compensate for the agrarian decline and offer townspeople alternative ways of earning a living.

As early as 1960, members of the town council proclaimed that the future of the community lay in developing the service sector of the economy rather than agriculture. Three years later, the *alcalde* of Aracena publicly invited "all sectors and classes" of local society to join him in his efforts to build a "more modern" town and declared that "on the three pillars of tourism, housing, and cultural services we will raise a new Aracena that will escape the morass and inactivities of past years" (DPS 1963). This speech signaled a shift in the governing strategies of local officialdom and announced a new era of authoritarian populism that was inspired by and dependent on both the industrial "takeoff" of the national economy and the development of the redistributive mechanisms of an embryonic welfare state in the early 1960s. Strongly influenced and aided by the progressive, "technocratic" power bloc within the Franco regime (see Chapter 9), local officials henceforth devoted relatively little attention to instilling townspeople with a sense of respect for order and hierarchy and chose instead to expend their energy on efforts to convince their neighbors that a new day of prosperity, if not political freedom, had dawned. Their efforts were thus both motivated by local conditions and guided by the newly emergent strategy of the Franco regime, which sought to divert attention from political discontents by fomenting economic development.[10]

The immediate upshot of this shift in political and ideological tendency in Aracena was an extended campaign of public relations and civic boosterism that generated countless ideas for the beautification and modernization of the community. A partial list of the proposals that poured from the town hall and other local agencies during the period suggests the flurry of activity involved in the effort to revitalize the town. Plans called for the completion of a *gran vía* for shops and promenades, the construction of a new municipal garden, increased support for an olive oil cooperative, the construction of publicly and privately financed apartment units, the enlargement of the municipal market, the establishment of an association for the promotion of the sierra, the conversion of the empty tuberculosis sanatorium into a national tourist inn, the celebration of a fiesta of sierran ham, the opening of a regional health center, the planting of trees along the main streets of town, and the construction of a municipal swimming pool and other sports facilities. There was even a publicly avowed and fairly determined effort on the part of local officials to improve the conditions of life in the much-neglected outlying hamlets of the township. Funds were allocated to improve the water supplies of the *aldeas* and thereby prevent outbreaks of typhoid fever; electricity lines were extended to the principal hamlets (a half-century after they were installed in Aracena proper); primary schools were built; and telephone services were begun.

Even so, the new populist spirit of progress and reconciliation was not without limits and drawbacks. Although the projects undertaken to "improve social conditions" were attractive to most members of the community, the benefits derived from them were unevenly distributed. While working-class people gained from the employment the projects generated and from the general improvements made in the local "ambience" and infrastructure, well-connected members of the old gentry and *comerciante* families and a few other enterprising individuals owned most of the properties that were eventually developed and also ran the construction firms that were awarded the largest contracts. Moreover, the strategy of tapping the largess of the state in order to compensate for the loss of a strong productive base made it necessary for town officials to engage in an intense and somewhat corrupt backroom politics of favoritism, brokerage, and patronage with regional and national bureaucrats, which did nothing to foster a sense of confidence in the fairness and disinterest of politicians among most townspeople (see Chapter 9).

Despite these circumstances, the leaders of the community were largely successful in making a new Aracena based on "tourism, housing, and cultural services" because they initiated their efforts just at the time when state bureaucracies were rapidly expanding and assuming greater control over such matters as education, health care, retirement pensions, and employment. As the head of a *partido judicial,* Aracena benefited greatly from an influx of civil servants who brought new services, government funds, public sector jobs, and their own salaries to town in the period from 1950 to 1982.

In addition to the expansion of the courts, notary offices, and registry of property of the *partido judicial,* Aracena gained branches of many provincial and national bureaucratic agencies, including El Instituto Nacional de Asistencia Social (social security), El Instituto Nacional de Empleo (employment), El Servicio de Extensión Agraria (agriculture), and El Instituto Geológico y Minero (geology and minerals). Most important, El Instituto Nacional de Bachillerato Mixto, a coeducational high school, was founded. The presence of the "Instituto," along with seven state and church schools for children under the age of fourteen, made the town into a regional educational center of considerable importance.

The steady flow of money into the local economy from the public sector facilitated the gradual expansion of private commerce. By 1980, there were over 170 commercial enterprises in the town—about one business for every 40 inhabitants—and 263 people identified themselves as *empresarios* (businesspeople, building contractors, commercial agents, or salespeople). As is typical of businesses in "modernized" but "underdeveloped" and marginal zones of advanced industrial economies, most of these enterprises were of extremely small scale. There was, for example, a seemingly endless series of tiny bars, grocery stores, and fruit and vegetable stands on every corner and more still in the covered area of the municipal market. But there were also nearly fifty retail and wholesale businesses of larger size, including banks, savings and loans, hotels, restaurants, and car dealers. Although the range of goods and services was not broad in any particular category, there was some selection of virtually every commodity that could be found in cities such as Seville or Madrid, including "high-technology" items such as video recorders, photocopiers, and electronic games. While most businesses would stand little chance of surviving if state institutions and agencies were not present, the town continues to serve as a marketing center for the many smaller *pueblos* of the eastern sierra, few of which have more than two or three small stores.

In addition, the rise of the town's service economy has made it a more attractive place for tourists, as the *alcalde* predicted.[11] Thousands of people, mostly Spaniards, visit Las Grutas de las Maravillas each year. Although most visitors arrive in busloads, stay only a few hours, and do not ordinarily wander far from the entrance to the caverns, they patronize a number of nearby shops, bars, and restaurants that provide a means of livelihood for a score of families. At least as important is the annual influx of summer vacationers, some of whom remain for a month and swell the local population by a thousand or more during the period from late July to early September. In the past, summer visitors were mostly members of the Seville elite. However, such people currently prefer the more expensive and fashionable resorts of the Costa del Sol and Costa de la Luz. Fortunately, the desertion of the well-off has been more than compensated for by the great increase in the number of predominantly urban working-class and lower-middle-class visitors. Many of these people can afford no more than to rent cheap rooms in a local school, but their cumulative contribution to local businesses is significant, particularly for the many bars and restaurants that take in a large proportion of their annual income during the summer. The annual arrival of working-class vacationers is linked in a fundamental way to the economic transformation of the region. Vacationers are not merely attracted by the town's ambience, the caverns, or the sierra's natural beauties. The great majority return year after year because they were born in Aracena or surrounding *pueblos*.

The Domestication of Conflict, Resentment, and Desire

The processes of modernization involved in the expansion of the public and service sectors of Aracena's economy in tandem with other political and cultural factors led to a radical transformation of rural class society. The change in the occupational structure of the township and the more equitable distribution of jobs, income, and property were also accompanied by a change in the dynamics of class relations in the town. To gain a sense of the impact of these changes on local social life, it is necessary to look no further than the former palace of the *marqués* of Aracena, which is located in the center of town. In 1973, the heirs of the *marqués* decided to sell the palace to a local *comerciante*, who promptly turned it into an appliance and furniture store. Since this conversion, townspeople who were once excluded from the elegant salons of the *marqués* can behold frescoed cherubs trumpeting the glories of gas stoves and washing machines whenever they wish.

With the decline of agriculture, many former working-class *jornaleros* and artisans were able to find relatively secure "blue-collar" jobs as mechanics, carpenters, waiters, janitors, plumbers, truck drivers, road-workers, and so forth. Some members of the postwar generation who were fortunate enough to have a few years of education became clerks or salespeople and see themselves as belonging to a "white-collar working class." Although only a small minority of these workers earn incomes comparable to their urban counterparts, the relatively low cost of living in Aracena permits most families to own their own homes and cars and to afford occasional luxuries such as nights out on the town and fashionable clothes. Neither the blue-collar nor the white-collar workers draw any sharp lines between themselves and the poorer people who lack a steady means of support and have to scramble to get temporary menial jobs in the countryside or the town. Currently, the poorest people in town are in this position because of old age, lack of pensions, mental or physical disability, alcoholism, the death of a key wage earner, or a combination of factors such as these. Although people with steady jobs may count themselves as more fortunate, harder-working, or more deserving than members of the poorest households who often have to rely on state disbursements to survive, they do not consider themselves as belonging to a distinct social group.

Chronic unemployment, underemployment, and low wages are characteristic of working life in Aracena, as in other areas on the margins of industrial society. Most businesses, offices, and shops in the town are overstaffed, and many people have little to do. Young people of all classes find it especially difficult to find secure jobs, and older people usually rely on very modest pensions. The well-off frequently take advantage of the free time that underemployment in their primary professions or posts creates in order to engage in a variety of profitable entrepreneurial activities. Most working-class families try to devise a variety of part-time occupations that compensate for underemployment and low wages and give the family some security through diversification of money-making activities. In one rather energetic working-class household in 1981, for example, the father of the family worked as a clerk in a hardware store and augmented his meager salary by playing in the town's band; his teenage son was a part-time waiter; his daughter had a job for a few hours a week in the public library; and his wife was a dressmaker and sold milk from the family's two cows and vegetables from their *huerta* (small irrigated garden) in the country.

Most people work at such ad hoc jobs because they want to accumulate money to spend on the comforts and luxuries that the new *sociedad de consumo* (consumer society) offers them. The importance of material symbols of prosperity is most apparent in matters relating to the household. Throughout the 1960s and 1970s, local landlords whose incomes were suffering because of the agrarian crisis sold many rental properties to working-class tenants. When these tenants became homeowners, they wanted their dwellings to have all of the modern conveniences and thus invested large sums to modernize and repair old houses. Now that "everybody owns his own house," the first thing a visitor is proudly shown by the working-class homeowner is the new and lavishly appointed tile bathroom, which has come to be regarded as the manifest proof of the new-found prosperity of ordinary towns-folk. The ability to undertake such projects has had a strong impact on social attitudes in Aracena because it has encouraged people to hope that the decades of truly desperate poverty that afflicted their parents and grandparents are over.

The experience and attitudes of Mari Carmen, a member of the postwar generation, are fairly typical. Mari Carmen was born into a poor family in 1939. She left school when she was eight years old to work in the fields and try to help her family through the many days when they lacked enough to eat. At fifteen, she began to work in a local bar and restaurant and still held this job when I met her in 1981. She was single and lived with her brother, who was a bricklayer, and her aging mother. No one in the household made a good wage. Mari Carmen earned the equivalent of about $130 a month; when her brother was working full-time (which was not often), his maximum earnings were about $250 a month; and their mother received a small government pension. Yet despite the household's tight budget, the family was able to save enough in the prosperous decade of the 1960s to buy the house they had rented for years in a working-class *barrio*. The house had cost them less than $1,000, but they spent nearly $7,000 in the 1970s to remodel it and buy modern furnishings. In 1980, when they had nearly paid off their debts, they had a telephone installed and put a down payment on a new car. Referring to these things, Mari Carmen said she was *más contenta* (more content, happier) now than in the past: "Life is better now. We work hard, but we have things like other people. Before, we worked just as hard and had nothing."

Like Mari Carmen, most townspeople have experienced an improvement in their basic conditions of life and hope for continued modest gains in the future, and they insist that life is better and that social relations are more "equal" than ever before. This perception of social leveling and overall progress has gone far in reducing the class tensions that once pervaded daily life. Old antagonisms have been mitigated by the awareness that now "even the rich have to work" and cannot afford to lead lives of idleness and leisure. One poor woman, for example, made the following comparison of her own situation with that of one of the town's oldest and wealthiest *comerciante* families: "Well, they aren't so much richer than us. They all have to work like everybody else, and look how many of them there are. The father has to give jobs to his children, his brother, his nephews and nieces. You can't keep your money that way."

Reinforcing such perceptions of greater equality is the widespread idea that the old class structure of the town has all but disintegrated and that even the poorest people have some chance of growing rich. Working-class townspeople especially like to talk of two social phenomena that have clearly emerged in the last two decades: that of being a *"Don sin Din"* (i.e., a gentleman [*Don*] without money [*dinero*]) and that of being a *"Din sin Don"* (i.e., a rich man lacking the status of a gentleman). The first category includes members of the old gentry who failed to educate their children for nonagricultural careers. The second includes men of working-class background who in one way or another took advantage of the construction boom of the late 1950s and 1960s to acquire considerable holdings in local real estate. The attitudes of most townspeople toward this second group of men are mixed. On the one hand, they tend to be regarded as traitors to their class who "changed their shirts" from "red to blue" (i.e., from leftist to Falangist) in order to make the political connections necessary to satisfy their personal ambitions. On the other hand, they are grudgingly admired for their enterprise, hard work, and shrewdness.

Class tensions have also been eased by a shift in the dynamics of labor and political relations. While many townspeople believe that the distribution of property and wealth is still unjust both nationally and locally, relatively few people feel directly exploited and there is little open conflict over economic issues. The absence of any large-scale agrarian or commercial enterprises has had the effect of personalizing most economic disputes. Rather than invoking the old language of general conflicts between wealthy *patrones* (patrons) and humble *obreros* (workers), these days people tend to describe disputes over wages and working conditions in terms of particular disagreements between a *jefe* (boss) and an *empleado* (employee). In addition, even before the end of the Franco dictatorship in 1975, a more egalitarian political ethos had emerged in Aracena. Although the continuing influence of a group of "strong families" was commonly deplored, no cohesive class group such as the old agrarian gentry completely dominated local affairs. Those in charge of the municipality during the last years of authoritarian rule were usually not members of the old oligarchy, since most of the latter group had either migrated to the cities or had little interest in running local affairs. Thus, the last *alcalde* of the Franco era was an assistant manager of a bank, an amiable and unpretentious man of modest means who had considerable understanding of and sympathy for the problems and aspirations of working-class townspeople. As a result of such shifts in attitudes, the significance of class distinctions between *ricos* and *pobres* (the rich and the poor) or proprietors and workers has been considerably altered for most townspeople, and almost everyone judges the overall social ambience of the town to be amiable and "tranquil." Put another way in relation to the class conflicts and repression of the past, life in the present seems peaceful and perhaps a bit monotonous.

Nevertheless, sharp disparities in wealth, education, political influence, and status still exist in Aracena and strongly affect virtually every aspect of social relations. By reputation and probably in fact, the wealthiest people in Aracena now are a dozen or so lawyers, private physicians, and other professionals who visibly maintain a standard of living similar to that of Andalusia's urban upper-middle class. Most of these people are the offspring of old gentry families, and their professional fees are augmented by income obtained from their rural land, by rents received from apartment houses and commercial buildings that they own in town, and in some cases by the salaries they receive from state bureaucracies. Though most of these wealthy professionals are politically conservative and regard themselves as the superiors of ordinary townspeople in education, breeding, and general culture, they are not unaware that from a broader national perspective they are seen as provincials and their social position is not a particularly envied or prestigious one.

There are two other middle-class groups that are less conspicuously affluent than the professionals but equally important in the life of the town. One of these groups consists of the many small shopkeepers, bank managers, businesspeople, and members of the old *comerciante* families. These people who manage the local service economy are civic-minded and regard themselves as the true pillars of the community. The other group includes the various ranks of civil servants and teachers whose educational qualifications and bureaucratic functions differentiate them from working-class townspeople. Many in this particular group are *forasteros* (nonnative residents) who expect to live in the town for only a few years and have not fully incorporated themselves into local life. Especially the younger members of the group tend to be more socially liberal and politically progressive than the native members of the middle class.

It is these three middle-class groups—the professionals, the *comerciantes,* and the civil servants—that in various ways set the tone of social life in contemporary Aracena and play a directive role in the political, economic, and cultural affairs of the community. This is so not merely because members of the middle class possess greater resources and hence influence on the course of day-to-day events but also because the majority of working-class townspeople strive to emulate or imitate their patterns of work, consumption, and diversion. Most working-class people receive only modest *sueldos* (wages) and thus long for the financial security they associate with middle-class *carreras* (careers or qualifications for specific jobs). And they also strive to keep up with the latest sophisticated fashions, modern opinions, and convenient innovations, which middle-class people are almost always the first to adopt in the town.

The overall effect of the processes of modernization described above has been to efface the once clearly etched lines that separated one social group from another. Class differences have not by any means been eliminated. Rather, these days socioeconomic differences have increasingly tended to be finely estimated in terms of the relative degree of influence and power and especially the amount of cash that people have at their disposal. This is particularly true among working-class people, who often choose to minimize the importance of differences in family background, life prospects, education, and the less immediately visible or exchangeable forms of cultural and economic capital that are vital to the sense of identity of the town's middle classes and who tend to stress instead how much more "equal" everyone has become in terms of the freedom to buy and consume.

The increasing dominance of this microcalculus of social differences in daily life, together with the preoccupation of most people with earning a living, paying off debts, and maintaining at least the appearance of a prosperous life-style, has domesticated sociopolitical conflicts, aspirations, and antagonisms of all kinds. This was particularly apparent in the way townspeople dealt with the political issues that arose during the transitional period from an authoritarian to a democratic regime in the years from 1975 to 1981. While the great majority of townspeople were sympathetic to the ideals and policies of national and local socialists and found the rhetoric of reform, "change," and social justice deeply appealing, they nonetheless cast their votes for conservative parties and candidates in local and national elections. People most often accounted for this disparity between conservative voting patterns and progressive political sympathies by stressing that they were generally content with the material and social gains they had made over the previous two decades despite the sharp economic downturn of the late 1970s and early 1980s. In addition, the prospect of rapid reforms worried them because they thought such reforms might be coupled with a reemergence of the class and political conflicts that had led to the destruction of the Second Republic. Hence, they voted for conservative candidates with links to the defunct Franco regime as a sort of insurance against the deterioration of local and national political and economic conditions. There was, of course, nothing unusual about this sort of cautious response to the perceived dangers of the transition period.[12] Organs of the mass media communicated similar interpretations of the basic political situation, and even the leaders of El Partido Socialista Obrero Español (PSOE) appeared quite content to remain in opposition and seemed in no hurry to form a national government. Moreover, fears of a reactionary military coup were well founded, as the Tejero affair demonstrated in early 1981.

However, the contrast between the conservative behavior and the leftist sympathies of Aracena's voters does indicate something of importance about the character of their community. The susceptibility of the townspeople of Aracena to conservative fears suggests that the social character of their town was unlike that of the many rural Andalusian communities that voted for leftist parties in national elections and often elected radical socialists and communists to local office. While the electoral returns of these rural communities deviated from national patterns, the returns of Aracena did not. This and other evidence indicates that the values, attitudes, and aspirations of Aracena's people varied relatively little from national and urban norms and also suggests that Aracena was as much a well-cultivated suburban backyard as a neglected rural backwater of Spanish society. Yet neither of these images fully captures how townspeople talk of their relations to contemporary Spanish society either as individuals or as members of a rural community. Instead, they tend to represent these relations in terms of a complex set of discourses concerning what it means to be "modern" or "traditional."

CULTURAL LIBERALISM AND THE RECONFIGURATION OF TRADITION

According to local legend, the first television set arrived in Aracena in 1961. In the same year, daily round-trip bus service to Seville was established. The town had never been isolated from the city or state, but the advent of such means of mass communication initiated a more immediate and comprehensive interaction between local and society-wide currents than had existed in the past. By the early 1980s, the force of these currents was everywhere apparent: two local rock bands were playing at dances and fiestas and performing songs by the Rolling Stones and David Bowie along with traditional Sevillanas; a group of teenagers and young adults called "*los pasotos*" (bums or hippies) were reputed to be using hashish; and there was a new "disco-bar," complete with wood paneling, ferns, overstuffed chairs, cocktail peanuts, and a giant-screen color television with a videotape player. Five national newspapers representing a broad range of political opinion were available daily in Aracena (increased from two in the 1970s), and local kiosks carried a large selection of periodicals and reviews, among which gossip and movie star magazines were especially well represented. Fueled by such sources, speculations about the drowning of Natalie Wood in Hollywood and the wedding of "La Princesa Di" in London were the stuff of daily conversation among townswomen. In the streets, there were sounds of children humming and whistling catchy commercial jingles for Nestle's candy. In the bars, men who held lottery tickets or had placed their bets on national soccer matches waited to hear the results. So pervasive was the impact of mass commercial culture that no trend, style, or fad that reigned in the cities lacked defenders and imitators in Aracena.[13]

During the period from 1960 to the early 1980s, a parallel process of transformation also affected the cultural institutions of the town. This process was perhaps most evident in the realm of formal education. Throughout the 1950s, the principal educational institution in Aracena was El Instituto Laboral, which was intended to prepare the youth of Aracena and surrounding *pueblos* for trades directly tied to the agrarian economy of the sierra and to indoctrinate them in the precepts of "National Catholicism." A large proportion of the students' time was devoted to religious instruction, and there were several Catholic youth clubs that sponsored special programs and lectures on themes such as "The Apostolate of Charity for Women" and "The Historical Figure of Saint Thomas Aquinas." Indeed, encouraged by their teachers, students founded a new lay brotherhood in 1956 whose members marched in the processions of Holy Week alongside those of the three brotherhoods that had been organized before the turn of the eighteenth century (see Chapter 8).

In the early 1960s, however, El Instituto Laboral was replaced by El Instituto Nacional de Bachillerato Mixto, whose curriculum was designed to prepare students for university and technical training relevant to the requirements of an advanced industrial society. With this transformation, religious instruction was reduced and a new emphasis on humanistic and scientific education became dominant. Practical and general "preparation for life" was the primary aim and no longer took second place to the glorification of Spain as the "spiritual reservoir of Europe."

This process of the secularization of secondary education was inadvertently accelerated by the dissolution of the alliance between the church and the authoritarian state, which further helped to open the way for the dissemination of "modern" cultural orientations and values in the town. During the 1960s, the members of the postwar generation of Spanish clergy were inspired by the spirit of institutional and liturgical reform of the Second Vatican Council, and they sought to disassociate the church from the neotraditionalist ideology of the Franco regime. The clergy of Aracena were generally sympathetic to these aims and to the new evangelical message to laymen, which emphasized the personal character of faith and the moral obligation to foster brotherly love. As a result, a deep impression was made on the town's most devout middle-class Catholics in 1971 by the news that the majority of churchmen at a national assembly of bishops had voted for a proposal that requested pardon of the Spanish people for the church's partisan role in the Civil War.

These developments went far in depoliticizing the church, and in Aracena the force of anticlericalism diminished greatly.[14] But the effect of this depoliticization was not the desired one of prompting a resurgence in orthodox devotion. Although popular religious feeling is strong, the resentments of the past have been replaced by a considerable degree of indifference toward official church teachings and ritual, and few people attend mass or participate in church-centered activities. The sermons delivered by the priests on special holy days almost invariably contain a rebuke to the many people who are "strangers to the church" for most of the year and think that all that is involved in religion is marching in processions and making *promesas* (promises, vows) to the Virgin.

As the influence of the church on official culture in Aracena waned, the teachers and students of the Instituto and some other townspeople took a leading role throughout the 1970s and 1980s in organizing exhibitions, forums, and seminars that were intended to foment an interest in liberal, democratic values and nonreligious artistic and literary culture. For example, the "Cultural Week" sponsored by the students and teachers of the Instituto in 1980 was wholly secular and mostly progressive in its themes. The events of the week included a play by Lope de Vega, an exhibition of the work of local artists, a lecture on Andalusian architecture, and, most significant, a seminar on family planning and birth control, which did not please the local clergy. Around the same time, a group of younger middle-class people revived *El Distrito,* but the contemporary version of the periodical contained no hint of Catholic social thought. Rather, its subject matter ranged from articles on the ecological movement in the mining zone of Río Tinto to discussions of Woody Allen as *auteur.*

Even so, the advent of the "modern" styles and cultural innovations of mass industrial society has not by any means led townspeople to reject local cultural traditions. On the contrary, almost all townspeople view traditions as vital for their community's identity. Depending on the particular context, they may describe Aracena either as a place where traditional and modern elements are ideally mixed or as a place that is a bastion of tradition. The first point of view is heard most often when townspeople compare Aracena with the smaller *pueblos* of the sierra, which are regarded as depressed and stagnant in contrast to the better material conditions, the more developed "culture," and the greater "prosperity" and "ambience" of Aracena. The second perspective is associated with the greater "tranquillity" and "security" that characterize the town in contrast to the "social ills" of the cities. This perspective was taken, for example, by a middle-class woman who decided to continue living in Aracena rather than accept a higher-paying and more prestigious job in Seville: "In Aracena, everyone knows everyone else—some more, others less—but still you know something about them, even if you don't say hello to them in the street. In Seville, everyone is a stranger. Life here is better, less complicated. The customs are different. People are happier."

This woman's opinions reflect the common local notion that Aracena is a place where egotism is restrained by traditional forms of behavior that enhance the intimate face-to-face character of social relations and make it easier to lead a virtuous and happy life. As a working-class man also remarked: "In other places, people seem to be friendly, but you never know what it means or what they want. It takes a long time to make friends—I know because I came here from Extremadura twenty years ago—but once you have a friend, he is a true friend that does more than say 'good morning.' Look, everyone knows everyone else here. No one can hide anything. Always there will be talk, so you are careful. . . . There are many good people here and also many sons of whores, but you know who they are."

The primacy of this populist pastoral version of tradition depends on a specific way of interpreting the town's history and its present circumstances. This view recognizes that during the early period of the dictatorship, an especially authoritarian, rigid, and intolerant form of traditionalism was imposed on the community. But it also attributes the present strength of tradition not to the strenuous efforts of the old regime's ideologues but instead to the ordinary townspeople's will to revive an archaic, essentially unchanging, popular and egalitarian set of values and customs that were long suppressed but never rejected or forgotten. This enduring legacy is now regarded as standing the townspeople as individuals and the community as a whole in good stead in the struggle to resist the oppressive disciplines and consuming compulsions of an increasingly bureaucratized and commodified mass society that encourages excessive egotism. Thus, townspeople view tradition both as a recovery of the distant past that has enabled them to overcome and correct the social effects of recent injustices and as an alternative set of autonomous local values that counterbalance contemporary pressures.

What this view tends to overlook, however, is the extent to which what counts as tradition these days has been shaped by the processes of politicoeconomic and cultural liberalization to which the community has been subjected. The clear distinction that people make between urban and rural life does not simply arise from their personal experience. This sort of distinction continually appears in the organs of the national mass media, which frequently publish or broadcast messages that plead for and praise the conservation and preservation of "colorful" and "authentic" rural customs. And one of the primary reasons that this pastoral rhetoric appeals to local people is that they have become increasingly interested in promoting tourism. Similarly, local politicians have actively promoted the notion that rural life is more "spiritual" than life in urban Spain, stressing the fact that its slower pace allows more chances for "contemplation" and the cultivation of intimate, personal relationships. Their efforts in this case have been related to the more mundane requirements of establishing the community's identity as an educational center. As Aracena's last *alcalde* of the Franco regime said in a farewell interview in 1976, "Industry does not count at present in Aracena. In the past, cork, hides, and pork constituted solid pillars. But . . . well, things change, and for this reason Aracena is now concerned with cultivating things of the spirit."

While processes of liberalization have disrupted some customs and traditions, they have also generated new forms of cultural representation. In order to understand the nature of these changes, it is necessary to explore several questions: How has tradition been reconfigured in relation to past formations? What forces have guided this reconfiguration, what individuals and groups have taken the leading role in this process, and in what ways does the present configuration of tradition influence and shape contemporary social practices and relations in the community?

The contrasts between the hypermoralistic, hyperpoliticized, class-divided, and directly ideological configuration of tradition that was dominant during the heyday of agrarian capitalism, the Civil War period, and the early years of the dictatorship on the one hand and the current egalitarian and populist sense of tradition on the other could hardly be more striking. These days when townspeople describe traditional culture, they do not mention religion per se in either its orthodox or popular variants, nor do they talk directly of the values of honor or ideals of patronage. Instead, they note the beauty and richness of community rituals and celebrations and usually mention the pageantry and processions of Holy Week and Corpus Christi, the excitement of the *feria* of August, and the camaraderie of participating in the *romería* (pilgrimage) to La Peña of Alájar in September. Formal rites and fiestas such as these are regarded as the highest expression of the life of the community and the epitome of traditional culture in the sierra because they communicate epic and pastoral images of personhood and community that are compelling to all townspeople, regardless of their class, individual moral values, religious convictions, or political opinions. Some customs involving habitual ways of speaking and acting, such as familiar forms of address, nicknames, the evening *paseo* (stroll), courtship, and mourning, are included within the realm of the traditional, of course, but are now considered more a matter of personal preference and conduct than of prescriptive community norms.

What is far stronger is the notion that people with a sense of the value of tradition embrace and manifest certain sorts of social virtues and personal dispositions. The most salient and frequently mentioned of these are "openness" and "grace" on the one hand and "shame" and "formality" on the other.[15] Each of these complex notions has spiritual, aesthetic, and moral resonances. Moreover, each has roots in the personalist culture of religion, honor, and patronage of the Ancient Regime. Thus, even though talk of "honor" is regarded as "old-fashioned" and is seldom heard and even though ideals of patronage are viewed by most people as socially regressive or downright "reactionary," social virtues intimately associated with these once-dominant discourses and modes of representation still persist in a modified and diluted but nonetheless compelling form.[16]

Briefly, the social virtues of being *abierto* (having the quality of openness) and having *gracia* (grace) reflect images of the self and community that are pastoral and "comic" (see Chapter 8). To be open involves not only a personal ability to be superficially friendly and intimate in ways that break down barriers of reserve between people but also a degree of genuine light- or open-heartedness, spontaneity, warmth, sympathy, trust, and generosity in relation to others. Similarly, *gracia* is attributed to people who show the sense, tact, skill, and wisdom to do the right thing in a particular situation. Thus, to show *gracia* may involve the capacity to make witty remarks, dance well, or recognize when it is appropriate to be "open" or "formal," but it implies that a person is especially favored by nature or nurture. Counterbalancing these pastoral virtues are the values associated with the capacity to feel *vergüenza* (shame) and to act with *formalidad* (formality, correct behavior), which involve the ability to restrain oneself and to regulate one's dealings with others in a way that maintains the integrity and good order of the person and community. These virtues of restraint reflect the epic and "tragic" or agonistic side of personal and social life (see Chapter 8) because they are based on the perception that vice and social evil will triumph unless natural desires are contained, self-control is exercised, and moral courage is cultivated.

Each of the key social virtues of openness, grace, shame, and formality is seen as complementary to the others and indicative of a moral capacity that facilitates rather than impedes relations of trust, concord, and intimacy. These social virtues are also strongly contrasted with "brutish," "closed," "cold," and "ugly" dispositions and actions, which are regarded as indications that a person is egotistic, self-serving, and a slave to the passions. Most important, however, each of the social virtues affects a fusion of style, manners, and morals so that it usually seems that the right thing to do is most often also the beautiful thing to do.

But what forces account for this reconfiguration of tradition? In its emphasis on egalitarianism and its deemphasis of orthodox religion, the contemporary form of traditionalism has clearly been shaped as a sort of antithesis to the religious and ideological formation of cultural authority that was imposed in the recent past by the local and higher-level officials of the Franco regime. However, more crucially, the contemporary form of traditionalism in many respects represents a positive synthesis of archaic and modern cultural elements. In particular, the structure of tradition in Aracena parallels in many respects the "high" or "elite" aesthetic culture of the arts and literature.[17] First, like "high" culture, tradition is defined in opposition to the dominant mass cultural forms of diversion, consumption, entertainment, and spectacle (sports, television, movies, fashion, and so forth). Second, the appeal or persuasiveness of tradition, like that of the high cultural domain of "art" (or at least the dominant "bourgeois" interpretation of this domain), is represented as a product of the way in which traditional works and performances such as rituals and fiestas span the distance between immediate social and sensual pleasures and enduring deep meanings. Third, tradition is thought to make life worth living not so much because it provides clear revelations of truth or definite moral guidelines but because it both inspires and expresses a diffused sensibility that informs a "way of life" that is civilized and beneficent in spirit (see Chapter 8). And, fourth, tradition provides alternative ways of construing and conducting personal and social relations, ways that challenge or at least compensate for rationalized, disciplined, abstract, and impersonal ways of representing persons and communities (for example, as citizens, workers, consumers, the public, and populations). Thus, the contemporary configuration of tradition in Aracena is fundamentally paradoxical. Although it is represented as the antithesis of the modern, it nonetheless seems to be structured in a distinctively "modern" way that bears more than mere traces of the influence of the aesthetic ideologies of "high" culture.

This particular configuration of tradition makes social sense in light of the fact that specific groups and individuals have played the leading role in the contemporary reform and resurgence of tradition in Aracena. While some of the town's old guard of Francoist notables still play a role in traditional cultural activities and organizations, the people who are most active in promoting local customs and particularly collective performances are the progressive, better-educated, and more civic-minded members of the middle class—that is, the same group of younger businesspeople, teachers, and office workers who were interested in ecology and Woody Allen and who organized the "Cultural Week" of 1980. Increasingly, this group is not only taking over and patronizing traditional rituals and performances (such as the processions during Holy Week) but also reviving traditions that had been abandoned (such as Carnival) and sponsoring new activities that are already dubbed "traditional" (such as early summer *romerías* to a chapel outside of town and to La Peña of Alájar). Given the group members' familiarity with the most modern themes and styles of contemporary Spanish culture, their mostly secular orientations, and their often progressive political attitudes, it is not surprising that their version of tradition—which is now indeed the dominant local version of tradition—should have a modern face.

It is, however, more difficult to describe the practical impact of this contemporary version of tradition on townspeople's lives. On the one hand, instead of limiting the scope of ordinary people's actions, tradition now offers new options. Traditional themes are invoked spontaneously in an enormous variety of ways and situations. Moreover, there is a constant tacking back and forth between different ways of describing the self and others and the character of life in the community. The possibilities for making unusual connections and odd contrasts that either reconcile or oppose new styles and attitudes with archaic images and imprecise notions of social virtue seem almost endless. On the other hand, while the general openness to cultural bricolage permits ample opportunities for ad hoc improvisations in the course of daily life, it creates considerable uncertainty about the general moral, political, and social significance of both old customs and new trends. The result is that virtually every aspect of life from local politics to teenage courtship is pervaded by a micropolitics of style, image, and interpretation, with townspeople often modifying their presentations of self and representations of the community in accordance with how they estimate what is at stake for themselves and others in particular situations.[18] Thus, despite the new options available for action, it is clear that gender, generation, and class, as well as individual goals, predispose people to take particular stances with respect to tradition. To illustrate how these factors interact with one another and shape the micropolitics of social relations in Aracena, I will recount an incident that occurred there in the summer of 1982.

One Saturday afternoon, my wife, Sharon, and I accompanied our friend, Miguel, the son of a prosperous merchant and clothing distributor, to the house of his much poorer fiancée in a nearby hamlet. Our intention was to collect Miguel's fiancée, Angelita, her younger brothers and sisters, and her mother and drive to a nearby reservoir for an afternoon of swimming and picnicking. When we reached the hamlet, however, we encountered some reluctance on the part of the mother to carry out our plan. The mother, whom everyone called La Madrecita both because of her diminutive stature and because of her aura of childlike innocence, was sixty years old and had been widowed ten months earlier. Despite the fact that she and her husband had been estranged for several years, she had been strict about observing the long period of mourning and confinement that local custom had traditionally required. Recently, she had even refused to indulge in her great passion for bullfights and had chosen not to attend the *corrida* celebrated in association with Aracena's annual fair. Yet in partial surrender to the enchantment of the arena, she had persuaded her future son-in-law (Miguel) to make a film of the event, which she had watched in the privacy of her own home; and in return for this favor, she had promised him that she would bring her period of seclusion to an end.

When the moment of truth arrived, however, La Madrecita, dressed head to toe in traditional black as she had been for months, declared that she was not going anywhere, because, as she said, people would certainly talk. This stance infuriated Angelita, who pointed out that her mother no longer felt really saddened by the loss of her husband, that she had promised Miguel that she would resume normal life, and that it was hypocritical to maintain the appearance of mourning while she enjoyed herself in private. Her daughter's charge put La Madrecita on the defensive, but she still refused to budge. Miguel, however, unbeknownst to anyone else, had anticipated La Madrecita's stubbornness and intervened in the argument by declaring that he had a marvelous solution to the problem that would surely silence wagging tongues and still permit La Madrecita to enjoy the afternoon with her children. With this statement, he reached into a bag that he had been carrying, pulled out a skimpy bikini bathing suit, and began waving it in the air. As he repeatedly and solemnly stressed, the bikini was black and therefore was totally appropriate for the occasion. Even La Madrecita smiled at this mock concession to tradition, and amidst peals of laughter from her children, she was more or less carted off to the beach. Nevertheless, once there, she kept on her mourning garb and also remained firmly tucked inside the car for most of the afternoon, saying that she preferred to stay there in her "*casa*" (meaning her "house").

Now what happened that afternoon can be understood from many different perspectives. Factors of youth and age, manhood and womanhood, and the social virtues of shame and grace were manifestly involved in this conflict of tradition and modernity. Indeed, at the time I had the feeling that we were foreign guests at a skilled cultural performance (a comic pastoral) that had at least partly been improvised and a touch overdramatized to be hospitable and to please and teach us something about local customs and values. Thus, in more ways than one, it seems to me that what occurred was fundamentally about how to adjust to modern conditions, events, things, and perhaps people by placing them in a traditional context and thereby "domesticating" them. In this case, La Madrecita had shown a willingness to take advantage of the technology of *la vida nueva* (the "modern" life) by earlier converting her house into a cinematic *plaza de toros*. After having made herself vulnerable to both traditional gossip and the compromises demanded by family reformers, she had allowed us to take her to the beach but had transformed the car into a fortress of tradition and once again reestablished a small if besieged domain of personal autonomy.

But what about Miguel, her leading adversary? At the time this incident occurred, he was thirty-one years old, in the process of taking over the family business from his aging father, and a backer of the Socialist party. In challenging the virtue of La Madrecita's extended period of mourning, he was attacking a specific rule-governed domain of tradition that he regarded as retrogressive and oppressive. This sort of challenge was consistent with his general stance concerning such matters. Indeed, his romance with Angelita can be seen in these terms, since many older *comerciantes* of Aracena, including his parents, saw their courtship as a shocking class misalliance.

But in many respects, Miguel was far from thoroughly modern. From his own perspective, his love for Angelita also confirmed and ex-

pressed his quite traditional sense of his own identity and solidarity
with the *pueblo*. Far from being hostile to tradition, Miguel felt a deep
attachment to it and was always one of the leading supporters and participants in community rituals and celebrations. Thus, while his good-
natured conflict with La Madrecita may seem a straightforward
conflict between modernity and tradition, the social and cultural factors shaping the incident were far more complexly articulated than it
would appear at first sight. In fact, Miguel was well on the way to establishing himself as the new paterfamilias and benevolent patron of
Angelita's family, and the issue between him and La Madrecita was not
really whether she should abandon her peasant life-style and switch to
haute couture but instead concerned which particular version of traditional virtues should prevail in the family and by extension in the
community.

The version that Miguel and many of his peers would like to prevail in Aracena is one that opposes not only the old-fashioned rules of
conduct but also the contemporary forces of the market, the bureaucratic state, and the mass media. While many have successfully resisted
the former, they can generate little practical resistance to the latter. Put
slightly differently, like many middle-class people in Aracena, Miguel
realized that he could exercise little direct control over the encompassing forces of commodification, bureaucratization, and cultural liberalization and diversification. In compensation for and under the pressure
of these forces, he therefore embraced and also actively recreated what
it means to be traditional in order to adjust to these modern forces and
to some extent manage his relationship with them.

In sum, then, the contemporary configuration of tradition in
Aracena is a by-product of hegemonic processes of liberalization.
While it serves to distinguish the identity of local people and the community as a whole in opposition to dominant cultural forces, it does so
in a way that enables rural people to accommodate themselves to their
marginal and subordinate position in relation to urban centers of
power. The dynamics of tradition thus reflect not the degree of residual "backwardness" or even "underdevelopment" of the town so much
as the manner of its active incorporation into the larger society. In relation to the recent past, cultural domination today is far less oppressive and less dramatic or obvious. But, as the next two chapters
demonstrate, it would be foolish to imagine that contemporary modes
of domination are less efficacious in establishing, maintaining, and
producing practical relations of social inequality. The liberalization of
tradition cannot be simply equated with the progress of liberation, autonomy, and freedom.

8

The Presence of Tradition

I wanted to tell them . . . that beauty gives us an excuse to cross our arms, and that to escape our lot we should resist the temptation to feel like a postcard or museum piece.
—JUAN GOYTISOLO
The Countryside of Níjar

THE AESTHETIC APPEAL OF TRADITION

WHEN I ARRIVED in Aracena, one thing that everyone was willing and indeed eager to talk about was the town's traditional community celebrations of major religious holidays. Since the next one on the calendar was the *romería* (pilgrimage) to La Peña of Alájar to celebrate the birth of the Virgin Mary in the month of September, people tended to talk about this ritual more than the others. Joining the people of Aracena in the *romería*, I was assured, would let me witness and experience the "truly authentic life of the sierra." Like my new friends and companions in the *romería*, I thoroughly enjoyed the activities that brought together people from fifteen or so different *pueblos* of the sierra. What I liked most about the *romería* was its bricolage of sacred and secular elements and the "animation"—one of the key local social and aesthetic criteria by which rituals and celebrations are evaluated—that resulted from having thousands of people march to La Peña and participate in dancing, drinking, eating, and praying together on the tiny hilltop (see Chapter 4). Later that autumn, I was also moved by the series of smaller religious processions in which many of the more devout women of Aracena participated and expressed their devotion to the Virgin.

These experiences led me to eagerly anticipate Aracena's celebration of the feast of the Epiphany, which is commonly called "El Día de los Reyes Magos" (Three Kings' Day) and which several people told me was one of the most important celebrations of the year. This was also stressed in a conversation I had with a local lawyer and a visitor from Madrid a week or so before the event. Describing the great beauty of the *pasos* (floats) in the evening procession of Three Kings' Day, the lawyer concluded with the heartfelt declaration that "as men of culture, we understand that customs reflect the art of life, and this town is a place where customs remain strong." In saying this to two outsiders, he captured the spirit of the contemporary "best of both worlds" configuration of pastoral epic by implying that genuine urbanity was a matter of cultivating and appreciating the local and the traditional. At the time, I could not have agreed more.

But I confess to having been disappointed and even disenchanted by the celebrations of the Epiphany that began on 6 January around noon. At this time, three men, one in blackface and all three dressed as magi, established a court in the main plaza where they received the town's children. One by one, the children approached the kings and gave them notes or whispered requests for gifts. Proud family members looked on and occasionally snapped photos. The proceedings lasted an hour or so, with the municipal band playing in the background. When the last child had visited the kings, the families returned to their homes to eat and exchange gifts. The first phase of the celebration differed little from children's visits to a shopping-mall Santa in the United States.

In the evening, everybody took to the streets, which were illuminated with thousands of colored electric lights, to watch the cavalcade of the three kings. The cavalcade consisted of musicians and fifteen or twenty *pasos* that were decorated with colored paper, aluminum foil, and so forth and were similar to though less elaborate than the sort of thing found in the United States in New Year's Day parades. But in this case, each of the floats carried young children and teenagers who were in costume and remained motionless in tableaux that represented beatific moments in the life of Christ and the Virgin. The most elaborately decorated and important float was the one that carried a teenage girl dressed as the Queen of Heaven and surrounded by a court of cherubs and angels. In the days before the cavalcade, a competition had been held to decide who would have the honor of representing the Queen of Heaven, and the girl who won achieved a status similar to that of a homecoming queen in American high schools. Many *pasos* also carried youngsters who were dressed in red suits as elves and tossed handfuls of candy to the crowd. Excited groups of shouting children chased after these floats with plastic bags in hand, tried to gather as much candy as possible, and greatly added to the noise and confusion of the cavalcade. After the procession had made its way to the plaza facing the town hall, municipal officials distributed a small present such as a plastic doll or toy motorcycle to every child.

At the time, I viewed the whole episode as a demonstration of just how deeply penetrated and subverted local customs had become through exposure to the saccharine sentimentality and Disneyland diversions of the commercialized mass media. Everyone who participated seemed out to have fun, and having fun in this case meant indulging children in a frenzy of consumption, holding a popularity contest for the position of the Queen of Heaven, and putting on as gaudy a spectacle as possible. I was further distressed to discover that the increase in both the size of the annual cavalcade and the popularity of the day's events represented perhaps the most dramatic development in the annual cycle of community rituals and secular celebrations in Aracena since 1960 and that the modern form of the cavalcade was contrived in hopes that it would eventually rival the much grander, more serious (and highly lucrative) processions of the neighboring town of Higuera de la Sierra, which have drawn visitors from neighboring towns, Seville, and as far away as Portugal since the 1920s.[1]

It was with some relief that I also soon discovered that despite the popularity of the proceedings, the general consensus in Aracena seemed to be that the cavalcade of the three kings was, as one man put it, "pretty, but of no importance." A minority even found the whole affair "very ugly" and unfavorably contrasted the cavalcade to other popular religious rituals and secular celebrations such as the *romería* to La Peña of Alájar in September, All Souls' Day, the Marian devotions of autumn, and, above all, the rites of Holy Week and the feast of Corpus Christi. Unlike the cavalcade, these rites were regarded as "beautiful and unchanging" reflections of the moral and spiritual character of the community. This particular view of tradition was emphasized by a town official in a set of notes concerning local rituals and included in the program of the annual *feria* (fair) in 1976:

> The character of the people of this population also merits attention. The love that all feel for the *patria chica* [i.e., Aracena] is unanimous, although some may be distant from her. Her traditional rites have not suffered the least variation throughout the centuries. Baptism, marriage, burial, the *quintos* [celebrations attendant upon the induction of young men into the armed forces; see below], the visit every Friday to the *patrona*, La Virgen del Mayor Dolor, with her throne in the church of "El Castillo" . . . are all customs deeply cherished by townspeople. . . . [As epitomized in traditional rites and customs] the beauties and sorrows of life are the patrimony of all, and so too always has been mutual support and it continues being so.

The distinctions that townspeople and I made between the pristine eternal heart of tradition and the "modern tradition" of the cavalcade were, of course, overdrawn. And contrary to the view that traditions "have not suffered the least variation throughout the centuries," even the rites of Holy Week and Corpus Christi in the 1980s were hardly the same as they were in 1955 much less the sixteenth century. In fact, when I asked people in Aracena about such matters, no one had any difficulty or reluctance in citing dozens of instances of change.[2] Similar examples of changes in other towns have been noted by recent ethnographers of Andalusian popular culture who have stressed how community rituals serve as arenas of class struggle.[3] The issue is therefore not whether traditional cultural forms have changed but, rather, in what ways, to what ends and purposes, and under what sorts of contemporary pressures and constraints they have been recast.

To address these problems in relation to Aracena, this chapter first describes recent enactments of the "great rituals" of Holy Week and Corpus Christi and indicates the major ways in which townspeople interpret the significance of these rites. However, instead of devoting exclusive attention to how the rites themselves condense and manifest contemporary social, cultural, and political conflicts and concerns as most accounts of Andalusian popular culture have tended to do, the next part of the chapter focuses on a case study that describes how the images of personhood and community which are communicated by the rituals were appropriated and redeployed by a group of townspeople as they went about their ordinary affairs. As this case history of a modern romance emphasizes, traditional culture in Aracena plays a direct expressive role in representing relations of domination, and it also plays an indirect instrumental role in maintaining and altering such relations in the micropolitics of everyday life.

The Heart of the Heart of Tradition: Contemporary Enactments and Interpretations

Tragic Epic: The Processions of Holy Week

The rites of Holy Week in Aracena represent the tragic pole of popular religious culture and are pervaded by an agonistic vision of existence and by images of pain and bereavement.[4] The week's rituals are organized by the four lay penitential *cofradías* of the town, and each of these brotherhoods has its own procession depicting a crucial phase in the passion of Christ. While the four processions represent the themes of suffering and sacrifice in slightly different ways, the elaborate baroque images of the Virgin and Christ that are carried through the streets of town are at the center of each stage of the ritual observances and depict the empathetic spiritual identification and disconsolate solitude of Mother and Son. The representations suggest that the Virgin and Christ are bound to one another by the experience of the passion and at the same time tragically separated from one another by it. The focus in this discussion will be on the first and last of the processions of the week, which townspeople describe as including *el pueblo entero* (all the people, the whole community), in contrast to the middle processions of the Nazarenos and the "student" *cofradía,* which involve people with a "special" faith and a "particular" devotion (see table 2 for a schematic comparison of the processions and *cofradías* in 1982; see Maddox 1986 for a more detailed discussion of all four processions).

The first procession of Holy Week is that of La Cofradía de la Vera Cruz, which departs from the church of "El Castillo" on Thursday an hour or so before sunset. The members of the Vera Cruz number almost two thousand men, women, and children. Although the question of precedence is disputed by the partisans of La Cofradía del Santo Entierro de Cristo, the supporters of the Vera Cruz claim that it is the oldest of the town's penitential brotherhoods and was active in the mid-sixteenth century. According to the traditional view, the Vera Cruz is the *cofradía* of workers and country people, although currently it includes townspeople of many occupations and is led by a group of middle-class *comerciantes* (merchants and shopkeepers) and members of the "white-collar" working class. But whatever the precise history of its membership, there is little doubt that the Vera Cruz has always been the most inclusive and egalitarian of the brotherhoods. The popularity of the *pasos* of this brotherhood is immense, and there are few dissenters from the opinion that one of the most beautiful sights in Spain is the procession of the Vera Cruz departing from the ancient hilltop church of "El Castillo" and solemnly wending its way down into town as the evening sun etches the hills of the sierra in sharp relief.

In 1982, as in most years, a large crowd of townspeople and visitors had gathered around the church doors by early evening to await the procession. After what seemed hours of delays, trumpets sounded and from the doorway of the church emerged the image of the Vera Cruz, a bare six-foot cross of polished dark wood capped in silver, carried by a *penitente* dressed in the sky-blue pointed hood and white gown of the brotherhood. Following the cross was a group of young *penitentes,* some holding the banners of the brotherhood and others carrying the thick, long candles of devotion that light the way of the procession after nightfall. Next came a small group of town officials led by the Socialist *alcalde* (mayor).

Table 2. Characteristics of the Holy Week Procession in Aracena

Procession	Theme	*Cofradía* Sponsoring the Procession	Characteristics of the *Cofradía*	*Pasos* Depicting (1) Christ and (2) the Virgin
First procession, beginning Thursday before sunset	Flagellation	La Cofradía de la Vera Cruz (Brotherhood of the True Cross)	Founded in early or middle 16th century; the most popular and most egalitarian brotherhood; predominantly workers and country people; about 2,000 members in 1982.	(1) Jesús Flagelado (Christ flagellated by two Roman legionnaires); (2) La Virgen del Mayor Dolor (Virgin of Great Sorrow).
Second procession, beginning Friday before sunrise	Carrying the cross	La Cofradía de Nuestro Padre Jesús Nazareno (Brotherhood of Our Father, Jesus of Nazareth)	Founded in 17th century; predominantly shopkeepers and artisans; about 1,000 members in 1982.	(1) Jesús Nazareno (Christ carrying the cross), accompanied by Simon of Cyrene; (2) La Virgen del Rosario (Virgin of the Rosary), accompanied by John the Evangelist.
Third procession, beginning Friday evening	Crucifixion	La Cofradía del Santísimo Cristo de la Plaza (Brotherhood of the Most Holy Christ of the Plaza)	Founded in 1950s by students of El Instituto Laboral in Aracena; predominantly leading members of the middle class (former students); about 1,000 members in 1982.	(1) Santísimo Cristo (Christ nailed on the cross); (2) La Virgen de Gracia y Esperanza (Virgin of Grace and Hope).
Fourth procession, beginning Saturday evening	Death	La Cofradía del Santo Entierro de Cristo (Brotherhood of the Holy Interment of Christ)	Founded in middle 16th century; predominantly the old elite; about 300 members in 1982.	(1) Santo Entierro (Christ in a glass coffin); (2) La Virgen de Soledad (Virgin of Solitude).

Table 2 (cont'd). Characteristics of the Holy Week Procession in Aracena

Procession	Number and Garb of *Penitentes* in the Procession	Other Participants in the Procession	Route and Approximate Duration of the Procession
First procession	About 130 people in white gowns and sky-blue hoods	The carrier of the bare cross (La Vera Cruz); the Socialist *alcalde* (mayor) of town and other town officials; the municipal band; drum and bugle corps; 30–40 people fulfilling *promesas*.	Exit from church of "El Castillo," an ancient church occupying the highest peak in town; tour throughout town, with stops at convents and the hospital for the aged; return to "El Castillo" (7 hours).
Second procession	About 130 people in black gowns and dark purple hoods	The municipal band; drum and bugle corps; 18–20 people fulfilling *promesas*.	Exit from the parish church in La Plaza Alta; tour throughout town, with stops at convents and the hospital for the aged; return to parish church (5 hours).
Third procession	About 60 people in white gowns and red hoods	The municipal band; drum and bugle corps; fewer than 10 people fulfilling *promesas*.	Exit from the parish church in La Plaza Alta; tour throughout town, with stops at convents and the hospital for the aged; return to parish church (5 hours).
Fourth procession	About 40 people in white gowns and black hoods, joined by members of the 3 other brotherhoods in their own garb	Conservative politicians leading the procession; 2 uniformed officers of the Guardia Civil carrying weapons; 2 drum and bugle corps, one headed by men carrying flags of Aracena, Andalusia, and Spain; the municipal band; very few people fulfilling *promesas*.	Exit from church of El Carmen, a church favored by the local elite; short tour through neighborhoods of the elite, with a stop at a wealthy widow's house; return to El Carmen (3 hours).

Source: Historical data and observations of the processions in 1982.

When the elaborate gilt and silver *paso* of Christ became visible, the crowd first gasped in fear and then briefly applauded as it became clear that the *costaleros* who supported the lurching platform from below had managed to slowly maneuver it through the narrow doorway of the church. The images of this *paso* portrayed the flagellation in a startlingly dramatic manner: two bare-chested men, arms raised, whips in hand, directed their blows to the bloody back of Christ, who was bound by his wrists to a post. The sense of gravity inherent in the representation of secular power was enhanced by the militant anthems and slowly rolling cadences of the drum and bugle corps following immediately behind.

As the *paso* of La Virgen del Mayor Dolor emerged from the church, the silence of the crowd was broken by long applause and cries of admiration prompted by the beauty of the silver *paso* covered with fresh flowers. Around the shoulder of the Virgin hung an elaborately embroidered cape that stretched ten or twelve feet behind and on which the seal of the town was stitched in multicolored threads. On the Virgin's cheek was the mark of a single tear, and a dagger's handle above her breast showed that underneath her splendid gown was a heart pierced by sadness for the suffering of her son. As the *paso* began its progress, the *capataz* in front barked commands to the *costaleros* hidden under the platform, and the entire *paso* with its elaborate hinged canopy above it began to sway back and forth in complex rhythms. Behind the *paso* was a group of thirty to forty women and men, some barefoot, who had made *promesas* to follow the Virgin in her passage around the town. As the procession stretched out in its slow march down the hill toward La Plaza Alta, 130 *penitentes* in their brilliant blue hoods, followed by the municipal band, brought up the rear. By the time the *paso* of the Virgin had covered the thousand paces from "El Castillo" to La Plaza Alta and made its customary stop in front of El Hospital de la Misericordia, an hour had passed and night had fallen.

The procession made its way toward La Plaza Mayor, the stops becoming more frequent in order to allow the *costaleros* to rest. On seven or eight occasions throughout the evening, the procession halted to permit one of the townspeople to offer a *saeta* (a song; the word literally means "an arrow") in honor of the Virgin.[5] From a balcony, a man or woman would look into the Virgin's eyes and sing of her beauty, the depth of her sorrow, or the love the singer felt for her. Most moving were the songs of the better women singers, whose words seemed to establish a direct bond of communication with the Virgin as a bereaved mother. Amidst the conversations of the onlookers, one could often hear people make observations on the sadness and suffering of Christ and the sorrow of the Holy Mother in the same vein as the songs, and exclamations marking the beauty of the scene were interspersed with murmurs of *Qué pena, Qué triste,* and *Qué barbaridad* (What pain, How sad, and How barbarous). As the hours passed and more and more people retired to their houses, the *saetas* seemed more elemental and desolate. It was nearly two in the morning when the last of the *penitentes* returned to the church of "El Castillo." By this time, the faces of the *costaleros* were pale with exhaustion, and as they removed the thick rolls of white cloth that protected their shoulders from the wooden braces of the *pasos,* they looked as chastened as the images they had labored to support.

Within two hours, the procession of the Nazarenos departed from the parish church with one *paso* depicting Christ carrying the cross and accompanied by Simon of Cyrene and another *paso* showing La Virgen del Rosario being consoled by John the Evangelist, popularly considered to be the brother of Jesus. In the early evening of Good Friday, the "student" *cofradía* founded in the mid-1950s brought forth its *pasos* of the crucifixion and La Virgen de Gracia y Esperanza.

The last of the processions of Holy Week, that of La Cofradía del Santo Entierro de Cristo, emerged from the church of El Carmen near La Plaza Mayor on Saturday evening. Although people say that this procession is always an affair of *el pueblo entero,* it is so in quite a different way than is the case with the procession of the Vera Cruz. Rather than being popular in spirit, the procession of Santo Entierro stresses social and symbolic differences among townspeople. El Carmen has always been a place of worship highly favored by the local elite, and the brotherhood centered there has only about three hundred members, the great majority of whom are from the town's old landowning and commercial families. As a result, the small but relatively rich association has for decades been unable to muster a sufficient number of *penitentes* to do justice to its prestige, influence, antiquity, and honored position as the last brotherhood to mark the observance of Holy Week.

This problem has been met by inviting brothers of the other *cofradías* to participate in the march of Santo Entierro. Thus, about twenty-five brothers of the other three associations normally join the march. However, it is clearly the brothers of Santo Entierro who govern the procession, and only their banners are carried. The necessity of including members of the other *cofradías* has been turned into a factor of crucial cultural significance by the way in which the procession is organized. In contrast to the earlier processions, the community is presented as separated into three corporate bodies encompassed by a fourth group of people who appear to be their patrons and governors—and perhaps even their captors. A stark representation of social hierarchy and worldly power is thus conveyed.

The *pasos* of Santo Entierro rival those of the Vera Cruz in their splendor, and they are even more somber. In the first *paso,* the body of Christ, gray and bloody, lay enclosed in a gold-framed, glass-walled coffin on whose top roosts a grotesque pelican with a gaping, voracious beak—a symbol of Christ's sacrifice and of worldly rule (see Portier 1984:11). Flanking this *paso* in 1982 were uniformed officers of the Guardia Civil carrying heavy automatic weapons. In the second *paso,* La Virgen de Soledad, standing on a huge silver platform and dressed in white lace and a massive black cloak, was shown weeping amidst white flowers and candles. As always, the *penitentes* of Santo Entierro were wearing jet-black hoods and pure white robes. Dressed in these funereal and absolute colors, they surrounded the *penitentes* of the other brotherhoods, who seemed to move within a closed circle.

The devotees who followed behind La Virgen de Soledad in 1982 were few in number, reflecting the fact that the procession of Santo Entierro is generally not popular. Scarcely two hundred nonparticipants were present to watch as the procession rounded the corner from the church and the Virgin's *paso* was turned and dipped to bow before the mansion of the old, wealthy, and haughty Viuda de Sánchez. This extraordinary gesture of respect for the widow whose family members have long been sponsors of the brotherhood was in striking contrast to gestures of the other *pasos* of Holy Week, which were dipped only before the convents and the hospitals for the aged.

With the procession of Santo Entierro, Holy Week ends—at least as a popular religious celebration. Images of death, social hierarchy, and worldly power are the final representations visible in the streets. The doctrine of the resurrection scarcely seems to enter into the popular comprehension of the drama of the passion and certainly finds no expression in the collective rituals.[6] Heaven, hell, and salvation seem irrelevancies. As a result, the dominant note in popular interpretations of the passion is not of a rebirth of hope but, rather, of tragic fatalism and identification with the humanity of Christ and the Virgin. As one man said, "That's the way life is. . . . Men bleed, mothers cry, . . . nothing more." A woman remarked, "It is the same now as always; men kill each other and the women are left alone to starve." Thus, the tragic vision that the rites of Holy Week convey gathers most of its force through the tensions existing between the domestic and political realms. People interpret the rites in ways which stress that the destiny of men is primarily determined by their relation to other men and that the destiny of women follows and is contingent upon what happens to their sons and husbands. But the tragedy of Holy Week represents only one pole of popular religion; the celebration of the feast of Corpus Christi, as described below, addresses the other pole and offers a contrasting view of the relationship between the domestic and political realms.

Comic Pastoral: The Celebration of Corpus Christi

The feast of Corpus Christi, which commemorates the Eucharist in the Catholic calendar, is held on the first Thursday after Trinity Sunday, which is usually in early June. Aside from Holy Week, it is probably the most important collective religious celebration in Aracena each year, but it is also the least typical of all the traditional popular religious observances in the town. Centered on the celebration of the first communion of the children of Aracena, it is the community ritual that is most closely linked to the church, most joyous and celebratory in tone, and most inclusive and egalitarian in its social implications. All of this is in striking contrast with the past. In the early twentieth century, the celebrations of Corpus Christi were austere and intensely orthodox, and participation in the rites was apparently confined almost entirely to ultraconservative *comerciantes* and members of the agrarian gentry. It is only since the late 1960s, with times of general prosperity, broad elementary education, and Vatican II reforms, that the celebrations have held much attraction for ordinary townspeople.

In 1982, the celebration began at ten in the morning with a high mass in the parish church attended by perhaps five hundred people, including a hired choir, the officers of the most important of the town's *cofradías*, many children, and a far larger number of men than is usual for church services even on days of fiesta. The high point of the mass was the first communion of seventy children between the ages of seven and twelve. While, in principle, taking communion is an act of the utmost sacredness and seriousness, as the children approached the altar one by one to receive the sacraments, the mood in the sanctuary was, in fact, anything but solemn. Excited by the occasion, most of the children plopped on their knees without regard for proper decorum and botched the prayers they had memorized. Moreover, as they turned toward the congregation after receiving the wafer and wine, they all bore the puzzled look of having swallowed something peculiar. Seeing this, the adults tittered with laughter and a few succumbed to the temptation to crack jokes. As the last of the children took the sacraments, they all ran toward their parents and everyone began talking at once. A moment later, a priest with a microphone began to shout instructions concerning how the procession should be conducted—i.e., reverently, prayerfully, and silently—but no one showed any sign of hearing, much less heeding, his directives.

A quarter of an hour passed before the procession was brought into a semblance of order outside the church in La Plaza Alta. Six boys holding banners of La Cofradía Sacramental headed sex-segregated groups of the new communicants. Nuns hovered around and prompted the children to sing the songs they had been taught in praise of the Lamb of God for the old people and sisters gathered in the doorways of El Hospital de la Misericordia adjacent to the parish church. Afterward, the procession began a slow march down the hill in the direction of La Plaza Mayor a few hundred paces below. Every girl carried a basket of rose petals, and the young communicants were followed by a simple wooden *paso* that had an image of Christ as the Young Shepherd and was carried by four teenage boys.

The adult participants in the procession were led by the officers of La Cofradía de la Reina de los Angeles, who held the banners of the brotherhood or their staffs of office. Next came representatives of the four penitential brotherhoods of Holy Week, followed by the adult members of La Cofradía Sacramental in the place of honor before the *paso* of the blessed sacrament. In contrast to the other brotherhoods, the formation of La Cofradía Sacramental was headed by a group of forty matrons, almost all of whom were well past childbearing age. A few men wearing ordinary suits trailed behind them. The officers of the brotherhood, a group of choirboys singing hymns, and the parish sacristan swinging a censer that filled the air with incense preceded the elaborate silver *paso,* which supported a six-foot-high silver monstrance holding the blessed sacrament. White carnations and sprigs of ripe wheat were strewn around the base of the monstrance. The parish priest followed, praying in a soft voice and walking under the shelter of a large canopy carried by six brothers of La Cofradía Sacramental. Behind him, there were about twenty older women and a few men who had made vows to march in the procession. At the rear, members of the municipal band marched along playing anthems.

As the long procession made its way through the streets, the participants were able to admire the dozens of embroidered shawls and bedspreads hung from balconies. The doors of many houses had been opened to reveal small domestic shrines graced by images of the child Jesus. Three of the most orthodox Catholic households had erected larger shrines on the sidewalks in front of their houses, with carpets extending into the middle of the street. The most elaborate of these shrines was a large carved table covered with flowers and candles and displaying a figure of Christ as the Good Shepherd with his arm raised in a gesture of blessing. As the first communicants reached each of these altars, they halted, sang a hymn, and bent to pick up one of the evergreen boughs that covered the carpets. Later, when the monstrance passed, members of the households with shrines emerged to throw flower petals on the *paso*.

The procession took about two hours to complete its circuit around the town center. All this time, the streets were lined with people looking on or chatting and strolling up and down the length of the procession. Many younger children darted in and out of the procession and teased the first communicants, who had been instructed not to talk and to be suitably pious and formal. When the first communicants reached La Plaza Alta, they formed two files through which the whole procession reentered the church, and as the monstrance passed, the young girls tossed their rose petals into the air. Then the new communicants and most of the crowd retired to their homes for formal dinners with their families and visiting relatives.

The celebration of Corpus Christi with the rite of first communion follows immediately upon the confirmation of the children by the church and represents a popular ritual recognizing that the children have reached the age of moral and spiritual discretion. Their new status and responsibilities are reflected in the practice of permitting the children to lead the procession. However, the celebration represents more than the beginning of a passage from childhood to adult status for the communicants. In the final moments of the rite, the roles of children and adults are reversed, since it is the children who form the protecting files through which the adults pass into the church, and in this way the young and innocent ones who have been ritually purified by the sacraments are momentarily cast into the role of spiritual patrons and guardians. Thus, the child-centered vision of social life communicated by the rites of Corpus Christi entails a dimension of spiritual regeneration and rebirth for the community as a whole. Through their common concerns as parents and guardians of the next generation, the adults of the community are united as a single social body. Moreover, Corpus Christi is the only occasion in the annual cycle of rituals when the clergy and all the lay brotherhoods of the town unite and participate in a single grand procession, and even though the various brotherhoods are differentiated from one another, the symbolic primacy of the children undermines the sense of social divisions and corporate hierarchies.

By these means, the rite merges and identifies the domain of personal and familial life with the public corporate realm in ways that enhance the spirit of community. The display of shawls and bedspreads, the opened doorways, and the extension of the household shrines into the streets both literally and figuratively accomplish an interpenetration of family and community and eliminate boundaries between the domestic and sociopolitical spheres that normally are highly marked. The combined impact of the focus on the beauty and innocence of children, the transcendence of images of social hierarchy, and the domestication of the broader community generates a joyous atmosphere that prompts people to describe the town as "one great family." Particularly noteworthy in this respect is the purified representation of manhood in the rite. Men are ordinarily depicted as being weighed down with burdens in an agonistic world and obliged to defend their honor. In Corpus Christi, however, men appear only as innocent boys, loving fathers, or benevolent patrons, as if every man were a priest. This beatification of manhood is made obvious through the various ways of representing Christ. The Lamb of God, the Good Shepherd, and indeed the Host itself are images that portray corporal and material life in the most innocent, pure, and spiritualized forms. The suffering tragic Christ of Holy Week is nowhere evident, and the alternative images are notably pacific and abstract in comparison with the starkly emotional depictions of the passion. The incarnated blood and body of Christ are represented by rose petals and sprigs of wheat. Thus, the images and sentiments of joy, harmony, unity, and equality created by the rite are essentially comic and pastoral: their cumulative impact is to constitute a vision of rural society as a self-renewing natural body that incorporates every person in ways that lead to a fulfillment of human desires and aspirations.

The celebration of Corpus Christi and the rites of Holy Week both use the same set of elements and themes—such as the tension between spiritual and corporal being, representations of gender, discriminations of the domestic from the public, and images of hierarchy and equality—but they enact opposite visions of human destiny. Yet taken together, the two great rituals of popular religion constitute a tragicomic vision of life in this world, a vision in which the seeds of hope and love are contained in the experience of defeat, suffering, and death, and vice versa.

In one form or another, this tragicomic vision is evident in virtually all of the traditional religious and secular celebrations in Aracena. Each in varying ways uses images of sacrifice, regeneration, gender, and the tensions between spiritual-moral values and the constraints of natural existence to shape a complex and rich but thematically integrated cultural configuration. In the closely linked secular celebrations of the *corrida de toros* (the "bullfight") and the *feria* (fair), for example, the tragicomic spirit of Holy Week and Corpus Christi is transposed into a this-worldly cultural register, with the moral concerns of the great rituals recast into nonreligious, aesthetic idioms of commensality, conviviality, bodily integrity, grace, courage, and the domestication of brute nature through heroic action, all of which resonate with traditional notions of honor and patronage.[7] Despite the wide range of themes and styles that these various cultural forms embody, they all focus attention on the dilemmas, virtues, actions, and fate of exemplary persons—be they Christ, the Virgin, and the Lamb of God in religious celebrations or be they the generous host and brave torero in secular celebrations such as the *feria* and the *corrida*. And in addition to providing these various images of personhood, each offers an image of the community that stresses its hierarchical and agonistic aspects or its egalitarian and mutualistic aspects.

But what is the sociopolitical significance of these various figurations of the relation of personhood to power in contemporary Aracena? One way to address this question would be to focus on the rites and celebrations themselves as an arena of struggle over meanings. Indeed, there are some townspeople who are not reluctant to affirm that the enactment of communal rituals and celebrations is and should be a contested terrain. Moreover, it is quite common for those involved in communal celebrations to voice ad hoc and partial interpretations of tradition that draw attention to some of the political, class, and historical factors that have shaped collective performances. For example, during the Holy Week procession of Santo Entierro, one older working-class man, before being hushed by his wife, loudly commented as the *paso* carrying the coffin flanked by the gun-toting Guardia Civil approached, "Look at Franco's legionnaires," and thus managed in a phrase to link the crucifixion to more recent defeats of the poor and humble by worldly authorities. Similarly, during the procession of Corpus Christi, more than a few townspeople commented sardonically to the effect that the rich are hypocrites who only cast open the doors of their houses to their neighbors once a year when they are sure no one will venture inside.

Yet important as it may be to recognize that traditional cultural performances represent a locus of class and political conflict (see Chapter 9), a directly ideological reading of these traditional cultural performances is at best incomplete and at worst misleading and distorted because it tends to minimize the extent to which there is a consensus about tradition. While townspeople readily admit that there are conflicting interpretations regarding certain aspects of the rites and celebrations and recognize that different sorts of people will discover different values and meanings in conventional images of personhood and community, this fact is itself one of the things that leads them to affirm a broad consensual vision of the significance of tradition as a whole and to maintain that traditional rites and celebrations embody profound and timeless truths about the human condition. Moreover, while they often declare that they participate in the cultural life of the community because of the immediate social interests and aesthetic pleasures that are involved in the rites and celebrations, they also affirm that traditional cultural performances express the enduring virtues that define the essential moral character of the community.

It therefore seems that what makes traditional rites and celebrations vital and compelling to townspeople is their capacity to express and focus local concerns and conflicts over values and meanings and at the same time to associate local and transitory matters with "transcendent" humanistic values (see Fernandez 1984). Out of the enactment, contemplation, representation, and juxtaposition of both social and symbolic forms of diversity and conflict springs a sense of cultural unity, identity, and concord. This logic of the reconciliation of disparate values and concerns reflects the contemporary "best of both worlds" configuration of the traditional cultural genre of pastoral epic and suggests that tradition has to be understood primarily in terms of encompassing hegemonic processes of incorporation rather than in terms of direct ideological processes of cleavage and conflict.[8] To understand the particular hegemonic force and authority of tradition in contemporary Aracena, it is therefore necessary to consider not simply how collective performances serve as occasions for the expression and mediation of social conflicts but also how the traditional images of personhood and community offered by these performances are reinterpreted and used by townspeople as they confront the problems and dilemmas of ordinary social life.

Modern Romance as Pastoral Epic: Courtship, State Power, and the Reproduction of Class Society

The most direct bridge connecting formal ritual processions and secular fiestas to the daily round is the custom of the *paseo,* the late afternoon and evening stroll when people put aside the work of the day and gather with their friends and family in the doorways, plazas, bars, and cafes of the town. The *paseo* is the central social event of everyday life and has something of the character of an improvised procession during which images of the self and the community are presented and contested. In no other aspect of daily life is the extraordinary importance townspeople attribute to maintaining appearances (in both the literal and figurative senses) so clearly manifest as in the *paseo,* the time par excellence for conducting much of the politics of daily life and for forming and revising social reputations, alliances, and antagonisms.

The general tone of the *paseo* is comic; it is a celebration of sociability and the social virtues of formality, grace, and openness during which the greatest emphasis is placed on the joys of being with others and the exchange of drinks, witticisms, and news. Nevertheless, much of the fascination and interest of these hours of leisure comes from the knowledge that it is always possible that an offhand remark, a barbed comment, or a stray bit of gossip can transform the usually good-natured competition to appear more generous, shrewd, or knowledgeable than one's companions into a genuinely heated dispute or conflict that sunders relations among members of the community. In this sense, the *paseo* also has a dark side that expresses the tragic, agonistic dimension of social relations.

For young couples, the *paseo* represents the primary time of *noviazgo* (courtship) and often poses the challenge of trying to work out personal conflicts while concealing them from public scrutiny. Because of the high emotional and social stakes involved in courtship, it embodies the dynamics of the *paseo* and the politics of daily life in a particularly dramatic way and thus provides a key to understanding the hegemonic force of traditional images of personhood and community in contemporary Aracena and particularly the relation of tradition to processes of the social, political, and economic production and reproduction of rural class society.

Like all other aspects of life in Aracena, courtship practices have undergone a great transformation, particularly in the years since 1960. Courtship in Aracena was traditionally governed by a narrow set of severe restraints.[9] For centuries, the avowed social ideal was of "equal marriages" between "equal partners," with courtship operating to guarantee this outcome. Determining whether a union would be equal involved making precise calculations and negotiations concerning how much and in what form each person would contribute to the partnership. This meant, of course, that class equality was the sine qua non of suitable marriage. All evidence indicates that the courtship system worked with great efficiency to preserve the basic structure of social inequality in Aracena.

Many aspects of traditional courtship still remain important in contemporary Aracena, but the overall pattern of courtship has been fundamentally altered in recent decades. Townspeople still use traditional terms such as *noviazgo de la plaza, noviazgo de la calle,* and *noviazgo de la casa* (the progressive stages of talking in the plaza, strolling and meeting in the streets, and then entering the *novia*'s house for

evening visits), but their social significance is no longer clear-cut because courtship practices have been liberalized. There has also been a
shift in the order of importance of the factors influencing the choice of
partners: personal character and attraction and the compatibility of the
couple now seem to be more decisive than considerations of property
and parental approval. This shift is related to the broader socioeconomic changes that occurred with the collapse of the old agrarian system. Since that time, the perceived importance of inherited property
in determining social destinies has declined; the social chasm separating the richest from the poorest townspeople has considerably nar-
rowed; and job training, education, and certain character traits that
can be considered "personal capital" have become more important. All
of these factors have reinforced the personal and romantic side of
courtship and made it more difficult for parents to control and limit
the choices of their children.

The cumulative effect of these changes has been to make it less obvious than in the past that courtships are begun and marriages are
made almost entirely within fairly narrow boundaries of class groups.
While the range of potential marriage partners may be somewhat
wider than previously, few class "misalliances" (such as that of Miguel
and Angelita, discussed in Chapter 7) have in fact occurred. Like falls
in love with and still marries like. That this happens, however, is less
a result of parental surveillance and intrusions than of the force of indirect selective pressures that are exerted in many ways. Among such
impersonal pressures, those brought to bear by the educational system
and military obligations rank high.[10]

Courtship and Social Discipline

Probably the most important but by no means the only mechanism of "social sorting" is the educational system imposed by the state.
Children complete the general basic education course at the age of
fourteen, and then they have the option of continuing their schooling
at the Instituto. In Aracena, most of those who have the desire and
money to continue are the children of the town's and region's old elite
and commercial classes. Because attending the Instituto sharply sepa-
rates the members of the student group from their working-class peers
at precisely the time when teenagers become most acutely aware of the
attractions of the opposite sex, the state's educational system essentially operates in loco parentis to preserve patterns of class differentiation (and, ultimately, inequality) in rural society.

The students of the Instituto have exclusive clubs, sporting teams,
and associations and their own favorite places for meeting, such as the
courtyard of the school and certain bars that nonstudents do not fre-

quent. Because the students spend most of their time with their male and female companions, they also have ample opportunity to develop close nonromantic friendships. They are exposed daily to the "modern" values of their teachers, and they expect to attend universities and technical institutes and are well aware that they may never reside in Aracena as adults. Since their expectations for the future differ from those of nonstudents, their romantic relationships are not thought of as necessarily leading to marriage, and they follow a set of courtship practices similar to American "dating." The term *novios* is out of fashion with the student group, and even romantically involved couples are usually referred to as "friends."

More traditional styles of courtship persist within the nonstudent group, which consists primarily of working-class youth and some members of the commercial class. Most of these young people hope to find adequate employment to remain in Aracena as adults and expect to find their future spouses among the people they already know. Therefore, they are generally more sensitive to community traditions and gossip than are their peers at the Instituto. Moreover, because most of their time is spent either at home or at work, their contact with the opposite sex tends to be more univocally "social" than that of the students, and this encourages a greater self-consciousness and formality in their relationships and a stronger awareness of the potential seriousness of romantic attachments. Thus, some though not all working-class *novios* follow many of the traditional courtship customs, such as the formal avoidance of their parents, and are acutely concerned with maintaining their reputations.

In addition to the educational system, other bureaucratic mechanisms influence courtship patterns during the critical period of transition from youth to adulthood. Every young man in Spain faces the prospect of military service for a year to eighteen months.[11] Normally, this period in the *"mili"* intrudes around the time when couples are first beginning to think seriously of marriage, and few young men look forward to leaving their native town and *novias*. Like the end of schooling at age fourteen, the period of military service is a watershed whose timing in the lives of working-class youth is determined by the state. Only the physically or mentally incapable are routinely exempt from compulsory military service. However, military experience is different for university students than it is for nonstudents. Because the students usually fulfill their military obligations during short periods in the summer rather than in a single long stretch, service in the military does not represent a significant break in their lives. In addition, the student soldiers are separated from ordinary conscripts. Thus, the "social sorting" initiated by the educational system is maintained by the military structure. Indeed, especially for the ordinary conscripts, the military usually represents a severe education in social discipline and ideological indoctrination, since many members of the officer corps continue to consider themselves the national guardians of Spanish tradition and regard it their duty to subject the ordinary conscripts to the sacrifices required by honor, *patria,* and the Catholic faith.

The prospects of a long forced absence, imposed discipline, and the usually rather remote but nevertheless real dangers of military life all make the weeks before induction a highly charged time in the lives of the conscripts, their families, and, of course, their *novias*. The branch of the military in which a youth will serve is determined by lottery, and the branch affects the length and place of service. In Aracena, the lottery results are supposed to be posted in late January, but posting always seems subject to inexplicable delays that cause a lot of anxiety. Once the decree of the state is known, the youths begin to prepare for their departure, which is commonly one or two months later. These preparations are punctuated by a set of cultural observances of great importance for the conscripts. The *quintos* (cohorts of young conscripts) organize and attend a series of meals given in turn by the parents of one or another of the future soldiers, and they spend many afternoons in the countryside on group picnics. These feasts and picnics are often rowdy affairs, with a good deal of singing, dancing, and noisy outbursts encouraged by copious supplies of food and drink. During this time, the silence of the early morning hours is frequently disturbed by bands of young men roaming about town, yelling, joking, taunting each other, and loudly serenading the darkened windows of their *novias'* houses. Most people respond to these displays of aggressive male camaraderie with remarkable indulgence and good humor because they recognize that the celebrations provide the last opportunity for the youths to do as they please before entering the service. Indeed, the celebrations of the *quintos* are regarded as a sort of comic farewell to boyhood; when the veteran soldiers return, they are expected to act as adults and are presumed to be ready to fulfill the responsibilities of manhood.

As the partying subsides in the last week before their departure, the conscripts spend more time with their immediate families, close friends, and *novias,* and the cultural forms of pastoral epic associated with this period reflect more somber and even tragic themes of isolation, social hierarchy and authority, and the need for patronage and protection. In the church of "El Castillo," a novena is celebrated. The first masses are attended primarily by the mothers and *novias* of the conscripts. The final mass, which is followed by a public ceremony, is attended by the conscripts and everyone in their families. A local official makes a speech bidding the conscripts farewell and enjoining them to act in ways that maintain the honor and good name of their native *pueblo*. In private and public prayers, the patron saint of Aracena, La Virgen del Mayor Dolor, is beseeched to watch over the departing sons of the *pueblo,* guard them from danger, and bring them safely home again. Many *novias* and mothers make vows to show their devotion to the Virgin in exchange for gaining her particular favor and protection for their loved ones. These community traditions surrounding conscription thus represent a response to the demands of the state, one that reaffirms both the masculine values of honor and comradeship and the domestic feminine side of popular religion. They also reaffirm traditional forms of community identity and solidarity in opposition to but in compliance with the regulations of a key bureaucratic state institution.

As even this brief description of the cultural, economic, and political forces affecting courtship in Aracena indicates, modern romance in the town is by no means a matter of freely following whatever the heart desires, as it sometimes appears to be. This point is further demonstrated in the following case history of a contemporary working-class courtship in Aracena. While the story of Carmen and José shows that traditional images of personhood and community continue to be adopted by people in their efforts to adjust to forces largely outside of their control, it also suggests some of the limits on this traditionalizing strategy that are pertinent to understanding the general dynamics of tradition in Aracena.

The Courtship of Carmen and José

A match surely made on earth and not in heaven, José and Carmen were brought together by the background they shared. When they first became *novios* at the age of seventeen, neither had any but the most fleeting and intermittent experience with members of the opposite sex. José was shy and immature for his age, and after he had left school, he spent most of his time in the company of one or two male friends. Carmen was also shy and retiring and had spent her early teenage years close to home. Both came from working-class families and had never given serious thought to continuing their education beyond the age of fourteen. These superficial similarities in adolescent experience do not, however, go very far in explaining why they were immediately attracted to each other or why they have stuck together in spite of strong opposition to their courtship.

Carmen and José are in fact two very different sorts of people. Carmen, though shy and modest, is also highly intelligent, earnest, kindhearted, and—with those she knows well—lively and quick-witted.

She is a hard worker, and many townswomen come to her when they want a sweater knitted or a dress sewn. Indeed, knitting and sewing are her *arte,* and she can copy any design shown to her after casually glancing at an example or even a picture in a magazine. Her work is completed rapidly and flawlessly; and because it is her "art," she usually charges her clients only for the raw materials she uses. In short, Carmen commands all the domestic virtues and feminine skills respected in the town. At his best, José has a boyish charm and playfulness that make him attractive. But he is also somewhat self-absorbed, mumbles rapidly in the thickest of local accents, and pouts when his whims are not indulged. His greatest love and talent is for music, and he has taught himself to play the guitar and other instruments and to sing the popular folk songs of Andalusia.

Although José and Carmen are different in personality, they seemed to understand and genuinely care for each other. This was perhaps because there were some affinities in their childhood experiences that enabled each to strike a chord in the sentiments of the other. Carmen's parents were terribly poor when she was born, and her mother died of a heart disease when Carmen was hardly over a year old. This left her father, Juan, in difficult circumstances. Though a hard worker, he was also known for being outspoken and proud; and in the political circumstances of the 1950s, he had great difficulty in finding work. Like other young working-class men of the period, he decided to emigrate to escape what was for him an intolerable situation. Carmen was left in the care of her father's sister, Amalia, who was married and soon had two children of her own. Juan made his way first to Barcelona and eventually to West Germany, where he found a good-paying factory job that enabled him to visit Aracena during his vacation every summer. Meanwhile, Carmen was raised in the unhappy household of her aunt and uncle.

Carmen's uncle had been injured at work in the fields, and because of his "bad back," he was never able to contribute much to his family's livelihood. Pain and embitterment drove him to drink heavily and to make life miserable for the whole family. It took him over ten years to die of the effects of alcoholism and inactivity, a period during which scarcely a day passed without conflict between husband and wife. Carmen, who was a few years older than her cousins, cared for them while her aunt worked as a domestic servant. The money Juan sent from Germany for Carmen's support was critical to the support of the whole family.

Shortly after the death of his brother-in-law and Carmen's fourteenth birthday and graduation from grammar school, Juan decided to return permanently to his native *pueblo*. Having risen to the position of foreman in a machine tool factory, an unusual accomplishment for a "guestworker," Juan came back a changed man. He had lived frugally and saved a great deal of money; he had become a highly skilled technician; and he had adopted some of the values and expectations of German middle-class people, whom he admired. Within a few months of his return, he opened a bar and restaurant in a *barrio* near Las Grutas de las Maravillas (the caverns), which soon attracted a fair portion of the daily tourist trade. Amalia became the cook, Carmen became her assistant, and Carmen's cousins helped the waiters Juan had hired. Juan himself managed the operation, and with good reason he took pride in his accomplishments. His intelligence, sacrifice, and hard work had improved the life and prospects of Carmen and his sister's family, and he had won the respect not only of his old friends but also of many middle-class businessmen of the town, who treated him as a social equal, or nearly so.

Juan was not pleased when Carmen began to see José, which was about two or three years after his return from Germany. After his long absence, Juan had become deeply attached to his daughter and perhaps overly protective of her, and he hoped she would find a *novio* of a reputable and prosperous family. Such a pairing would confirm his own newly achieved status within the *pueblo*. Thus, it was partly snobbery that led Juan to disapprove of José, who was the eldest of two sons of a poor and often unemployed mason. Even so, snobbery does not adequately explain the intensity of Juan's hostility toward José. It was not simply that José's family was of a humble background; Juan was proud to say that his own background was humble, too. Rather, he perceived in José a character similar to that of his late brother-in-law. Not only was José unambitious, but his father was a notorious alcoholic who often made life miserable for his wife and children. Juan saw José as a true son of his father, and Amalia (Carmen's aunt) feared the same. Carmen, in contrast, seemed to be attracted to José precisely because he had suffered considerably from his father's meanness and drinking, as she and her cousins had suffered from her uncle's similar faults.

From its very beginnings, then, the courtship of Carmen and José was rocky. Amalia and Juan lost no opportunity to criticize José, and they invented numerous strategies to impede Carmen from seeing him. Juan suddenly seemed to discover that his daughter (who had never shirked any responsibility) was lazy, and he invented tasks for her in the restaurant that made it difficult for her to find an hour to spare in the evenings. Amalia, always a person who hated being alone, would sulk whenever Carmen's evenings with José left her without company. Carmen insulated José from this hostility by steering him clear of any potential interaction between him and his enemies. As a result, he mistook her guardians' opposition for the aloofness and formal distance a *novia*'s family traditionally maintained toward a suitor. This misinterpretation only led him to blame Carmen all the more for the times when she was unable to meet him, and he soon began to fly into fits of undirected jealousy that tormented Carmen. Caught in the middle, Carmen suffered most and was criticized from all sides. During some bad times, she actually became ill from the stress and felt she could please no one. Worst of all, she began to half believe that she was indeed a lazy, inconsiderate, and selfish woman.

This cycle of recriminations and disputes continued for three years, sometimes with greater intensity and other times with less. During the whole period, José never approached closer than half a block from Carmen's house; Juan's opinion of him did not change; and José, who was usually unemployed, spent most of his time at home or wandering about the streets with his friends while Carmen was at work. Although Carmen began to assemble her trousseau, her joy at collecting sheets, silverware, and the other things she would need for her household after marriage was diminished by Amalia's continual observations that José would never be able to support a wife and family. Such pressures as these made the relationship tenuous, and indeed the courtship almost ended once when José demanded that Carmen quit working for her father and look for employment elsewhere so she would have more time to spend with him in the evenings. Even Carmen saw this as an irresponsible and senseless demand and upbraided José for being too timid to attempt to win the favor of Juan, who was as devoted to his daughter as he was prosperous and in an excellent position to help his future son-in-law find work if he chose to do so.

Thus, the courtship of José and Carmen was plagued by the tensions inherent in their class backgrounds and family situations. On the one hand, Juan's hard work and energy had permitted him to transcend the condition of local poverty and underemployment. On the other, both his own family and that of José had not escaped the consequences of the past. Carmen's uncle and José's father had both been frustrated by their continual failure to improve their conditions or even simply to maintain the support of their wives and children and had thus turned to drink in a futile effort to evade their sense of hopelessness. After three years of courtship, José and Carmen as a couple had not been able to achieve any significant degree of acceptance from their families. In traditional terms, they seemed stuck in the second phase of courtship, *noviazgo de la calle*. Ironically, a nearly total disruption in their courtship enabled them to move beyond this phase and establish their relationship on firm ground. This disruption was caused by José's induction into the Spanish marine corps, and it was in conjunction with the distressing separation forced on them by the state that Carmen and José managed to present their courtship in the best possible light through their invocation and use of traditional cultural images of the pure and virtuous woman and the honorable young man.

When José's year to serve arrived, both he and Carmen were disturbed by the prospect of his imminent departure, and their participation in the celebrations of the *quintos* did more to exacerbate than relieve their worries. Of the dozens of youths whose names were in the military lottery for the year, José was almost the last to discover his fate. Carmen suffered deeply from the uncertainty and could not enjoy the parties and other activities being held for José's cohort. She was distracted and in a daze. Finally, unable to bear the tension any longer and mustering all her courage, she took the bold step of calling the regional military authorities and demanding to be told what José's assignment would be. What she learned was the worst possible news. José was one of the few local men drafted into the marines, and this meant he had to serve a full eighteen months at a post so far from Aracena that he would be unable to come home on weekend passes. This was devastating for José and Carmen, and the sympathy of their friends, who had all fared much better in the lottery, was small consolation.

The courtship was already threatened by the opposition of Carmen's family, and now it seemed to everyone that the courtship would be destroyed by the long period of separation. Indeed, Juan and Amalia were almost openly jubilant at the chance of ridding themselves of the unfortunate suitor once and for all. But the bad news nonetheless had the effect of bringing Carmen and José closer to one another than they had been for some time. José was moved to declare his love for Carmen once again, and for the first time both began to speak openly to their friends of their plans for marriage. In token of this renewed commitment, José (in close consultation with Carmen and his mother, Juana) extended an invitation to Carmen to have dinner at his house. This unusual step reversed the order of invitations in traditional courtships, but in light of the hostility of Carmen's family, it was the only measure the couple could devise to make public and formal their private intention to wed. Although the dinner greatly annoyed Juan and Amalia, at the time it seemed little more than a futile gesture. However, the invitation to José's house later proved important not only because it showed that José's family approved of Carmen but also because it established an alliance between Carmen and Juana—an alliance that Carmen used to full advantage in the battle to win her family's consent to her union with José.

The character of the alliance between Carmen and Juana, which set the cultural tone for the ensuing months, was demonstrated as soon as the bus carried José away to basic training. Together Carmen and Juana made their way back from the bus stop toward Juana's house. As they walked arm-in-arm, Juana cried over and over again, "*Ay, mi hijo; ay, mi hijo; Dios mío; ay, mi hijo*" (Oh, my son; my son; my God; my son). Carmen, crying no less and no less upset, repeatedly whispered the phrase, "*Mi niño, mi niño*" (My little boy, my little boy). The mother and the young *novia* were mourning in an idiom that was unmistakable in its religious reference and invoked the most powerful of cultural images. Together they were Mother and Virgin lamenting the passing of a suffering Son. And it is indeed as a virgin of solitude that Carmen acted and represented her situation in the weeks and months that followed.

José's departure brought about an immediate shift in Carmen's behavior and a radical redefinition of her social persona. In José's absence, Carmen almost entirely stopped seeing their mutual friends. Each day, she wrote to José and passed by the house of José's mother for a few minutes to see if she had received word from her son. Otherwise, her only activity was to attend mass, which she did four or five times a week, occasionally alone but usually in the company of Juana or another older woman. The change in her habits could hardly have been more striking, for Carmen had never before shown much interest in the church or things religious and in most respects was as thoroughly modern as any of the young working-class women of Aracena, who often sought her advice on matters of fashion.

Nor was Carmen at all unaware of the cultural supports for her metamorphosis, as revealed by a conversation that my wife, Sharon, and I had with her one day. Carmen had just received a letter from José and was crying. To tease her, her aunt said to us, "Look at her sitting there like the Virgin of Anguish." We then had the following discussion with Carmen:

Rick: You think more about the Virgin when José is gone, Carmen?

Carmen: Yes, of course.

Rick: Why do you think that's so?

Carmen: Because you think more of her when something or someone is lacking. She understands love and suffering.

Sharon: You mean because she lost her son?

Carmen: Well, yes, but that's more the part of the mother. José's mother put a photo of him under the glass of the image of the sacred heart of Jesus that hangs in her room, so that when she prays she always thinks of her son. For me it's different. I don't pray to the Virgin in the same way, but I think of her as a friend. José's mother asks for strength, but my anguish is less than hers. So for me the Virgin is like a friend who understands the things of my life and my love for José. She understands these things too.

Rick: Your aunt says you try to be like the Virgin in your actions. Is that true?

Carmen: *Hombre!* That is too much. I am just trying to be a good person.

Sharon: But the Virgin is also a good person.

Carmen: Yes, it's true—the purest woman, the Mother of God.

Carmen's understanding of her own situation was subtle and complex, but it was centered on the double significance of Mary as pure maiden and holy mother. As a young woman, Carmen offered her support to the anguished mother of José and also regarded the Virgin as her own friend and confidante who showed her how to be a good person and lead a good and simple life while waiting for José's return.

The shift in Carmen's social persona had far-reaching effects on her courtship. Despite her longing for her *novio*, Carmen's life was otherwise happy and seemed untroubled and carefree in comparison with the period of the courtship before José's departure. Her quiet life put her beyond the criticism of her father and aunt, since they could no longer say she was shameless in seeing too much of José and lazy because she wanted a few hours in the evening in order to do so. More confident of herself, Carmen began to redefine her relationships with others. For example, she began to refer to José's mother as her *suegra* (mother-in-law), obviously a term loaded with assumptions about the future. Just as important, Carmen constantly spoke of José as her *niño* (her little boy), a term that took away all hint of the romantic and erotic side of the courtship, stressed the maternal desires of Carmen, and indeed reflected the way many wives tend to regard their relationship with their husbands.

Calling José her *niño* was one element in a complex reconstitution of José as a social persona that was complementary to Carmen's own self-transformation. For Carmen and her *suegra*, José was a little boy, a suffering son comparable to Jesus, and simultaneously an honorable hero. As José's letters arrived, Carmen would read parts of them to anyone who would listen. In them there were tales of the hardships and discipline of military life and declarations of loneliness and homesickness. To impress Carmen, José also wrote of the long hours of guard duty and exaggerated the dangers of his situation by repeating rumors that there might be battles with the British over Gibraltar (this was the period of the Falkland Islands war). However, the dominant theme in José's letters was of the honors he was winning as a good recruit. He had been made leader of his squad, and his correspondence included a seemingly endless string of ribbons, citations, certificates, and so forth. The most interesting of these items provided by the state was a trick photograph that showed José's face bathed in misty light and swathed in gauzy clouds, looking benignly down on a Spanish battle cruiser slicing through rough seas—an image of heroism that spoke volumes about sacrifice, honor, and faith.

With this ammunition at hand, Carmen and Juana sang the praises of José; and since they were the only ones who had any direct news from José, Juan had nothing upon which to base his hostility and could only listen in disparaging silence to tales of José's accomplishments. All of these factors operating together over a period of three months or more—Carmen's restrained and impeccable traditional behavior, her close friendship with Juana, and the news of José's triumphs in the marines—subtly shifted the play of forces in the courtship. This was most obvious in the more benevolent attitude adopted by Amalia, who liked Juana and said less and less about her doubts concerning José's character. Indeed, Amalia began to express much more sympathy for Carmen's situation than she ever had before. Moreover, neither Juan nor Amalia could find much fault in Carmen's close friendship with Juana, a woman worthy of respect and in need of moral support because of her difficult domestic situation.

At this point, a crisis arose and effectively isolated Juan in his opposition to the couple and inhibited his capacity to take effective measures against the future marriage. The crisis arose in conjunction with a traditional event sponsored by the military and held when conscripts complete basic training and are ready to be assigned to their permanent duty posts. The event, known as "El Día de las Madres" because the ceremonies honor the mothers of the soldiers, coincides with the fiesta of La Virgen del Pilar, a patron saint of the Spanish armed forces. Invitations are extended to the soldiers' families weeks in advance, and most of them are eager to attend the colorful ceremonies. This was particularly the case with José's relatives because they had not seen him since his induction and because his new duty post was nearly as far away as his training camp, which meant that he would rarely be able to go home for visits in the coming months. Juana said she was determined to have her "whole family" around her on the "special day," and she not only invited Carmen to accompany her but also enlisted her help in planning the trip.

Both money and a means of transportation had to be found. Traveling by train was expensive and impractical because of the many connections that had to be made. The family car rarely made it as far as the other end of town without a breakdown, and as usual Juana had barely enough money on hand to feed her family. Because of these difficulties, Carmen and Juana decided to consult Amalia (an eminently practical woman) about the trip, and she was quick to offer suggestions. When it became clear to Amalia that Carmen intended to accompany José's family, she did not protest but she warned Carmen that Juan would never permit her to go. Juan was told nothing about the trip both because everyone agreed there was no need to upset him prematurely and because no one had the courage to broach the subject. In effect, then, Amalia became almost by accident a coconspirator of Juana and Carmen.

It was not until two days before leaving that Juana finally arranged to borrow a car and some money from relatives who lived in a neighboring town, and when the morning of departure arrived, Juan still remained in ignorance. Finally, a few minutes before Juana and her family arrived, Carmen mustered her courage and went to Juan with tears in her eyes and told him of her plans. Predictably, Juan flew into a frightening rage, forbade Carmen to leave the house, and went so far as to call her "a shameless whore" and a disgrace to him. But at this moment, Amalia (who had been hovering in the background) physically interposed herself between Juan and Carmen, pushed Carmen toward the door, and told her to go. Juan was shocked and momentarily dumbfounded by this, and Carmen escaped.

It was Amalia who suffered most from Juan's anger. He blamed her for not having watched over her niece with more care and for having betrayed him. Again and again he upbraided her with diatribes like the following:

What have you done? This is not right. You make my daughter a whore. This man who makes demands on Carmen, who tells her she must go with him at whatever hour of the day or night. . . . It is a bad thing. He's lazy, uncultivated, he can't talk properly, he has no education, he doesn't work. What's more, his whole family is the same—no formality, *sin vergüenzas*. It's not just my opinion. I knew nothing about his house. It was Antonio who first told me. He tried to give the father work but he is a drunk. It is into this house that you want Carmen to marry? Where is your shame? Why do you let this continue?

Amalia (and Carmen after her return) generally bore such outbursts in resentful silence, and weeks passed before relations among the three of them returned to something approaching normal. But Juan's effective resistance to the courtship of Carmen and José was at an end. Somehow he had lost his ally, Amalia. The fact that he had failed to prevent Carmen from accompanying José's family meant either that he had failed in his own paternal duty to protect his daughter or that he had entrusted the protection of her virtue to the vigilance of Juana, thus undermining his own hostile view of the family of José. If he protested too harshly and too publicly, his protests would amount virtually to an indictment of himself and an admission of his own failure as a paterfamilias. Thus, after Carmen's return, Juan increasingly confined his protests to the circle of his closest friends, and his public attitude toward the courtship gradually began to shift from one of determined resistance to rueful resignation.

The shift in the balance of forces was made evident to all when José finally secured a special leave that is granted to soldiers so that each can attend the *feria* or patron saint's day of his native *pueblo*. At Carmen's instigation, José nervously came one evening for the first time to her family's house and restaurant to find his love. Dressed in his uniform, he breached the fortress of paternal opposition and was met with only token opposition by Juan, who simply ignored his presence. The victory had clearly gone to the young couple. After that evening their courtship was relatively untroubled, and they were married two years later.

What kind of victory was the courtship of José and Carmen? At first sight, it may seem a victory of traditionalist working-class youth over a "modern" father whose migrant experience had imbued him with upwardly mobile middle-class aspirations and prejudices. But such a conclusion is surely wrong. For one thing, when push came to shove, Juan acted the traditional role of an authoritarian paterfamilias out to guard his daughter's virtue, and his own honor and thus his investment in what townspeople consider to be traditional values were no less great than José's or Carmen's. More important, however, José and Carmen's embrace of traditional images of personhood and community was less than definitive. When José became a civilian again, he dropped most of his talk of honor, heroism, and courage, and Carmen stopped attending mass and more or less ceased to act the part of a modest young virgin. Instead, the couple devoted themselves to planning their married life, accumulating the household goods they needed to set up an apartment, arranging outings with their friends to Seville, and convincing Juan that José was capable of helping him in his business and eventually of managing it. In other words, their aspirations differed little from Juan's, and their actions were virtually indistinguishable from the most modern sector of Aracena's youth.

Rather than being a pure and simple victory of traditionalism, the triumph of José and Carmen indicates that the force of tradition is of a limited, qualified, and occasional character and that it is complexly linked with contemporary social pressures and dispositions. Thus, when Juan represented José as an unambitious good-for-nothing of doubtful moral fiber and attacked Carmen's shameless behavior, and when the courtship reached a crisis point as a result of the intervention of the state in the couple's lives, Carmen and José were able to make the best of a bad situation by adopting traditional personae that cast themselves in the best possible light. They accomplished this by redefining the disparate threats to their relationship as a test of their character and virtue to which they could respond by imitating cultural models that represented the epitome of honor, grace, and formality. In so doing, they managed to domesticate a situation fraught with uncertainties and ambiguities. From this perspective, the primary practical efficacy of traditional images of community and personhood would appear to lie in their ability to offer an alternative means of construing the significance of social relations in situations in which the community as a whole or some of its members find themselves at a disadvantage. In such situations, traditional images provide an important defensive redoubt in the politics of self-presentation. Indeed, it is precisely the ease with which townspeople switch from modern to traditional images and idioms that lends credence to their "best of both worlds" contemporary version of pastoral epic.

Even so, it is clear that tradition is a redoubt that presents little serious threat to the contemporary status quo in Aracena or to the dominant political, economic, and cultural forces that are shaping contemporary Spanish society. Just as the transcendent humanistic interpretation of communal rites reflects the capacity of encompassing forces of cultural liberalism to neutralize social differences and conflicts, and just as the observances of the *quintos* and the novena in "El Castillo" when young men are about to enter the military define the local community in ways that concede and even celebrate the subordination of townspeople to state power, so too the courtship of José and Carmen demonstrates the efficacy of the various mechanisms that ultimately maintain the basic structure of class inequalities that characterizes rural society. In the case of José and Carmen, the outcome of the courtship was the union of two people of strikingly similar class positions, experiences, and dispositions. In this sense, the courtship manifested what Pierre Bourdieu (1976:140) has called an *amor fati,* a falling in love with one's own social destiny, which brings together socially compatible partners by way of apparently free choices whose results turn out to be far from unpredictable and arbitrary. Moreover, the traditionalizing strategy that José and Carmen followed in fulfilling their romantic desires involved them in a process of complying with and seeking the approval and recognition of higher authorities and a disciplinary state apparatus in order to gain a marginal advantage in their domestic struggle. It is hard to see this surrender as an assertion of personal freedom. Having won Juan's tolerance by surrendering to the power of the state, the couple later did everything they could to secure his active approval of their marriage at least in some measure because they realized that their future livelihood depended on it. And in this process, they gave up much of the independence they had won from parental authority.

So it is with traditional culture in contemporary Aracena more generally: the practical social outcome of the great cultural energies expended in distinguishing local values, virtues, customs, and people from those of the larger society is not so much to improve the conditions of life within the community as it is to render these conditions of relative dependence and subordination more tolerable and palatable. This is not to say of course that the hegemonic force of tradition in contemporary Aracena makes no difference in townspeople's lives. On the one hand, the notion that tradition provides an alternative set of values and satisfactions that partly compensate for townspeople's underprivileged position in the corporate bureaucratic state system of contemporary Spain is not by any means wholly illusory. On the other hand, as the courtship of Carmen and José clearly demonstrates, the tactical victories and marginal gains that the embrace of tradition enables townspeople to achieve tend in the long run to lead them to accommodate themselves to social destinies over which they have only limited control.

9
The Politics of the Commonplace

[He] is the most motherly father of all fathers. . . .
We were nothing until he came; we owe everything
to his initiative.
—MIGUEL DELIBES
The Hedge

TRANSITION AND CONSENSUS

THE MOST critical difficulties of the passage from an authoritarian dictatorship to a liberal parliamentary democracy had already been successfully negotiated by the time I arrived in Aracena for an extended stay in the summer of 1981. The legal and institutional framework of a constitutional monarchy had been approved by the Spanish electorate in 1978, national elections had been held in 1977 and 1979, the Basque country and Catalonia had been established as autonomous political entities, and other regions such as Andalusia had nearly achieved this status. In February 1981, shortly after the resignation of Adolfo Suárez, the head of government and principal engineer of the transition since 1976, the long-anticipated attempt of the far right to resurrect Francoism had occurred when Colonel Tejero of the Guardia Civil in collusion with a group of high-ranking army officers had seized the Cortes and held virtually the entire political class of Spain hostage for almost twenty-four hours. Thanks largely to the determined action of King Juan Carlos, the coup attempt had quickly crumbled, thereby greatly diminishing the most serious threat to the liberal political order.

But the next year and a half was hardly an uneventful political period. From the collapse of the coup until the national elections of October 1982, violence in the Basque country continued; arguments about the laws governing the autonomy process intensified; the center-right coalition party of La Unión Centro Democrático (UCD), which had governed Spain during the transition period, disintegrated into competing factions; and La Alianza Popular, a party led by former Francoists and financed by banking interests, attracted widespread support. Yet despite the continuing political turmoil, the leaders of Spain's political parties managed to suspend their differences at least to the extent that they cooperated to ensure the survival of the constitutional system. The sweeping victory of El Partido Socialista Obrero Español (PSOE) under Felipe González in the elections of 1982 was, as most commentators have observed, the culminating event of the transition period, an event signaling the consolidation of Spanish democracy and the beginning of a new phase in the political history of the country.[1]

Most people in Aracena, of course, followed the news coverage of these developments with a considerable degree of interest. But during the period I lived there, the most dramatic political event that occurred in the town itself was a whistle-stop campaign speech given by Manuel Fraga Iribarne, the leader of the conservative Alianza Popular. Fraga arrived in town a couple of hours behind schedule one evening in the early summer of 1982 and rushed into the less-than-well-furnished town cinema to give a speech to an overflowing crowd that even included a few militants of the local socialist party. This ex-minister of the dictatorship had staked out a conservative political position that appealed to "sociological Francoists" (Preston 1986:108). Though unimpressive in appearance, Fraga was a bundle of energy and had a commanding and even intimidating personal presence. In a speech that lasted barely twenty minutes, he heaped scorn on the activities of labor unions, called for increased activity by the forces of order to suppress the violence in the Basque country, and appealed to traditional ideals of patriotic love for the Spanish nation and respect for family values and religion.

Although nothing Fraga said came as any surprise to his audience, his booming voice had a power all its own. Even members of the audience whose political positions were diametrically opposed to Fraga's were moved by his rhetorical powers, and they applauded him. And as Fraga rushed from the theater, he received a standing ovation. For many days afterward, the visit was a principal topic of conversation. At first, it seemed as if Fraga had succeeded in winning at least a few converts to his cause. As the excitement of the speech waned, however, the sense of political caution usually evident in townspeople's political talk reasserted itself, and expressions of dislike for Fraga became the rule. He was continually unfavorably compared with his primary political adversary, Felipe González, who was represented as less personally ambitious and far more committed to democratic reforms. In the long run, it became clear that Fraga was not trusted, while González was admired because of his moderation and good sense and because of the egalitarian principles he represented.

The reaction to Fraga's visit reveals a good deal about political life in Aracena during the period of transition. In addition to reflecting the political caution of most townspeople, it showed the tendency of local public opinion to swing back and forth between attitudes of hopeful optimism and disenchanted skepticism regarding the people and events in national politics. But perhaps the most puzzling thing that Fraga's rather unextraordinary visit and overly enthusiastic initial reception by townspeople indicates is just how uninteresting, undramatic, and even dull the political life of the community really was during this critical period in modern Spanish history. Despite the bitter memories of local class conflict and oppression and the fact that townspeople were well aware of what was at stake in terms of their own and their country's future during the transition period, there was little excitement generated over national or local politics and even less commitment to active involvement in political parties and processes.

For this reason, the key questions to be answered concerning the political life of Aracena during the transition period carry a negative connotation: Why was community politics characterized by a lack of engagement, animated debate, conflict, and drama? What forces contributed to an effective practical depoliticization of local culture precisely at a time when there were ample reasons to imagine that the contrary might well have been the case? To address these questions, this chapter first examines the political legacy of the last years of the Franco regime, next investigates how local politics were conducted during the transition period, and then describes some of the contemporary socioeconomic pressures that have generated consensus and imposed limits on dissent in Aracena. It concludes that the way in which processes of political and economic liberalization were construed in terms of tensions and convergences between traditional and modern values played a vital role in convincing townspeople that social progress depended on concord rather than struggle and that the price of prosperity in the future was acceptance of the community's dependent and marginal status in the present.

THE LAST PATRON AND THE LEGACY OF AUTHORITARIAN POPULISM

The most important political figure emerging from Aracena in the post–Civil War period was "Don Enrique," a consummate academic politician in a country where a university career has long been a well-traveled path to the summit of state power. Throughout his distinguished career in national politics, Don Enrique never forgot his native *pueblo,* and the history of his involvement with Aracena reveals a great deal about how encompassing hegemonic forces and local conditions affected political culture in the town during the period of transition from dictatorship to democracy.

Don Enrique was born in Aracena in the first decade of the twentieth century. His parents were members of the middle class and far from wealthy. After his father's early death, he was raised by his widowed mother, for whom he maintained the greatest devotion in his later years. As a young student, Don Enrique showed great promise and attracted the attention of the editor of *El Distrito,* José Andrés Vázquez, a novelist whose literary talent and intimate acquaintance with the *marqués* and other members of the grand bourgeoisie of Seville and the sierra made him influential in academic circles. Befriended by Vázquez and aided by the *marqués,* Don Enrique was able to pursue university studies. His social connections and an honorable war record in the Nationalist army led him eventually to secure a prestigious appointment in the school of Spanish-American studies of the University of Seville. As an historian with an interest in the golden age of exploration, conquest, and empire in the New World, he was ideally matched to the hypernationalism that characterized the ideology of the Franco regime in the first years after its victory.

After 1947, Don Enrique became increasingly influential in the intellectual circles of the regime and gained a succession of important posts. He served as director general of propaganda in Seville; as secretary of the review *Arbor,* a key journal of El Consejo Superior de Investigaciones Científicas; and, until 1957, as president of the Ateneo of Madrid. These offices gave Don Enrique tremendous influence over official intellectual life and the award of university appointments and fellowships throughout Spain. At the same time, he was active as a scholar and wrote a number of monographs on Spanish history and many essays on religious and humanistic themes with titles such as "Liberty, Tradition, and Monarchy" and "We, the Christians," in which he took positions on the ideological questions of concern to the regime in the 1950s and 1960s. Throughout the 1960s, Don Enrique continued to be an important figure within the ministry of education and was well connected to several of the influential "families" or factions that controlled the state apparatus. After holding a succession of prestigious bureaucratic and academic posts, he capped his career by serving as director general of fine arts from 1970 to 1973.

The key to Don Enrique's eminent position throughout his career was his leading role in Opus Dei, a semisecret devotional organization of Catholic laymen whose members sought to live pious lives while pursuing successful secular careers.[2] In their first years of activity in Franco's Spain, the leaders of Opus Dei expounded a doctrine of "integrism" of church and state and attacked remaining traces of liberalism in the elite circles of the regime. The "integrist" doctrine had great appeal for many officials in the regime, and men reputed to be members of Opus Dei were able to establish strongholds in the ministries and departments of education, tourism, and fine arts and then maintain them for decades. Moreover, by the mid-1950s, technocrats of Opus Dei began to hold sway in the economic and financial community and engineered a shift away from economic autarky and toward neoliberal policies of governmental and foreign investment, which stimulated the industrial development of Spain and the economic boom of the 1960s.

Some of the ideological groundwork for this policy shift had already been laid by such intellectuals of Opus Dei as Don Enrique and his friend and mentor, Rafael Calvo Serer. Even before 1955, these men had turned away from the doctrine of "integrism" and defined themselves as a "third force" in opposition both to Falangists on the far right and to Catholic liberals on the far left of the spectrum of political opinion tolerated within the regime. This "third force" supported a "traditional, social, popular monarchy" that would not be dogmatically opposed to a gradual and orderly political and economic evolution of Spanish society (Carr and Fusi 1981:171). By 1960, Don Enrique and a powerful minority faction within Opus Dei had shifted their position still farther to the left and essentially reached an accommodation with political and economic liberalism. Don Enrique now envisioned a "universal Catholicism" that maintained an "open" attitude toward capitalist economic development and the influence of the democratic societies of western Europe. Indeed, by the end of his career, Don Enrique had gone so far as to cautiously espouse the ideal of a democratic monarchy for post-Franco Spain and had thus disassociated himself from the politicians of the "bunker" who wished to preserve the basic institutions of the authoritarian regime.

Even though Don Enrique had left the rural life of his boyhood days in Aracena far behind him and played an active role in the factional politics at the highest levels of the Francoist state, he did not forsake his birthplace and he visited his native *pueblo* as often as he could. Moreover, during the entire postwar period, he did everything within his considerable power to improve the conditions of life in the town. For years, no delegation sent from Aracena to Madrid on local business failed to call on him for advice and favors on matters important for the town, and on his own initiative Don Enrique used his

influence with the higher levels of the national bureaucracy to promote many local projects. Among his other achievements, Don Enrique managed to persuade the Opus Dei leaders of Seville to choose
a site in Aracena on which to build a large mansion (complete with
swimming pool and tennis courts) to serve as a retreat and conference
center. But his most important practical contribution to the town was
in the field of education. It was Don Enrique who first proposed to the
town council in 1951 (ACM, 1 Dec. 1951) the project of founding El
Instituto Laboral, and his continuing patronage was instrumental in
bringing the long process of establishing the school to a successful
conclusion. It was also Don Enrique who originated the idea that
Aracena build a school preparing students for advanced technical and
university education in the early 1960s. Such projects contributed directly to the town's development and helped facilitate the transition
from an agrarian to a service-oriented economy. Equally important,
however, was Don Enrique's leading influence on the emergent ideology of authoritarian populism within the community in the 1960s
and early 1970s. Under his influence, the political culture of Aracena
in the waning years of Franco's Spain represented a curious mixture of
state authoritarianism and socioeconomic populism.

Local officials took care to return the concrete favors and astute advice of Don Enrique with profuse expressions of gratitude and ful-
some praise. In fact, they had little else to offer, since he had no vital
local political interests and did not require local support to sustain his
influence within the regime. Thus, the town council honored Don Enrique as a benevolent patron and over the years heaped accolade after
accolade upon him. He received the bronze, silver, and gold medals of
virtue from the town and was designated a favorite son. The plaza of
the Instituto was named after his mother, and the statue dedicated "to
all the mothers of Aracena" in its center is reputed to bear a strong
resemblance to her. As a final gesture of gratitude and homage shortly
before his death, the town council decided to place a statue of Don
Enrique near the entrance to the church of "El Castillo." With this
measure, Don Enrique was received into the official pantheon of the
town's honored patrons. The grateful council eulogized him as one
who had always "extended his generous hand toward us to aid us in
every just and noble aspiration" (ACM, 15 July 1973).

Before his death, Don Enrique had eagerly embraced the role of
patron, and his writings, which are in the best tradition of pastoral
epic, testify to his intense heartfelt attachment to the town. On one
occasion, for example, he wrote of how a visit to Aracena awoke in his
spirit "deep maternal and childhood echoes and bittersweet memories
of boyhood and youth" and of how it pleased him "to magnify such

memories" by telling himself that they represented "*la vida más mía*" (the most authentic and deepest aspect of his life). As such passages make clear, Don Enrique's sense of social obligation to his birthplace was based on a pastoral vision of rural life, and his interest in his native town, which was so important for the community in a pragmatic sense, was nevertheless for him mostly a matter of nostalgic ties to an idealized, half-remembered past. Thus, while Don Enrique's explicit political and ideological orientation had changed dramatically in the postwar period, his evolution toward democratic liberalism scarcely altered his sense of himself as a person, which continued to be centered on romantic notions of benevolent patronage, authority, personal honor, and social hierarchy. What his ideological evolution did do, however, was lead him to describe the essence of traditional culture in his native town in terms of pastoral, egalitarian, and populist idioms and images.

Don Enrique died in 1973, two years before Franco, and under the new democratic regime, no comparable figure has achieved or is likely to achieve his stature as a patron of the community. Indeed, Don Enrique left two great political legacies that continued to influence the politics of the transition period in Aracena. The first was a willingness and even eagerness to increase the town's economic dependence on the largess of state bureaucracies and to make every effort to attract new agencies, civil service jobs, and programs. The second legacy was a "best of both worlds" policy that associated material progress with an increased capacity to preserve a distinctive traditional way of life in the community. Both of these legacies were well expressed in Don Enrique's last project for the improvement of the quality of life in Aracena and the one that was perhaps closest to his heart: the project of securing state funds to found a museum of the sierran folk arts that would bring tourists to Aracena and the region.

The museum eventually failed because it was underfunded, attracted few visitors, and represented a considerable drain on the town's finances. But faith in Don Enrique's "best of both worlds" approach to the contemporary dilemmas facing Aracena continued, with the great majority of the community adopting the practical political goal of ensuring the town's economic viability by accepting the benefits (and costs) of state support and by maintaining a balance between tradition and modernity. As a result of these attitudes, community politics tended to be dominated by two interrelated concerns during the transition period: concerns about which people and parties could best maintain relations with the higher reaches of officialdom and which of them could offer the best blend and synthesis of local customary values with the forces of sociopolitical progress. The focus on political style and personal character severely limited the amount of local debate about substantive issues. And as discussed below, since the socialists of the PSOE were best able to present themselves as friends rather than patrons of the *pueblo* and as the political defenders and paragons of traditional social virtues, they were able to consolidate their hold on municipal offices during the latter phases of the transition period.

ELECTORAL POLITICS AND THE PERSONALIZATION OF CLASS DIFFERENCES

The 1979 municipal elections were the first democratic local elections in forty-three years. The parties and politics surrounding them and resulting from them had both general parallels with and essential differences from the politics of the Second Republic in Aracena. As in the past, class-based voting was the general pattern, although there were enough exceptions to the rule that votes were nearly evenly divided between parties of the left and the right.

On the right were two parties: (1) a local branch of the UCD, the conservative party in power nationally; and (2) El Grupo Independiente de Aracena (GUIA), a smaller local party. The UCD's local electoral list was headed by politicians and officeholders of the Franco regime, but most of these men were, like Don Enrique had been, fairly moderate in their political positions. However, most of the militants of the UCD were also from the old landowning families of the town and a number of them were professionals, especially lawyers. The core group of the GUIA consisted of a number of middle-class businessmen, most from old *comerciante* families.

On the left were three parties: (1) a local branch of the PSOE, the main national opposition party; (2) El Partido Socialista Andaluz (PSA), a regional party that was committed to securing and developing the autonomy of the eight provinces of Andalusia in the new organization of the Spanish state; and (3) La Organización Revolucionaria de Trabajadores (ORT), a party farther to the left than either of the above socialist parties. In Aracena, the leader of the small group of radical men and women in the ORT was a popular young man who had considerable support in his own neighborhood and almost won a seat on the town council. Otherwise, few townspeople were attracted by the youthful ardor of the ORT. Most of the loyalists of the parties of the left were from the white-collar working class and skilled trades, although professionals, civil servants, students, small businessmen, and agrarian workers were also represented on their party lists.

The municipal electoral campaign was cautious in tone. The parties on the left called for a new era of progress and social justice that would correct the inequities of the past. The UCD claimed that its previous experience and solid connections with the political officials of the province would bring concrete benefits to the town. The GUIA cast itself as the voice of moderation, stressed its nonideological character, and argued that it would serve the interests of the community rather than those of the national parties. While none of the leaders on the left had any voice in previous political affairs, they argued that they could best carry forward reforms in local government. The townspeople were thus presented with a choice between those who adopted a rhetoric of patronage, influence, and experience and those who identified themselves as friends of the people and pledged fair treatment for all members of the community.

The results of the election left no party with a clear majority, and the vote count of one of the electoral districts was challenged in a way that was highly reminiscent of the chicaneries of the Second Republic. The dispute was eventually settled by provincial authorities, who awarded the PSOE four seats on the town council; the PSA, three seats; the UCD, four seats; and the GUIA, two seats. The socialist parties formed a coalition that gave them a seven-to-six majority, sufficient to control the council and to name an *alcalde* (mayor) from the PSOE. However, the majority coalition did not attempt to control all of the working committees of the council (as had been the case in the Second Republic), and each party had at least one representative on the "permanent commission" (the day-to-day administrative committee). This moderate stance meant that there would be no walkouts as occurred in the Second Republic. But it also meant that the council could potentially become an arena of intense partisan debate.

Yet once the council had been established, it became increasingly apparent that the various parties had little to disagree upon in terms of the day-to-day overseeing of practical affairs or in the matter of long-range policy goals. On the contrary, there was a consensus that the best course for the future lay in continuing the policies established in the era of Don Enrique. In pursuing these policies of community boosterism and state support, a spirit of caution and cooperation prevailed on both the right and the left. Although none of the parties on the council proved itself particularly more adept than the others at achieving their common goals, each devoted considerable energies to convincing townspeople that it had best reflected the general values of the community and should be given a vote of confidence in the next round of municipal elections.

The primary difficulty faced by the local socialists was that of allaying the fears of the conservative sectors of the middle class, who believed that the party members were closet radicals despite their professed moderation. The conservatives had the burden of convincing at least some members of the working-class majority that they were genuine democrats rather than secret Francoists. In the long run, the socialists were far more successful in overcoming townspeople's reservations about them because they followed a traditionalizing strategy of presenting differences in class position and interest in terms of the personal character flaws and lack of social virtues of the leading members of the opposition. By personalizing and domesticating class differences, they managed to cast their opponents in a bad light and at the same time were able to reaffirm their own claims to be moderate and reasonable defenders of the values of the whole community.

One of the most revealing issues that emerged in the first year of democratic government was a dispute over the question of whether the *alcalde* should receive a salary. The socialist *alcalde* worked in the office of a bus company and had a modest income, but his political duties caused him to miss a great deal of work and thus suffer financially. The parties on the left argued that the post of *alcalde* should be established as a salaried job. Members of the UCD protested that the post was an honor and that the incumbent should resign if he could not afford to continue. The issue generated a bitter debate and created enduring resentments among some council members—particularly the *alcalde* and the head of the UCD, a lawyer of independent means from an old gentry family. Eventually, the issue was decided in favor of the *alcalde,* but its broader political impact was to enable the socialists to portray their adversaries as personally haughty, mean-spirited, and shamelessly manipulative.

A second issue that attracted public attention in the early months of democratic government concerned the *casetas* of the *feria* (fair). The *casetas* were tents set up by private groups who hired cooks, bartenders, and musicians to serve and entertain them during the three or four days of *feria* celebrations in August. Because of the costs involved and also because previous town councils had tended to grant permission to establish *casetas* only to upper-class and well-heeled middle-class groups with "correct" political opinions, most of the community had no *casetas*.

The majority coalition on the council seized on the issue of the *casetas* soon after the elections. The socialists of the PSOE and PSA proposed that entertainment for future *ferias* be publicly sponsored, open to all, and financially supported by the municipality. The conservative forces of the UCD and GUIA opposed this on the grounds that it was an attack on the town's traditions and an unwarranted drain on municipal funds. The socialists continued to declare in the closed sessions of the council that the *feria* should be "eminently popular" in character and meet the needs of the general public rather than special groups, and they also began to make the issue public in hopes of creating a tide of popular support for their plans. This strategy generated arguments, proposals, and counterproposals from all quarters. The conservatives were forced to soften their initial opposition and eventually proposed that funding for public entertainment be increased. But they continued their efforts to convince middle-class members of the community that the socialist council members were ignorant men who had no sense of formality and were willing to destroy the beautiful "ambience" of the *feria* simply to pander to vulgar tastes.

Despite this charge, the majority on the council insisted on adopting a policy that relegated private *casetas* to the side streets and alleyways around La Plaza Mayor. This rule effectively destroyed the "ambience" of the *casetas* by removing them from the center of *feria* activities, and although the private groups bravely put on a show of enjoying themselves during the first "popular" *feria* in 1979, the *casetas* languished in the years that followed. By the time of the *feria* of 1982, only one *caseta* remained. According to the socialists, the *feria* had become "truly popular" and "more animated" thanks to the free entertainment and municipally sponsored, low-cost drink and food concessions.

The issue of the *casetas* represented an ideal opportunity for the socialists because it permitted them to attack a residual "privilege" of the old elite, to associate themselves with the "comic" rather than "tragic" aspects of community traditions, and to accomplish both of these ends without making themselves vulnerable to the charge that they were irresponsible radicals. Indeed, throughout the debates on the *feria*, they somewhat disingenuously insisted that their purpose was not to abolish the *casetas* but simply to give a more central role to forms of entertainment and diversion open to the whole community. Yet by putting the *casetas* in their proper place, they managed to isolate their political opponents by defining the conservative position on the *feria* as one representing the interests of a narrow, exclusive social group.

The debates surrounding the *alcalde*'s salary and the *feria* set the tone, defined the principal types of issues, and gave the socialists the initial advantage during the first year of the new democratic political regime in the town. And as time passed, the socialists were repeatedly able to capitalize on their initial success. One of the key ways in which they did this was to create difficult situations for their opponents and then by means of rumors, jokes, and various other forms of insinuation to associate the conservatives' awkward responses to these situations with some of the worst memories of past injustices.

For example, in early 1981, two cultural events were scheduled (probably not by accident) to occur on the same afternoon. One was the *pregón* of Holy Week, a speech announcing the current plans and recounting the history of the penitential brotherhoods. The other was the annual fiesta of the patron saint of a small *aldea* (dependent hamlet). The *pregón*, which is generally attended by all the officers of the penitential brotherhoods and the more pious members of the middle class, had a particularly reactionary stamp on this occasion because the honored speaker was an aging and somewhat decrepit but well-known and thoroughly unrepentant Francoist. The *aldea*'s fiesta was, in contrast, a minor and usually sparsely attended but purely popular, working-class affair. Not surprisingly, all of the leading conservative politicians of the town decided to attend the *pregón*. Meanwhile, however, unbeknownst to the conservatives, the *alcalde* and other leading socialists took the unprecedented step of showing up en masse in the *aldea* and played a prominent role in the day's modest celebrations. The news of this spread rapidly through town, and people naturally interpreted the politicians' choices as reflecting their basic political loyalties and class allegiances. The socialists' clever move had made it appear as if the conservatives disdained ordinary townsfolk and preferred the verbal meanderings of an old reactionary.

Around the same time that the events described above occurred, a witticism concerning one of the town's conservative politicians was also being repeated in all of the town's bars. This humorous gossip centered around the politician's involvement in administering the town's tourist attraction, Las Grutas de las Maravillas (the marvelous caverns). The politician was the head of the committee responsible for the upkeep of the caverns and was a lawyer from an old gentry family. He had held a number of important political offices in the town and the province during the last years of the Franco regime, and he had been elected to the town council on the strength of campaign promises to use his provincial connections for the benefit of his constituents. Although he was competent, openhearted, and moderately progressive in his political opinions, he was rather shy and extremely formal in dealing with ordinary townspeople and had perhaps an overly cultivated and refined manner. Probably to avoid having much to do with people he did not know well, he had the habit of walking about the streets gazing upward in what seemed to be rapt meditation. This mannerism had earned him the nickname "Milagros" (miracles) because it appeared that he was constantly expecting a miracle from heaven. The invocation of this nickname continually worked to his political disadvantage because it was commonly remarked that he had worked no "miracles" through his connections with higher powers.

But the political prestige of this man as well as that of his conservative allies suffered a really serious blow in connection with the refusal of the town council to extend his committee's authority over other matters affecting tourism. Ordinarily, this rather minor defeat attributable to the socialist majority on the town council would have caused little stir, but a socialist wit summarized the outcome of the issue by declaring that "*las putas de Milagros no tienen nada más que Las Grutas de las Maravillas*"—a statement that could be interpreted in several ways, including "the followers of Miracles have control only of the caves" or, more colorfully, "the miraculous whores have nothing but their marvelous cavities." Moreover, in the days that followed, the observation underwent a series of transformations playing on the complex meanings of the verb *ganar*, which can signify "to earn" or "to win" or "to allure" (e.g., "the miraculous whores allure because of their marvelous cavities"). All of these observations cast aspersions on the moral character of the conservative politicians both by "feminizing" them in ways that conformed to gender prejudices and by implying that they were motivated by self-interest and greed. Most important, however, the witticism was damaging to the conservatives because, as one man explained, it reminded people of the not too distant past when the old gentry oligarchy controlled the caverns and were commonly thought to skim vast sums of money from their income.

The incidents of the *pregón* and the caverns helped the socialists in their efforts to cast the town's conservatives as back-room plotters and malcontents more interested in their own power and prestige than in the community's general welfare. But it is important to realize that these oblique attacks on the reputation and character of political opponents were efficacious not so much because the charges and slurs were taken seriously by townspeople in political or ideological terms but, rather, because they reduced community politics to a micropolitical level of personal reputation. And at this level, it was possible for the socialists to take advantage of class-influenced differences in styles of social interaction and represent their opponents as less fairminded and openhanded and more egotistic and pretentious than themselves. As a result of this strategy of personalizing the political, the key factor in determining the popularity of politicians during the transition period was the extent to which their actions could be construed in terms of their desire to act the part of superior patrons or of equal friends and representatives of ordinary townspeople. Two contrasting stories that concern the manner in which personal favors were negotiated will serve to illustrate what was involved in winning the trust and confidence of the community and suggest why the socialists were so successful in casting the worst possible light on their opponents by exploiting minor differences.

The first story concerns a middle-aged working-class couple from an *aldea* who came one morning to a local employment office directed by Paco, an influential member of the local branch of the UCD. The aim of their visit was to have their eighteen-year-old son's name restored to a list that determined the order in which assignments to public works projects were awarded to the unemployed. After a delay of fifteen or twenty minutes, Paco called to the couple from his desk and bade them enter his office. The man came in, stopped four or five steps short of Paco's desk, took off his hat, and waited silently. His wife stood behind him. Paco proceeded to shuffle papers and allow time to pass before he looked up and asked the man what he wanted. Nervously fingering his cap, the man hesitantly began to address "Don Paco." With eyes averted, he told the story of how his son had unavoidably missed work one day a couple of weeks earlier and had his name removed from the list. Paco listened with a look of indifference on his face, all the while fiddling with the cord of a window blind wrapped around his finger. After a minute or so, he interrupted the countryman's story and declared that there was nothing he could do until a new list was posted at the first of the month (i.e., three and a half weeks hence). Then he observed that if the family needed money, they should have seen to it that their son appeared for work on the right day. Hearing this, the countryman's wife thrust herself in front of her husband and interrupted Paco with repeated invocations of the Virgin. The first words of her speech, which were delivered with dramatic gestures and in a tone of righteous indignation, were more or less as follows: "Mother of God! Mother of God! What are we to do? Is my family to go hungry because my son took his father to the doctor? How can a family live without work? Are we to be gypsies in the street when we have one who can work? This is a shame—to live without a *duro* to buy bread. And you say you can do nothing, Paco? You don't have a family? Mother of God!"

Paco was visibly amused by this diatribe but again said there was nothing he could do, although his tone was less firm and peremptory. Detecting this shift, the woman repeated her speech again with a few variations and even more loudly. When she had finished, Paco looked at her askance, told the couple to wait, and went into another office. He returned a minute or two later, shaking his head sadly and saying how difficult the matter was. Finally, he said he would see what he could do and dismissed the couple from his presence. The following week, the son's name reappeared on the work list.

Dramas of this kind were an everyday occurrence in Paco's office and usually unfolded along predictable lines, with Paco taking every opportunity to indicate his superior status and authority but then granting the requests. He seemed to think that he was thereby securing the political loyalty and gratitude of those who came to him. But the agonistic style of the interaction, which pitted the bureaucracy and its impersonal rules against the townspeople and their personal, informal, domestic idioms, was bound to work to Paco's disadvantage. Although by no means all of the conservative politicians of the town were so inept or insensitive as Paco in their dealings with ordinary townspeople, many clearly found it difficult to adopt a more egalitarian style and were not comfortable in their role as servants of the people.

In contrast, interactions between the socialists and their constituents were usually conducted in an informal, familiar, and "comic" style. An example is the way in which a delicate situation was handled by Alberto, a member of the PSOE, a resident of an *aldea,* and a *vicealcalde* of Aracena, when one of his neighbors needed a favor at the time of year when families of the *aldeas* customarily slaughter one or two hogs to provide meat for the household (see Chapter 5 and Capel 1982). Until the last decade or so, virtually every household with sufficient means raised hogs for this purpose, and the "whole *pueblo*" worked together, first helping one family with its *matanza* and then being helped in return with the labors of slaughtering the hogs and preparing the hams and sausages. Not everybody raises hogs now, and to invite neighbors who have no hogs of their own to a *matanza* is tantamount to demanding hours of labor without compensation. Except in the case of close friends, extending an invitation under these circumstances would be shameful because it amounts to asking for charity or to be patronized.

This, at least, is how one woman who was the head of a household of five children felt as the time approached to butcher her hogs. Because of a long drought, most people had decided not to keep any hogs that year in order to avoid the daily burden of carrying water to them. Nevertheless, María was not really worried about having enough help to prepare the meat before it spoiled; her children could work, and she had a number of close friends among the women of the *aldea.* What troubled her was the problem of who would actually butcher her hogs. This job, which is traditionally men's work, requires considerable strength and skill. Unfortunately, María's husband, who supported his family by working in a factory in northern Spain, had exhausted his vacation time and had written that he would be unable to return for the slaughter. Her three sons were too young and inexperienced to be of other than peripheral assistance. In these circumstances, the obvious person to invite to the slaughter was Alberto, who had a reputation as the best butcher in the hamlet. Moreover, his wife, Margarita, was an acknowledged mistress of the art of sausage making. However, María was not particularly close to the couple; they had no hogs that year; and Alberto's job and political duties in Aracena kept him busy and away from home. María's friends advised her to invite Alberto and Margarita anyway, but María could not bring herself to ask the favor. Instead, she declared that if no one else was available on the day of the *matanza,* her eldest son (a teenager) would butcher the hogs.

This proved unnecessary. When the appointed day arrived, Margarita and Alberto came uninvited to María's house, equipped with knives and other needed articles. Alberto said he recalled the many times in the past when María's husband had helped other men of the hamlet with the task of killing and how skillful he was in ensuring that no blood from the animals was lost. He then modestly offered to do the killing, although he warned that he was not a very good butcher himself. Obviously overjoyed but struggling to act matter-of-factly, María thanked Alberto, and he and Margarita proceeded to take over the whole business. After the hogs were killed, their bristles burned away, and the carcasses quartered, Alberto offered his apologies and quickly rushed off to Aracena. María, in gratitude and friendship, later carried a bundle of the choicest bits of meat to the house of Alberto and Margarita. Alberto protested that María was being excessively generous, but he eventually accepted the gift with many thanks.

In effect, Alberto, Margarita, and María had all silently conspired with one another to interpret the situation not as an act of patronage or exchange of unequal favors but instead as an occasion for maintaining a voluntary and equal friendship based on principles of generalized reciprocity and gestures of mutual goodwill. Alberto, in particular, had not only voluntarily helped María but also proved himself a master of tact and grace by doing everything in his power to underplay the generosity of his action. By acting as he did, he virtually guaranteed that few people in the *aldea* would forget what sort of person he was at election time.

In public politics, as in the private interactions in these two examples, the focus was on personal reputation and class relations. Most of the issues that emerged as topics of public discussion resonated with the townspeople's mundane concerns regarding how to deal with one another as they went about the affairs of daily life. From this perspective, what was striking about community politics was its lack of differentiation from the micropolitics of daily life. Despite the force of bureaucratic procedures, the requirements of elections, and the formal responsibilities of office, the dominant tendency was to domesticate the political by reabsorbing it culturally into the realm of quotidian social values and styles of social interaction. Moreover, to the extent that this domestication occurred, it gave a political advantage to the socialists because their class backgrounds and ideological predispositions generally made them appear "more equal" or more egalitarian than their opponents and because they had the social skills to know how to present themselves to ordinary townspeople as paragons of the social virtues of openness, formality, and grace and as defenders of the traditional moral values of the community. In short, the socialists were masters of the common touch. Their awareness of the broad sociopolitical implications and cultural resonances of their positions on such issues as the *feria* and more generally their ways of interacting with their constituents helped them convince the townspeople that they could adapt to new conditions and opportunities without undermining the town's identity as a traditional community.

The political payoff of the socialists' campaign of personalization and domestication of class issues came in 1981, when forces within the town council realigned, enabling the PSOE to strengthen its hold in Aracena. Both internal and external factors brought about the realignment. In the elections of 1979, the regional socialists of the PSA had taken the lead in supporting the establishment of the eight provinces of Andalusia as an autonomous political entity within the Spanish state. However, within a year or so of the elections, the PSOE had managed to deprive the PSA of its distinctive position on the autonomy issue by adopting a similar stance and playing a leading role in the negotiations concerning the constitution of the regional government. In danger of losing its identity as an independent political force, the PSA began to pull out of its alliance with the PSOE. The general breakdown of the alliance on the regional level provoked a crisis in the town council of Aracena because it destroyed the majority coalition of the PSOE and PSA and opened the possibility for the conservative minority on the town council to take control of local affairs.

This, however, did not occur. Instead, the PSOE socialists were able to convince the local middle-class conservatives of the GUIA to enter into an alliance with them. This realignment isolated members of the UCD (on the right) and the PSA (on the left) and gave the new centrist coalition of PSOE socialists and GUIA independents a working majority on the council. The cultural and economic factors that led the conservatives of the GUIA to be willing to forge an alliance with the socialists of the PSOE are worth discussing because they suggest how finely attuned the socialists' political tactics were to encompassing hegemonic processes of corporate and bureaucratic domination and how difficult such processes are to resist.

INVESTMENTS IN TRADITION: LOCAL CREDIT, THE TRIUMPH OF THE SOCIALISTS, AND THE POPES OF ROCK 'N' ROLL

For most of the twentieth century, Aracena's more prosperous *comerciante* (merchant) families had ranked as the town's most orthodox and pious Catholics and had been the political dependents of the agrarian gentry. These families and other middle-class businessmen and shopkeepers had positioned themselves politically as defenders of the local community, claiming that they were not tied to specific parties and that they were nonideological conservatives and moderates. Nevertheless, it was this group that was represented by the GUIA during the period of transition. Its members were particularly wary of residual anticlericalism among the parties of the Spanish left and were hardly the natural allies of the PSOE socialists. And even though they decided it was to their advantage to form a coalition with the PSOE, this decision was not based on any change in the explicit political principles of either group. Rather, it stemmed from the dramatic shift in local socioeconomic conditions in the twenty years before 1980, a shift that altered the pattern of social relations and economic interactions between middle-class merchants and working-class townspeople.

Until the 1960s, local merchants (with the exception of most grocers and food vendors) were far more eager to extend credit for purchases to one another and to well-off professional and gentry families than they were to the impoverished working classes. In particular, the economic preeminence of the landowning families was such that they could command credit on easy terms in exchange for their continuing patronage of local businessmen who were their dependents both politically and economically. In contrast, credit was easily extended to poor people only for the bare necessities of life. For other purchases, credit was granted grudgingly and only for small amounts because most merchants viewed the extension of credit to the poor as either foolhardy economic miscalculation or concealed charity. As a result of this and other factors, social relations between the *comerciante* group and most of the town's working class were generally distant, tense, and full of mutual mistrust. This pattern is still evident among some elderly working-class people who regard well-established shopkeepers with great suspicion, complain constantly about prices, carefully count their change, and worry about possible chicanery in bookkeeping practices.

However, the general pattern of merchants' relations with ordinary townspeople has greatly improved since the early 1960s, when the community became more exposed to the temptations and pleasures of consumerism, the economic dominance of the agrarian gentry declined, and most working-class people began to have more disposable income. As merchants came to depend more and more on the collective purchasing power of the whole community for their livelihoods, both their credit policies and their general attitude toward working-class people softened. These days, merchants are not only willing but indeed eager to extend credit to almost anybody from the town and *aldeas* of Aracena, although they are still a bit cautious in their dealings with the people from surrounding *pueblos*. And younger buyers seem to have few qualms about merchants or about going into debt.

The extension of credit is necessary and attractive to the merchants and customers for a number of reasons. First, local merchants have difficulty matching the prices of the large stores of Seville to which townspeople have increasingly resorted. The extension of easy credit and the convenience and availability of local service compensate to some degree for the difference between local and city prices. Second, extending credit increases the number of purchases of nonessential and expensive goods, such as appliances and television sets. Most households have reliable if modest incomes, and people find it easier to set aside small amounts of money to repay their debts than they do to save large sums. Third, the amount of disposable income of local farmers, young people with sporadic employment, and bar and restaurant workers who are dependent on tourism and summer visitors varies considerably from time to time, and extending credit to these people increases the amount of "impulse" buying of luxury items.

Indeed, in some families, the memory of abject poverty in the past and anxieties about the economic future powerfully contribute to a desire to enjoy the relative prosperity of the present for as long as it lasts. As a result, luxury purchases on credit have a tendency to wreak havoc with family budgets. In one case, for example, the mother of a working-class family was counting on the money her son earned during six weeks of back-breaking work in the fields to supplement the household budget for the winter, but the son suddenly decided to spend all of his earnings to pay the first installment on a gold bracelet for his fiancée. The mother did not complain even though the whole family had to eat *miga* (a pan-fried dish of bread, potatoes, garlic, and onions) for two weeks. The factors involved in purchases such as this provide a clear economic rationale for local merchants to give credit to those denied it in the past.

Despite the manifest practical sense of extending credit, the way the credit system actually operates in local stores bears little resemblance to the financial pattern that prevails in the cities, where charge accounts, credit cards, and consumer loans with high-interest fixed-repayment schedules are the rule. Merchants in Aracena charge virtually no interest; there are no fixed monthly payments; and many small debts are kept on the account books for years. Merchants point to such practices to support their claim that they make no money by giving credit. They like to assure people that extending credit is an informal gesture of goodwill and neighborliness.

There are indeed good reasons for denying the profit-making, calculating side of local credit, and these reasons involve more than the simple matter of public relations. Suppressing the direct economic character of credit transactions is crucial if the merchants want to be repaid with any degree of promptness. As mentioned above, suspicions of the trustworthiness of businessmen persist among older people, and for any merchant to resort to legal mechanisms to force repayment is likely to be far more perilous for the merchant than for the debtor and might well lead to a drastic decline in business. Resorting to the law would be seen as a violation of community values, just as in the political sphere excessive regard for bureaucratic regulations is seen as a sign of misplaced allegiances. As one merchant said, to take legal action or even to pressure malingering debtors for payment is almost unthinkable because it would destroy people's "confidence" in the merchant's character. What makes the local credit system work is not coercive threats but the desire of both parties in a transaction to maintain their reputations as people with a sense of "formality" and obligation. The repayment of debts is a matter of pride, and most townspeople make every effort to make regular payments. Even during times of domestic crisis, they generally deliver token amounts of money to their creditors on the first of the month.

Of course, not all people are sufficiently concerned with their reputations to repay their debts. For example, one family man of sufficient means made a small down payment on a refrigerator, took it home, and then made almost no payments for the next eight years. The merchant involved in this transaction chose to write off the debt as a loss. Instead of taking legal action, he simply told the story of his patience and forbearance and of his debtor's irresponsibility to anyone who would listen. This redounded to his credit and his debtor's loss. Merchants generally handle bad debts in this way, and this strategy of underplaying the economic, calculating side of credit transactions and emphasizing the moral and social character of obligations between merchants and their customers seems, on the whole, remarkably successful.

Moreover, it is noteworthy that in all but the most mundane exchanges, the idea seems to be that money should change hands more or less under the table and, if possible, silently. For example, when rent is paid to a landlord, the tenant will often devise an excuse for the visit and leave the money on a desk or table at the conclusion of what is ostensibly treated as a social call. Direct offers of payment are usually initially met with an outright refusal to accept or a wave of the hand suggesting the unimportance of the matter. Thus, day-to-day transactions are generally characterized by an exaggerated desire of the parties involved to avoid the appearance that they are motivated by narrow considerations of economic self-interest. There is little haggling over prices, and when townspeople do bargain, it either tends to be done in a joking manner or else indirectly and cautiously with comments on prices directed vaguely into the air rather than toward the other person involved.

Indeed, it usually appears as if money is a secondary consideration in commercial transactions and that the central aim of the negotiation is to nourish the friendship of the two parties and maintain it on an equal basis.[3] Great care is taken in matters of debt and credit to avoid the appearance that one party is patronizing the other, and credit arrangements are treated as a simple matter of mutually convenient and beneficial arrangements between friends. The interactions involved in an extended credit-debt relationship are frequently conducted as a series of gift exchanges. Thus, when the final payment is made on a substantial debt, the merchant generally responds by giving the faithful customer something of value. For example, when the time came for a man to make his last payment on some furniture, he sent his two teenage nieces to pay. They anticipated a gift and were given one by the dealer. This gesture of sending "ambassadors" reasserted the debtor's equality and affirmed his friendship with the dealer by placing both the debtor and the dealer in the position of patrons of the young women.

As this brief description of local trade suggests, credit practices have generally been thoroughly integrated within the encompassing customary patterns of interactions of daily social life that revolve around the exchange of favors and debts and the honoring of personal obligations. For their shops and businesses to prosper, merchants must maintain friendly relations with everyone in town, rich and poor alike, and must stress the importance of mutual moral obligations and fair dealings among social equals and members of the same community.

It is in these concerns that the merchants represented by the GUIA had much in common with local socialist politicians of the PSOE during the last phase of the transition period. For somewhat different reasons, neither group had an interest in stirring up past class conflicts that would exacerbate social tensions in the community, and neither wanted to be associated too closely with impersonal corporate or bureaucratic ideologies, institutions, and procedures. The merchants had no wish to remind working-class townspeople of their former affiliations with the agrarian gentry, and they had to differentiate their way of doing business from that of the large enterprises of Seville in order to compete. The socialists, without betraying their dedication to democratic, egalitarian principles, wanted to answer charges that they were intemperate radicals intent on either resurrecting old class conflicts or imposing ill-considered reforms that would threaten the possibility of continuing social and economic progress. To steer through these dangers and win the confidence of fellow townspeople, both groups sought to personalize and domesticate political and economic relations within the community. The natural outgrowth of these tactics was the promotion of a "best of both worlds" vision of Aracena as a place where the need for progress was counterbalanced by the love and respect for local customs and virtues. Thus, both the merchants and the socialists embraced traditional idioms and images of pastoral epic as a means of making the best of the politicoeconomic pressures and constraints of the transition period.

The political wisdom of the PSOE-GUIA coalition was confirmed in the second round of municipal elections that occurred in 1983. In this round, the GUIA no longer existed as a formal group, but former members of the party won more seats on the new council than the PSA socialists did. The conservatives of the UCD were routed in their bid for reelection and as an organized group were no longer a force in local politics. The PSOE, in contrast, obtained a majority on the town council and assumed almost unchallenged leadership in community affairs. Overall, then, the second round of municipal elections represented a decisive triumph of the forces of the center-left and for all practical purposes concluded the period of transition from dictatorship to liberal democracy in the town. This triumph was in keeping with trends in national politics, which had given the PSOE a large majority in the national elections of the autumn of 1982, and it reflected not only the consolidation of parliamentary institutions in Spain but also the emergence of a broadly based national social democratic consensus concerning the governance of the country.

Yet from the perspective of Aracena, many of the contemporary concomitants and implications for the future of middle-of-the-road social democracy were disturbing. The transition period extended and even deepened the dependence of the town on the redistributive mechanisms of the state—the key political legacy of Don Enrique. Moreover, there were few genuine local reforms enacted during the transition period, since the socialists' efforts to assuage local fears, particularly those of the middle class, imposed strict limits on what they attempted to accomplish. Indeed, because the whole thrust of their strategy was to avoid provoking new class struggles while at the same time evoking past ones in a half-comic, low-key manner that was intended to discredit and isolate conservatives, even such modest measures as increasing municipal property taxes were beyond serious consideration. As a result, the local triumph of social democracy was attained at the cost of a substantial depoliticization of community affairs.

Instead of addressing questions about the relation of the community to the national state or its place within the autonomous region of Andalusia, the PSOE socialists' tactics of personalization and domestication tended to obscure such issues by creating the impression that local social tensions and political disputes were attributable to the character flaws and outmoded prejudices of their opponents rather than to the persistence of patterns of class inequalities. In addition, while members of the PSOE and GUIA continually affirmed that the customs, manners, and morals of Aracena were distinct and should be preserved, they did little to impede or alter the impact of economic forces that were transforming the town into a rural outpost of consumer society. Thus, although the rhetoric and images of tradition had a central place in the political culture of the transition period, the principal effect of their use was the hegemonic one of ensuring that the community's incorporation into the emergent corporate and bureaucratic liberal state system was comfortable, smooth, and all but painless.

But this is not quite the whole story of the transition period. In spite of the deep investment of the leading sectors of local opinion in the new liberal regime, among some townspeople there was an often expressed sense that something was missing, some opportunities were being lost, and some aspirations were being cast to the wayside in the rush to get the institutional vehicles of liberalism up and running and on the road to the future. By no means everyone was convinced that the new order represented an ideal balance of local traditions and contemporary forces of cultural and political change. What the mass media were fond of calling *el desencanto* (the disenchantment) was evident in Aracena in expressions of apathy, impatience, and resentment directed primarily toward national and local politicians. And while the PSOE's and GUIA's embrace of the modern variant of pastoral epic made it difficult to criticize the dominant point of view that things were about as good in the town as it was realistically possible to expect, those whose voices had been muted during the process of the transition, particularly the supporters of the PSA and the national parties of the far left, were not completely bereft of cultural resources. Indeed, even amidst the PSOE's celebrations of victories such as their successful effort to popularize the *feria*, voices of resistance and proclamations of a sharply different view of the relation of local customs and traditions to contemporary sociopolitical forces could be heard.

One such voice was that of Antonio Vargas, a man who was in his early sixties during the transition period. Vargas had been born into an impoverished working-class family from one of Aracena's *aldeas*, and his elder brother was one of the leading revolutionaries of the mid-1930s. Vargas himself had participated in the working-class movement of the period, but thanks to a stroke of bad luck, he had been forcibly drafted into the Nationalist army after the capture of Aracena. His outstanding war record and his marriage to a woman from a well-connected, right-wing, middle-class family had enabled him to prosper in the postwar period, and he had kept his leftist political opinions to himself. In the waning years of the Franco regime, however, he had increasingly felt freer to speak out and had soon become somewhat notorious as one of those who had "changed his shirt" from blue (the color of the Francoist Falange) to red. Always something of a social and political misfit, by the early 1980s Vargas was one of the few people of any influence in Aracena to express support for the positions of the Spanish Communist party, although he never became a party member.

During the town *feria* of 1982, an event occurred that gave Vargas an opportunity to express his disillusionment with the state of community politics. This event was a performance by a nationally famous rock band that had been invited to the town in conjunction with the PSOE's efforts to create a "truly popular *feria*." Most (though not all) of Aracena's younger generation enthusiastically welcomed the band, and the performance was a glitter rock spectacular with images from 1950s horror films and commedia dell'arte mixed in. For weeks afterward, it seemed that every bar with a youthful clientele was constantly blaring the band's songs into the streets—much to the annoyance of many of the town's older inhabitants, who were almost equally vocal in expressing their disapproval of the whole affair. Vargas was especially incensed by the event, although his opinions otherwise corresponded with those of most of his neighbors. They were shocked by the fact that crowds of youths from nearby towns had camped in the streets and plazas after the concert ended at four in the morning and were less than pleased that the event had the official imprimatur of the town council. Again and again, Vargas denounced the whole business to anyone who would listen. One of his more colorful speeches went like this:

> Why did the town council bring them here? They have no public here. Those *sin vergüenzas* [shameless ones] sleeping in the streets are not from Aracena. That rock group is Basque, and they sing about drugs. . . . *Qué barbaridad!* [How barbarous!] They are nothing but an instrument of propaganda promoting drugs because they want to appear to have a special truth. They are as bad as the priests, who never stop whispering of the mysteries of the faith and obedience to the pope. No, they are worse. They are the true anarchists *sin formalidad* [without formality, manners, and a sense of virtuous behavior], and the authorities brought them here. That is what happens in this so-called democracy. It is an abuse, and the fault is with the parents, the teachers, and the sons of whores on the town council. . . . But let me tell you, better the pope than these degenerates with respect for nothing.

It is perhaps tempting to dismiss this diatribe as the reactionary ravings of an eccentric. The international youth subculture is not held in esteem in many quarters, but it is only rarely compared to the Catholic church. Although most of those who heard Vargas were amused by his vehemence, they did not think what he said was nonsense. On the contrary, his speech about the popes of rock 'n' roll was compelling precisely because it drew together many serious matters of concern to ordinary townspeople in an unusual but revealing way. For many in Aracena, the local appearance of the band was a perfect example of the intrusive and increasingly fluid flow of images, information, and performers associated with encompassing processes of liberalization in the post-Franco era. It was experienced as a violation of the cultural boundaries of the community that had transformed a traditional local festival into an unanticipated and undesired celebration of modernity. In response to this event, Vargas's speech reasserted a set of local and traditional values, including those of "formality," "respect," and a sense of "shame," in opposition to the external sources of cultural authority represented by the pope and the rock band. But his speech did more than reconstruct the moral boundaries of the community; it redrew those boundaries in a highly politically charged manner that was intended to provoke conflict and debate by lumping together and excluding from the moral community the wayward youth, indulgent parents, socialist members of the town council, teachers, and other local agents of the state.

By associating the rock band with the pope and by associating drugs with the mysteries of the faith, Vargas conveyed the message that one form of cultural hegemony which reinforced authority and discipline (the Catholic church) was rapidly being supplanted by another form which was market-driven and centered on consumption and diversion. At the same time, however, he also conveyed the sense that it was still pretty much the same old story of exploitation and subordination albeit in a new and slicker guise. His invocation of the frustrated will of the people of the community recalled and reanimated for his listeners the old revolutionary ideals of local autonomy that had shaped the class conflicts during the Civil War period, but it was also designed to criticize and undermine the emergent center-left political and cultural hegemony of the life of the town, region, and nation by directing attention to the complicity and involvement of the local socialists with contemporary forms of domination closely linked to the dissemination of the commodity culture of international capitalism. These juxtapositions, contrasts, and identifications challenged conventional notions of progress and reaction. Thus, Vargas's diatribe attempted to alter his listeners' sense of the cultural and political possibilities in the present by presenting in a highly condensed form an alternative view of local history that undermined the widespread notion that local customs and values represented an ideal synthesis of the new and the old, a notion that had become dominant during the transition period.

Vargas's act of resistance demonstrated that it was possible to reappropriate and reinterpret traditional images and idioms in a way that permitted them to function as a critical horizon of cultural and political possibilities in contemporary Aracena. In particular, the political implications of the remarks of Vargas and of other local expressions of resistance and dissent seemed to point toward the possibility of transcending the politics of the commonplace within the community by renewing an interest in issues critical to the vitality of the parties and currents of opinion dedicated to increasing Andalusian autonomy. Yet in the aftermath of the transition and throughout the 1980s, such issues did not generate much popular debate or result in any firm support for alternative political agendas within the town. The general failure to question the political agenda and the very ingenuity and creativity that Vargas had to show in order to make his points both testify to just how effective the political culture of pastoral epic that was increasingly embraced during the transition from dictatorship to democracy had been in converting the more or less compliant but discontented subjects of an authoritarian regime into the more or less docile and contented if somewhat uneasy citizens of an advanced liberal capitalist state system. Having come to regard the strength of traditional customs and values as the signs of the vitality of a uniquely beautiful and moral way of life, townspeople felt themselves well compensated for the sacrifices they had to make in order to survive in a subordinate rural community.

Postscript and Conclusions: 1992 and Beyond

Everything that exists, no matter what its origins,
is periodically reinterpreted by those in power in
terms of fresh intentions.
—FRIEDRICH NIETZSCHE
The Genealogy of Morals

IT IS A FINE summer evening and I have contrived to begin this
summation of my research while seated atop the *monte* of "El
Castillo." A decade will soon have passed since my "official" period of fieldwork came to an end in late 1982. On a visit to Aracena in
1985, it seemed to me that very little had changed in the town. But
this is no longer the case. The streets are now jammed with cars; there
are many new apartment buildings and stores; a large health clinic has
been erected; a clinic of veterinary medicine has recently opened; the
meat, fruit, and vegetable stands are now housed in a modern, two-
story edifice; the park at the entrance to the town is freshly landscaped;
a new hotel with a private bath in each room is currently available to
accommodate the tastes of foreigners, who for the first time represent
a significant number of visitors to Las Grutas de las Maravillas; and the
ayuntamiento (town hall), library, and notary offices have been moved
to a large modern complex on the other side of town.

It is apparent that the local socialists, who were cautious in their
proposals during the transition period, now govern without opposition and have a free hand in sponsoring projects to improve the quality
of life in the community. As I look out over the rooftops, I can see five
cranes engaged on construction sites. The parish church is being restored, and an even more luxurious hotel is rising in the *barrio* of San
Pedro. The long-abandoned sixteenth-century town hall, which has recently been declared a monument of historical and artistic value, is be-

ing reconstructed stone by stone. The highway from Aracena to Seville is also being improved, and the trip from the town to the city will soon take less than an hour. But people need not travel to Seville to encounter big-city prices. In Aracena, the costs of ordinary goods have risen dramatically to levels equaling and in some cases exceeding those of urban centers in the member countries of the European Community (EC).

While the price hikes are linked to Spain's entry in the EC, the projects in Aracena are more directly tied to the massive preparations for the Universal Exposition that will be held in Seville in 1992 to commemorate the fifth centennial of the "Discovery of America" and to celebrate "Man's Quest for Knowledge." The exposition is expected to attract eighteen million visitors and to transform Seville from the capital of an underdeveloped and marginal region of Spain into a southern center of high technology and administration—in short, into a center of "the new Europe." At least 110 countries will be represented at the exposition, and there will be parking spaces for forty thousand cars. In the sierra not far from Aracena, a palace in which Seville dignitaries will receive official guests is under construction. Many people in Aracena believe that the exposition will bring a flood of ordinary visitors from Seville and will permanently alter the relation between the town and the city.

But what is becoming of tradition in the town? And how does this relate to longer-range historical and cultural processes? If, as throughout this study, tradition is thought of as a set of strategies that involve using cultural materials from the past to authorize contemporary relations of domination, then the answer to the first question is that tradition is thriving. "After all," as a local brochure puts it, "history and tradition are a tourist attraction of the first order." However, as earlier chapters have shown, more is involved in the contemporary configuration of tradition than exploiting a market niche. In recent years, for example, two new penitential brotherhoods began to take part in the processions of Holy Week in Aracena, an event that few tourists ever attend. And, more generally, it appears that the cultivation of traditional sorts of events, crafts, and folk arts in the town has become the primary avocation of a large group of middle- and working-class townspeople who seem more interested in entertaining, edifying, and defining themselves and their community than in selling their wares to outsiders. Indeed, even though promoting Aracena's reputation as a highly traditional community helps attract tourists and serves to incorporate the town into the contemporary Spanish and European socioeconomic order, traditionalism for most townspeople continues to be the primary means to assert cultural distance and difference.

In this regard, I am reminded of an incident that has vexed me for years and forced me on several occasions to rethink how I should describe the contemporary force of traditional culture in Aracena. The incident involved a snapshot of a man and woman on horseback that I took during the *romería* to La Peña of Alájar several weeks after I arrived in Aracena in 1980. In the snapshot, the young man is doffing his hat, while his companion, attired in the traditional Sevillana dress, is smiling demurely. The horse seems carefully posed. It could be a scene from the land of happy tourists and colorful peasants that Juan Goytisolo (1977) calls "sunnyspain." A few seconds before the shutter clicked, however, the street had been full of shouting riders and panicked horses that could not maintain their footing on the slick cobblestones. A friend of the rider in the photo had lost his hat, and I had stepped from the sidewalk to return it to him. We shook hands, I gestured with the camera, and he nodded his assent to being photographed.

Occupied with his own mount, the young man in the photo had seen none of this. But when he regained control, he noticed me pointing the camera in his general direction. Obviously annoyed, he said something to the woman seated behind him which made her laugh and bite her lip. Then he turned toward me, adopted the pose of the photo, and began to sing. The song praised the pastoral beauties of the sierra and expressed love for Aracena. But it was sung in a booming voice that seemed almost to parody the genre and to turn an act of hospitality into an aggressive challenge. Confused by what was happening, I responded awkwardly and predictably like most tourists would. In other words, to my embarrassment, I took the photo.

This was the sort of incident that Antonio Vargas, the man who criticized the popes of rock 'n' roll, would have loved to recount. Demonstrating both an acute awareness of the distorted views others have of Andalusian culture and a sense of self-irony, the young man had nonetheless been able to reaffirm a distinctively Andalusian cultural identity by patronizing an apparently arrogant outsider. Although his response to what he clearly perceived as an act of cultural aggression was neither embittered nor extreme, his gesture of resistance recalled something of the spirit of defiance and integrity that had animated many of those who burned the churches of the town in 1936. But rather than attempting to destroy the icons of patronage and hierarchy as the church burners had done, it was sufficient for him to have undermined a familiar image of cultural subordination by shifting the way it can be interpreted.

With 1992 approaching, the issue of cultural identity has taken on even greater significance for the people of Aracena. This is particularly evident in the expressions of skepticism concerning the Universal Exposition and its aftermath. One form of this skepticism is defensive and centers on concerns for Andalusia as well as Aracena. Many townspeople resent the imposition of schemes for the socioeconomic transformation of Andalusia by central bureaucrats and corporate planners and express doubts about whether these schemes will succeed and about who will be the real beneficiaries if they do succeed. In this context, townspeople stress the "traditional" cultural identity of themselves and other Andalusians as a way both to explain and to displace responsibility for whatever failures, shortcomings, and pitfalls the next few years hold in store. As one local businessman put it, "Andalusians are not the sort of people who can do a project of this kind; Seville is a city of folklore, and others are taking advantage of our lack of experience."

The other form of tradition-based skepticism is more aggressive and focuses on concerns for Aracena itself. Many townspeople, including businesspeople with deep local roots, fear that the changes looming on the horizon may lead to something like a complete suburbanization of Aracena and that soon "the *pueblo* will not be a *pueblo*." While they expect (and to some degree, of course, eagerly await) an influx of money and visitors from Seville, they do not want the town to be taken over by outsiders and outside financial interests. They seem determined to increase local solidarity to ensure that it is the townspeople who prosper, profit, and decide what happens in the day-to-day life of the community. Whether this strategy will work is doubtful, but it is clear that the practical social dynamics of organizing traditional rites and celebrations that bring people together in voluntary cooperative efforts and strengthen the general sense of a distinctive community identity are critical to the framing and fate of issues of local control.

From one perspective, this strategy reproduces the fundamental social and cultural dynamics of pastoral epic. Local businesspeople, officials of the town hall, and professionals are taking a leading role in cultivating local customs. In their efforts, they are especially eager to encourage the young and underemployed men and women who are anxious about their futures to become involved in the cultural life of the community. This enables the members of the leading group to present themselves as persons with the collective interests of the community at heart and to assume the role of mediators between the townspeople and the outsiders who are imagined to have primarily self-interested motives. Thus, in reanimating traditional rites, celebrations, and images of personhood and community, the leading members of the community have occupied the high ground of patronage and once again managed to maintain their influence over local affairs. The *hidalgo* oligarchs of the eighteenth century, who were inspired by figures such as Madre María and Don Gerónimo Infante, did much the same when they affirmed the noblest values of honor and orthodoxy even as they engaged in high-stakes politicoeconomic duels with one another and higher authorities. Similarly, the twentieth-century agrarian gentry under the guidance of men such as the *marqués* and Don Enrique acted as the benefactors of local culture and thereby enhanced their positions of power and authority.

But if this wide-angle view of the contemporary politics of tradition in Aracena reveals that certain aspects of the sociopolitical and cultural dynamics of tradition have endured, it should not be allowed to obscure the ruptures and discontinuities that separate the past from the present. During the Ancient Regime, Catholic orthodoxy, formalized codes of honor, and ideals of religious and worldly patronage were the central elements in a dominant cultural formation that largely equated truth with tradition and ceded preeminent authority over both to defenders of the dual institutional hierarchies of a militant church and a protobureaucratic monarchy. With the triumph of the liberal state and agrarian capitalism and the weakening of the church in the nineteenth century, the direct linkage of traditional forms of cultural authority with institutional power was radically altered. The disintegration of old orthodoxies and patterns of social relations compelled and enabled the contending groups of rural class society to reinterpret tradition in the light of contemporary conflicts and interests. As a result of this process of cultural displacement and reconfiguration, the images and idioms of religion, honor, and patronage became central elements in the hypermoralized ideologies of revolution and reaction that informed and aggravated the sociopolitical conflicts of the first half of the twentieth century.

In recent decades, the relationship between traditional values and discourses and contemporary patterns of social life in Aracena has once again undergone a profound transformation in conjunction with the impact of encompassing processes of politicoeconomic and cultural liberalization on the community. Traditional idioms and practices have increasingly operated not to exacerbate but instead to diffuse tensions and soften conflicts that have arisen both within the town and between outsiders and members of the community. Reconstructing a traditional cultural identity for themselves has helped townspeople adapt to their marginal and subordinate position in contemporary Spanish society by enabling them to represent their lives as an ideal blend of time-hallowed spiritual, moral, and aesthetic values and progressive concerns for social welfare, equality, and justice.

Over the long run, the historical trajectory of these shifts in the ways in which traditional discourses and images have articulated with day-to-day social practices and hegemonic strategies of domination in Aracena has been determined by the emergence, rise, and triumph of the rationalized and impersonal modes of cultural authority involved in the development of modern bureaucracies and technologies, large-scale capitalist corporations, and the nation-state. As social life has become increasingly subject to secular, instrumental, and objectified forms of knowledge and techniques of management and control, tradition has been gradually transformed from a repository of revelatory truths about the human condition and the character of the social order into one among a number of cultural alternatives and possible value orientations that address problems of meaning, shape motives, guide actions, and construct specific visions of the good life.

As a result of these processes of cultural and sociopolitical transformation, what it now means to be religious or nonreligious, to act honorably, or to be a patron and benefactor of the community bears little resemblance to what it meant at different times in the past. Despite the fact that the dominant groups of every epoch of the town's history have reinforced their preeminent social position by acting as the guardians of traditional values, not even the *marqués* and his working-class adversaries, much less Madre María and the countrymen of the Ancient Regime, would feel at home in present-day Aracena. Although they might be comforted by some familiar scenes and customs, they would eventually be induced and compelled as people always are by hegemonic pressures and constraints to reconsider the significance of everything they experienced in accordance with the contemporary state of affairs in the town and in the larger society; and in the course of this process of adjustment, their sense of themselves as persons would also be transformed.

Indeed, at the most basic level, hegemonic processes involve the continual formation and re-formation of the interpretations, dispositions, motivations, and actions of subjects as they are confronted with the dominant discourses and practices of the day. In this sort of contemporary "war of positions" (Gramsci 1971:229–36), the wisest way of using the resources provided by the idioms and images of local and regional traditions may not lie in pursuing efforts to construct a fixed or definitive version of cultural identity, since what in fact counts most is the way in which strategies of representation and action articulate with whatever cultural and politicoeconomic arrangements and tendencies happen to be prevailing at a given point in time.

As noted above, today in Aracena and in Andalusia more generally, it is the Universal Exposition that is most powerfully influencing people's sense of identity and of the possibilities of the present. In cultural terms, the exposition is doing this primarily by generating a vision of the past that is finely adjusted to the requirements of present regional, national, and international political and economic interests. Harking back to the "golden age" of Spanish discovery, continental hegemony, and global empire is the strategy that the designers of the exposition are employing to define, foster, and predict a new and vital role for Andalusia as a European gateway to Africa and Latin America. To represent history in these terms will very likely involve suppressing people's awareness of the intervening centuries of Andalusian poverty, conflict, marginalization, and subordination and relegating any critical scrutiny of the less glorious aspects of the region's past to a realm of fine-print qualifications in the mass media, cautionary footnotes to impressive exhibits, and scholarly conferences at luxury hotels. Only by such means can the exposition positively construe the relation of regional history and tradition to the epic story of the emergence, development, and progress of the modern world.

But it is not necessary to visit the site of the Universal Exposition to discover the increasing force of similar cultural strategies in Andalusia. The impact of analogous views of the harmonious relation of tradition to modernity is already evident in Aracena. The newest, most highly visible expression of this relation is the monumental array of El Museo de Arte Contemporaneo, an impressive open-air sculpture garden near the entrance to Las Grutas de las Maravillas on the southern edge of town. More than a dozen works of art, most of them abstract and all of them sculpted by well-known Spanish artists, are displayed in an elegant plaza bordered by palm trees. On a terrace two meters above the plaza is the ancient *barrio* chapel of San Pedro. The chapel has been fully integrated into the museum. It overlooks a fountain whose waters flow from one end of the plaza to the other, and next to the chapel doors are sculptures that pay homage to the sanctuary's graceful lines. Inside, behind the altar is a restored Gothic carving of Saint Peter seated on a throne and holding the keys to the kingdom— by far the finest of the few images of the saints that survived the Civil War. The chapel still serves as a center of religious devotion, but it is also frequently used to house exhibitions and sales of the folk arts of the sierra.

Like "El Castillo," which towers over it, El Museo de Arte Contemporaneo links rural culture to the high culture of urban centers in the best tradition of pastoral epic. The juxtaposition of the religious and secular and of the ancient and contemporary in the outdoor museum lends a sacred aura to the works of high modernism and simultaneously suggests the sophistication of the forms and values embodied in tradition. The effect of this is to weaken the sense of art and religion as separate cultural domains and to strengthen the aesthetic configuration of traditional culture that has predominated in the town since the post-Franco period of cultural liberalization. Not without reason, the townspeople are proud of their open-air art museum. The museum project was organized by the town council and carried out by local contractors and workers, and it has won the support of virtually everyone in the community. Many people speak of it as an act of collective patronage.

The fact that townspeople are able to build on the foundations of their past belies the notion that traditions are impediments to the future. It also belies the notion that tradition is an assortment of customs and beliefs that are handed down from one generation to the next and simply passively accepted. What most strongly shapes the politics of tradition is instead the constant process of interpreting the experiences of day-to-day life in terms that make sense of the relation between local interests, conflicts, and aspirations on the one hand and encompassing social forces and forms of cultural authority on the other. And what is most striking in light of the history of social injustice and the contemporary struggles to carve out a future is just how active and imaginative the process of reclaiming the past continues to be for the people of Aracena.

NOTES

Introduction: Space Inscribed

1. My use of the term "pastoral epic" obviously draws its inspiration from literary criticism, and I have benefited from the work of Eagleton (1988), Frye (1971), Poggioli (1975), and Williams (1973) on pastoral and epic. I have also benefited from Fernandez's (1988a, 1988b) essays exploring the play of pastoral and other images in the popular poetry of Asturia and the work of Spanish folklorists. While Fernandez's work clearly shows that revealing connections can be made between the "high" literary forms of pastoral and epic and other modes of cultural representation in Spain, I make no systematic attempt to explore these connections, nor to explore the social or political significance of traditional literary genres per se. Rather, I use the term "pastoral epic" to identify and illuminate the relations among a number of seemingly disparate themes, images, and idioms evident in a broad variety of materials from Aracena, materials that are largely nonliterary and range from architectural arrays and communal rituals to bureaucratic documents and ordinary conversations.

2. My account of these complex cultural processes in Aracena has been influenced by Williams's (1977) general discussion of dominant, residual, and emergent moments of hegemonic processes. I have adapted his terms (with modifications) for use in this study and have added the notions of "displacement," "resurgence," and "reconfiguration" to describe other aspects of the dynamics of traditionalism in Aracena.

3. For a discussion of the "modern" aspects of Spanish culture in the seventeenth century, see Maravall's (1986) *Culture of the Baroque: Analysis of a Historical Structure*.

4. The fading or death of traditions is by no means inevitable, nor is this phenomenon as widespread as is commonly supposed. In Spain, it appears to have occurred primarily in small, relatively egalitarian, "postpeasant" communities (such as those studied by Behar [1986] and Harding [1984]) in which cultural idioms and institutions were linked in a fairly direct and unmediated way to a particular set of archaic and no longer viable social and economic arrangements. For other perspectives on the relation of traditional culture to processes of modernization in Spain, see Aceves and Douglass 1976; and Aceves, Hansen, and Levitas 1976.

5. See, for example, M. Sahlins's (1981, 1985) development and use of the concept of the "structure of the conjuncture" as a way of analyzing processes of sociocultural transformation. For a more sociological approach to the analysis of these processes, see Giddens's (1984) theory of the processes of "structuration."

6. For critical discussions of the relevance of these developments for Mediterranean studies, see Herzfeld 1987. For positive overviews of the theoretical and ethnographic implications of recent trends, see Clifford and Marcus 1986, Marcus and Fischer 1986, and Rosaldo 1989. For a sharply dissenting view of many of the ideas advanced in the three works cited above, see Sangren 1988.

7. My approach to sociocultural analysis takes as its starting point Foucault's (1981:78–109; 1983:208–28) concept of power as a strategic relation between forces and between subjects. I use the concepts of hegemony and hegemonic processes to describe the effects of domination generated by the manner in which the more or less formalized and rationalized discursive formations of primary institutions such as the church and state are articulated with the ideological representations of sociopolitical blocs and the socially embedded signifying practices of everyday life. This perspective assumes that hegemonic effects of power are multidimensional and complex and that they include but are by no means limited to the legitimation of authority and inequality, the muting and marginalization of oppositional discourses and practices, and the constitution, deflection, and deferral of subjects' desires and interests. For a discussion of the relation of Foucault's analytics of power to Gramsci's concept of hegemony, see Smart 1983 and 1985. Cultural genealogy I take to be a matter of doing "history backward" in order to know how the present emerged "out of a certain situation obtaining in the past" (Geertz 1968:59).

8. Among the most notable exceptions to this generalization concerning Mediterranean ethnography in the 1960s and 1970s are the works by Blok (1974) and Schneider and Schneider (1976) on the culture and political economy of Sicily. A more recent work that uses the Weberian notions of rationalization and disenchantment to relate long-range patterns of cultural and sociopolitical domination to contemporary processes of modernization is Holmes's (1989) *Cultural Disenchantments: Worker Peasantries of Northeast Italy.*

9. Herzfeld (1987:133–41, 201) has elaborated two useful concepts, "diglossia" and "disemia," to capture the contrast and interrelation between official and socially embedded discourse. This distinction, however, must not be allowed to obscure what Bakhtin (1981) called the "heteroglossia" of all discourse, including the official and socially embedded types. This point is an important one in the present context: while each of the hegemonic cultural

discourses of religion, honor, and patronage contrasts and interrelates with the others, each of them is also expressed in official and socially embedded idioms.

10. As Gramsci (1971:97) states, "By intellectuals must be understood not those strata commonly described by this term, but in general the entire social stratum which exercises an organizational function in the wide sense— whether in the field of production, or in that of culture, or in that of political administration." More recently, McDonogh (1986:202–11) has called for further analysis of the roles and culture of elites. Although he discusses urban and national elites in this context, many of his points about the importance of studying these groups are relevant to the study of rural and local elites as well.

11. See, for example, Blok and Driessen 1984, Brandes 1980, and Gilmore 1980. For a discussion of negative and positive ethnographic representations of Andalusian culture, see Fernandez 1983.

12. For some recent examples of functionalist approaches to the cultural analysis of Spain and the Mediterranean in general, see Gilmore 1987a and 1987b. For a discussion of the persistence of functionalist arguments and models even in the work of cultural anthropologists who have criticized functionalist theory, see Rosaldo 1986.

13. For similar formulations of a cultural studies project, see Bourdieu 1977, Lyotard 1984, and M. Sahlins 1976. In spite of the great differences separating these writers, all three in one way or another call for what Sahlins (1976:101) termed "a pragmatics of cultural forms." In my judgment, however, Hall's (1980, 1983, 1985, 1988) discussions of hegemony, articulation, and the dynamics of social formations have gone the furthest in clarifying the theoretical and political implications of what is at stake in such a project.

14. For discussions of the relation between Andalusian and Spanish cultural identity, see Acosta Sánchez 1978 and 1979 and Mitchell 1990:83–92.

Chapter 1: Local Polities

1. Research on the province of Huelva during the Ancient Regime began to expand in the late 1970s, but knowledge of the region is still scanty in comparison to what is known about other areas of western Andalusia (see, however, González Gómez's [1977] *Moguer en la baja edad media, 1248–1538,* for a fine study of a town in southern Huelva during the period). The first certain mention of Aracena dates from the thirteenth century, the period of the wars for the reconquest of Seville and western Andalusia, but it is not clear whether the name identifies a permanent settlement or simply an easily defended hill. What is evident in the early documents (F. Pérez-Embid 1975; Terán 1976) is the strategic importance of the location. In the first decades of the thirteenth century, the whole area was being fought over by the Moors, whose strength

lay to the south; by the Portuguese, to the west; and by the Castilians, to the northeast. Though the sierra was a sparsely populated border march, whatever force held it would pose a threat to the great prize of Seville. Thus, even after the defeat of the Moors in western Andalusia, Aracena changed hands several times as the Castilians and Portuguese jockeyed for position in the following decades. It was not until 1267, when the Treaty of Badajoz was signed, that the skirmishes between the contending Christian forces subsided and Aracena was permanently incorporated into the Crown of Seville. Shortly thereafter, the location was certainly permanently settled. By 1290, the newly built castle of Aracena was one of several fortresses in the region garrisoned to defend against further Portuguese intrusions. Near its walls stood the foundations of the church of Santa María de Aracena.

As late as the fifteenth century, the sierra was still wild country. In 1407, the huge township of Aracena, many times larger in area than it is today, could count only 234 *vecinos* (heads of households), and the exercise of formal authority of any kind appears to have been rather nominal. During the next decades, there were frequent reports of outlaw activity, including smuggling and thievery, and local officials of the garrison of Aracena complained that the countryside suffered from a total absence of governance and that many official posts were vacant in the town (see Moreno Alonso 1979).

However, by the middle of the sixteenth century, the picture appears quite different. Increases in wealth, population, and social complexity are apparent in all the documents of the period. It is clear that a small group of gentry and notables had established themselves as the arbiters of local affairs, and an impressive new stone *ayuntamiento* (town hall) as well as the grandiose parish church of Santa María de la Asunción, two monasteries, and a convent bore witness to their prosperity.

2. Núñez Roldán's (1987) analysis of the Ensenada materials concerning the present province of Huelva in *En los confines del reino: Huelva y su tierra en el siglo XVIII* is indispensable for understanding the history and political economy of the sierra during the Ancient Regime. For illuminating essays on the towns of the present province, see J. Pérez-Embid and Rivero Galán 1988. For broader historical overviews of seventeenth- and eighteenth-century Spain, see Anes Alvarez 1975, Domínguez Ortiz 1970 and 1976, Hamilton 1947, Kamen 1980, and Lynch 1989.

3. Calculating the population of Aracena and other towns and hamlets of the sierra during the Ancient Regime is a difficult matter not only because of the unreliability of the data but also because the census reports list *vecinos* rather than the total number of inhabitants. According to the Catastro de Ensenada, *respuestas generales* (general reponses) for question 21, in 1753 the number of *vecinos* of the town center and hamlets was 1,367, distributed as follows: Aracena, 540; Campofrío, 177; Linares, 170; Corteconcepción and Puerto Gil, 97; Puerto Moral, 78; Valdearco, 70; Los Marines, 59; La Gra-

nada, 50; Corterangel and Castañuelo, 45; Carboneras, 34; Valdezufre and Jabuguillo, 25; La Umbría, 14; and Las Granadillas, 8. To estimate the overall population of Aracena using the number of *vecinos* as a base, I have employed the 3.60 conversion coefficient suggested for the sierra by Núñez Roldán (1987:88–91).

It is important to keep in mind that the population of townships such as Aracena shifted rather dramatically whenever one of their hamlets broke away and became established as an autonomous political unit. In addition, the population of Andalusia was increasing during this period, as was that of Spain as a whole (see Nadal 1976; Núñez Roldán 1987), and Aracena was not unusual in this respect.

4. Information on local agriculture in Chapter 1 is based partially on the document of Zapata (a governor of Aracena) in 1723 but is derived primarily from the *respuestas generales* of the Catastro de Ensenada. For example, the answer to question 10 was that Aracena had 1,216 "measures" of land of "first quality," 6,728 "measures" of "second quality," and 33,055 "measures" of "third quality." Wheat and barley were sown in a proportion of about two to one, and on the best lands, techniques of extensive cultivation usually produced only one crop every three years. On the poorest lands, this figure dropped to one crop in fourteen years.

5. For comparable socioeconomic data on the towns of Huelva during this period, see Núñez Roldán 1981 and 1987. While what is most striking about his account is how untypical Aracena was in relation to the small, poor, and egalitarian *pueblos* of the sierra region of Huelva, it is clear that from a broader regional and national perspective, Aracena was by no means exceptional in its degree of stratification nor in the diversity of its economic links to other rural towns and cities such as Seville and Cádiz during the Ancient Regime. As Herr (1989) demonstrates in his valuable account of the political economy of seven towns in Andalusia and Castile in the late eighteenth century, many rural populations in Andalusia were highly stratified and had strong orientations to external markets. Indeed, many other aspects of Aracena's sociopolitical and economic structure appear to have been similar to those of towns located in the richer sections of the Guadalquivir basin in Jaén and described by Herr (1989:560–61). Like these Andalusian towns and unlike the more egalitarian and homogeneous communities of the sierra, Salamanca, and much of northern Spain (see Behar 1986; Reher 1990; Vassberg 1978, 1984), Aracena was dominated by an economically aggressive and self-perpetuating *hidalgo* oligarchy.

6. My figures on the distribution of land in Aracena should be taken as rough estimates. Information from the Catastro de Ensenada provided to me by Francisco Núñez Roldán of the University of Seville indicates that 30 percent (4,087 measures) of the land surveyed by the compilers of the Catastro de Ensenada was "beneficial" (i.e., ecclesiastical land dedicated to the support of

members of the clergy). Another 8 percent (1,133 measures) was "patrimo-nial" (i.e., owned by proprietors who were members of the clergy). The re-maining 62 percent (8,337 measures) was "secular" (i.e., owned by laymen of all ranks and classes). However, this survey gives no direct indication concern-ing the crucial matter of the degree of concentration of property among lay-men, nor does it evidently take into account the thirty-four tracts of common lands (*propios* and *tierras baldías*) that were administered by the town *cabildo* (council).

My estimates that the local gentry were direct proprietors of about 40 per-cent of the township's area and that nearly 50 percent of the township's land was under the control of lay and ecclesiastical authorities thus involve certain inferences concerning both the degree of concentration of property among laymen and the land area of the town's commons. Overall, it is quite clear that private lands were concentrated in the hands of a few proprietors. The wills and testaments recorded by local notaries show that the town's elite had large estates; the township had few *vecinos* who were classified as *labradores* (small landholders); most of the population consisted of landless laborers; and a handful of clerical proprietors of patrimonial lands held fully 8 percent of the area surveyed, which suggests that clerical members of the local elite were generally well endowed. Moreover, on the matter of the area of the common lands, nineteenth-century sources suggest that these lands, though not insig-nificant, were also not extensive; they probably constituted between 8 and 12 percent of the area of the township. When the figures given in the Ensenada materials are adjusted to take this evidence into account, it appears that the local gentry administered nearly 50 percent of the township's land and were the direct proprietors of something like 40 percent of the land.

Accurate calculation of the distribution of agrarian property in the town-ship is extremely difficult because several different units of land measurement were used during the Ancient Regime. The "measure" of land generally used by the compilers of the Ensenada materials in Aracena was the *fanega de tierra* of Seville (0.58 hectare), but the compilers were not always consistent in their usage. The standard measure of land in Aracena was the *fanega de puño*. De-pending on the quality of land, one *fanega de puño* was calculated as being the equivalent of either two or four *fanegas de tierra*. Because of the uncertainties arising from this and related factors, there are severe problems in arriving at any precise idea of who owned or controlled how much land in Aracena, and thus the margin of error in the estimates given in the text may be considerable.

7. The *alcabala* was originally a sales tax levied on basic commodities. However, it became common practice for towns to negotiate with higher au-thorities to fix the tax at a certain settled sum. In Aracena, the bulk of this sum, which was owed to the House of Altamira, was derived from the income produced by the *tierras baldías*.

8. The number of *regidores* (council members) varied over time. There were only two in 1723, but there were usually six in the mid- and late eighteenth century.

9. For more extensive accounts of municipal offices and government in Huelva during the eighteenth century, see Núñez Roldán 1987:59–78 and J. Pérez-Embid et al. 1988:231–318.

10. For a discussion of the types, uses, and extent of common lands during and after the Ancient Regime, see Nieto 1964 and Vassberg 1974, 1975, and 1984.

11. For a more detailed account of Aracena's religious institutions in the early years of the eighteenth century, see Candáu Chacón 1988.

12. *El libro del mayor hacendado* of 1752 (an Ensenada source) listed the convent of Santa Catalina as the institution or person with the greatest annual income in the township of Aracena. Although there is no reason to doubt that the income of the convent was reported accurately, greater skepticism is in order concerning the claim that the convent had the largest annual income in the township. Several private and politically influential landowners had properties and cash reserves many times greater than those of the convent, and it seems unlikely that they managed their estates less efficiently than the convent. Moreover, the local gentry had both the opportunity and the motive to cheat in reporting income. All of the men who compiled the Ensenada report were members of the gentry elite, and one of them (a member of the Villafranco family; see Chapter 3) was probably the richest man in the township. The convent's status as a corporation of the church exempted it from taxation, whereas the private incomes of the great landowners were potentially liable to such levies. Thus, designating the convent as the *mayor hacendado* did no harm to the institution and stood to benefit the landowners if, as seems likely, they were willing to lie about their own incomes. However, see Núñez Roldán 1987 for a defense of the general accuracy of the reports in *El libro del mayor hacendado*.

13. One *fanega* as a measurement of a quantity of grain (rather than land) is the equivalent of an English bushel.

14. Charity, the access of ordinary householders to the smaller parcels of ecclesiastical lands, the modest incomes of many of the clergy, and the direct administration of larger church properties by laymen rather than clerical officials were factors that insulated the church and made it less vulnerable to charges of dishonesty and greed than were the town's secular authorities. Nevertheless, individual members of the clergy by no means escaped such accusations, and the populace apparently disliked the fact that ecclesiastical authority was concentrated in Aracena and most of the clergy of the township were affiliated with the *priorato* (priory) of Aracena. Indeed, it seems that lay protests about these matters had some influence in the breakup of the *priorato* in 1787. This reorganization abolished the control of the senior priests of

Aracena over the parish clergy of the surrounding towns and hamlets of the region.

15. For an illuminating account of intervillage and intertown politics in another border zone of Spain during this period, see P. Sahlins's (1989) *Boundaries: The Making of France and Spain in the Pyrenees.* For an extended discussion of the role of the state in the sale of privileges to towns, see Nader's (1990) *Liberty in Absolutist Spain: The Hapsburg Sale of Towns, 1516–1700.*

Chapter 2: The Dominions of Spirit and Flesh

1. Lorea's biography of Madre María also includes some reflections written by the holy woman herself, and it concludes with a postscript that was contributed by an anonymous contemporary of Lorea and describes the celebrations marking the foundation of a convent of Dominican nuns in Aracena. The biography has not been published in English; all quotations in English are my own translations. For an overview of the role of *beatas* in the founding of Dominican convents in early modern Spain, see Miura Andrades 1989.

2. Both the levels of literacy and the extent to which literacy reinforced religious conformity or fostered the emergence of Protestant or secular values are, of course, matters of critical interest to historians of early modern Europe (see, for example, Burke 1978; Davis 1975). Because the Inquisition exercised tight control over printed matter in Spain, it appears that printing primarily represented a means of promoting the doctrines and views of the Counter-Reformation church. Even so, Spanish secular and ecclesiastical officials feared the possible effects of literacy and discouraged its spread in the sixteenth century. As a result of hostile official attitudes and policies, literacy rates (which were perhaps as high as 50 or 60 percent for males in parts of Castile in the late 1500s) sharply declined in the seventeenth century. For illuminating discussions of literacy and its impact on Spanish society during this period, see Kagan 1974 and Nalle 1989. In Aracena, overall levels of literacy during the seventeenth and eighteenth centuries appear to have been quite low, judging from the number of townspeople who were unable to sign their names to notarial documents. Nevertheless, virtually all the male members of the local elite of officials, large landowners, and *hidalgos* and at least some of the women of this group appear to have been literate. But neither their close family ties to members of the clergy nor their general social and political interests (see Chapter 3) would have much inclined them to seek out banned books or embrace suspect ideas. On the contrary, literacy represented one of the things they had in common with the great princes and prelates and the orthodox authorities of the realm on whom they were in critical ways dependent.

3. For a discussion of the early development of the concept of the duality of human being and its effects on medieval sociopolitical thought, see Duby

1980. For an extended account of Western conceptions of the self, see Dumont 1986.

4. Consider, for example, this passage from Paul's Epistle to the Romans (8:5–9, 12–13): "For those who live according to the flesh set their minds on the things of the flesh, but those who live according to the Spirit set their minds on the things of the Spirit. To set the mind on the flesh is death, but to set the mind on the Spirit is life and peace. . . . So then, brethren, we are debtors, not to the flesh, to live according to the flesh—for if you live according to the flesh you will die, but if by the Spirit you put to death the deeds of the body, you will live."

5. In their work on contemporary Andalusian culture, Corbin and Corbin (1987:15–32) argue that the tensions between the spiritual and material dimensions of human being continue to pervade Andalusian culture, and they use the model of a great chain of being to describe this cultural structure. While I am sympathetic to their efforts, I believe this model oversimplifies the relation between spirit and flesh and represents only one among a number of representations of the world evident in Andalusian culture and history. Even if this structure had been dominant at some point in the past, it is difficult, given the impact of liberal and secular ways of representing individuals and society, to accept the notion that it is the key to understanding contemporary Andalusian culture.

6. Many scholars (see, for example, Bennassar 1979; Castón Boyer 1985; Maravall 1986; Mitchell 1990) stress the dramatic, emotional, romantic, and especially the "baroque" character of Andalusian and Spanish culture and religion, using figures such as Don Quixote, Don Juan, Manuel Manara, Saint John of the Cross, and the characters in the dramas of Lope and Calderón to illustrate their point. From these extreme examples, we get the impression that Spaniards in general and Andalusians in particular are prone to extremes of pious and mystical visions and devotion or are obsessed with worldly honor and reputation. And, indeed, such extremes do circumscribe the cultural limits and represent the tensions that have existed and, to a much lesser extent, still exist. It is important, however, to remember that most people most of the time have led far more ordinary and middling lives and have tried to reconcile, to alternate between, or even to ignore the tensions arising from different value orientations and forms of cultural authority. How they attempt and often succeed in doing this in their religious and daily life is far more important in understanding hegemonic processes of domination than most accounts suggest, and it is for this reason that I stress the convergences, compromises, and positive articulations among the idioms and values of religion, honor, and patronage in this chapter.

7. This integration of the secular and religious in Spain may also be seen as the first stage of what Bossy (1985:153) has generally described in Europe as a "migration of the holy," a process that eventually invested the sovereign state

with an aura of virtually autonomous sacrality. For another recent overview of how religious authority and crusades for reform were involved in newly emerging strategies of political and economic domination during the early modern period, see J. Schneider 1990.

8. The anthropological literature on the topics of honor and patronage in the Mediterranean and elsewhere is vast, but relatively little explicit attention has been given to how the ideas, images, and values of honor, religion, and patronage have been interwoven. The basic works on honor and patronage in the Mediterranean remain the collections edited by Peristiany in 1965 and Gellner and Waterbury in 1977. On patronage in Spain, see Kenny 1960, MacLachlan 1988, and Maravall 1979. On honor, see Gilmore 1987b and Bourdieu 1979. Thompson's (1985) work on the "Christianization of *hidalguía*" in the seventeenth century, which describes how the concept of nobility was keyed to the quasi-religious notion of "willing sacrifice," offers a highly illuminating discussion about the accommodation of worldly and spiritual values in early modern Spain.

In general, Counter-Reformation theologians continually emphasized the distinctions between religious and secular values and stressed the contradiction between the evangelical message of forgiveness, humility, and love and the worldly ethos of honor and nobility, an ethos that envisioned life in this world as inevitably full of antagonism and conflict and therefore placed the highest possible value on the "natural" virtues of courage, wary prudence, pride, and the defense of personal integrity. But even though Catholic moral teaching sharply distinguished the ascetic disciplines of self-sacrifice practiced by saints and martyrs from the worldly pursuit of honor and glory, the church inevitably had to reach some accommodation with worldly power. Thus, the devaluation of the heroic and noble ethos of civic virtue, which had inspired the classical civilizations of the Mediterranean, was far from total, and the pursuit of honor was rarely wholly condemned by the church. Rather, it was construed as a positive ideal that encouraged princes and those who shared in their functions to promote the limited goods of worldly existence and thereby provide an indispensable defense of the faith. Since the principal imperatives of honor were to manifest, guard, and strengthen the integrity of the body politic whether this be the (socialized, physical) body of the person or the frontiers of the kingdom, honor could be regarded as a line of moral defense that protected the spiritual interior from the forces of sin and corruption that raged in a fallen world full of sin, suffering, and death. To the extent that the values of honor fortified the will and disciplined the passions of believers, honor could be embraced by the church as complementary to religious life even if, as a worldly ethos, it had in principle to be subordinated to higher spiritual concerns, just as the life of the flesh had to be subordinated to the life of the spirit.

9. For a fascinating account of the origins and functions of cults of the saints, see Brown's (1981) *The Cult of the Saints: Its Rise and Function in Latin*

Christianity. Brown argues that the emergence of saint worship was linked to the sociopolitical dominance of wealthy and powerful "friends and patrons" in late antiquity. For a stimulating general account of "traditional religion" in the early modern period, see Bossy's (1985) *Christianity in the West, 1400–1700*. Bossy stresses the extent to which local religion was based on notions and ties of "natural" kinship and friendship. For more information about popular religious forms and customs in Spain during and after the early modern period, see Alvarez Santaló, Buxó i Rey, and Rodríguez Becerra's (1989) *La religiosidad popular* (3 volumes); especially useful for purposes of comparison are the contributions by Driessen (1989:82–104) and Sánchez Herrero (1989:268–307) in the first volume. On the whole, the religious life of Aracena does not appear to have differed greatly in either its basic emphases or social dynamics from that of other Andalusian communities of roughly equal size and complexity.

10. There were two basic types of brotherhoods in Aracena: penitential and parish-centered. The functions of the penitential brotherhoods of Holy Week were almost exclusively devotional and focused on processional celebrations. The brotherhoods depended on nominal membership fees, the sponsorship of communal feasts, the gifts of patrons, and, occasionally, the allotments from secular authorities to meet their expenses. Since the fees and formal obligations imposed on the brothers were minimal, membership sometimes cut across the boundaries separating social ranks and neighborhoods.

While penitential brotherhoods tended to be centered in rural chapels or the places of worship of the religious orders, brotherhoods of the second type were centered in the principal parish churches of the town and hamlets. Both types had devotional and cultic features, but the parish-centered brotherhoods also served ends that were partly practical in nature. For example, they functioned as mutual aid societies for particular hamlets, neighborhoods, parishes, and, perhaps, occupational groups, and their membership therefore tended to consist of people of the same general social status. They usually also acted as burial societies and made contributions for the support of poor widows and children of deceased members. Unlike the penitential brotherhoods, the parish-centered associations were often endowed with some property to meet these ends, and parish clergy seem to have played a fairly active role in them. With one important exception (see Chapter 3), the patrimonies of the parish-centered brotherhoods were never extensive and usually amounted to a few small plots of land and a herd or two of goats consigned to the care of a senior brother.

The best general discussion of the many roles and functions of lay religious brotherhoods in rural Spain during the Ancient Regime is found in Christian's (1981b) *Local Religion in Sixteenth-Century Spain*. My description of the types of brotherhoods focuses on those found in Aracena and varies a bit from Christian's description.

11. The clergy's efforts to curb popular excesses were, of course, part of a much broader strategy of orthodox princes and prelates to impose religious and cultural uniformity and to foster church-sponsored forms of devotion. For a discussion of Catholic disciplines, see Bossy 1970.

12. Regarding the widespread occurrence of visions and apparitions in early modern Spain, see Christian 1981a and Velasco 1989.

13. For an account of emotionalism in Spanish religion during this period, see Christian 1982.

14. For accounts of the lives of prostitutes, *beatas,* and women in general in Spain during this period, see Bilinkoff 1989 and Perry 1985 and 1990.

15. The exaggerated strength of "familial particularism" (see Pérez Díaz 1976) in southern Spain and elsewhere in the Mediterranean has been linked to many social factors and particularly to the family's role in the holding and transmission of property. Codes of honor have been analyzed as an ideology structured by economic imperatives, and without question there is a connection between economic interests and practical ethics (J. Schneider 1971). This is obvious in Lorea's anecdote: Madre María was concerned that her nephew be "accommodated." However, her motives involved more than pragmatic family "interests," and to focus on this alone would be more obscuring than clarifying in understanding Madre María's actions. Of vital importance in this case was the way in which the particular worldly interest of her nephew in retaining his commission—an interest that everyone involved in the matter no doubt recognized—could be construed, incorporated, and transformed into something more profound by representing it in relation to the spiritual and honorable values that constituted what it meant to be a person and a member of a family. Thus, in order to understand Madre María's motivations, it is essential to consider how her actions were shaped and pragmatic interests structured by the religious and secular meanings and values associated with the complex notions of family and kinship and, by extension, patronage. For a fuller account of how the family was doubly constituted as a spiritual community of love and a secular community of honor, see Maddox 1986: 197–203.

Chapter 3: Patronage, Patrimony, and Oligarchic Domination

1. In his last letter (1693) to Aracena, Captain Gerónimo Infante stated that he had sent the equivalent in gold, silver, and coin of forty thousand pesetas (i.e., pesetas españoles) in eight shipments to found his *patronato* and aid his relatives.

2. The personal and family names of the "Villafranco" and "Granvilla" lineages discussed in this chapter are pseudonyms. Information in some cases was derived from documents from private sources (DPS), which townspeople were gracious enough to let me study. I have used pseudonyms to fulfill

pledges to protect the confidentiality and privacy of the living, rather than to preserve the reputations of those long dead. For the same reason, I have followed a similar procedure in Chapter 4, which discusses the family history of the *marqués* of Aracena and his ties to the "Villafrancos," "Granvillas," and other local gentry families.

3. For illuminating discussions of shifts in the notions and values of honor and nobility in the seventeenth and eighteenth centuries in Spain, see Callahan 1972, Maravall 1979, and Thompson 1985.

4. For a discussion of the forms of spirituality expressed in the last wills and testaments of Andalusians during this period, see Rivas Alvarez 1986.

5. The 1787 Censo de Floridablanca (see Documents Cited) lists the number of *hidalgos* in Aracena as twenty-six, the greatest number cited for any of the towns of present-day Huelva province. Presumably this figure refers to the number of adult males of this rank.

6. For a general account of the privileged classes of Spain during the early modern period, see Domínguez Ortiz 1973. For a fine discussion of the cultural dimensions of the relatively open system of oligarchical control that existed in Barcelona from the late fifteenth to the early eighteenth century, see Amelang 1986.

7. Practices relating to the preservation of the patrimony, the strategies of marriage, and the mode of inheritance for both ordinary peasant-workers and for the local elite in Aracena seem to have varied little from the overall patterns of practices dominant in Castile and for that matter in most of rural Europe. For discussions of these general patterns, see Creighton 1980; Flandrin 1977; Goody 1983; and Goody, Thirsk, and Thompson 1976.

8. For a concise presentation of the issues involved in understanding the emergence of capitalism and liberalism in eighteenth- and nineteenth-century Andalusia, see Gilmore 1990b.

Chapter 4: *Liberalism,* Caciquismo, *and Cultural Enterprise*

1. In 1798, war with Great Britain had strained Spanish national finances to the breaking point. In a desperate attempt to raise money, the royal government mandated the sale of some of the endowments of the church. Portions of the property of ecclesiastical institutions were auctioned to individuals, and the proceeds went to the national treasury. In compensation, the religious institutions received 3-percent bonds equal to the price of the sales. By the time the sales ended more than a decade later, about one-sixth of all the vast properties of the church in Spain had been sold (for an extended discussion, see Herr 1989; see also Herr 1974:68 and 1971a). These sales to private persons constituted the first phase in the process of disentailment (or "disamortization") of ecclesiastical and communal properties, a process that

culminated in the second half of the century and contributed to the development of agrarian capitalism in Andalusia and elsewhere in Spain.

2. Since the holdings of the brotherhoods (with the exception of the endowments of La Cofradía de San Pedro) were numerous but of modest proportions, the impact of the sales was greater in cultural and social terms than it was from a purely economic perspective. Most of the brotherhoods' small properties were added to the already large estates of the local gentry, particularly those charged with administering the sales. However, a land-poor but prosperous local trader who drew on financial support in Seville managed to secure two very large properties of La Cofradía de San Pedro. Although these sales did not destroy the brotherhood, they brought to a permanent halt its accumulation of property (see Chapter 3), and after the 1830s its importance as a charitable and financial institution slowly eroded. The trader's coup in securing these large properties immediately made him one of the township's largest landowners.

3. My account of the liberal period in the sierra in the early 1820s is indebted to Moreno Alonso's discussion of this period (1979:154–58) and draws on the excerpts he quotes from a diary kept by a priest of Alájar during the 1820s (1979:298–306). Few local sources of information on Aracena during the early nineteenth century have survived. Fires set in the course of later class struggles took their toll on the local archives that would have been most valuable for understanding the period. While the available sources provide a basic outline of what happened in the township during this crucial period of Spanish history, much remains obscure about the underlying factors that influenced the course of events. What the surviving documents reveal most clearly is an acute sense of politicoeconomic instability, uncertainty, and crisis.

4. For a description of the emergence of Andalusian and Spanish "proto-Carlism," see Cuenca Toribio 1971 and Torras 1976.

5. At mid-century, for example, there were about 440 men in Aracena who qualified as electors (Mádoz 1845–50), and this number included the more prosperous *labradores* (small landholders) and *comerciantes* (merchants and shopkeepers) of the town as well as the old elite.

6. The most critical factor in this accumulation of property by gentry families was the sale of ecclesiastical and communal lands, which transpired in three phases. The first phase, which has already been described, occurred in the early decades of the century and involved the alienation of the properties of the lay religious brotherhoods and some of the endowments of the religious orders. The second phase began after 1836, the year when the disentailment laws of Mendizabel were passed by the Cortes. In Aracena during the late 1830s and early 1840s, this legislation led to the sale of most of the remaining properties of the religious orders as well as to the alienation of some of the lands and houses of the parish churches and chaplaincies. The third phase of disentailment, initiated by the Mádoz legislation of 1855, mandated the sale

of remaining ecclesiastical properties and also stipulated the auctioning of all municipal and royal lands not worked in common. During this phase, huge tracts of Aracena's institutional land were purchased on credit.

While all three phases of the disentailment process were instituted by governments principally because of the need for increased revenues for the state's treasuries, in the case of the Mendizabel and Mádoz legislation, this aim was accompanied by liberal hopes that the nation's wealth would be increased and a class of prosperous independent farmers would be created. However, no general mechanism to help the poorer classes buy land was ever created; and in places such as Aracena, where economic resources and political influence were already unequally distributed, the results were predictable.

For accounts of the disentailments in Spain, see Nieto 1964, Rueda Hernanz 1981, Simón Segura 1973, and Tomás y Valiente 1974. For a discussion of the disentailments in Aracena and Huelva province in the period from 1836 to 1844, see Capelo García 1979.

7. The many lacunae in local records have made it impossible to determine the exact amounts of property that passed from the corporate to the private domain in Aracena during the nineteenth century, but there is no doubt that the sales involved vast amounts of land (and also many houses). I have been able to document 126 sales spanning the period from 1800 to 1895. The parcels involved in these sales ranged greatly in size from a few square meters to 300 or 400 hectares. The quality of the lands involved also varied greatly; for example, some small irrigated gardens were worth as much as large tracts of hilltop scrub. In total, these 126 alienations involved the transference of 2,408 hectares. The amounts of land sold in the various categories were as follows: 1,310 hectares of town lands and commons, 422 hectares of parish chaplaincies, 301 hectares of the lay religious brotherhoods, 287 hectares of the religious orders, and 88 hectares of the parish churches. The 1,310 hectares of town lands and commons probably represent almost all of the secular corporate lands of Aracena; however, the ecclesiastical lands listed probably represent only a small part of the properties that were transferred from the clergy, religious brotherhoods, and church to private individuals. Indeed, local documentation of another 35 sales of ecclesiastical properties has survived; but because the records do not indicate the size of the properties alienated, these sales are not included in the figures cited above. Nevertheless, the prices and descriptions of these parcels suggest that they ranked among the largest tracts sold. In addition, the names of numerous tracts owned by individuals by the end of the century—for example, La Capellanía de Escribanos (145 hectares), El Monte de Frailes (238 hectares), Obra Pía (267 hectares), and Huerta Abad (472 hectares)—suggest that many of them were once ecclesiastical properties.

The precise number of hectares of town and ecclesiastical lands sold in the nineteenth century is also difficult to calculate because of the problems involved in some instances in converting traditional measures of land (such as the *fanega de tierra*) into hectares. Some of the local documents indicate that a *fanega* ranged from as little as 0.36 hectare to as much as 0.80 hectare. The average size of a *fanega* was close to 0.63 hectare, and I have used this standard conversion rate to arrive at the figure of 2,408 hectares.

8. For an account of how land was accumulated and transferred within bourgeois families of Seville province in the nineteenth century, see Heran 1980.

9. Many historians have traced the so-called bourgeois revolution that transformed Spanish rural society in the nineteenth century to the sales of ecclesiastical and common lands. Important as these sales were, it is nonetheless possible to overestimate the global impact of the privatization of communal property on rural society (see Herr 1976:108ff.). In economic terms, while the sales (and, later, the increased markets for local agricultural commodities) in Aracena did not overturn the existing economic structure, they did magnify certain aspects of the archaic agrarian system. Private lands had always been unequally distributed in the township, and even during the Ancient Regime, members of the local elite had been the primary though not the sole beneficiaries of the fruits of corporate endowments. Although cork represented an immensely profitable new product, the leading sector of the local economy had always been oriented toward production for markets. In this sense, there was no far-reaching economic revolution in the township. Similarly, there was no far-reaching political revolution, because the heirs of the old gentry retained control of local affairs even if the strategies and tactics of political domination underwent radical change. Nevertheless, the cumulative effect of these economic and political changes in conjunction with other sociocultural processes was a revolutionary transformation characterized by the intensification of most of the worst aspects of the society of the Ancient Regime. For a description of the general effects of nineteenth-century political and economic developments on Spanish society, see Nadal 1975 and Shubert 1990.

10. Artola, Bernal, and Contreras (1978:105–11) indicate that the oak groves of the sierra, which provided fodder for pigs, greatly expanded after 1850 and argue that this transformation was associated with an increase in grain production by lowland cultivators and a consequent reduction in the amount of land they devoted to raising livestock. In Aracena during the period between 1850 and 1940, it appears that the amount of land devoted to groves of cork-oak trees increased by about 20 percent (i.e., to roughly one-third of the surface area of the township) while the area of land dedicated to grains declined proportionately. This estimate of shifts in land usage is based on inferences from mid-eighteenth-century information and on comparisons of land usage data from 1910, 1936, and 1940 derived from public and private documents (AA 1910; DPS 1936; AA 1940). Because of the time and costs involved in planting new oak and cork groves (there is a delay of over two decades before the trees become fully productive), this transformation was

necessarily slow albeit steady. Nevertheless, the old elite of the town, such as those who had purchased the endowments of the church and the town commons, were the great beneficiaries of this transformation in local agriculture and external demand both because they were able to purchase already existing oak and cork groves rather than create new plantations and because only they possessed sufficient holdings to make replanting worthwhile and could afford to wait out the long period necessary before acorns could be gathered, cork bark stripped, and profits made.

11. Moreno Alonso (1978:44) states that 394 men of Aracena worked in the mines of Río Tinto in the century after 1870. There is also evidence that a steady stream of men and women migrated from Aracena to Seville.

12. For historical overviews of the role of the church and religion in Spanish society in the period from 1750 to 1975, see Callahan 1984, Cuenca Toribio 1980, Lannon 1987, and Ullman 1983.

13. Table 1 is based on the *catastro* compiled by the town council of Aracena in the 1940s. A comparison of this survey with late nineteenth-century data from the registry of property in Aracena strongly suggests that there were no great changes in either the pattern of land ownership or the manner of exploitation from the 1880s to the 1940s. The nineteenth-century sales of corporate properties and the other processes that led to the concentration of property in the hands of a few large proprietors thus created the basic conditions of twentieth-century agriculture.

However, land distribution was even more unequal than the raw data cited in table 1 suggest. Ten of the forty largest proprietors were wives of men in the "large holdings" category, and their *fincas* (agricultural properties) were worked jointly with those of their husbands. In addition, many proprietors of great estates in Aracena were to be numbered among the largest landowners in nearby townships such as Corteconcepción and Zufre. In Corteconcepción, four estates owned by residents of Aracena accounted for 3,018 hectares (or 62 percent of the township's lands), and in Zufre, twenty-five estates owned mostly by people from Aracena and Seville encompassed 21,041 hectares (or 63 percent of the township's lands). These global figures on the concentration of agrarian property in towns surrounding Aracena are derived from Carrión (1975:242–48). The incompleteness of the surveys upon which Carrión's analysis was based led him to slightly underestimate the degree of concentration of property in Aracena, although he does state that nine estates comprised 29.28 percent of the township's land. His figures for surrounding towns probably also reflect minor miscalculations.

14. Ideally, the parcels of a small landholder included a *huerta* (small irrigated garden), a small stand of fruit trees, an open or fenced field or two, and a stand of oak trees. The holdings of a medium landowner often consisted of essentially the same kinds of plots but of larger size and perhaps with the addition of a pasture and olive or chestnut grove. In addition to the holdings

described above, the great latifundia included large *dehesas* (cultivated groves of oak and cork trees) and tracts of *monte bajo* (hillsides of scraggly *matorral* growth interspersed with trees).

Most of the properties in the range from 20 to 100 hectares represented the holdings of *labradores*. Many of the landowners in this category hired temporary labor when it was needed, but most of them together with their families also directly engaged in agricultural work. Hiring workers was less common among owners of properties in the range of 5 to 20 hectares both because there was less need for additional hands and because holdings of this size were barely able to support a household. Similarly, *fincas* of less than 5 hectares, no matter how intensively worked, were normally inadequate to support a household. The produce of such *fincas* supplemented the incomes either of *jornaleros* (agrarian day laborers) or of artisans and others primarily involved in nonagricultural occupations.

15. To ensure good crops of acorns and a thick growth of cork bark, trees had to be pruned and the ground between them cleared of the weeds, brush, and *matorral* that constantly threatened to overrun the *dehesas*. The two main seasons for the *poda* (pruning) and *arrancado* (clearing of brush) were late summer and late winter.

16. Data on market prices for cork and pork cited in the text are derived from biweekly quotations of prices that appeared in *El Distrito*.

17. For overviews of the emergence of rural working-class movements in nineteenth- and twentieth-century Spain, see Bernal 1979 and Lida 1972.

18. While there had been protests against the loss of the common lands of the townships of the sierra in the 1850s and 1860s and much sympathy in Aracena with the cantonalist programs of the Republicans in the 1870s, collective actions and strikes over agrarian wages and working conditions were slow to emerge in the sierra and particularly in Aracena. In 1888, however, local workers as well as many proprietors supported the demonstrations and protests organized against the Río Tinto Company's open-air *teleras* (smelting pits) whose noxious fumes were poisoning miners and villagers and destroying the agriculture of the mining zone. In February 1888, an anarchist-organized mass demonstration in the mining zone, which was intended to shut down the *teleras* and win better wages, led to a violent confrontation during which dozens and perhaps as many as one hundred or two hundred protesters were massacred by forces under the command of the civil governor of Huelva. In response to the heightened militancy of the workers of the region, a "workers' center" and mutual aid society with 156 members was established in Aracena in 1894. But it is unclear to what extent this organization was independent of the control of the large landowners of the township. For accounts of the labor conflicts in the mining zone in the late nineteenth and early twentieth centuries, see Avery 1974, Harvey 1981, and Kaplan 1982.

19. Spain was neutral in World War I, and the early years of the war were difficult for the miners of Río Tinto because of the restrictions imposed on international trade. By late 1914, some of the miners were unemployed and the remainder were on short hours. Some of these unemployed miners returned to live with their families in the *pueblos* of the sierra (*El Distrito*, 14 Nov. 1914). Although the mining economy soon revived, the presence of the desperate miners in the sierra worsened an already difficult local agrarian situation and greatly exacerbated politicoeconomic tensions. For a general account of the Spanish left during these years, see Meaker 1974.

20. In order to protect the confidentiality of local informants, some details of Don Francisco's family history and political career have been altered.

21. The general framework of the discussion of *caciquismo* and some of the information concerning Don Francisco's political career owe a great deal to Tusell's (1976, 1977) historical studies of Andalusian politics from 1890 to 1931. For complementary accounts of the politics of the period, see Boyd 1979 and Kern 1974.

22. In the earlier decades of the twentieth century, Montano's persona was involved in the cultural politics of Aracena and the region in several ways. The members of an esoteric, theosophical group with political overtones adopted him as their spiritual master (see Chapter 5). In response to this, a writer in *El Distrito,* the local newspaper and key ideological organ of the agrarian gentry, represented Montano as a forerunner of progressive Catholic social thought. The ensuing flurry of debate led to a general revival of Montano's reputation, and the gentry of the sierra decided a statue should be erected in his honor. Money was raised through donations, and a heated dispute arose between the towns of Aracena and Alájar about whether to erect the statue in Aracena or at La Peña. (La Peña is closer to Alájar and is inside its present municipal boundaries, although during Montano's lifetime, Alájar was a dependent hamlet of Aracena.) Alájar won the battle, and the statue stands today at La Peña. Despite the defeat, Aracena by no means forsook Montano's memory. The casino of the town's former elite and a Catholic school, both eminently conservative cultural organizations, still bear Montano's name, and the exterior of the casino is adorned with his image.

23. Even today, La Peña remains an important focal point of regional culture in the sierra, and its structure reveals the continuing importance of the traditional themes of religion, honor, and patronage. For further discussion of La Peña as a symbolic space, see Maddox 1986:46–51.

Chapter 5: Class Cultures and Ideologies

1. Landowners generally managed their estates with the assistance of bailiffs and foremen, and those among the agrarian elite who were also lawyers or physicians generally practiced their professions in a desultory manner.

2. In some respects, this concern with nobility harked back to the Ancient Regime. Although *hidalgo* rank was a dead letter, families in Aracena cherished their breeding and bloodlines and delighted in claiming exalted forebears. In a practice that was followed as late as the 1950s, the names of deceased members of elite families were often carved on a stone tablet near the altar in the church of "El Castillo." A number of the people honored by their inclusion in this list of natives of *esclarecidos linajes y claras estirpes* (illustrious lineages and unblemished origins) were indeed descendants of *hidalgos,* but others were simply wealthy and respectable members of the landowning bourgeoisie who sought to add a patina of nobility to their more modest names. In any case, presenting an image of a cultivated person was an adequate substitute for a good bloodline in creating and maintaining the marks of upper-class distinction.

3. Access to motorcars made it possible to spend a day or two in Seville whenever business or pleasure demanded, and a few among the local gentry had houses and apartments in the city, where they resided during the worst months of winter. Nevertheless, it was not necessary to travel to be attuned to the currents of urban life. Aracena's dress shops, furniture stores, and jewelers and tailors kept abreast of urban styles, and anyone with sufficient money could look fashionable during the evening *paseo* in La Plaza del Marqués. In addition, the town could boast of the sine qua non of elegant urban life: a large and well-appointed hall, El Teatro Ayala, in which traveling companies frequently performed *zarzuelas* (Spanish operettas) and sometimes edified the audience with presentations of the dramas of the *siglo de oro.*

4. The *cacique* wrote sentimental verses such as the following, in which a pastoral effect is achieved by associating the sierra with motherhood: "Madre, madre, si me pierdo / No me busqué en otra parte / Que en esta calle de Zufre / Que se llama 'Los Lineares' / Que otra calle más bonita / No he visto en el mundo, madre." (Mother, mother, if I am lost / Do not look for me anywhere else / Than in this street of Zufre / That is called "Los Lineares." / A street prettier than this / I have not seen in the world, mother.)

Although many local writers and artists did not greatly surpass this level of accomplishment, Aracena's cultural florescence did produce a number of competent essayists and two writers of some renown. José Nogales, who wrote novels and short stories around the turn of the century, had a fine eye for satirical detail and great skill in composing simple narratives and succinct descriptions of social mores (see the epigraphs to Chapters 5 and 7). José Andrés Vázquez, who as a young man followed Nogales to the summit of local letters, eventually became the editor of an important historical and literary journal and developed a national reputation as the novelist of *la buena gente* (the "good people"—i.e., the upper class) of Seville.

5. The three topics of bulls, politics, and agriculture were in fact intimately interrelated, since talk of the bravery, breeding, and sacrifice of bulls obliquely

reflected many of the practical concerns of the gentry about the masculine virtues required to maintain their social power, position, and reputation by ensuring that wild workers as well as savage animals were well managed. For discussions of authoritarian aspects of the culture of bullfighting, see Marvin 1988 and Mitchell 1991.

6. For a discussion of the importance of notions of breeding and cultivation among the urban elite of Barcelona during this period, see McDonogh 1986:108–40.

7. *El Distrito* was founded in response to the rural unrest of 1912 and rapidly became the main forum for upper-class discussion of the local scene. Although the review was published for only a few years, it was instrumental in shaping the conservative monarchical and Catholic ideology of Aracena's elite, which persisted with few minor modifications until after the destruction of the Second Republic. Many of the more intellectually inclined proprietors and professionals of the sierra contributed to the periodical, and a range of conservative opinions were expressed in its pages. Even so, the differences among its authors were relatively insignificant in comparison to the broad consensus on most social and political questions.

8. Two *sindicatos* (syndicates) were founded in Aracena as vehicles to promote mutualism, and each boasted a center dedicated to educational and recreational pursuits. The first was El Sindicato Católico, presided over by a lawyer who was also one of the largest landowners of the region. The second was El Sindicato Agrícola de Trigueros, which was affiliated with Los Sindicatos Agrícolas Católicos Españoles. But after a decade or so of ineffectual and halfhearted efforts, the local *sindicatos* "disappeared with neither pain nor glory" to their credit (Ordóñez Márquez 1968:240). The ideology of mutualism had little success in assuaging worker demands in Aracena or for that matter in Spain in general. For a contrasting case in which the church managed to neutralize working-class radicalism, see Holmes's (1989) discussion of the Catholic workers' movement in northeast Italy.

9. For a fascinating account of the impact of scientific culture on Spanish society, see Glick 1988.

10. In keeping with the notion that working-class families were discrete social isolates, working-class women were especially praised because they upheld the essentially reticent and defensive virtue of *vergüenza* (shame), as indicated in the following passage from *El Distrito* (5 Oct. 1914): "Thanks be that great numbers still maintain that powerful bastion of defense of the Spanish woman. I am referring, gentlemen, to 'shame,' which the woman of the sierra has in such a considerable quantity that it is her characteristic quality—a color that beautifies her face, tints her virtues—precious stone of her customs and sister of her continence."

Above all, however, feminine virtues of modesty and shame were praised because local commentators (*El Distrito*, 5 Oct. 1914) believed that a woman's sense of honor naturally inclined her to nurture and raise patient, humble children who would become respectful and obedient members of society: "The woman of the sierra looks to her heart above all and puts the honor of her family according to the rank and hierarchy of its race above all else. [For this reason] the necessary goal of her conduct is the rich and abundant fruits her children will gather in the future. The church and the state that will receive [these children] as members will exalt her and eternally bless her memory."

11. Roso de Luna's account of a spiritualist quest, *De Sevilla al Yucatán: Viaje ocultista a través de la Atlántida,* contains an extended description of Aracena and some of his friends there. His work, published in 1920, greatly influenced local theosophy enthusiasts, and it appears that much of the rhetoric of esoteric republicanism in Aracena was inspired by Roso de Luna's flights of spiritualist fancy.

12. Despite Arias Montano's contributions to the Council of Trent, the esoteric republicans were convinced that Montano was a secret forerunner of the theosophists. This conviction has received some indirect and inconclusive support from Rekers (1973) in his biography of Montano, which argues that Montano was a member of the Brotherhood of Spiritual Love, a quasi-clandestine group that was inspired by the teachings of Erasmus and had an interest in the emotional and experiential aspects of Catholic faith. Although there is no substantial evidence that Montano was attracted by Neoplatonic mysticism or cabalist esoterica, it does seem that he was involved in a form of spirituality which was deeply mistrusted by orthodox authorities.

13. From the perspective of Aracena, it seems absurd to blame any of the disasters of national and local political life on the machinations of Masonic conspirators intent on subverting the church and every other bulwark of authority, truth, and reason, as some right-wing Catholic historians (for example, Ordóñez Márquez 1968) have tended to do.

14. Ordóñez Márquez (1968:184–85) recounts how the "*espiritistas y teósofos*" (spiritualists and theosophists) of Alájar were considered "bad dogs" and mocked by other villagers. He also relates that an attempt by a local republican leader to hold a "Masonic funeral" for his mother was disrupted by the local inhabitants. The spiritualists of Aracena were more circumspect in making public their beliefs, but they were also reportedly subject to the same general sort of criticism.

Chapter 6: Tradition in Ashes

1. For general accounts of the history of the Second Republic and Civil War, see Jackson 1965, Preston 1978, and Thomas 1961. On the historiography of the war, see Preston 1984b. For an account of agrarian conflicts during the Second Republic, see Cevallos 1983.

2. Early studies tended to view the phenomenon of violent anticlericalism as one of the virtually diagnostic signs that rural radicalism represented a premodern and often irrational political mentality. Brenan, for example, in his seminal study on the origins of the Civil War (first published in 1943), noted the highly moralistic character of working-class ideologies and argued that rural anarchists could be considered millenarian heretics whose fanaticism sprang from the view that the Catholic church represented the Antichrist (1960:189–90). In his account in *Primitive Rebels* (1965), Hobsbawm considerably refined Brenan's characterization but concurred with his point of view. Provocative recent work by J. Corbin (1986), Lincoln (1985, 1989), and Mitchell (1988) dealing with the ritualized aspects of violence during the Civil War period has to a certain extent both revitalized and offered alternatives to the classic millenarian approach to understanding working-class movements. There remain, however, many unaddressed problems with the millenarian theory and related "symbolic" approaches as general frameworks for understanding radical action and attitudes in Andalusia. For one thing, the rural bourgeoisie in places such as Aracena can hardly be characterized as having a premodern mentality, and they responded to the brief period of working-class rule at the outbreak of the war with every bit as much emotionalism, "religious" fervor, and violence as their class enemies. This fact alone creates skepticism toward evolutionary schematizations that center on the contrast between "modern," "rational" modes of political organization and supposedly "primitive" political movements by emphasizing the moralism, religiosity, and fanaticism of the latter.

Several other accounts of rural radicalism, including those of Kaplan (1977) and Mintz (1982), have extensively criticized the millenarian theory. These studies have stressed the immediate political contexts, rational planning, considerable degree of organization, and pragmatic aims of working-class actions in order to reverse the impression that phenomena such as anticlerical violence and strikes represent spontaneous outbursts of revolutionary fanaticism. The effect (perhaps unintended) of this counterargument has been to underplay the significance of church burnings and attacks on the clergy by conveying the sense that they can be satisfactorily understood as incidental assaults on the property and representatives of a key ideological institution.

Proponents of the millenarian and symbolic approaches and their critics usually overdraw the distinction between pragmatic and symbolic action, and their accounts are weakened by a common tendency to place the variety of intentions and understandings evident among the anticlericals into narrow and opposed analytical straitjackets. By implicitly or explicitly engaging in a debate concerning the distinction between rational and nonrational political mentalities, both approaches tend to obscure how revolutionary anticlericalism resulted from a convergence of manifold political and cultural processes of differing duration, intensity, and force. Because they refuse the temptation to dichotomize expressive and practical action, Gilmore (1986, 1989) and Sánchez (1987) give more balanced accounts and suggest a number of useful lines of inquiry.

3. For a full account of the dictatorship of Primo de Rivera, see Ben-Ami 1983.

4. A tone of political elegy had already been sounded the year before in an open letter written to *El Liberal* (13 Aug. 1930) by one of the oldest and closest allies of the *marqués*. Addressing the letter to a "friend" who had refused to join the Conservative party, the writer admitted that the "grave symptoms" afflicting the district of Aracena could be cured only by the "work of freedom and intelligence, the work of youth," and he declared that "the middle classes have been converted into the major class" and prophesied that they were destined to supersede "the forces of the nobles." This was more wishful thinking than accurate prognostication, but it does reflect the general recognition that times had changed and a younger generation of politicians would henceforth be responsible for the conduct of local affairs.

5. Although the matter is by no means certain, one informed account indicates that the rift in the local working-class movement had originated in the period of the dictatorship. In Aracena, many working-class people had greeted the dictatorship with considerable enthusiasm. Although Primo clamped down on strikes and protests, he promised reforms; there was some hope that the nineteenth-century alliance between progressive forces and some sectors of the army could be revitalized; and Primo's earthy personality and considerable (rather bombastic) charm appealed to many. But when the desire for reform (particularly agrarian reform) was frustrated, a cleavage was generated between those who had welcomed the dictatorship and those who had not. The former group blamed the old politicians of the constitutional monarchy for Primo's downfall, while the latter criticized those sympathetic to the dictator and were further disillusioned with the possibility of reaching any agreement with political moderates. A somewhat analogous cleavage had occurred on the national level when the Socialist union (La Unión General de Trabajadores) led by Largo Caballero had reached an accommodation with Primo and was accused of being a traitor to the working class by the anarchists who had been forced to go underground in response to the dictator's repressive measures.

6. In 1934, however, the local Republican bloc fragmented when the national Radical Republicans moved to the right and adopted a conciliatory position on the issue of the church. At this point, some of the local Republicans shifted to the side of the Catholic right while others affiliated themselves with the strongly anticlerical splinter group, the Unión Republica headed by Martínez Barrios. As was the case with the other blocs that dominated the town's political life during the Second Republic, the course of development of the

local Republican group was closely tuned to the continual jostlings, realignments, and power struggles among national parties and also to the more general process of political and class polarization that characterized the whole period in Aracena and the rest of Spain.

7. The increase was in accord with new legislation which mandated that local wages and working conditions be set by a commission of town councilors, workers, and employers. For overviews of the impact of this legislation, see Malefakis 1970:166–70 and Preston 1984a:159–81. For a detailed account of the sorts of political conflicts associated with these commissions in the Sierra de Aracena, see G. Collier 1987.

8. Information on the fifty-five properties that local officials identified for possible confiscation under the laws of agrarian reform was supplied to me by George Collier and is based on the records of the Registry of Expropriable Property in Madrid.

9. During this whole period and especially after the victory of the CEDA in the national elections of November 1933, the Republican town council sharply moderated its rhetoric and actions. Nonetheless, the council persisted in pursuing certain reforms and attempted to provide employment for the poor in several ways. Though finances were strained, the council still contrived to build a school, improve education, construct new quarters for the Guardia Civil, and build a road to connect the hamlet of Jabuguillo with the Seville highway.

10. Ordóñez Márquez (1968:546–56, Appendix 5) lists the voting results for each of the townships of the province of Huelva in the national elections of February 1936. His figures for Aracena show that about fifteen hundred votes were cast for each of the CEDA and Popular Front slates of candidates. It should be borne in mind, however, that this somewhat distorts the overall alignment of political forces in the town, since many working-class people sympathetic to the left either refused to vote because of their disillusionment with democratic processes or else were afraid to vote because of right-wing intimidation.

11. The dismissal of one functionary in particular—the secretary of the *ayuntamiento* (town council), who was difficult to dislodge from his post because of his civil service status—led to the most vindictive sorts of exchanges among the local politicians. After his dismissal, the secretary went about town fomenting "rebellion and resistance" against the town council, which responded with a suit (ACM, 2 May 1936). This was merely the most serious of several such cases. A schoolteacher and a municipal employee lost their posts for "slandering" the council, and another town official who refused to give up his job quietly was dismissed and jailed for two weeks for "corruption and slander" (ACM, 25 May 1936). Some of these municipal employees bore much of the responsibility for the purges that ensued after the capture of the town by Nationalist forces and later became leaders of the local Falange.

12. Both of these pat answers have to be treated with some caution, for they clearly echo the general view of the victorious Nationalists and have to be seen in light of the ideological pressures exerted during the decades of repression that followed the Civil War. Thus, those who characterize the burning of the churches as the work of "the Marxist hordes" are almost invariably to be counted among the supporters of the postwar authoritarian regime, and their characterization represents a way of justifying that regime by spreading the blame for church burning as broadly as possible among the working classes. In contrast, those who blame "a few fanatics" are usually poorer people who are attempting to avoid the implication that they or their friends and neighbors were in any way sympathetic to such extreme actions. Both responses are "interested" and reveal as much about post–Civil War conditions of life as they do about what actually happened in August 1936.

13. One might initially suspect that this third characterization of the church burners is also an "interested" view because it casts the crowd as youths, hamlet dwellers, and miners and is thus largely consistent with the notion that those who burned the churches were not full members of the community in one way or another. However, there is good reason to think that this recollection of events in Aracena is accurate, since most accounts of church burnings in the sierra indicate that the crowds in other towns were young and led or influenced by miners (for example, see G. Collier 1987:148–49; Ordóñez Márquez 1968:183ff.). In Aracena, most of the people who described the crowd as young and from the hamlets were either working-class youths or hamlet dwellers themselves in 1936; and if they had wanted to absolve themselves from blame, they would hardly have described the crowd in this way. Moreover, while it is reasonable to suppose that the young and those whose ties to the community were most tenuous were therefore more willing to engage in acts of wholesale destruction than older lifelong residents of Aracena, this likely tendency is only a secondary factor in understanding the nature and character of the crowd and should not be allowed to obscure the directly political factors that influenced those who participated in the church burnings. More immediately decisive than residence, age, or membership in the community per se was the fact that it was young men, miners, and hamlet dwellers who were most enthusiastic about making a revolution.

14. For a fascinating discussion of how religious symbols and experiences could unite Spanish conservative forces during this period, see Christian 1987.

15. My description of the confrontation between the anticlericals and Acción Católica over the issue of the crucifixes in the schoolrooms varies somewhat from that of Ordóñez Márquez (1968:179) and is based on the recollections of three townspeople, who stressed the provocative character of the activities of Acción Católica during the incident. Although Ordóñez Márquez estimated that eight hundred workers were involved, the townspeople thought the number was considerably smaller.

16. Because confession involves the impositions of penances and priestly absolution and because communion entails receiving the sacraments on one's knees, both forms have been regarded as offensive to human dignity. The depth of resistance to such subordination is suggested by the remark of one devout man who was a close friend of a priest and was not reluctant to praise his friend as a paragon of virtue. Nevertheless, when asked if he would attend a mass his friend was celebrating, he thought for a moment and responded sadly, "No, because then we would no longer be friends." His attitude is a reflection of a more general pattern of noncompliance in which Andalusian men, in particular, often go to great lengths to avoid symbolic subordination to priests. They attend mass only under extraordinary circumstances such as the death or marriage of a close relative, and even on such special occasions as these, they sometimes demonstrate their independence by gathering outside the church doors and chatting with their friends while the ceremonies are in progress.

In light of such attitudes, it is tempting to regard traditional anticlericalism as a latent "Protestant" dimension of Catholic culture. This led Brenan (1960:188ff.) to advance the idea that rural anarchism represented a Protestant movement within Catholic culture. While this is perhaps not altogether inaccurate, it may be an anachronistic and misleading comparison, for criticisms of the doctrines and dogmas of the church are a secondary and relatively minor element in traditional anticlericalism in Andalusia.

17. Brandes (1980) and Gilmore (1986, 1987a) have discussed Andalusian misogyny, machismo, and notions of homosexuality at considerable length and analyzed their relation to anticlericalism, politics, and other matters. They and others have argued that ribald tales and anecdotes of priestly seduction of other men's wives reflect deep-seated anxieties and fears concerning the lack of autonomy or the tenuous control of working-class men over their women, their households, and their political and economic lives.

18. For another view of the relation of blasphemy to the politics of resistance in the Mediterranean, see Herzfeld 1984. For an illuminating discussion of the relationship between religiosity and anticlericalism in Portugal, see Riegelhaupt 1984.

19. A similar ironic response was made by another man when he was asked about his refusal to take communion or comply with the Easter duty: *"Qué barbaridad!* [How barbarous! How ridiculous!] This body of Christ thing . . . the little bits of wine and bread of the priest are not food for a man. From God you receive even less than from the rich, and God wants everything. You know what happened to his son."

20. From this perspective, the attack on the church and sacred images appears to have been neither essentially religious in character nor a spontaneous and irrational outburst, as the proponents of the millenarian theory would have us believe. The millenarian theory is correct in supposing that the sig-

nificance of burning the churches and destroying the images cannot be understood without reference to traditional culture; however, to regard revolutionary irreligion in terms of an iconoclastic frenzy of aberrant spiritual enthusiasm is to distort and oversimplify a complex interplay of historical and cultural continuities and discontinuities.

The actions of the church burners were political, ideological, and, above all, moral in their intent and were not in any particularly meaningful way "religious." Moreover, rather than being a matter of spontaneous inspiration, the church burnings represented a calculated stratagem of the most committed revolutionaries, who acted in ways consistent with the crisis and the limits and potentialities of the revolutionary moment. For these men, it was not senseless to attack the churches and destroy the images. On the contrary, their assault was a gesture supersaturated with meaning because it challenged conceptions of personhood, power, and society that exerted pressures and constraints on virtually every aspect of social life.

21. No official records of the executions were kept, of course, so it is difficult to say whether seventy or two hundred is the more accurate figure. The higher number probably takes into account those men from neighboring towns who were killed in Aracena.

Chapter 7: Mass Culture and Local Custom

1. For good general accounts of recent Spanish history and contemporary Spanish society, see Carr and Fusi 1981, Hooper 1986, and Pérez Díaz 1987. For an account of the recent history and present structure of Spanish political and economic institutions, see Donaghy and Newton 1987. For discussions of the urban social dynamics, see Buechler 1983, Gregory 1983, Kenny and Knipmeyer 1983, and Press 1979.

2. Regarding the general history and structure of the Franco regime, see Linz 1976 and Payne 1987.

3. For a discussion of retrospective village versions of the events of the Civil War, see Harding 1988 and G. Collier 1987.

4. For accounts of the modernization of agriculture in Andalusia and northern Spain, see Gilmore 1980, Greenwood 1976, Harding 1984, and Martínez-Alier 1971. For an analysis of Andalusian economic dependency and marginality, see Delgado Cabeza 1981.

5. The decline of agriculture in Aracena was also linked to the industrialization and urbanization of Spanish society in general during the period from 1955 to 1970. As late as 1950, more than half of the working population of Spain was still tied to the land, and industry was largely confined to the Basque provinces and Catalonia. But after about 1955, foreign investment and government policies promoting industrialization began to make an impact; and by the 1960s, Spain's rate of economic growth was only exceeded by

that of Japan. This rapid process of economic development was markedly uneven and centered on expanding metropolitan poles such as Madrid and Barcelona, which attracted vast numbers of immigrants from the countryside of Andalusia and Castile. The process also created severe problems for Spanish agriculture, which was relatively unproductive and archaic in its methods. The nature of the problems created is best suggested by comparing prices in the agricultural and industrial sectors of the economy: while the value of industrial goods rose dramatically in the 1950s and 1960s, agrarian prices and production levels remained relatively stagnant. For detailed analyses of the problems confronting agriculture in the sierra, see Durán Alonso 1985, Márquez Fernández 1977, and Roux 1975. For general descriptions of the course of national economic development, see Carr and Fusi 1981 and Lieberman 1982.

6. Spaniards had long favored sierran hogs, which are fed acorns for about eighteen months before they are ready for slaughter, at which point almost 50 percent of their weight is fat. While this is ideal for the sausages and lard of the traditional diet, urban consumers have increasingly preferred the leaner meat of imported breeds. Although imported breeds have the advantage of requiring a shorter period before they are ready for market, they have to be fed on grains that cannot be grown in the sierra; the costs of transporting and buying feed thus make it prohibitively expensive to raise nonnative hogs. As a result of these problems, local hog production has fallen dramatically.

7. Scholars attempting to calculate the declining impact of agriculture on local society can be misled by raw quantitative data. Although figures from the mid-1970s state that 54 percent of Aracena's working population were involved in agriculture, the town's economy was nevertheless already dominated by the service sector, and there were relatively few households whose *primary* source of income came from working the land. In tandem with the transformation of the large estates, there has been a progressive decline in the number of small exploitations. Thus, active exploitation of the land is largely confined to the relatively few medium to large estates ranging from twenty to three hundred hectares. In the case of small garden plots and holdings of up to one hundred hectares, vegetables, fruits, and meat are produced for the family table, for barter with neighbors, and to a limited extent for sale in the town; but full-scale production for external markets is becoming less common, and, in general, households depend on pensions, social security payments, or part-time or full-time employment in the service sector as the primary source of income. The data are skewed by the fact that those who identify themselves as agrarian workers include teenagers and aging men who are unemployed many months of the year and are dependent on the earnings of others engaged in nonagricultural pursuits. The number of households in which all members are actually engaged in agricultural work is small, and the incomes of such households are, at best, moderate. As a consequence of

agricultural decline, the social impact of the archaic agrarian system on local society has been drastically reduced. Agriculture is presently the key factor in Aracena only in the sense that other sectors of the town's economy serve the primarily agrarian producers of the surrounding villages.

8. For an account of the impact of migration on an Andalusian town, see Gregory 1978. For accounts regarding other regions of Spain, see Brandes 1975, W. Douglass 1975, and Margolies 1980.

9. All six of Aracena's *aldeas* (dependent hamlets) underwent radical declines in population. The most extreme case of depopulation was that of the *aldea* of Corterangel, which had 138 people in 1950 and 3 in 1980. In some cases, the people from the *aldeas* moved only as far as Aracena.

10. For discussions about the general impact of processes of modernization on Spanish rural communities, see Aceves 1971; Aceves and Douglass 1976; Aceves, Hansen, and Levitas 1976; Barrett 1974; Cazorla 1980; and Pérez Díaz 1974 and 1976. On the role of local and regional elites in fostering these processes, see especially Hansen 1977; Pi-Sunyer 1974; and Schneider, Schneider, and Hansen 1972.

11. For studies of the initial impact of tourism on Spanish communities, see Greenwood 1972 and Pi-Sunyer 1973.

12. For analyses of election returns and party politics during the period of the transition and after, see D. Bell 1983 and Gunther, Smith, and Shabad 1988.

13. For discussions about the impact of recent politicoeconomic changes on the culture of Andalusian towns, see Gilmore 1983 and 1987a:180–86 and Provanzal 1984.

14. For ethnographic accounts of recent religious and political change in Spanish communities, see Behar 1990, Brandes 1976, Freeman 1978, and Frigolé Reixach 1983. For broad sociological and historical perspectives, see Lannon 1987 and Linz 1980.

15. These historically "sedimented" (Gramsci 1971:324) and "socially embedded" (Herzfeld 1987:201) moral, spiritual, and aesthetic notions both express and shape a commonsense and practical consciousness of what is at stake in social relations. In Bourdieu's (1977, 1985) terminology, they are key to understanding the traditional dimensions of the contemporary "habitus" of Aracena. For recent discussions of honor and shame and related notions such as formality, openness, and hospitality, see Gilmore 1987b. For accounts of ideas of grace, see Mitchell 1990:31–32 and Pitt-Rivers 1989.

16. For a discussion of the political dynamics of the decline of ideals and relations of patronage, see Frigolé Reixach 1977.

17. My discussion of the hegemonic dynamics of the emergent and predominately aesthetic constitution of tradition in Aracena is indebted to Adorno's (1973, 1984) critical theory. While the discussions of "artificial negativity" by Luke (1978), Piccone (1977, 1978), and the staff of *Telos* (1990) are also helpful in some respects, I do not regard tradition in Aracena

as either completely "artificial" or "negative" in these authors' sense of the terms. For illuminating discussions of the constitution of the realm of the aesthetic and high art in modern culture, see Brenkman 1987, Burger 1984, and Eagleton 1990.

18. For another perspective on the larger sociopolitical and cultural significance of fashion and style in rural Andalusia, see J. Collier 1986.

Chapter 8: The Presence of Tradition

1. Fernandez (1984) offers a more positive view of the paradoxes involved in contemporary Spanish fiestas. He indicates, for example, that the "ironic play of tropes" in a northern Spanish kayak festival expresses a transcendent humanism. For a discussion of shifts in Spanish religious styles, see also Freeman 1978.

2. In particular, townspeople cited the loss of vitality in *barrio* (neighborhood) fiestas and the reforms of the annual *feria* (fair) undertaken by the Socialist-controlled town council (see Chapter 9) as examples of changes in tradition.

3. For ethnographic accounts of the ritualization of class conflict, see Driessen 1984 and 1989 and Gilmore 1975.

4. The ethnographic literature on the lay religious brotherhoods and processions of Holy Week in Andalusia is large. For historical and ethnographic overviews and detailed discussions of the customs of Holy Week and other religious celebrations such as Corpus Christi, see Alvarez Santaló, Buxó i Rey, and Rodríguez Becerra 1989 (especially volume 3); Castón Boyer 1985; Maldonado 1975; Moreno Navarro 1974; and Rodríguez Becerra 1985. For accounts of how the processions of Holy Week are organized and conducted in particular towns, see Aguilar Criado 1983, Aguilera 1978, Briones 1985, Driessen 1984, Luque Requeray 1980, Mitchell 1988, and Moreno Navarro 1972. For accounts of Holy Week in Seville, see Mitchell 1990 and Moreno Navarro 1982. Regarding Seville, the two accounts diverge sharply in their interpretations of crucial matters concerning the emotional tone and degree of subjective investment in the rites. Mitchell (1990:179–80) focuses on the "incarcerating" and "defensive emotionality" of the processions and underplays their political aspects. Moreno Navarro (1982:222–34) stresses the political dimensions of the processions and emphasizes the casualness of attitudes and broad range of emotional and cultural stances that Sevillanos adopt in relation to the processions. Moreno Navarro's descriptions seem far more appropriate to the Holy Week celebrations of Aracena.

5. Based on the forms of Andalusian *cante hondo* (deep song) from which flamenco also developed, these *saetas* are more or less extemporaneous compositions delivered as anguished or ecstatic cries of passion in a wrenching, trilled vibrato that seems to be both a call to prayer and a cry of sensual longing.

6. Throughout the week of the passion in 1982, townspeople kept telling my wife and me what would come next. But nobody even bothered to mention the events following the entombment of Christ. The masses of Easter Sunday were not well attended. While a few people followed the custom of taking a picnic lunch consisting of a paschal loaf and hard-boiled eggs to the countryside, most appeared to do on Easter Sunday what they would do on any other Sunday. For a discussion of the lack of emphasis on the resurrection in Andalusian religion, see Mitchell 1990:164–66.

7. For a fine comprehensive account of *la corrida de toros* (the "bullfight"), see Marvin 1988. For discussions of the cultural significance of the *corrida*, see C. Douglass 1984, Marvin 1986, Mitchell 1988 and 1991, and Pitt-Rivers 1984.

8. For a discussion of the broader hegemonic significance of the theme of diversity in unity in European culture, see Herzfeld 1987:77–94.

9. For accounts of the courtship system in a small *pueblo* near Aracena, see G. Collier 1983 and Price and Price 1966a and 1966b. For an extended account of the folklore of Spanish courtship, see Taggart 1990. For a discussion of the politics of gender relations in contemporary Andalusia, see Gilmore 1990a.

10. For a general account of how state power and bureaucratic disciplines have affected families in France and elsewhere under liberal regimes, see Donzelot 1979.

11. The discussion of military conscription here pertains to the early 1980s. In recent years, the number of conscripts has declined, and it is likely that the laws and policies regulating military service will be significantly changed in the near future.

Chapter 9: The Politics of the Commonplace

1. For general political histories of the transition, see Gilmour 1985; Graham 1984; Gunther, Smith, and Shabad 1988; Preston 1986; and Share 1986.

2. For accounts of Opus Dei in Spain, see Moncada Lorenzo 1974 and Moreno 1977.

3. For a discussion of the rhetoric of friendship and exchange in Andalusia, see Gilmore 1991.

DOCUMENTS CITED

AA, or *apuntes históricos de Aracena y su distrito*. A fire that destroyed the parish church of Aracena in 1936 also resulted in the loss of almost all of the town and parish archives. In 1948, wishing to ensure the preservation of the scanty remaining information concerning the town's past, the town council hired Victor González Tello, a local man, to compile a collection of partial transcriptions and summary descriptions of documents and a set of notes on local history. The work of González Tello leaves much to be desired in terms of complete referencing and other matters. In addition, his strong political opinions colored his comments on the materials he preserved. Nevertheless, his compilation contains a good deal of miscellaneous information on the town from its earliest days through the mid-1940s, and this part of his work appears to be fairly accurate when compared with data from other sources or witnesses. Thus, approached with caution, the work is a valuable source. The *apuntes* are kept in the *ayuntamiento* (town hall) of Aracena. Parenthetical references to the *apuntes* in the text—for example, (AA 1757)—indicate the source (AA) and the date or approximate date (1757) of the documents transcribed, cited, or described by González Tello.

ACM, or *actas de la comisión municipal*. This source is a set of handwritten minutes of weekly or biweekly town council meetings held in Aracena. Minutes from the pre-1920 period were stored in the parish church of Aracena. Many of them were apparently lost in the fire that destroyed the church in 1936. From 1920 on, minutes were recorded on a fairly regular basis and kept in the *ayuntamiento* of Aracena. Although the minutes from 1920 to 1982 vary from fairly detailed descriptions of debates within the council to brief notes of council decisions, they are an invaluable source on community politics and many other aspects of local affairs. Parenthetical references to the *actas* in the text—for example, (ACM, 2 June 1931)—indicate the source (ACM) and the day, month, and year of the town council meeting.

AN, or *archivo de la notaría*. This archive in Aracena contains documents made by professional notaries from before the turn of the sixteenth century until the present and includes materials from Aracena and all of the other towns of the *partido judicial* (judicial district). Documents filed after

1836 consist mostly of wills, testaments, and records of land sales and other commercial transactions and include some judicial records. Before 1836, however, and especially in the period from about 1650 to 1800, the scope of the documentation is considerably broader and includes such things as legal pleas and decrees of the secular and ecclesiastical *cabildos* (councils) and the religious communities and brotherhoods of the town. The *archivo* is an indispensable source of information on Aracena and the sierra during the Ancient Regime, even though it is difficult to use because of its lack of organization and inadequate indexing of records. The *archivo* is housed in the office of the notary in Aracena. Parenthetical references to the *archivo* in the text—for example, (AN/mlv 1759:10)—indicate the source (AN), the notary's initials appearing on the spine of the volume cited (mlv), the year of the document (1759), and in cases in which the volume is paginated, the page or folio number (10).

Catastro(s) de Aracena. Two tax lists with the names of landowners and the size of their holdings were available in the *ayuntamiento* of Aracena during 1981–82. The more recent *catastro* dates from 1972. The earlier one was compiled in the 1940s and was rather haphazardly and partially revised in the 1950s and 1960s to reflect shifts in ownership through sales and inheritance.

Catastro de Ensenada. During 1752–54, the *marqués* of Ensenada undertook a general survey of the wealth of the Crown of Castile. This survey provides a general picture of numerous townships, including the township of Aracena, in the mid-eighteenth century. I have relied most heavily on the *respuestas generales,* a series of forty questions and answers concerning institutions, taxes, and the local economy. The *respuestas generales* for Aracena are housed in El Archivo General de Simancas (Libro 560, Tomo 1, pp. 720–47) in the town of Simancas, near Valladolid. In addition, I have drawn on data about Aracena generously provided to me by Francisco Núñez Roldán, who transcribed the information from two other Ensenada sources, *El libro del mayor hacendado* (Simancas) and *Los estados generales* (Archivo Nacional, Sección de la Hacienda, Madrid). The former describes the amount and bases of the income of the convent of Santa Catalina in Aracena, and the latter reveals the overall distribution of land among three categories of property holders: laymen, beneficed clergy, and clergy with patrimonial endowments.

Censo de Floridablanca. This census of 1787 gives the population of Aracena by age, sex, marital status, and occupation or rank of adult males and also provides some information on the organization of the town's monasteries and convents. It is preserved in El Real Academia de la Historia (*legajo* 9/6245) in Madrid.

DPS, or *documents from private sources*. A number of people in Aracena per-mitted me to use documents that were once in the public domain but are now privately owned. Considerations of confidentiality prevent me from discussing these documents in greater detail. Parenthetical references to these documents in the text—for example, (DPS 1756)—indicate the source (DPS) and the date or approximate date (1756) of the document.

DZ, or *document of Zapata*. This is a general description of Aracena, written in 1723 by Zapata, a governor of the town. The complete text of the doc-ument has recently been published. See González Sánchez 1988:555–87.

EL, or *electoral lists*. Lists of eligible voters in Aracena in the period from 1890 to 1930 are available in El Archivo de la Diputación Provincial, lo-cated in Huelva, the capital of the province. These records are of value for understanding local politics. They also provide some information on lev-els of literacy and list the occupation of every adult male voter. Paren-thetical references to these lists in the text—for example, (EL 1920)—indicate the source (EL) and the date (1920) of the document.

RP, or *registro de propiedad*. The registry gives details of property transactions from the mid-nineteenth century until the present for all of the townships of the *partido judicial*. It is a particularly valuable source for the last phase of sales of ecclesiastical and common lands. The *registro* is kept in the of-fice of the registry of property in Aracena. Parenthetical references to the *registro* in the text—for example, (RP 1896:2737)—indicate the source (RP), the year (1896), and the number of the transaction (2737).

REFERENCES CITED

Aceves, Joseph
1971   *Social Change in a Spanish Village*. New York: Schenkman.
Aceves, Joseph, and William Douglass, eds.
1976   *The Changing Faces of Rural Spain*. New York: Schenkman.
Aceves, Joseph, E. Hansen, and E. Levitas, eds.
1976   *Economic Transformations and Steady-State Values: Essays in the Ethnography of Spain*. Flushing, N.Y.: Queens College Press.
Acosta Sánchez, José
1978   *Andalucía: Reconstrucción de una identidad y la lucha contra el centralismo*. Barcelona: Anagrama.
1979   *Historia y cultura del pueblo andaluz*. Barcelona: Anagrama.
Adorno, Theodor
1973   *Negative Dialectics*. E. B. Ashton, trans. New York: Seabury Press.
1984   *Aesthetic Theory*. C. Lenhardt, trans. London: Routledge and Kegan Paul.
Aguilar Criado, Encarnación
1983   *Las hermandades de Castilleja de la Cuesta: Estudio de antropología cultural*. Seville: Ayuntamiento de Sevilla.
Aguilera, Francisco
1978   *Santa Eulalia's People: Ritual Structure and Process in an Andalusian Multi-Community*. St. Paul, Minn.: West Publishing Company.
Alvarez Santaló, Carlos, María Jésus Buxó i Rey, and Salvador Rodríguez Becerra, eds.
1989   *La religiosidad popular*. 3 vols. Barcelona: Anthropos.
Amelang, James
1986   *Honored Citizens of Barcelona: Patrician Culture and Class Relations, 1490–1714*. Princeton: Princeton University Press.
Anes Alvarez, Gonzalo
1975   *El antiguo régimen: Los Borbones*. Vol. 4 of *Historia de España Alfaguara*. Madrid: Editorial Alfaguara.
Artola, Miguel, M. Bernal, and J. Contreras
1978   *El latifundio: Propiedad y explotación, siglos XVIII–XX*. Madrid: Servicio de Publicaciones Agrarias.

Avery, David
　　1974　　　*Not on Queen Victoria's Birthday: The Story of the Río Tinto Mines.* London: Collins.

Avila Fernández, Domingo
　　1981　　　*Campofrío: Una forma de vida entre la sierra y la mina.* Huelva: Instituto de Estudios Onubenses "Padre Marchena."

Bakhtin, Mikhail
　　1981　　　*The Dialogic Imagination.* Michael Holquist, ed. Austin: University of Texas Press.

Barrett, Richard A.
　　1974　　　*Benabarre: The Modernization of a Spanish Village.* New York: Holt, Rinehart, and Winston.

Behar, Ruth
　　1986　　　*Santa María del Monte: The Presence of the Past in a Spanish Village.* Princeton: Princeton University Press.
　　1990　　　"The Struggle for the Church: Popular Anticlericalism and Religiosity in Post-Franco Spain." In *Religious Orthodoxy and Popular Faith in European Society,* ed. Ellen Badone, 76–112. Princeton: Princeton University Press.

Bell, Aubrey F. G.
　　1922　　　*Benito Arias Montano.* Oxford: Humphrey Milford.

Bell, David, ed.
　　1983　　　*Democratic Politics in Spain: Spanish Politics after Franco.* New York: St. Martin's Press.

Ben-Ami, Shlomo
　　1983　　　*Fascism from Above: The Dictatorship of Primo de Rivera.* Oxford: Oxford University Press.

Bennassar, Bartolomé
　　1979　　　*The Spanish Character: Attitudes and Mentalities from the Sixteenth to the Nineteenth Century.* Benjamin Keen, trans. Berkeley: University of California Press.

Bernal, Antonio
　　1979　　　*La lucha por la tierra en la crisis del antiguo régimen.* Madrid: Taurus.

Bilinkoff, Jodi
　　1989　　　*The Avila of Saint Teresa: Religious Reform in a Sixteenth-Century City.* Ithaca: Cornell University Press.

Blok, Anton
　　1974　　　*The Mafia of a Sicilian Village, 1860–1960: A Study of Violent Peasant Entrepreneurs.* Oxford: Basil Blackwell.

Blok, Anton, and Henk Driessen
　　1984　　　"Mediterranean Agro-Towns as a Form of Cultural Domi-

nance with Special Reference to Sicily and Andalusia." *Ethnologia Europaea* 14:11–24.

Bossy, John
1970   "The Counter-Reformation and the People of Catholic Europe." *Past and Present* 4:51–70.
1985   *Christianity in the West, 1400–1700*. Oxford: Oxford University Press.

Bourdieu, Pierre
1976   "Marriage Strategies as Strategies of Social Reproduction." In *Family and Society: Selections from Annales,* ed. R. Forster and O. Ranum, 117–44. Baltimore: Johns Hopkins University Press.
1977   *Outline of a Theory of Practice*. Richard Nice, trans. New York: Cambridge University Press.
1979   "The Sense of Honour." In *Algeria 1960,* trans. Richard Nice, 95–132. Cambridge: Cambridge University Press.
1985   *Distinction: A Social Critique of the Judgement of Taste*. Richard Nice, trans. Cambridge, Mass.: Harvard University Press.

Boyd, Carolyn
1979   *Praetorian Politics in Liberal Spain*. Chapel Hill: University of North Carolina Press.

Brandes, Stanley
1975   *Migration, Kinship, and Community: Tradition and Transition in a Spanish Village*. New York: Academic Press.
1976   "The Priest as Agent of Secularization in Rural Spain." In *Economic Transformations and Steady-State Values: Essays in the Ethnography of Spain,* ed. Joseph Aceves, E. Hansen, and E. Levitas, 22–29. Flushing, N.Y.: Queens College Press.
1980   *Metaphors of Masculinity: Sex and Status in Andalusian Folklore*. Philadelphia: University of Pennsylvania Press.

Brenan, Gerald
1960   *The Spanish Labyrinth: An Account of the Social and Political Background of the Spanish Civil War*. Cambridge: Cambridge University Press.

Brenkman, John
1987   *Culture and Domination*. Ithaca: Cornell University Press.

Briones, Rafael
1985   "La semana santa de Priego de Córdoba: Funciones antropológicas y dimensión cristiana de un ritual popular." In *La religión en Andalucía,* ed. Pedro Castón Boyer, 43–71. Seville: Biblioteca de la Cultura Andaluza.

Brown, Peter
1981   *The Cult of the Saints: Its Rise and Function in Latin Chris-
               tianity.* Chicago: University of Chicago Press.

Bruner, Jerome
1986   *Actual Minds, Possible Worlds.* Cambridge, Mass.: Harvard
               University Press.

Buechler, Hans
1983   "Spanish Urbanization from a Grass-Roots Perspective." In
               *Urban Life in Mediterranean Europe: Anthropological Perspec-
               tives,* ed. Michael Kenny and David I. Kertzer, 135–61. Ur-
               bana: University of Illinois Press.

Burger, Peter
1984   *Theory of the Avant-Garde.* Michael Shaw, trans. Minneapo-
               lis: University of Minnesota Press.

Burke, Peter
1978   *Popular Culture in Early Modern Europe.* New York: Harper
               and Row.

Calero, Antonio M.
1977   *Movimientos sociales en Andalucía, 1820–1936.* Madrid: Siglo
               Veintiuno.

Callahan, William J.
1972   *Honor, Commerce, and Industry in Eighteenth-Century Spain.*
               Boston: Harvard Graduate School of Business.
1984   *Church, Politics, and Society in Spain, 1750–1874.* Cam-
               bridge, Mass.: Harvard University Press.

Candáu Chacón, María Luisa
1988   "Presencia y jurisdición eclesiásticas en la sierra de Huelva:
               Aracena y sus aldeas a comienzos del siglo XVIII." In
               Huelva en su historia, vol. 2, ed. Javier Pérez-Embid and En-
               carnación Rivero Galán, 401–36. Huelva: Colegio Univer-
               sitario de la Rábida.

Capel, José Carlos
1982   "La matanza en Andalucía." In *Manual de la matanza,* ed.
               J. V. Suiero et al., 219–65. Madrid: Penthalon.

Capelo García, María Luz
1979   *Contribución al problema de la desamortización en la provincia
               de Huelva, 1836–1844.* Huelva: Instituto de Estudios
               Onubenses "Padre Marchena."

Caro, Rodrigo
1896 (1634)   *Antiquedades y principado de la ilustrísima ciudad de Sevilla y
               corografía de su convento jurídico o antigua cancellería.* Seville.

Caro Baroja, Julio
1957   "El sociocentrismo de los pueblos españoles." In *Razas,
               pueblos y linajes.* Madrid: Revista de Occidente.

1963   "The City and the Country: Reflections on Some Ancient Commonplaces." In *Mediterranean Countrymen*, ed. J. Pitt-Rivers, 27–40. The Hague: Mouton.

1966   "Honour and Shame: A Historical Account of Several Conflicts." In *Honour and Shame: The Values of Mediterranean Society,* ed. J. G. Peristiany, 79–138. Chicago: University of Chicago Press.

1978   *Las formas complejas de la vida religiosa: Religión, sociedad, y carácter en la España de los siglos XVI y XVII*. Madrid: Akal Editor.

Carr, Raymond
1982   *Spain, 1808–1975*. Oxford: Clarendon.

Carr, Raymond, and Juan Pablo Fusi
1981   *Spain: Dictatorship to Democracy*. London: Allen and Unwin.

Carrión, Pascual
1975   *Los latifundios en España*. Barcelona: Ariel.

Castón Boyer, Pedro
1985   "La religiosidad tradicional en Andalucía: Una aproximación sociológica." In *La religión en Andalucía,* ed. Pedro Castón Boyer, 97–129. Seville: Biblioteca de la Cultura Andaluza.

Castro, Concepción de
1979   *La revolución liberal y los municipios españoles.* Madrid: Alianza.

Cazorla, José
1980   "Mentalidad 'modernizante': Trabajo y cambio en los retornados andaluces." *Revista Española de Investigaciones Sociológicas* 11:29–53.

Cevallos, Fernando Pascual
1983   *Luchas agrarias en Sevilla durante la Segunda República*. Seville: Diputación Provincial de Sevilla.

Christian, William
1981a   *Apparitions in Late Medieval and Renaissance Spain*. Princeton: Princeton University Press.

1981b   *Local Religion in Sixteenth-Century Spain*. Princeton: Princeton University Press.

1982   "Provoked Religious Weeping in Early Modern Spain." In *Religious Organization and Religious Experience,* ed. J. Davis, 105–12. New York: Academic Press.

1987   "Tapping and Defining New Power: The First Months of Visions at Ezquiroga, July 1931." *American Ethnologist* 14:140–66.

Clavero, Bartolomé
1974   *Mayorazgo: Propriedad feudal en Castilla, 1369–1836*. Madrid: Siglo Veintiuno.

Clifford, James, and George E. Marcus, eds.
1986   *Writing Culture: The Poetics and Politics of Ethnography.*
          Berkeley: University of California Press.

Collier, George
1983   "Late Marriage and the Uncontested Reign of Property."
          Paper presented at the 1983 annual meeting of the Ameri-
          can Anthropological Association, Washington, D.C.
1987   *Socialists of Rural Andalusia: Unacknowledged Revolution-
          aries of the Second Republic.* Stanford: Stanford University
          Press.

Collier, Jane
1986   "From Mary to Modern Woman: The Material Basis of
          Marianismo and Its Transformation in a Spanish Village."
          American Ethnologist 13:100–107.

Corbin, John
1986   "Insurrections in Spain: Casas Viejas 1933 and Madrid
          1981." In *The Anthropology of Violence,* ed. David Riches,
          28–49. Oxford: Basil Blackwell.

Corbin, J. R., and M. P. Corbin
1984   *Compromising Relations: Kith, Kin, and Class in Andalusia.*
          Aldershot, England: Gower.
1987   *Urbane Thought: Culture and Class in an Andalusian City.*
          Aldershot, England: Gower.

Creighton, Colin
1980   "Family, Property, and Relations of Production in Western
          Europe." *Economy and Society* 9:129–67.

Cuenca Toribio, José Manuel
1971   *La iglesia español ante la revolución liberal.* Madrid: Alianza.
1980   *Estudios sobre la iglesia andaluza moderna y contemporanea.*
          Córdoba: Instituto de Historia de Andalucía.
1984   *La Andalucía de la transición: Política y cultura.* Madrid:
          Mezquita.

Davis, Natalie
1975   *Society and Culture in Early Modern France.* Stanford: Stan-
          ford University Press.

Delgado Cabeza, M.
1981   *Dependencia y marginación de la economía andaluza.* Cór-
          doba: Monte de Piedad.

Domínguez Ortiz, Antonio
1970   *La sociedad española en el siglo XVII.* 2 vols. Madrid:
          ISTMO.
1973   *Las clases privilegiadas en la España del antiguo régimen.*
          Madrid: ISTMO.

1976   *Sociedad y estado en el siglo XVIII español*. Barcelona: Ariel.

Domínguez Ortiz, Antonio, and Francisco Aguilar Piñal
1976   *El barroco y la ilustración: Historia de Sevilla*. Vol. 4. Seville:
               Universidad de Sevilla.

Donaghy, Peter J., and Michael T. Newton
1987   *Spain: A Guide to Political and Economic Institutions*. Cam-
               bridge: Cambridge University Press.

Donzelot, Jacques
1979   *The Policing of Families*. Robert Hurley, trans. New York:
               Pantheon.

Douglass, Carrie B.
1984   "*Toro muerto, vaca es:* An Interpretation of the Spanish Bull-
               fight." *American Ethnologist* 11:242–58.

Douglass, William A.
1975   *Echelar and Murelaga: Opportunity and Rural Exodus in Two
               Spanish Basque Towns*. London: C. Hurt.

Driessen, Henk
1984   "Religious Brotherhoods: Class and Politics in an Andalu-
               sian Town." In *Religion, Power, and Protest in Local Commu-
               nities: The Northern Shore of the Mediterranean*, ed. Eric
               Wolf, 73–92. Amsterdam: Mouton.
1989   " 'Elite' versus 'Popular' Religion? The Politics of Religion
               in Rural Andalusia: An Anthropological Perspective." In *La
               religiosidad popular*, vol. 1, ed. Carlos Alvarez Santaló, María
               Jésus Buxó i Rey, and Salvador Rodríguez Becerra, 82–104.
               Barcelona: Anthropos.

Duby, Georges
1980   *The Three Orders: Feudal Society Imagined*. Arthur Goldham-
               mer, trans. Chicago: University of Chicago Press.

Dumont, Louis
1986   *Essays on Individualism: Modern Ideology in Anthropological
               Perspective*. Chicago: University of Chicago Press.

Durán Alonso, Antonio
1985   *Estructura socio-económica de una comarca deprimida: La sierra
               de Aracena*. Huelva: Diputación Provincial de Huelva.

Eagleton, Terry
1988   "The Critic as Clown." In *Marxism and the Interpretation of
               Culture*, ed. Lawrence Grossberg and Cary Nelson, 619–
               32. Urbana: University of Illinois Press.
1990   *The Ideology of the Aesthetic*. Oxford: Basil Blackwell.

Elliott, J. H.
1986   *The Count-Duke of Olivares: The Statesman in an Age of De-
               cline*. New Haven: Yale University Press.

Fernandez, James

1983   "Consciousness and Class in Southern Spain." *American Ethnologist* 10:165–73.

1984   "Convivial Attitudes: The Ironic Play of Tropes in an International Kayak Festival in Northern Spain." In *Text, Play, and Story: The Construction and Reconstruction of Self and Society,* ed. Edward M. Bruner, 199–229. Washington, D.C.: American Ethnological Society.

1988a   "Andalusia on Our Minds: Two Contrasting Places in Spain as Represented in a Vernacular Poetic Duel of the Late Nineteenth Century." *Cultural Anthropology* 3: 21–35.

1988b   "El dominio del tropo: Poesía popular y convivencia social, Gracián y Costa en el campo." *Anales de la Fundación Joaquín Costa* 5:21–35.

Flandrin, Jean-Louis

1977   *Families in Former Times: Kinship, Household, and Sexuality.* Richard Southern, trans. New York: Cambridge University Press.

Foucault, Michel

1981   *Power/Knowledge: Selected Interviews and Other Writings, 1972–1977.* Colin Gordon, ed. New York: Pantheon.

1983   "Afterword: The Subject and Power." In *Michel Foucault: Beyond Structuralism and Hermeneutics,* ed. Hubert L. Dreyfus and Paul Rabinow, 208–26. Chicago: University of Chicago Press.

1984   "Nietzsche, Genealogy, History." In *The Foucault Reader,* ed. Paul Rabinow, 76–100. New York: Pantheon.

Fourneaux, Francis

1980   *Huelva hacia el desarrollo: Evolución de la provincia durante los veinte últimos años.* Huelva: Instituto de Estudios Onubenses "Padre Marchena."

Freeman, Susan Tax

1978   "Faith and Fashion in Spanish Religion: Notes on the Observation of Observance." *Peasant Studies* 7:101–23.

Frigolé Reixach, J.

1977   " 'Ser cacique' y 'ser hombre' o la negación de las relaciones de patronazgo en un pueblo de la Vega Alta de Segura." *Agricultura y Sociedad* 5:143–73.

1983   "Religión y política en un pueblo murciana entre 1966–1976: La crisis del nacionalcatolicismo desde la perspectiva local." *Revista Española de Investigaciones Sociológicas* 23: 77–126.

Frye, Northrop
1971   *Anatomy of Criticism: Four Essays*. Princeton: Princeton University Press.
Geertz, Clifford
1968   *Islam Observed*. Chicago: University of Chicago Press.
Gellner, E., and J. Waterbury, eds.
1977   *Patrons and Clients in Mediterranean Societies*. London: Duckworth.
Giddens, Anthony
1984   *The Constitution of Society*. Berkeley: University of California Press.
Gilmore, David D.
1975   "*Carnaval* in Fuenmayor: Class Conflict and Social Cohesion in an Andalusian Town." *Journal of Anthropological Research* 31:331–49.
1980   *The People of the Plain: Class and Community in Lower Andalusia*. New York: Columbia University Press.
1983   "Culture Change in Post-Franco Spain: Preliminary Report from an Andalusian Town." *Anthropology* 7:31–42.
1986   "Andalusian Anti-Clericalism: An Eroticized Rural Protest." *Anthropology* 3:31–43.
1987a   *Aggression and Community: Paradoxes of Andalusian Culture*. New Haven: Yale University Press.
1987b   *Honor and Shame and the Unity of the Mediterranean*. Washington, D.C.: American Anthropological Association.
1989   "The Anticlericalism of Andalusian Rural Proletarians." In *La religiosidad popular*, vol. 1, ed. Carlos Alvarez Santaló, María Jésus Buxó i Rey, and Salvador Rodríguez Becerra, 478–98. Barcelona: Anthropos.
1990a   "Men and Women in Southern Spain: 'Domestic Power' Revisited." *American Anthropologist* 92:953–70.
1990b   "The Spanish Disentailment Reconsidered: A New Look at the Old Regime." *Peasant Studies* 17:73–95.
1991   "Commodity, Comity, Community: Male Exchange in Rural Andalusia." *Ethnology* 1:17–30.
Gilmour, David
1985   *The Transformation of Spain*. London: Quartet Books.
Glick, Thomas
1988   *Einstein in Spain: Relativity and the Recovery of Science*. Princeton: Princeton University Press.
González Gómez, Antonio
1977   *Moguer en la baja edad media, 1248–1538*. Huelva: Instituto de Estudios Onubenses "Padre Marchena."

González Sánchez, Carlos Alberto
    1988   "El principado de Aracena en dos fuentes documentales del siglo XVIII." In *Huelva en su historia,* vol. 2, ed. Javier Pérez-Embid and Encarnación Rivero Galán, 555–88. Huelva: Colegio Universitario de la Rábida.

Goody, Jack
    1983   *The Development of the Family and Marriage in Europe.* New York: Cambridge University Press.

Goody, Jack, Joan Thirsk, and E. P. Thompson, eds.
    1976   *Family and Inheritance: Rural Society in Western Europe, 1200–1800.* Cambridge: Cambridge University Press.

Goytisolo, Juan
    1977   *Juan the Landless.* Helen R. Lane, trans. New York: Viking Press.

Graham, Robert
    1984   *Spain: Change of a Nation.* London: Michael Joseph.

Gramsci, Antonio
    1971   *Selections from the Prison Notebooks of Antonio Gramsci.* Quinton Hoare and Geoffrey Nowell Smith, eds. and trans. New York: International Publishers.

Greenwood, Davydd
    1972   "Tourism as an Agent of Change: A Spanish Basque Case." *Ethnology* 2:80–91.
    1976   *Unrewarding Wealth: The Commercialization and Collapse of Agriculture in a Spanish Basque Town.* Cambridge: Cambridge University Press.

Gregory, David
    1978   *La odisea andaluza: Una emigración hacia Europa.* Madrid: Tecnos.
    1983   "The Meaning of Urban Life: Pluralization of Life Worlds in Seville." In *Urban Life in Mediterranean Europe: Anthropological Perspectives,* ed. Michael Kenny and David I. Kertzer, 253–72. Urbana: University of Illinois Press.

Gunther, Richard, Giacomo Smith, and Goldie Shabad
    1988   *Spain after Franco: The Making of a Competitive Party System.* Berkeley: University of California Press.

Hall, Stuart
    1980   "Cultural Studies: Two Paradigms." *Media, Culture, and Society* 2:57–72.
    1983   "The Problem of Ideology: Marxism without Guarantees." In *Marx 100 Years On,* ed. B. Matthews, 57–86. London: Lawrence and Wishart.
    1985   "Signification, Representation, Ideology: Althusser and the

Poststructuralist Debates." *Critical Studies in Mass Communication* 2:91–114.

1988   " 'The Toad in the Garden': Thatcherism among the Theorists." In *Marxism and the Interpretation of Culture,* ed. Lawrence Grossberg and Cary Nelson, 35–74. Urbana: University of Illinois Press.

Hamilton, Earl J.
1947   *War and Prices in Spain, 1651–1800.* Cambridge, Mass.: Harvard University Press.

Hansen, Edward C.
1977   *Rural Catalonia under the Franco Regime: The Fate of Regional Culture since the Spanish Civil War.* New York: Cambridge University Press.

Harding, Susan
1984   *Remaking Ibieca: Rural Life in Aragon under Franco.* Chapel Hill: University of North Carolina Press.

1988   "Narrative Resistance: The Village Version of the Spanish Civil War." In *Meanings and Memories,* Harvard University Center for European Studies Working Paper Series, 1936–1986: From the Civil War to Contemporary Spain, 24–32. Cambridge, Mass.: Harvard University.

Harvey, Charles E.
1981   *The Río Tinto Company: An Economic History of a Leading International Mining Concern, 1873–1954.* Penzance, Cornwall, England: Alison Hodge.

Heran, François
1980   *Tierra y parentesco en el campo sevillano: La revolución agrícola del siglo XIX.* Madrid: Ministerio de Agricultura.

Herr, Richard
1958   *The Eighteenth-Century Revolution in Spain.* Princeton: Princeton University Press.

1971a   "Hacia la derrumbe del antiguo régimen: Crisis fiscal y desamortización bajo Carlos IV." *Moneda y Crédito* 118: 37–100.

1971b   *An Historical Essay on Modern Spain.* Berkeley: University of California Press.

1974   "El significado de la desamortización en España." *Moneda y Crédito* 131:55–94.

1976   "Spain." In *European Landed Elites in the Nineteenth Century,* ed. David Spring, 98–125. Baltimore: Johns Hopkins University Press.

1989   *Rural Change and Royal Finances in Spain at the End of the Old Regime.* Berkeley: University of California Press.

Herzfeld, Michael
    1984   "The Significance of the Insignificant: Blasphemy as Ideology." *Man* 19:653–64.
    1987   *Anthropology through the Looking-Glass: Critical Ethnography in the Margins of Europe.* Cambridge: Cambridge University Press.

Hobsbawm, Eric
    1965   *Primitive Rebels: Studies in Archaic Forms of Social Movements in the Nineteenth and Twentieth Century.* New York: Norton.

Hobsbawm, Eric, and Terence Ranger, eds.
    1983   *The Invention of Tradition.* Cambridge: Cambridge University Press.

Holmes, Douglas
    1989   *Cultural Disenchantments: Worker Peasantries of Northeast Italy.* Princeton: Princeton University Press.

Hooper, John
    1986   *The Spaniards: A Portrait of the New Spain.* New York: Viking Press.

Jackson, Gabriel
    1965   *The Spanish Republic and the Civil War, 1931–1939.* Princeton: Princeton University Press.

Kagan, R. L.
    1974   *Students and Society in Early Modern Spain.* Baltimore: Johns Hopkins University Press.

Kamen, Henry
    1980   *Spain in the Later Seventeenth Century, 1665–1700.* London: Longman.

Kaplan, Temma
    1977   *Anarchists of Andalusia, 1868–1903.* Princeton: Princeton University Press.
    1982   "Class Consciousness and Community in Nineteenth-Century Andalusia." *Political Power and Social Theory* 2:21–57.

Kenny, Michael
    1960   "Patterns of Patronage in Spain." *Anthropological Quarterly* 33:14–23.

Kenny, Michael, and Mary C. Knipmeyer
    1983   "Urban Research in Spain: Retrospect and Prospect." In *Urban Life in Mediterranean Europe: Anthropological Perspectives,* ed. Michael Kenny and David I. Kertzer, 25–52. Urbana: University of Illinois Press.

Kern, R. W.
    1974   *Liberals, Reformers, and Caciques in Restoration Spain.* Albuquerque: University of New Mexico Press.

Lannon, Frances
1982   "Modern Spain: The Project of National Catholicism." In *Religion and Nationalism,* ed. Stuart Mews, 567–90. Oxford: Basil Blackwell.
1987   *Privilege, Persecution, and Prophecy: The Catholic Church in Spain, 1875–1975.* Oxford: Clarendon.
Leach, Edmund
1964   *Political Systems of Highland Burma.* Boston: Beacon Press.
Lida, C.
1972   *Anarquismo y revolución en la España del siglo XIX.* Madrid: Siglo Veintiuno.
Lieberman, Sima
1982   *The Contemporary Spanish Economy: An Historical Perspective.* London: George Allen and Unwin.
Lincoln, Bruce
1985   "Revolutionary Exhumations in Spain, July 1936." *Comparative Studies in Society and History* 2:241–60.
1989   "Revolutionary Exhumations in Spain." In *Discourse and the Construction of Society,* 103–27. New York: Oxford University Press.
Linz, Juan
1976   "An Authoritarian Regime: Spain." In *Politics and Society in Twentieth-Century Spain,* ed. Stanley Payne, 160–207. New York: Franklin Watts.
1980   "Religion and Politics in Spain: From Conflict to Consensus above Cleavage." *Social Compass* 27:255–77.
Lison-Tolosana, Carmelo
1983   *Belmonte de los Caballeros: Anthropology and History in an Aragonese Community.* Princeton: Princeton University Press.
Lorea, Antonio de
1854   *Vida y virtudes de la venerable Madre Sor María de la Santísima Trinidad, de la tercera orden de Santo Domingo, escrita año 1671.* Seville: Imprenta de Don José María Geofrin.
Luke, Tim
1978   "Culture and Politics in the Age of Artificial Negativity." *Telos* 35:55–72.
Luque Requeray, J.
1980   *Antropología cultural andaluza: El viernes santo al sur de Córdoba.* Córdoba: Monte de Piedad y Caja de Ahorros de Córdoba.
Lynch, John
1989   *Bourbon Spain, 1700–1808.* Oxford: Basil Blackwell.

Lyotard, Jean-François
1984   *The Postmodern Condition: A Report on Knowledge*. Geoff Bennington and Brian Massumi, trans. Minneapolis: University of Minnesota Press.

McDonogh, Gary
1986   *Good Families of Barcelona*. Princeton: Princeton University Press.

MacLachlan, Colin
1988   *Spain's Empire in the New World: The Role of Ideas in Institutional and Social Change*. Berkeley: University of California Press.

Maddox, Richard
1986   "Religion, Honor, and Patronage: A Study of Culture and Power in an Andalusian Town." Ph.D. diss., Stanford University.

Mádoz, Pascual, ed.
1845–50   *Diccionario geográfico-estadístico-histórico de España y sus posesiones de ultramar*. 16 vols. Madrid.

Maldonado, Luis
1975   *Religiosidad popular*. Madrid: Editorial Cristianidad.

Malefakis, Edward
1970   *Agrarian Reform and Peasant Revolution in Spain: Origins of the Civil War*. New Haven: Yale University Press.

Maravall, José Antonio
1979   *Poder, honor y élites en el siglo XVII*. Madrid: Siglo Veintiuno.
1986   *Culture of the Baroque: Analysis of a Historical Structure*. Terry Cochran, trans. Minneapolis: University of Minnesota Press.

Marcus, George E., and Michael M. J. Fischer
1986   *Anthropology as Cultural Critique: An Experimental Moment in the Human Sciences*. Chicago: University of Chicago Press.

Margolies, Luise
1980   "The New Ghost Towns: Rural Exodus in Modern Spain." *Reviews in Anthropology* 7:107–18.

Márquez Fernández, Dominga
1977   *La geoeconomía forestal de Huelva y el dilema de sus eucaliptales*. Seville: Universidad de Sevilla.

Marriott, McKim
1955   "Little Communities in an Indigenous Civilization." In *Village India*, ed. McKim Marriott, 171–222. Chicago: University of Chicago Press.

Martínez-Alier, Juan
1971   *Labourers and Landowners in Southern Spain.* London: Allen
                and Unwin.

Marvin, Gary
1986   "Honour, Integrity and the Problem of Violence in the
                Spanish Bullfight." In *The Anthropology of Violence,* ed.
                David Riches, 118–35. Oxford: Basil Blackwell.
1988   *Bullfight.* Oxford: Basil Blackwell.

Meaker, Gerald
1974   *The Revolutionary Left in Spain, 1914–1923.* Stanford: Stan-
                ford University Press.

Menéndez Pidal, Ramón
1966   *The Spaniards in Their History.* Walter Starkie, trans. New
                York: Norton.

Mintz, Jerome R.
1982   *The Anarchists of Casas Viejas.* Chicago: University of Chi-
                cago Press.

Mitchell, Timothy
1988   *Violence and Piety in Spanish Folklore.* Philadelphia: Univer-
                sity of Pennsylvania Press.
1990   *Passional Culture: Emotion, Religion, and Society in Southern
                Spain.* Philadelphia: University of Pennsylvania Press.
1991   *Blood Sport: A Social History of the Bullfight.* Philadelphia:
                University of Pennsylvania Press.

Miura Andrades, José María
1989   "Milagros, beatas, y fundaciones de conventos: Lo mila-
                groso en las fundaciones domínicas desde inicios del siglo
                XV a finales del siglo XVI." In *La religiosidad popular,* vol. 2,
                ed. Carlos Alvarez Santaló, María Jésus Buxó i Rey, and Sal-
                vador Rodríguez Becerra, 443–60. Barcelona: Anthropos.

Moncada Lorenzo, Alberto
1974   *El Opus Dei: Una interpretación.* Madrid: Indice.

Montero, José
1977   *La CEDA: El catolocismo social y política en la Segunda Repú-
                blica.* 2 vols. Madrid: Editorial de la Revista del Trabajo.

Moreno, María
1977   *El Opus Dei.* Barcelona: Planeta.

Moreno Alonso, Manuel
1978   *Colonización agraria y poblamiento en la sierra de Huelva: Ro-
                sal de la Frontera en el siglo XIX.* Huelva: Caja Rural Pro-
                vincial de Huelva.
1979   *La vida rural en la sierra de Huelva: Alájar.* Huelva: Instituto
                de Estudios Onubenses "Padre Marchena."

1981   *Historia general de Andalucía.* Seville: Argantonio Ediciones Andaluzas.

Moreno Navarro, Isidoro

1972   *Propriedad, clases sociales, y hermandades en la Baja Andalucía: La estructura social de un pueblo del Aljarafe.* Madrid: Siglo Veintiuno.

1974   *Las hermandades andaluzas: Una aproximación desde la antropología.* Seville: Universidad de Sevilla.

1981   "Rechazo de la dependencia y afirmación de la identidad: Las bases del nacionalismo andaluz." In *Jornadas de estudios socioeconómicos de las comunidades autónomas,* vol. 3, 87–106. Seville: Universidad de Sevilla.

1982   *La semana santa en Sevilla: Conformación, mixtificación y significaciones.* Seville: Ayuntamiento de Sevilla.

1984   "La antropología cultural en Andalucía: Estado actual y perspectiva de futuro." In *Antropología cultural de Andalucía,* ed. Salvador Rodríguez Becerra, 98–107. Seville: Consejería de Cultura, Junta de Andalucía.

1985   *Etnicidad andaluza.* Seville: Universidad de Sevilla.

Nadal, Jordi

1975   *El fracaso de la Revolución Industrial en España, 1814–1913.* Barcelona: Ariel.

1976   *La población española, siglos XVI a XX.* Barcelona: Ariel.

Nader, Helen

1990   *Liberty in Absolutist Spain: The Hapsburg Sale of Towns, 1516–1700.* Baltimore: Johns Hopkins University Press.

Nalle, Sara T.

1989   "Literacy and Culture in Early Modern Castile." *Past and Present* 125:65–96.

Nieto, Alejandro

1964   *Bienes communales.* Madrid: Revista de Derecho Privado.

Nogales, José

1901   *El último patriota.* Barcelona: Casa Maucci.

Núñez Roldán, Francisco

1981   "Condiciones naturales y paisaje agrario en Huelva en el siglo XVIII: Un análisis comarcal—El Andevalo y la costa occidental." *Archivo Hispalense* 193–94:213–33.

1987   *En los confines del reino: Huelva y su tierra en el siglo XVIII.* Seville: Universidad de Sevilla.

Ordóñez Márquez, Juan

1968   *La apostasía de las masas y la persecución religiosa en la provincia de Huelva, 1931–1936.* Madrid: Consejo Superior de Investigaciones Científicas.

Ortner, Sherry
  1984   "Theory in Anthropology since the Sixties." *Comparative Studies in Society and History* 26:126–66.
Parsons, J.
  1962   "The Acorn-Hog Economy of the Oak Woodlands of Southwestern Spain." *Geographical Review* 52:211–35.
Payne, Stanley G.
  1987   *The Franco Regime, 1936–1975*. Madison: University of Wisconsin Press.
Pérez Díaz, Victor
  1974   *Pueblos y clases sociales en el campo español*. Madrid: Siglo Veintiuno.
  1976   "Processes of Change in Rural Castilian Communities." In *The Changing Faces of Rural Spain*, ed. Joseph Aceves and William Douglass, 115–35. New York: Schenkman.
  1987   *El retorno de la sociedad civil*. Madrid: Instituto de Estudios Económicos.
Pérez-Embid, Florentino
  1975   *La frontera entre los reinos de Sevilla y Portugal*. Seville: Universidad de Sevilla.
Pérez-Embid, Javier, and Encarnación Rivero Galán, eds.
  1988   *Huelva en su historia*. Vol. 2. Huelva: Colegio Universitario de la Rábida.
Pérez-Embid, Javier, et al.
  1988   "El concejo de Gibraleón de la edad media a la moderna." In *Huelva en su historia*, vol. 2, ed. Javier Pérez-Embid and Encarnación Rivero Galán, 231–318. Huelva: Colegio Universitario de la Rábida.
Peristiany, J. G., ed.
  1966   *Honour and Shame: The Values of Mediterranean Society*. Chicago: University of Chicago Press.
Perry, Mary
  1985   "Deviant Insiders: Legalized Prostitutes and a Consciousness of Women in Early Modern Seville." *Comparative Studies in Society and History* 27:138–58.
  1990   *Gender and Disorder in Early Modern Seville*. Princeton: Princeton University Press.
Piccone, Paul
  1977   "The Changing Function of Critical Theory." *New German Critique* 12:29–38.
  1978   "The Crisis of One-Dimensionality." *Telos* 35:43–54.
Pike, Ruth
  1972   *Aristocrats and Traders: Sevillian Society in the Sixteenth Century*. Ithaca: Cornell University Press.

Pi-Sunyer, Oriol
1973   "Tourism and Its Discontents: The Impact of a New Indus-
            try on a Catalan Community." *Studies in European Society*
            1:1–20.
1974   "Elites and Noncorporate Groups in the European Mediter-
            ranean: A Reconsideration of the Catalan Case." *Compara-
            tive Studies in Society and History* 16:117–31.

Pitt-Rivers, Julian A.
1961   *The People of the Sierra.* Chicago: University of Chicago
            Press.
1966   "Honour and Social Status." In *Honour and Shame: The Val-
            ues of Mediterranean Society,* ed. J. G. Peristiany, 19–77. Chi-
            cago: University of Chicago Press.
1984   "El sacrificio del toro." *Revista de Occidente* 84:27–49.
1989   "La gracia en antropología." In *La religiosidad popular,* vol. l,
            ed. Carlos Alvarez Santaló, María Jésus Buxó i Rey, and Sal-
            vador Rodríguez Becerra, 117–22. Barcelona: Anthropos.

Poggioli, Renato
1975   *The Oaken Flute.* Cambridge, Mass.: Harvard University
            Press.

Portier, Lucienne
1984   *Le pélican: Histoire d'un symbole.* Paris: Editions du Cerf.

Press, Irwin
1979   *The City as Context: Urbanism and Behavioral Constraints in
            Seville.* Urbana: University of Illinois Press.

Preston, Paul
1978   *The Coming of the Spanish Civil War: Reform, Reaction, and
            Revolution in the Second Republic.* London: Methuen.
1984a   "The Agrarian War in the South." In *Revolution and Civil
            War in Spain, 1931–1939,* ed. Paul Preston, 159–81. Lon-
            don: Methuen.
1984b   "War of Words: The Spanish Civil War and the Historians."
            In *Revolution and Civil War in Spain, 1931–1939,* ed. Paul
            Preston, 1–13. London: Methuen.
1986   *The Triumph of Democracy in Spain.* London: Methuen.

Price, Richard, and Sally Price
1966a   "*Noviazgo* in an Andalusian Pueblo." *Southwestern Journal of
            Anthropology* 22:302–21.
1966b   "Stratification and Courtship in an Andalusian Village."
            Man 1:526–33.

Provanzal, Danielle
1984   "Desarrollo, subdesarrollo, e identidad cultural: El caso de
            un pueblo de la provincia de Almería." In *Antropología cul-*

tural de Andalucía, ed. Salvador Rodríguez Becerra, 151–66. Seville: Consejería de Cultura, Junta de Andalucía.

Rebel, Herman
1983   *Peasant Classes: The Bureaucratization of Property and Family Relations under Early Hapsburg Absolutism, 1511–1636.* Princeton: Princeton University Press.

Redfield, Robert
1960   *Peasant Society and Culture.* Chicago: University of Chicago Press.

Reher, David Sven
1990   *Town and Country in Pre-Industrial Spain: Cuenca, 1550–1870.* Cambridge: Cambridge University Press.

Rekers, Ben
1973   *Arias Montano.* Angel Alcalá, trans. Madrid: Taurus.

Riegelhaupt, Joyce
1984   "Popular Anti-Clericalism and Religiosity in Pre-1974 Portugal." In *Religion, Power, and Protest in Local Communities: The Northern Shore of the Mediterranean,* ed. Eric Wolf, 93–115. Amsterdam: Mouton.

Rivas Alvarez, José Antonio
1986   *Miedo y piedad: Testamentos sevillanos del siglo XVIII.* Seville: Diputación Provincial de Sevilla.

Rodríguez Becerra, Salvador
1980   "Cultura popular y fiestas." In *Los andaluces,* ed. M. Drain et al., 447–94. Seville: Universidad de Sevilla.
1982   *Guía de fiestas populares de Andalucía.* Seville: Consejería de Cultura, Junta de Andalucía.
1985   *Las fiestas de Andalucía: Una aproximación desde la antropología cultural.* Seville: Biblioteca de la Cultura Andaluza.

Rosaldo, Renato
1986   "From the Door of His Tent: The Fieldworker and the Inquisitor." In *Writing Culture: The Poetics and Politics of Ethnography,* ed. James Clifford and George E. Marcus, 77–97. Berkeley: University of California Press.
1989   *Culture and Truth: The Remaking of Social Analysis.* Boston: Beacon Press.

Roso de Luna, M.
1920   *De Sevilla al Yucatán: Viaje ocultista a través de la Atlántida.* Madrid: Editorial Ibero-Africano-Americana.

Roux, Bernard
1975   *Crisis agraria en la sierra andaluza: Un estudio económico de las empresas ganaderas de la provincia de Huelva.* Michéle Saillant-Llorens, trans. Seville: Universidad de Sevilla.

Rueda Hernanz, Germán
1981   "Bibliografía sobre el proceso desamortizador en España."
             Agricultura y Sociedad 19:215–47.

Sahlins, Marshall
1976   *Culture and Practical Reason.* Chicago: University of Chi-
             cago Press.
1981   *Historical Metaphors and Mythical Realities: Structure in the
             Early History of the Sandwich Islands.* Ann Arbor: University
             of Michigan Press.
1985   *Islands in History.* Chicago: University of Chicago Press.

Sahlins, Peter
1989   *Boundaries: The Making of France and Spain in the Pyrenees.*
             Berkeley: University of California Press.

Sánchez, José María
1987   *The Spanish Civil War as a Religious Tragedy.* Notre Dame,
             Ind.: University of Notre Dame Press.

Sánchez Herrero, José
1989   "Algunos elementos de la religiosidad cristiana popular
             andaluza durante la edad media." In *La religiosidad popu-
             lar*, vol. 1, ed. Carlos Alvarez Santaló, María Jésus Buxó i
             Rey, and Salvador Rodríguez Becerra, 268–307. Barcelona:
             Anthropos.

Sangren, P. Steven
1988   "Rhetoric and the Authority of Ethnography." *Current An-
             thropology* 29:405–35.

Santos López, José María de los
1984   "La cultura andaluza como cultura de la dependencia." In
             Antropología cultural de Andalucía, ed. Salvador Rodríguez
             Becerra, 109–21. Seville: Consejería de Cultura, Junta de
             Andalucía.

Schneider, Jane
1971   "Of Vigilance and Virgins." *Ethnology* 9:101–24.
1990   "Spirits and the Spirit of Capitalism." In *Religious Orthodoxy
             and Popular Faith in European Society,* ed. Ellen Badone, 24–
             54. Princeton: Princeton University Press.

Schneider, Jane, and Peter Schneider
1976   *Culture and Political Economy in Western Sicily.* New York:
             Academic Press.

Schneider, Peter, Jane Schneider, and Edward Hansen
1972   "Modernization and Development: The Role of Regional
             Elites and Noncorporate Groups in the European Medi-
             terranean." *Comparative Studies in Society and History*
             14:328–50.

Serrán Pagán, Ginés
1980   "La fábula de Alcala y la realidad histórica en Grazalema: Replantamiento del primer estudio de antropología social en España." *Revista Española de Investigaciones Sociológicas* 9:81–115.

Share, D.
1986   *The Making of Spanish Democracy.* New York: Praeger.

Shubert, Adrian
1990   *A Social History of Modern Spain.* London: Unwin Hyman.

Símon Segura, Francisco
1973   *La desamortización española del siglo XIX.* Madrid: Editorial Instituto de Estudios Fiscales.

Smart, Barry
1983   *Foucault, Marxism, and Critique.* London: Routledge and Kegan Paul.
1985   *Michel Foucault.* London: Tavistock.

Taggart, James
1990   *Enchanted Maidens: Gender Relations in Spanish Folktales of Courtship and Marriage.* Princeton: Princeton University Press.

Telos
1990   "Does Critical Theory Have a Future?" *Telos* 82:111–30.

Terán, Antonio Collantes de
1976   "La tierra realenga de Huelva en el siglo XV." In *Huelva en la Andalucía del siglo XV,* 37–64. Huelva: Instituto de Estudios Onubenses "Padre Marchena."

Thomas, Hugh
1961   *The Spanish Civil War.* New York: Harper and Row.

Thompson, I. A. A.
1985   "Neo-Noble Nobility: Concepts of *Hidalguía* in Early Modern Castile." *European History Quarterly* 15:379–406.

Tomás y Valiente, Francisco
1974   "Recientes investigaciones sobre la desamortización: Intento de síntesis." *Moneda y Crédito* 131:95–160.

Torras, Jaume
1976   *Liberalismo y rebeldía campesina, 1820–1823.* Barcelona: Ariel.

Tusell, Javier
1976   *Oligarquía y caciquismo en Andalucía, 1890–1923.* Barcelona: Editorial Planeta.
1977   *La crisis del caciquismo andaluz, 1923–1931.* Barcelona: Editorial Planeta.

1984   *Franco y los católicos: La política interior española entre 1945 y 1957*. Madrid: Alianza.

Ullman, Joan Connelly
1968   *The Tragic Week: A Study of Anticlericalism in Spain, 1875–1912*. Cambridge, Mass.: Harvard University Press.
1983   "The Warp and Woof of Parliamentary Politics in Spain, 1808–1939: Anticlericalism versus 'Neo-Catholicism.'" *European Studies Review* 13:145–76.

Vassberg, David E.
1974   "The *Tierras Baldías:* Community Property and Public Lands in Sixteenth-Century Castile." *Agricultural History* 48:383–401.
1975   "The Sale of *Tierras Baldías* in Sixteenth-Century Castjle." *Journal of Modern History* 47:629–54.
1978   "Peasant Communalism and Anti-Communal Tendencies in Early Modern Castile." *Journal of Peasant Studies* 4:477–91.
1984   *Land and Society in Golden Age Castile*. Cambridge: Cambridge University Press.

Velasco, Honorio
1989   "Las leyendas de hallazgos y de apariciones de imágenes: Un replantamiento de la religiosidad popular como religiosidad local." In *La religiosidad popular,* vol. 2, ed. Carlos Alvarez Santaló, María Jésus Buxó i Rey, and Salvador Rodríguez Becerra, 401–11. Barcelona: Anthropos.

Weisser, Michael
1976   *The Peasants of the Montes: The Roots of Rural Rebellion in Spain*. Chicago: University of Chicago Press.

Williams, Raymond
1973   *The Country and the City*. New York: Oxford University Press.
1977   *Marxism and Literature*. Oxford: Oxford University Press.

Wolf, Eric
1982   *Europe and the People without History*. Berkeley: University of California Press.

INDEX

Acción Católica, 125–26, 147, 156, 158, 175, 292n15
Aceves, Joseph, 267n4, 296n10
Acosta Sánchez, José, 269n14
Adorno, Theodor, 296n17
Agriculture: during the Ancient Regime, 28–31, 271n4; during the nineteenth and early twentieth centuries, 101–2, 105–8, 282nn9,10, 283nn13,14; post–Civil War recovery and decline of, 174, 177–78, 294nn4,5, 295nn6,7; and rainfall and climate, 1–2. See also Cork industry; Grain; Labor; Markets; Pork industry
Aguilar Criado, Encarnación, 297n4
Aguilar Piñal, Francisco, 32
Aguilera, Francisco, 297n4
Alájar: peña of, 26, 134, 285nn22,23; romería to, 117, 193, 195, 199, 201; town of, 96, 280n3, 285n22, 288n14; town charter of, 25, 40
Aldeas (dependent hamlets), of Aracena: during the Ancient Regime, 25, 27–29, 39–46, 83, 88, 270n3; anticlericalism of, 157, 161, 292n13; decline in population of, 179, 296n9; during the nineteenth and early twentieth centuries, 96, 103, 114, 136–37, 153, 180; during the post–Civil War period, 2, 242, 244–46, 249, 296n9; and the process of gaining independence, 28, 40–46
Altamira, house and counts of, 32–34, 42–44, 84, 97, 99, 272n7
Alvarez Santaló, Carlos, 277n9, 297n4
Amelang, James, 279n6
Anarchism, 127, 143, 147, 284n18, 289n2, 290n5, 293n16
Ancient Regime: collapse of, 12, 95–98; domestic and political linkage during, 84–92; dominant cultural formation of, 49–53, 58–62, 275n7; dominant politicoeconomic processes during, 32–37, 40, 45–46, 80–92; and emergent capitalism, 72, 89–92, 279n8, 280n1, 282n9; general character of, 12, 32, 88–92; in the sierra and western Andalusia, 269n1, 270nn2,3, 271n5
Andalusia: medieval history of, 269n1; parliamentary politics in, 111, 113; popular political thought in, 139, 256; post–Franco politics in, 188, 247; regional autonomy and culture of, 21; and the Universal Exposition, 259, 260–61, 263–64. See also under Ethnographic studies
Anes Alvarez, Gonzalo, 270n2
Anthropological studies. See Ethnographic studies
Anticlericalism: and blasphemy, 127, 162–64, 293n18; and class conflict, 145–46, 153–65, 168, 248, 289n2, 290n6, 292nn12,13,15, 293nn18,20; depoliticization of, 190; millenarian and other theories of, 142, 145–46, 289n2, 293nn16,17,20; nineteenth-century emergence of, 102–4; and working-class culture, 141, 293nn16,17,19
Aracena's contemporary role: as an administrative center, 2, 6, 181; as an educational center, 6, 181, 189; as a marketing center, 4–5, 181; as the seat of a partido judicial, 2, 6, 181; as a tourist center, 5–7, 181–82, 258–59
Archives, 17–18, 299–301
Aroche, 2
Artola, Miguel, 89, 282n10
Authority. See Cultural authority
Avery, David, 284n18
Avila Fernández, Domingo, 2

Bakhtin, Mikhail, 268n9
Barrett, Richard A., 296n10
Barrios (neighborhoods), of Aracena, 4, 6, 136, 297n2

and personalism, 9–10, 62–70, 91–92, 193–94; of fashion, 297*n18;* functional analysis of, 15, 269*n12;* genealogical account of, 13, 268*n7;* and habitus, 296*n15;* and hegemonic processes of domination, 9–16, 21–22, 146, 267*n2,* 268*n7;* of honor, patronage, and religion in class society, 9–10, 118–22, 126–30, 135, 140, 144, 163–65, 168, 228–30, 261–63; of honor, patronage, and religion in estate society, 49, 53, 58, 61, 88–92, 98, 276*n8;* impact of science on, 126–28, 287*n9;* and the local elite, 15, 269*n10;* neofunctional and ideological theories of, 13, 15–16; official and informal dimensions of, 10–11, 14–15; and pastoral epic, 9–10; politics of, 285*n22;* symbolics and pragmatics of, 16, 269*n13*
Cumbres Mayores, 41, 54

Davis, Natalie, 274*n2*
Delgado Cabeza, M., 294*n4*
Discourse and rhetoric: of appeals to authorities, 42–46, 61, 244–46; of appeals to God, the Virgin, and the saints, 56–58, 61, 140, 219, 224–25, 244; blasphemous, 162–64, 255–57; of everyday speech, 136–44, 247, 255–57, 262–63; of formal documents and speeches, 27, 73, 232; of the gentry, 73, 116–17, 122–30, 144; of honor, patronage, and religion in class society, 122, 126–30, 140–44, 193, 218–19, 269*n9;* of honor, patronage, and religion in estate society, 10, 42–46, 52, 61, 73, 89, 269*n9;* of obligations, 42, 44–46, 137–40; of protest and resistance, 10–11, 42–46, 162–65, 176–77, 244, 255–57; and reproduction of inequalities, 268*n7;* of the spirit and the flesh, 49–62, 92, 126, 130, 192, 275*nn4,5,* 276*n8;* tension between formal and informal, 14–15, 268*n9;* of tradition, 88–92, 122, 144, 168, 252–53, 262–63
Documents, local, 17–18, 299–301
Domination: and the church, 156, 159, 163–65, 176; and the elite, 15, 72–74, 88–92, 114–15; and national political parties, 21; patterns of, 14, 21–22, 27, 229–30, 256–57, 268*n8;* rhetoric of,

42–46, 124–30; strategies of, 62, 70, 89–92, 117–20; and tradition, 10, 21–22, 198, 202, 259, 262–65. *See also* Cultural authority; Hegemonic processes
Domínguez Ortiz, Antonio, 32, 74, 270*n2,* 279*n6*
Dominican order, 8, 25, 35, 47, 48, 91, 103, 274*n1*
Donaghy, Peter J., 294*n1*
"Don Enrique" (pseudonym), 7, 8, 233–39, 252, 262
"Don Francisco" (pseudonym), 111–17, 120, 279*n2,* 285*nn20,21;* enlightened acts of, 116; ennoblement of, 117; as *marqués,* 8, 117–20, 122–23, 156, 234, 262, 263; politicoeconomic decline of, 133, 146–47, 149, 152, 182, 290*n4*
"Don Juan Duro" (pseudonym), 100, 111
Donzelot, Jacques, 298*n10*
Douglass, Carrie B., 298*n7*
Douglass, William A., 267*n4,* 296*nn8,10*
Driessen, Henk, 269*n11,* 277*n9,* 297*nn3,4*
Duby, Georges, 274*n3*
Dumont, Louis, 275*n3*
Durán Alonso, Antonio, 295*n5*

Eagleton, Terry, 267*n1,* 297*n17*
Economy: during the Ancient Regime, 28–32, 89–92, 270*n2,* 271*n5;* during the nineteenth and early twentieth centuries, 100–102, 105–8, 121, 126, 136, 282*nn9,10,* 283*nn13,14;* during the post–Civil War period, 172–73, 177–88, 259, 294*n5,* 295*n7. See also* Agriculture; Capitalism; Church property and endowments; Credit policies; Labor; Markets; Private property; Public property; Taxes
Education: Aracena's regional role in, 5–6, 181, 189, 236; and the church, 48, 104, 132, 134, 158, 189–90, 209; and courtship, 216–17; and culture, 122, 126, 130, 186, 190; as a mechanism of "social sorting," 216–17; and military service, 217–18; and the pursuit of careers, 132, 187, 189, 236; and teachers, 186, 189–90. *See also* Literacy
Egalitarianism: and anticlericalism, 160–61, 164; in Aracena versus other *pueblos,* 40, 43, 267*n4,* 271*n5;* ethnographic accounts of, 15; post–Civil War revival of, 12–13, 184–86, 237; and representa-

RICHARD MADDOX is an assistant professor of anthropology at Augustana College, Rock Island, Illinois, and has a Ph.D. in anthropology from Stanford University. His book *El Castillo* won the Social Science History Association's 1991 President's Book Award. His current research focuses on the politics of culture, history, and identity at the Universal Exposition of 1992 in Seville, Spain.